CONTENTS

		PAGE
INTRODUCTION		v
AS A MAN THINKS	*Augustus Thomas* .	1
THE RETURN OF PETER GRIMM	*David Belasco* . .	101
ROMANCE	*Edward Sheldon* .	215
THE UNCHASTENED WOMAN .	*Louis Kaufman Anspacher* . . .	359
PLOTS AND PLAYWRIGHTS .	*Edward Massey* .	483

INTRODUCTION

The plays here printed are not, of course, the only five which might have been selected. From the many possible American plays of the last ten years these five have been chosen because decided success has been theirs, and because today they are worthy of professional revival. There is, however, a third test which has excluded many plays otherwise desirable,—the selections made must show the greatest possible variety.

Romance, played very successfully in the United States for a season or two, was revived by Miss Doris Keane in London in War time. Its "run" was over a thousand nights, one of the longest on record. The central situation, an unsophisticated young man infatuated with an actress, is undeniably not new. We have seen it in *Nance Oldfield*, and more recently in Barrie's *Rosalind*, indeed, in a dozen other plays. What lifts *Romance* free of triteness is just what produced its unusual success, the characterization of Mme. Cavallini. So inseparably is the part associated with Miss Keane, who first acted it, that it is impossible exactly to distinguish the contributions of the author and the actress to the final effect of perfect characterization. After all, the drama is a collaborative art, and no rôle—even Hamlet or Lear—is seen at its best till an actor of such sensitiveness and matured technique plays it that not merely what the text obviously says, but its slightest implications are revealed. In Mme. Cavallini, as played, author and actress worked in perfect accord.

The heroine of *Romance* quickly wins, and thereafter holds, the sympathy of the audience. The fortunes of an

v

unsympathetic heroine, observers of our stage have repeatedly told us, an American audience follows unwillingly. It always resents, according to the same wiseacres, an unhappy ending. To all this the success of *The Unchastened Woman* has been a positive and a very desirable denial. Certainly Mr. Anspacher's task was not easy—to make a woman essentially repugnant to audiences compel their attention. Nor was it enough to make Caroline Knollys interesting. The public must recognize her as a type numerous enough and dangerous enough to warrant making her the center of a play, which inevitably sets an audience thinking how women like her may be kept from the tragedies they create. *Romance,* then, depends for its appeal on the dramatic interest with which it tells its story, and especially on the complete understanding with which it draws its heroine. *The Unchastened Woman,* too, draws its central figure with perfect comprehension, but it seeks to do what *Romance* does not,—move an audience to serious thinking about the social significance of that figure. The success of *The Unchastened Woman* undoubtedly helped prepare our audiences for their recent hearty approval of Mr. Ervine's *Jane Clegg* and Mr. O'Neill's *Beyond the Horizon.*

The Return of Peter Grimm and *As a Man Thinks* prove that our drama of the past ten years has tried to keep pace with the public in some of their thinking. Mr. Thomas has given a thoroughly dramatic presentation of one of the conservative answers to the feminists who have urged complete emotional freedom for women. Mr. Belasco dramatizes the borderland between the seen and the unseen of which Sir Oliver Lodge has written so persuasively. *As a Man Thinks* deals not with people of the theater, but portraits from the life of the moment. How well Seelig is done! How good, because how clear yet restrained, is the drawing of the Jewish side of his character! Again and again, too, the play solves the constantly recurring puzzle of the dramatist: How shall I translate this argument, this needed exposition of motives or central facts, into terms of absorbing drama? The seeming simplicity of the emphasis on the details which later make Clayton sure that it was his wife who went to De Lota's apartment proves its mastery. The central idea of *As a Man Thinks* may not be subtle, nor as difficult to convey in the theater as many others recently attempted by our dramatists, but it must be admitted that this play completely succeeds in translating its essential didacticism into genuine drama.

Anyone who saw Mr. Warfield in *The Return of Peter Grimm* as the dreamy idealist, the gentle but obstinate schemer, will be glad to hear that Mr. Belasco plans to revive the play. But there is more in the play to commend than central characterization. Deft touch after touch makes us swiftly feel that we are on the borderland between the real and the unreal: and the difficult atmosphere, once created, is perfectly sustained. Probably what is most remarkable in *Peter Grimm*, however, is the neatness and sureness of emphasis. By a well chosen phrase, by iteration, by illustration, by clever disguising of exposition as an emotional scene, Mr. Belasco puts into the minds of his audience the ideas as to the occult which are essential if the play is to develop with the emotional results he desires.

Plots and Playwrights, a decided success originally in The 47 Workshop and later with The Washington Square Players, is, of course, criticism made drama. So well has this been done that its three short scenes stir audiences emotionally, and its long burlesque moves to laughter or sympathetic tears according as an auditor has been well trained in the theater or has depended on more extravagant motion pictures and melodrama. Revived in 1918 at one of the large War camps, the three short scenes went rather tamely, but the burlesque was followed absorbedly. More than one hearer turned aside to brush from his manly cheek the furtive tear of sympathy for the ever trustful mother and the erring daughter!

Plots and Playwrights, with its prologue, three one acts slightly connected, its long burlesque, and its epilogue, is, too, an interesting example of the constantly increasing attempts to break free from the time-honored division of a play into three, four, or five acts.

Primarily, of course, this book is intended to make its plays more accessible for readers. Yet it will be disappointing if there are not two other results. From all over the country comes the demand of amateur actors for plays of literary quality from the professional stage. Will not acquaintance with such books as this lead readers to apply to the dramatists represented for acting rights? It is far more worth while to attempt the giving of a significant play than to act a bad play better. Originally *Plots and Playwrights* was produced by The 47 Workshop.

Even, however, if reading these plays does not lead to amateur production of all of them, surely it will create a demand for frequent revivals by local stock companies. We do not see enough of some American plays of the past three decades. Many years ago everyone was talking of Bronson Howard's *The Banker's Daughter.* His farce, *Saratoga,* was one of the earlier plays to conquer London. How many of the generation which has come into the theater since 1910 have had any chance to see either of these plays? Why should Clyde Fitch be a man of whom young people hear today, but whose plays they see hardly at all? No history of the American drama can neglect his work as do the managers of the stock theaters. If any

INTRODUCTION

American company would give them as well as the English actors at the Copley Theater, Boston, play the English pieces of his contemporaries, they would find a sufficient public to warrant the venture. There are people who still talk of James A. Herne's *Griffith Davenport* as notable among the first forerunners of the newer American drama. Even had the manuscript not been destroyed when Mr. Herne's house was burned, we should have seen few revivals of it. Surely books like this may do a little to overcome this foolish worship of the recent as the necessarily novel, this willingness to attend a poor play of the moment instead of a play of proved good quality from the nearer past. Of course, plays which seemed likely to have permanent attractiveness do become strange and uninteresting, but only by the sifting process of occasional revival shall we come to know which plays have for the public lasting significance.

Twenty years ago we had pretty well discarded adaptations from French and German farces which had been the great successes of an earlier period. We were just emerging from a time when the leading American managers relied principally on successes from London. Repetitions of plays by Henry Arthur Jones, Sir Arthur Pinero, Oscar Wilde, and G. B. Shaw were helping to shape the American drama in the first dozen years of the present century. The last ten years have shown that our public, while still enjoying many of the best plays from across the Atlantic, has welcomed most heartily the work of American dramatists. For some time it has been the custom to decry post-War conditions in the American theater. Nevertheless the recovery of the drama has been quicker in New York than in either London or Paris. The present American season has shown more really interesting plays, has brought forward more new writers of promise than has the

London season. A public which heartily welcomes *Beyond the Horizon* and *Jane Clegg* is not the old public. It seems now as if there really were in New York an audience large enough to make successful any kind of drama worthy attention. With that newer public created out of the War, with the probable greater effectiveness of the dramatists who have been writing successfully for us, with the promise shown by the newer writers, this is no time for pessimism. If the five plays chosen here from many other possibilities show the atmosphere, characterization, swift response to the interests of the public, and technique already remarked, surely we have the right to hope that the next decade will give us an American drama which, in its mirroring of American life, will be even more varied in form, even richer in content.

GEORGE P. BAKER.

AS A MAN THINKS

A Play in Four Acts

By

AUGUSTUS THOMAS

AUGUSTUS THOMAS was born at St. Louis, January 8, 1859. He was educated in the St. Louis public schools and studied law for two years. He has been variously page boy for the 41st Congress, special writer and illustrator on the St. Louis, Kansas City, and New York papers, editor and proprietor of the Kansas City *Mirror*. His plays are *Alabama, In Missouri, Arizona, The Earl of Pawtucket, The Education of Mr. Pipp, Oliver Goldsmith, On the Quiet, Mrs. Leffingwell's Boots, The Other Girl, The Burglar, The Embassy Ball, The Witching Hour, The Harvest Moon, As a Man Thinks, Rio Grande, Indian Summer, The Copperhead, Palmy Days.*

As a Man Thinks was first presented at the 39th Street Theater, New York, March 13, 1911, with John Mason as Dr. Seelig.

[Copyright, 1911, by Duffield & Company]

CHARACTERS

VEDAH
DR. SEELIG
HOLLAND, Seelig's footman
BUTLER
MRS. CLAYTON
JULIAN BURRILL
BENJAMIN DE LOTA
FRANK CLAYTON
MRS. SEELIG
SUTTON, Clayton's footman
MISS DOANE
JUDGE HOOVER
DICK

AS A MAN THINKS

ACT I

[*SCENE: Drawing Room of the residence of* DOCTOR SEELIG. *Two small sofas set at right angles to the fireplace form a kind of inglenook. At the outer ends of the sofas are two marble pedestals, each surmounted by an antique vase.*

Time: An afternoon in late September. VEDAH SEELIG, *a young girl, is at the piano and playing. After a few bars there is the sound of a door closing.* VEDAH *listens, then speaks.*]

VEDAH. Papa?

SEELIG. Yes.

VEDAH. Alone?

SEELIG. Alone. [*He enters from the hall.* VEDAH *meets and kisses him.*] Mother home?

VEDAH. She is lying down.

SEELIG. Is mother ill?

VEDAH. Only resting.

SEELIG. Ah—where is the tea?

VEDAH. It isn't time.

SEELIG. [*Regarding his watch.*] Quarter of five.

VEDAH. [*Laughing.*] But no company.

SEELIG. Company? My dear Vedah. Tea with me is not a function—it's a stimulant. [*He calls to a footman passing.*] Holland.

HOLLAND. [*Pausing at doorway.*] Yes, sir.

SEELIG. Tell the butler—some tea. [HOLLAND *goes.*]

VEDAH. Now, Papa.
SEELIG. [*Affectionately imitating her.*] "Now, Papa." *You* want to drive me into dissipation.
VEDAH. But the others will think they're late.
SEELIG. I shan't grudge them that accuracy—they *are* late. I don't wonder at some of them, but I'm astonished at De Lota.
VEDAH. [*Pause.*] De Lota?
SEELIG. Yes.
VEDAH. Is Mr. De Lota coming?
SEELIG. I asked him to come.
VEDAH. Why?
SEELIG. Meet your artist—
VEDAH. But, Papa—
SEELIG. [*Playfully.*] Well, scold me.
VEDAH. But—Papa.
SEELIG. First to famish for a little tea—and then to be reprimanded for inviting a prospective son-in-law.
VEDAH. I don't want Mr. Burrill and Mr. De Lota to meet.
SEELIG. Not meet—?
VEDAH. Just yet.
SEELIG. Why not?
VEDAH. I haven't told anybody of my engagement to Mr. De Lota.
SEELIG. Well?
VEDAH. Well—he carries himself so—so—
SEELIG. Proudly?
VEDAH. So much like a proprietor that it's hard to explain to others—strangers especially.
SEELIG. By "strangers especially" you mean Mr. Burrill?
VEDAH. Yes.
SEELIG. Is Mr. Burrill's opinion important?

Vedah. His refinement is important.

Seelig. Refinement?

Vedah. Yes—the quality that you admire in men—the quality that Mr. De Lota sometimes lacks.

Seelig. When—for example?

Vedah. I've just told you.

Seelig. Well, tell me again.

Vedah. When he gives the impression of—of—owning me.

Seelig. [*Pause.*] But after all, isn't there a compliment in that?

Vedah. There's considerable annoyance in it.

Seelig. Oh—[*A butler enters, gets tea table, which he places center and goes out.*] If you and De Lota announced your engagement his manner might—seem more natural—to strangers especially.

Vedah. I don't wish it announced.

Seelig. It was to have been announced in September, wasn't it?

Vedah. I know—but I'm waiting.

Holland. [*Appearing in doorway and announcing.*] Mrs. Clayton.

[Mrs. Elinor Clayton, *a blonde and blue-eyed woman of delicate charm and distinction, enters.*

Vedah. Elinor! [*Kisses her.*] How good of you to come so early.

Elinor. Doctor.

Seelig. [*Shaking hands with* Mrs. Clayton.] Elinor.

Elinor. [*Seeing the empty tea table.*] Am I the first?

Vedah. The very first.

Seelig. If I'm not—counted.

Elinor. *You're* first in every situation, Doctor. [*To* Vedah.] I hope to have a moment with your father before the others call.

AS A MAN THINKS [Act I

VEDAH. Professionally?
ELINOR. Don't I look the invalid? How's your mother?
VEDAH. Fine, thank you.
ELINOR. And to see her on a matter about as unimportant as my medical errand.
VEDAH. I'll leave you together while I tell Mama.

[*She goes out.*

ELINOR. [*Sitting.*] When I came to see you last time—?
SEELIG. Yes?
ELINOR. You told me the truth about myself?
SEELIG. My dear Mrs. Clayton.
ELINOR. Of course you did as far as you told me anything, but I thought you might be withholding something.
SEELIG. I don't know a woman in better physical condition. [*He takes a chair beside her.*]
ELINOR. Well, I want you to give me something to make me sleep.
SEELIG. Sleep!
ELINOR. I wake about four in the morning and—stay awake.
SEELIG. How often has this happened?
ELINOR. Ever since I came to see you—and a week before that.
SEELIG. 'M—[*Pause.*] Anything troubling you?
ELINOR. No.
SEELIG. Do you stay wide awake or—only partly so?
ELINOR. Awake.
SEELIG. Thinking?
ELINOR. Yes.
SEELIG. Of what?
ELINOR. Oh—everything.
SEELIG. But principally—?

ELINOR. Principally—[*Pause.*] That old trouble at Atlantic City.
SEELIG. Anything in Frank's conduct to revive that?
ELINOR. No—but—
SEELIG. What?
ELINOR. I think—sometimes that I felt that trouble more than any of us—even *I* thought I felt it.
SEELIG. You forgave Frank, didn't you?
ELINOR. Yes—but it was a good deal for a wife to overlook.
SEELIG. You mean you *didn't* forgive him?
ELINOR. I mean the hurt was deeper than I knew—deeper than I could know except as time taught me its depth.
SEELIG. Your thoughts on that are what wake you in the early morning?
ELINOR. And keep me awake.
SEELIG. Well, let's talk about it.
ELINOR. I don't wish to talk about it, Doctor.
[*She moves to a seat near the window.*
SEELIG. In surgery we sometimes find a condition where a wound has healed too quickly and on the surface only. The treatment is to re-open it entirely. A mental trouble has its analogy. Better talk of it. [*He goes to a seat beside her.*] Frank was foolish. Under the law you might have abandoned him to his folly. In that case, with his temperament—[*Pause.*] Two years? He'd have been—well—" a failure " is too gentle a description. As it is, consider his advancement in the two years—his development—power. All due to your wisdom, my dear Elinor—to your wisdom and forbearance—to your love for him—[*Pause.*] That sums it up—you do love him.
ELINOR. [*Earnestly.*] Yes.
SEELIG. Frank is important—he influences public opinion

with his magazines and papers. He addresses an audience of two millions, let us say. In the great scheme of the world Frank is a factor—a big factor—isn't he?

ELINOR. Yes—I suppose he is.

SEELIG. [*Cheeringly.*] Well, there you are. Your abiding love for him made all the difference between success and failure. All the forces radiating from Frank really do so because of your loyalty at a supreme moment. That's a large commission, isn't it? The fates made you their chosen instrument—their deputy. If Frank hadn't needed help you couldn't have given it, could you?

ELINOR. Of course not.

SEELIG. [*Rising energetically.*] Well, don't regret having been useful—be proud of it.

ELINOR. But a man who has once committed such a fault—may do so again.

SEELIG. [*Pleasantly.*] You're assuming that we learn nothing from our mistakes—we men.

ELINOR. Well, do you?

SEELIG. [*Smiling.*] As a physician—I'd hate to tell you how much.

ELINOR. I couldn't go through it again.

SEELIG. You won't have to.

ELINOR. [*Going to* SEELIG.] And you won't give me anything for my insomnia?

SEELIG. Isn't a point of view something?

ELINOR. Yes, if I can take it.

SEELIG. You did take it. I saw the care go out of those eyes—and the peace come into them.

ELINOR. [*Pause.*] You're a dear. [*She gratefully and impulsively takes* SEELIG's *hand.*]

VEDAH. May I come in?

SEELIG. Yes.

[VEDAH *enters.*

Act I] AS A MAN THINKS 9

VEDAH. Mama wants you to come up, Elinor.
ELINOR. Yes—[*As* VEDAH *starts with her.*] Oh, I'll go alone.
VEDAH. But don't desert me entirely.
[ELINOR *goes out.*
SEELIG. Mama not coming down?
VEDAH. No.
[*The* BUTLER *enters with tea service—lighted lamp, etc., which he puts on the table and goes out.*]
SEELIG. When did you first meet Mr. Burrill?
VEDAH. With you—at his exhibition.
SEELIG. That was in September.
VEDAH. Yes.
SEELING. [*Pause.*] Vedah, I want to help Mr. Burrill—
VEDAH. He has a lot of talent.
SEELIG. I'm going to take down my beautiful vases De Lota gave us. [*He caresses a vase on one of the pedestals.*]
VEDAH. They're deadly—
SEELIG. And put up Mr. Burrill's statuettes—
VEDAH. That's helping ourselves.
SEELIG. I'm going to enlist Clayton in Mr. Burrill's fight with the architects.
VEDAH. That's "copy" for Clayton's.
SEELIG. But Mr. Burrill is [*Pause.*] not a Jew.
VEDAH. [*Pouring tea.*] There's no race nor religion to art, is there?
SEELIG. There frequently is to the artist. [*Tenderly.*] Careful, my pet. Remember—your happiness will be—with your own race. [VEDAH *gives* SEELIG *his tea.*
HOLLAND. [*Appears and announces.*] Mr. Burrill.
VEDAH. Show Mr. Burrill in. [HOLLAND *goes.*
SEELIG. Second call this week, isn't it?
VEDAH. Yes.

SEELIG. You know, he has *some rights.*
VEDAH. You mean—?
SEELIG. *His* heart—
[*Enter* BURRILL, *a young man of twenty-eight years.*
VEDAH. Good afternoon.
BURRILL. How do you do? [*They shake hands.*]
SEELIG. How are you?
BURRILL. Fine, thank you.
SEELIG. Any more news of the court house decoration?
BURRILL. Nothing different.
VEDAH. How will you take your tea, Mr. Burrill?
BURRILL. Submissively. I take it only because I admire its preparation.
SEELIG. We still struggle along with our vases. [*He indicates the vases on the pedestals.*]
BURRILL. I understand your reluctance to move them.
SEELIG. Only waiting for your statuettes.
BURRILL. They haven't come?
SEELIG. No.
VEDAH. I think they did, Papa. Something dreadfully heavy came this morning.
SEELIG. Well!
VEDAH. I was afraid to unpack them.
BURRILL. [*Laughing.*] They're bronze.
[VEDAH *gives* BURRILL *his tea. She then goes to the door and pushes the electric button.*
SEELIG. Do you know Clayton—the publisher—Clayton's magazine?
BURRILL. Reputation.
SEELIG. He's a live wire—Clayton.
BURRILL. Yes.
[*The* BUTLER *enters.*
VEDAH. The expressman brought a package this morning?

BUTLER. Yes, M'm—two statues.
VEDAH. How do you know?
BUTLER. I opened it.
VEDAH. You opened it!
BUTLER. [*Looking to* SEELIG.] Mrs. Seelig told me to open it.
VEDAH. Mama told him to open it. Would you have thought it?
SEELIG. [*To* BURRILL.] How was the box addressed?
BURRILL. To you.
SEELIG. [*Dryly.*] I would have thought it—yes—
VEDAH. Bring the statuettes here.
BUTLER. They are in Mrs. Seelig's room.
VEDAH. I'll go with you and get them—Excuse me—
[VEDAH *and the* BUTLER *go out.*
SEELIG. I've asked Clayton to drop in on his way uptown.
BURRILL. I shall be glad to meet him.
SEELIG. *Mrs.* Clayton is here. Have you met *her?*
BURRILL. No.
SEELIG. She was a Miss Hoover. Judge Hoover's daughter.
BURRILL. [*Nodding.*] The newspapers keep one pretty well informed.
SEELIG. Unfortunate, that notoriety.
BURRILL. Can't be agreeable.
SEELIG. Prosperity tries a man more than poverty does—
BURRILL. So I've read—
SEELIG. Clayton makes two millions a year from his publications—
BURRILL. Think of it!
SEELIG. His temptations were proportionate to his sudden success and—well, she is a most sensible woman.
BURRILL. Forgave everything I believe.

SEELIG. Not too meekly—I assure you—but—they have a little boy and—as I say—she is a most sensible woman. As for Clayton—well I guess Clayton is sufficiently contrite.
[VEDAH *and the* BUTLER *re-enter, the* BUTLER *carries two bronze figurines.*
VEDAH. [*Indicating a pedestal.*] I think the *girl* on that pillar— And the man on that one—
SEELIG. I'd put the girl here—
VEDAH. Why?
SEELIG. See it first. [*He takes the female figure from the* BUTLER *who places the male figure on the floor and goes out.*]
VEDAH. She's too darling for anything.
SEELIG. [*Placing the statuette on the tea table.*] Your figures are even handsomer here, than at the exhibition.
BURRILL. The room helps them.
SEELIG. [*With the statuette which he displays.*] Look, Vedah! Isn't she graceful in every view?
VEDAH. She is.
SEELIG. Do you know your nymph reminds me of those stunning little things by Theodore Riviere?
BURRILL. That's very interesting. The girl that posed for this was a model for Riviere.
SEELIG. [*Playfully.*] Well, there you are—I shall set up as a connoisseur.
VEDAH. You promised to bring her photograph.
BURRILL. I have brought it.
SEELIG. [*Half anxiously.*] But—posing?
BURRILL. Oh, no—street costume.
SEELIG. Oh—
BURRILL. There—[*He takes a photograph from his pocket and hands it to* VEDAH.]
SEELIG. [*Sitting comfortably.*] I don't know why sculpture is so much more modest than photography—but—it is.

BURRILL. The artist is a mediator.
SEELIG. Does that explain it?
BURRILL. Doesn't it?
SEELIG. I don't know—I've never been an artist.
VEDAH. Nor a photographer.
SEELIG. Nor, for that matter, a beautiful female model.
VEDAH. [*Carrying the photograph to* SEELIG.] See, Papa—isn't that face angelic?
SEELIG. It is—It is—[*To* BURRILL.] And I dare say the lady herself was—[*Indicates abandon.*]
BURRILL. No—she wasn't a bad sort. She has a right to the face.
VEDAH. [*With girlish enthusiasm.*] Those eyes, Papa! And that beautiful nose and mouth. Why, anybody could *love* her.
BURRILL. Well—a good many did.
VEDAH. Of whom does she make you—think?
SEELIG. Some player.
VEDAH. Duse. [SEELIG *nods.*]
BURRILL. The resemblance is often remarked.
VEDAH. She should have been an actress.
BURRILL. [*Shaking his head.*] She tried acting and failed.
VEDAH. Did you see her?
BURRILL. Before my time. Antoine gave her a very good chance in his theater, but—she was only a model.
SEELIG. Yes, if Antoine couldn't make her act. [VEDAH *returns the photograph to* BURRILL.]
BURRILL. But—a fine girl for all that—warm hearted —most grateful to the man who had got her the chance.
VEDAH. Well, if anybody got me a place in Antoine's theater I'd be grateful. [*She returns to the statuette examining it closely.*] I'm sorry we can't see her mouth.
SEELIG. You can't? [*Also examines the statuette.*]

BURRILL. No—our early Greeks played with those pipes tied to the face.

VEDAH. I'm going to put her on her pedestal.

BURRILL. Let me. [*He takes the statuette from the table.*]

VEDAH. Take your old vases, Papa.

BURRILL. Old vases!

SEELIG. [*Taking the vases from the pedestals.*] The finest specimens in America, Mr. Burrill.

BURRILL. Exquisite—where did you find them?

SEELIG. Benjamin De Lota brought them from Genoa. De Lota does art and music for Clayton!

BURRILL. Charming.

SEELIG. I shall promote them to my library. [*He goes toward the door.*] I—I regard them somewhat as a bribe.

BURRILL. A bribe?

VEDAH. [*Expostulating.*] Papa!

SEELIG. De Lota gave them to me—and in the same interview asked me to—to become his father-in-law—an intimate and antique relation—a time-honored method. [*Regards vases.*] Ah, well. [SEELIG *goes out through the library door.*]

BURRILL. [*Dashed with the news.*] His father-in-law.

VEDAH. You hadn't heard? [BURRILL *shakes head, avoiding her gaze.*] Why, yes. [*Pause.*] May I pour you some more tea?

BURRILL. No, thank you. [*He walks away.*]

VEDAH. Do you know Mr. De Lota?

BURRILL. No.

VEDAH. He wrote that beautiful notice in Clayton's about your work.

BURRILL. [*Moodily at window.*] I know his articles, of course.

VEDAH. Shan't we put up the dancing man too?

BURRILL. [*Rousing himself.*] Let me. [*He puts the male figurine on the second pedestal.*]

VEDAH. They go well there, don't they?

BURRILL. Very well.

VEDAH. Attendant spirits of my fireside.

BURRILL. They are honored.

VEDAH. Do you know why I like them?

BURRILL. Why?

VEDAH. [*Impressively.*] They are just a girl and a man—nothing more—with their pan pipes—their freedom—the joy of existence—

BURRILL. [*Forcing a gayety.*] That sounds like paganism.

VEDAH. I am a pagan.

BURRILL. And the gentleman?

VEDAH. Mr. De Lota?

BURRILL. Yes.

VEDAH. Mr. De Lota—is a Jew.

BURRILL. [*Pause.*] Well, I'm a pagan myself—a Walter Pater pagan.

VEDAH. Oh, yes. I, too, must have the sunshine, the poetry, the festivals.

BURRILL. And you saw somewhat of that in my little figures?

VEDAH. Yes—

BURRILL. You hinted as much that day at the exhibition—thousands had walked by and looked at their catalogues—but you—only you—interpreted them. I can't tell you how much that meant to me.

VEDAH. I wonder if you know—that we—[*Pause.*]

BURRILL. We what?

VEDAH. Were never introduced to each other.

BURRILL. I hug that to my memory.

VEDAH. A friend offered—but I fibbed. I said I *knew*

you already. An introduction would have been—well—
[*Rises impatiently.*]

BURRILL. What?

VEDAH. A strait-jacket on your dancer. [*She pauses and comes near him.*] But it has been wrong to make you call here, hasn't it?

BURRILL. Has it?

VEDAH. Tell *me*.

BURRILL. [*With renewed fervor.*] Not if they are really to be the attendant spirits.

VEDAH. [*Evading his manner and going to the first statuette.*] Why did you get her a place in Antoine's theater?

BURRILL. I didn't.

VEDAH. Then how do you know she was grateful?

BURRILL. The man who got her the place—afterwards committed—committed a crime and was on trial in Paris. Mimi had then become a model and was posing for Riviere and me and other artists. She dragged us—Antoine—Riviere—me—everybody—to the court house in a frenzied effort to free him.

VEDAH. Maybe she loved him.

BURRILL. I think not—simply gratitude for his interest. But that's a rare virtue.

[MRS. ELINOR CLAYTON *returns to the room.*

VEDAH. Mrs. Clayton, may I present Mr. Julian Burrill, the sculptor.

ELINOR. Mr. Burrill. [*She gives* BURRILL *her hand.*]

VEDAH. Mrs. Clayton is *the* Mrs. Clayton.

ELINOR. You must look as though you knew.

BURRILL. My struggle is to conceal my knowledge—

ELINOR. [*To* VEDAH.] All that you've told me of him seems to be true.

BURRILL. So quickly?

VEDAH. One or two lumps? And look at my Greek playmates.

ELINOR. [*Seeing the statuettes.*] Charming. [*To* VEDAH.] Two please. [*She turns to the dancing nymph.*] Think of wanting to vote when one may do that.

BURRILL. Exactly.

VEDAH. And cream?

ELINOR. Lemon please. [*To* BURRILL.] You're a dangerous man.

BURRILL. I?

ELINOR. With that degree of flattery.

BURRILL. *That's* a servile portrait.

ELINOR. Really?

VEDAH. Show Mrs. Clayton the photograph.

BURRILL. [*Passing the photo to* ELINOR.] Model.

ELINOR. I know this woman.

VEDAH. Resembles Duse.

ELINOR. In Paris.

BURRILL. Yes.

ELINOR. She writes for the papers.

BURRILL. I hardly think writes for the papers.

ELINOR. French papers—yes. And she represents Mr. Clayton's publications.

BURRILL. I shouldn't have thought it.

VEDAH. You've met her?

ELINOR. A moment—yes—in this same hat and gown. [*She hands the photograph to* VEDAH.] Mr. Clayton said she spoke no English though she understood it fairly. Frank introduced her as a writer—she smiled assent—

BURRILL. [*Reclaiming the photograph.*] Possible.

HOLLAND. [*Entering and announcing.*] Mr. De Lota. [BENJAMIN DE LOTA *enters. He is a tall—aggressive and intellectual Spanish Jew of thirty-five years or so.*

[HOLLAND *goes out.*

VEDAH. Good afternoon.
DE LOTA. [*Taking her hand with much manner.*] Vedah.
VEDAH. Mrs. Clayton you know?
DE LOTA. Yes—how are you. [ELINOR *nods to him.*
VEDAH. And let me introduce Mr. Burrill.
DE LOTA. Mr. Burrill.
[*The men shake hands.*
BURRILL. [*Seriously.*] I've an impression of having met you in Paris.
DE LOTA. I'm often there.
VEDAH. Some tea?
DE LOTA. Not any, thank you. [*To* ELINOR.] I thought Frank was to be here?
ELINOR. He is.
DE LOTA. Good. [*To* BURRILL.] Doctor Seelig has told Frank—Mrs. Clayton's husband—about your row with the architects.
BURRILL. I hardly call it a row.
DE LOTA. Better call it a row and make it a row or you'll never get a chance at the big sculpture. Once let a ring do all the work and you young fellows can starve or be journeymen. Thank God, Clayton's a Westerner, believes in the open shop.
BURRILL. We want his influence, but not to involve him.
DE LOTA. Magazines must print something. [*He goes to* ELINOR.] Frank will clasp him and his row to our bosom with hooks of steel, won't he?
ELINOR. How do you spell steel?
DE LOTA. I follow the market. [*To* VEDAH.] Where's Papa?
VEDAH. Finding the post of honor in his library for your vases.
DE LOTA. [*Noting the pedestals.*] Oh—yours?

BURRILL. Yes.
DE LOTA. [*Regarding the dancing girl.*] Charming.
ELINOR. Does she impress you as a co-worker?
DE LOTA. Co-worker—no—co—respondent—yes.
ELINOR. I mean as a fellow member of the profession?
DE LOTA. Which profession?
ELINOR. Journalism.
DE LOTA. By nothing except the willingness to increase her circulation.
VEDAH. Mrs. Clayton says the lady represents your magazine in Paris.
DE LOTA. I dare say I'm dull—but—?
BURRILL. Not the statuette—the model—Mimi Chardenet.
DE LOTA. Mimi Chardenet—Europa?
BURRILL. Yes.
DE LOTA. Was Mimi your model? [BURRILL *nods.*] I might have known it. [*He turns admiringly to the bronze.*]
ELINOR. Why do you say "Europa?"
DE LOTA. Mimi *was* "Europa" at the Quat'z Arts ball this year.
ELINOR. Europa—mythological, isn't it?
DE LOTA. Yes.
VEDAH. [*As* ELINOR *looks to her.*] I remember something of Europa in our literature class—must be all right.
DE LOTA. Disappointingly proper.
ELINOR. But the lady at the ball?
DE LOTA. Costume—well, somewhat less than this.
ELINOR. Less?
DE LOTA. [*Nodding.*] Without the pipes—mounted on a sleek black bull which the students led about the ball room.

ELINOR. Show Mr. De Lota the photograph.
DE LOTA. [*Taking photo from* BURRILL.] That's Mimi.
ELINOR. Let me have it again.
>[DE LOTA *gives* ELINOR *the photograph.*]

BURRILL. Can she possibly have also written?
DE LOTA. Mimi a blue stocking? I leave it to you.
ELINOR. Frank knows this woman.
DE LOTA. Your husband?
ELINOR. Yes.
DE LOTA. Of course. I introduced him.
ELINOR. I was sure of it.
>[DE LOTA *is startled by* ELINOR's *seriousness.*]

SEELIG. [*Calling from the library.*] Vedah.
VEDAH. Yes, Papa.
SEELIG. You and Mr. Burrill come here a moment.
VEDAH. [*To* BURRILL.] He wants us—[*To others.*] He doesn't know you are here.
DE LOTA. Don't disturb him on my account.
VEDAH. Your vases anyway—I expect—
BURRILL. [*Excusing his going.*] Pardon.
>[ELINOR *nods.* VEDAH *and* BURRILL *go to the library.*]

DE LOTA. [*Alone with* ELINOR.] Well?
ELINOR. Well?
DE LOTA. We do meet, don't we?
ELINOR. Vedah didn't tell me you were to be here.
DE LOTA. The Doctor invited me.
ELINOR. Meetings of this kind—I can't help.
DE LOTA. But you won't ask me to your home.
ELINOR. Frank asks you.
DE LOTA. I'll come when *you* ask me.
ELINOR. I shan't ask you.
DE LOTA. Why?
ELINOR. [*Pause.*] You know why.

Act I] AS A MAN THINKS 21

De Lota. I don't.
Elinor. [*Going to the statuette.*] This model—you say you introduced Frank to her?
De Lota. Yes.
Elinor. When?
De Lota. This year.
Elinor. Where?
De Lota. Paris—Quat'z Arts ball. It was her pose as Europa that caught—Frank's—caught his eye.
Elinor. I remember the newspaper comment the day after. On that particular night—Frank went to a meeting of the American Chamber of Commerce.
De Lota. So did I. At those student dances the interesting things don't begin until midnight.
Elinor. I see.
De Lota. [*Insistently.*] But you're changing the subject. Frank and I see a good deal of each other at the office. He begins to think it strange I don't accept his invitations to the house.
Elinor. Why haven't you?
De Lota. He said he wanted me to call, to know you better—[*Smiles.*] I saw you'd told him nothing—so—I await *your* invitation.
Elinor. You were away when Frank and I first met. [De Lota *nods.*] Away when we married—[De Lota *nods.*] I suppose all husbands ask their wives if they've ever cared for anyone else—[*She leaves the fireplace and goes to the window.*]
De Lota. [*Pause.*] And you said—?
Elinor. I said no. Smile if you wish but—I hadn't loved anyone as I loved him.
De Lota. [*Following.*] Naturally.
Elinor. So what I said was true.
De Lota. By the feminine standard—yes.

Elinor. That's one of the things I always disliked in you, Ben.

De Lota. What?

Elinor. Your talk of feminine standards and masculine standards. In morals there is just one standard.

De Lota. [*Laughing.*] Were there *many* other things you disliked in me?

Elinor. This is one other.

De Lota. What?

Elinor. Your mood of cat-like cruelty.

De Lota. Cruelty—cat-like?

Elinor. Yes—cruelty—and it goes with your smile. That is like a cat's—your manner is like a cat's. When you play the piano it is a cat walking on the keys.

De Lota. There were times, however, when you asked me to play.

Elinor. There are times when I like cats.

De Lota. Elinor—[*He starts impulsively toward her.*]

Elinor. [*Avoiding him.*] No—

De Lota. [*Regarding her with admiration.*] Damn it—we'd have been happy together—you and I.

Elinor. No.

De Lota. The history of my people supports me.

Elinor. Spanish history?

De Lota. Jewish history. Our girls have often been unhappy when they've married outside. But our men—have absorbed the women of other races.

Elinor. You mustn't talk to me in that strain. [*She walks angrily away.*]

De Lota. A man in sentimental bankruptcy may at least enumerate his assets. We *would* have been happy.

Elinor. No.

De Lota. One of us would have been happy, of that—I'm sure. I loved you, Elinor, because you were a queen—me you sacrificed because—[*Pause.*] I was a Jew.

ELINOR. And because you are a Jew you still speak of it.

DE LOTA. Exactly.

ELINOR. But you must cease to speak of it.

DE LOTA. Not while you listen.

ELINOR. [*Starting toward the door.*] I will never be alone with you again.

DE LOTA. [*Interposing.*] Then I must tell you now.

ELINOR. [*Commandingly.*] Play something or I shall leave.

DE LOTA. Thank you—I prefer this way myself. [*He laughs and goes to the piano which he plays brilliantly and with passion.*]

[SEELIG, VEDAH *and* BURRILL *re-enter in turn and join* ELINOR.

[*Enter* HOLLAND *who whispers to* SEELIG. SEELIG *goes out with* HOLLAND *and returns with* CLAYTON *as piano ceases.*

VEDAH. [*Meeting* CLAYTON *and shaking his hand.*] We feared you were forgetting us.

CLAYTON. Never—[*He nods to his wife.*] my dear.

VEDAH. Mr. Clayton, may I present Mr. Julian Burrill.

CLAYTON. [*To* BURRILL.] I thought you an older man.

VEDAH. He is. [BURRILL *laughs.*]

CLAYTON. In the Salon six years ago, weren't you?

BURRILL. Yes.

CLAYTON. *Medal,* if I remember?

[BURRILL *nods.* CLAYTON *turns to* SEELIG *with a shrug.*

SEELIG. No justice at all in the discrimination of these architects.

ELINOR. [*Calmly.*] That is Mr. Burrill's latest work. [*She indicates the dancing figurine.*]

CLAYTON. Charming.

ELINOR. Do you recognize the lady?

CLAYTON. [*Playfully.*] I'd like to.

ELINOR. Mimi Chardenet.

CLAYTON. Chardenet?

ELINOR. You must remember—rode the black bull at the Quat'z Arts ball.

[*A swift glance passes between* DE LOTA *and* CLAYTON.

CLAYTON. Ah, indeed. [*To* BURRILL.] From that celebrated model. [BURRILL *nods.*

ELINOR. [*To* BURRILL.] Let Mr. Clayton see the photograph.

BURRILL. I can't think it would interest him.

[CLAYTON *tries to engage* SEELIG *in conversation.*

ELINOR. Oh, yes. [*To* CLAYTON.] Frank! [CLAYTON *turns to her.*] Look at this photograph—please. [*To* BURRILL.]

BURRILL. [*Reluctantly yielding the photograph.*] Miss Seelig had some curiosity about it.

CLAYTON. Oh, yes.

ELINOR. Mr. Burrill was inclined to doubt that the lady represented your magazines.

CLAYTON. [*Evasively.*] Oh, that arrangement was never completed—discussed but—[*He returns the photograph to* BURRILL.]

DE LOTA. [*Trying to help the strained situation.*] Mimi had more than one side to her.

ELINOR. [*Regarding the bronze.*] So it appears.

DE LOTA. I mean she could think. Antoine told me that she caught the meaning of a line—as quickly as any woman that ever came into his theater.

VEDAH. [*Starting at the name.*] Antoine?

DE LOTA. Yes, Antoine the manager. I got her a place in his company.

VEDAH. When was that?

DE LOTA. Oh, nine or ten years ago before she posed professionally.

[VEDAH *looks to* BURRILL *who avoids her inquiry.*

CLAYTON. She said she would write of the theater.

ELINOR. Well—I must go.

VEDAH. Really? Am I to be the only woman in this council of war?

ELINOR. Leave it *all* to the men, my dear.

CLAYTON. The car's at the door—take it if you wish.

ELINOR. [*Frigidly.*] I'll walk, thank you. [*Pause.*] Mr. Burrill, I'm very glad to have seen you.

BURRILL. Thank you.

ELINOR. And your model—well—a delightful reminder of Paris, Mr. De Lota. [DE LOTA *turns to her.*] As you also know the lady, Mr. De Lota—*you* shall tell me more of her. I hope you'll call on us. [*She gives* DE LOTA *her hand.*]

DE LOTA. I've been promising Mr. Clayton to do so.

ELINOR. You must—[*Going with* VEDAH *to the hall*]— You'll bring Mr. Burrill to see me too?

VEDAH. Delighted, Mrs. Clayton.

[VEDAH *and* ELINOR *go out.*

DE LOTA. I put my foot in it—but—hang it, I was completely off guard. Mrs. Clayton said "Why Frank knows this woman" and I blurted "of course—I introduced him." [*Turns to* BURRILL *for confirmation.*]

CLAYTON. Forget it.

SEELIG. Trouble?

CLAYTON. *En promenade* with the girl—Elinor met us. I said business.

SEELIG. [*Seriously.*] 'Mmm. Too bad after—the—the other trouble so soon.

CLAYTON. Damn it—a man can't go to Paris and live on bread and milk. I've got to know the world I live in. I publish three magazines and a metropolitan newspaper.

SEELIG. The wife met you walking with the woman?

CLAYTON. That's all—[*To* DE LOTA *with some anxiety.*] You told her nothing more?

DE LOTA. [*Expostulating.*] My dear Frank—

CLAYTON. [*Relieved.*] Oh, I can fix it.

[VEDAH *enters.*

SEELIG. Well—shall we discuss this business of the architects?

CLAYTON. Yes.

SEELIG. Suppose we go into the library—I've your papers there, Mr. Burrill.

CLAYTON. Yes. [*The men start to the library.*

VEDAH. Mr. Burrill! I'll send Mr. Burrill immediately.

BURRILL. [*To* SEELIG.] You permit me?

[SEELIG *pauses, regards* VEDAH *intently.*

[DE LOTA, CLAYTON *and* SEELIG *go out.*

VEDAH. [*In sudden alarm.*] He is the man—I saw your face when he said he had introduced this girl to Antoine.

BURRILL. Antoine's name startled me—that was all—and—

VEDAH. You thought you'd seen *him* in Paris.

BURRILL. Probably did—many times.

VEDAH. You think you saw him in that court room—on trial for a crime.

BURRILL. [*Evasively.*] No—no.

VEDAH. The man on trial had spoken to Antoine for the girl.

BURRILL. A dozen men may have done that. Engagements in the theater require many introductions.

VEDAH. I read the doubt in your heart. You're not the conventional coward that most men are—tell me. I am promised to *marry* Benjamin De Lota—doesn't that mean anything to *you?*

BURRILL. Mean anything!—[*He starts impulsively toward* VEDAH, *stops and after a moment's effort at self-control says calmly and tenderly.*] I love you! [VEDAH *inhales quickly, her glance falls before* BURRILL'*s look, she turns irresolutely toward the room into which* DE LOTA *has gone—a pause.*

Curtain.

ACT II

[*SCENE: Lounging room of* MR. FRANK CLAYTON'*s house. The walls are covered with green canvas on which is a profusion of illustrations furnished to* CLAYTON'*s magazines by various artists. The room, square and shallow and low, is furnished in mahogany and leather. Two five-foot "arches" on either side of center open to rooms back. That at right shows hallway in red, with staircase leading to second story. That at left shows music room in yellow with Chippendale furniture and pictures in gilt frames. A sofa above fireplace which is at right, stands at right angle to fireplace. A low table for tobacco is at end of this sofa. On this table is a big reading lamp. A large writing table is at back. A smaller table near the window at left side has a desk telephone.*

At Rise of Curtain the stage is empty. MRS. SEELIG *and* VEDAH *and* ELINOR *enter from the dining room by a door above the fireplace. They are in evening gowns.*

Mrs. Seelig. Vedah.

Vedah. Mama?

Mrs. Seelig. [*To* Elinor.] Mr. Clayton's found my gloves, but my handkerchief is gone.

Elinor. [*Starting back to dining room.*] I'll get it.

Mrs. Seelig. Let Vedah.

Elinor. No trouble.   [*She goes out.*

Vedah. See this picture, Mama.

Mrs. Seelig. Which?

Vedah. This.

Mrs. Seelig. What is it?

Vedah. At Jerusalem. "The Wailing Wall."

Mrs. Seelig. Poor fellows. It's dreadful to take religion so seriously.

[Elinor *enters.*

Elinor. Mr. De Lota is bringing your handkerchief—wouldn't let me have it.

Mrs. Seelig. An excuse to join us.

[De Lota *enters from the dining room waving a lace handkerchief playfully.*

De Lota. Found! Lady's handkerchief—no marks.

Mrs. Seelig. [*Extending her hand.*] Thank you.

De Lota. [*Withholding the handkerchief.*] On one consideration. [*To* Elinor.] Mrs. Seelig says the talking machine has spoiled—Celeste Aïda—for her ears—[*To* Mrs. Seelig.] If you think you are mistaken when you hear Caruso to-night—you must stand up and wave this to me as a signal of surrender.

Mrs. Seelig. I agree—[*Takes handkerchief.*] because we shall be too late to hear that solo.

De Lota. Sharp practice, madam.

Elinor. Are we so late!

Vedah. Oh—let's not hurry.

DE LOTA. This room attracts me more than the opera. [*He regards the drawings on the wall.*]

MRS. SEELIG. Originals, aren't they?

ELINOR. Yes. They were in the offices of the magazine when Mr. Clayton bought it.

DE LOTA. Here's one by Frost. I used to watch for his sketches when I was a boy.

[SUTTON, *the Clayton butler, enters with coffee.*

MRS. SEELIG. [*At another drawing.*] And Remington —[*To the butler.*] Thank you—[*Takes coffee.*]

[CLAYTON *and* BURRILL *come from the dining room.*

CLAYTON. You found the cigars?

DE LOTA. I'll take a cigarette. [*He does so.*]

ELINOR. [*To* BURRILL.] Here's a libretto of Aïda. Find that passage of which you spoke.

BURRILL. There were several.

MRS. SEELIG. Our coffee won't interfere with your cigars.

DE LOTA. Do you mind?

ELINOR. This room is dedicated to nicotine. [*To* MRS. SEELIG.] Besides, we're going to take Mr. De Lota to the piano.

DE LOTA. Are you?

ELINOR. [*To* VEDAH.] Aren't we?

VEDAH. We are.

BURRILL. Here's one place—[*His pencil breaks.*] Ah!

CLAYTON. [*Offering a pencil attached to his watch chain.* Here.

BURRILL. [*Giving libretto to* CLAYTON.] Just mark that passage—"my native land," etc. [*To* ELINOR.] Now follow that when Aïda sings Italian and note how the English stumbles.

ELINOR. Thank you. [*To* CLAYTON *as she takes book.*] Will you order the car?

CLAYTON. I have done so.

Elinor. [*To* De Lota.] Come.
  [Elinor, Mrs. Seelig, Vedah *and* De Lota
     go to the music room by the arch left.
Burrill. [*To* Clayton *with whom he is alone.*] See here—I've an idea you'd go to the opera if it weren't for me.
Clayton. My boy, a box at the opera is the blackmail —a man pays for a quiet evening at home.
Burrill. [*Laughing.*] Many men *do* go.
Clayton. And sleep on the rear chairs. No! I *planned* to stay home—you're part of the excuse. [Sutton *enters with a note.*] Excuse me. [*Pause. Reads superscription on the note.*] Vedah—[Burrill *gets a cigarette.* Clayton *goes to the door of the music room and calls.*] Vedah. [Vedah *comes to him.*] They pursue you even here. [*He laughingly gives* Vedah *the note which she opens and quickly scans.* Sutton *goes.*]
Vedah. [*Speaking to the ladies and* De Lota *who are not in view.*] Papa will be late. Mrs. Clayton mustn't wait for us.
Clayton. Our car carries seven.
  [Elinor *and* Mrs. Seelig *appear in the doorway—*
     De Lota *follows, they enter.*
Elinor. I'm sure we can make room.
Clayton. *Make* room! You're only four!
Elinor. Mr. De Lota and I are to stop for the Underwoods.
Mrs. Seelig. And we have our cousins Friedman.
De Lota. *I* can take a taxi.
Vedah. That won't help—Papa is *coming* here—but later.
Mrs. Seelig. You go ahead, Mrs. Clayton.
Vedah. Yes.
Elinor. [*To* De Lota.] What do you think?
De Lota. Any time for me—but—the Underwoods—!

[SUTTON *enters.*]

SUTTON. The automobile.

[ELINOR *nods;* SUTTON *goes.*]

MRS. SEELIG. It's all settled—you go. So much formality. [*She and* CLAYTON *go to music room.*]

ELINOR. Take this for me. [*Hands libretto to* DE LOTA.]

VEDAH. [*Going out with* ELINOR.] Papa will probably be here before you get away.

[ELINOR *goes upstairs talking with* VEDAH. *They disappear.*]

BURRILL. [*As* DE LOTA *starts to music room.*] Mr. De Lota—were you in Paris eight years ago?

DE LOTA. [*Returning.*] Yes—and twenty-eight years ago—I'm there every year.

BURRILL. Did you ever—visit the Cour d'Assizes?

DE LOTA. Occasionally—if some interesting case were on—

BURRILL. I remember one very interesting case—A husband punished his wife—and also her lover—by imprisonment.

DE LOTA. The French law *has* that absurd possibility.

BURRILL. The lover was sentenced to a year's imprisonment.

DE LOTA. He was fortunate—the court in its discretion might have given him two years.

BURRILL. You are more minutely informed on the subject than the average American.

DE LOTA. I am more minutely informed on *most* subjects that the average American. I know somewhat of character—of men's temperaments and motives, Mr. Burrill. And your interest in my life at Paris is very serviceable just now.

BURRILL. Indeed!

De Lota. Indeed yes. I've been at a loss to understand the change in Miss Seelig's deportment toward myself. I was charging it to your superior attraction. I see it was due to your power of insinuation.

Burrill. I have insinuated nothing about you.

De Lota. You have been direct?

Burrill. I've avoided discussing your life in Paris.

De Lota. That is wise, Mr. Burrill. In fact, you could do only one thing that would be more wise.

Burrill. Yes?

De Lota. Avoid discussing *any* of my affairs.

Burrill. My *instinct* is to do that.

De Lota. Thank you! [*He turns away.*]

Burrill. [*Following.*] Except with one person.

De Lota. You mean—the lady?

Burrill. I mean you. I expect to discuss them with *you* rather frankly.

De Lota. I shall be pleased. [*He throws the libretto on the table and confronts* Burrill.]

Elinor. [*Entering.*] Ready, Mr. De Lota?

De Lota. [*Smiling.*] You excuse me? [Burrill *nods.*]

[De Lota *disappears in the hallway.*

Elinor. I wish you were going with us.

Burrill. I wish I were.

[Clayton *re-enters from the music room.*

Elinor. You'll see Dick, won't you?

Clayton. Yes.

Elinor. He's not started to undress yet. Miss Doane never knows how to manage him.

[Burrill *joins* Vedah *and disappears with her in music room.*

Clayton. [*Alone with* Elinor.] Don't worry. Good night.

Elinor. Good night. [Clayton *offers to kiss her.*] No.

CLAYTON. Still cross patch?

ELINOR. We can't laugh it off, Frank.

CLAYTON. Think we can *pout* it off?

ELINOR. I think you can't tread my sensibilities into the mire by your affairs with other women and expect me to smile at cue.

CLAYTON. Women!—One girl—and a man's natural curiosity about her type. Hang it—there must be some freedom.

ELINOR. Do you suggest more than you've had?

CLAYTON. I suggest domestic peace—or any other punishment than this deadly sulking.

ELINOR. You've admitted you went to the woman's room.

CLAYTON. Admitted nothing. I candidly told you I had gone there—*told* you in order that you might know all.

ELINOR. All that you were willing to tell.

CLAYTON. I can't keep pace with your imagination.

ELINOR. Your wish to have me "know all" is six months after the fact and when her photograph accidentally exposed you!

CLAYTON. If you're kicking on the tardiness of your news service, I'm with you.

ELINOR. I'm resenting your breach of faith.

CLAYTON. Don't assume any covenant, my dear, that doesn't exist.

ELINOR. Do you deny your promises after the affair of two years ago?

CLAYTON. I didn't promise to stagnate. I'm a publisher with a newsman's curiosity about the world he lives in.

ELINOR. And what of a woman's curiosity?

CLAYTON. Colossal! But not privileged. Curiosity of that kind in a woman is idle and immoral!

ELINOR. And in a man?

CLAYTON. A man's on the firing line—a woman's in the commissariat.

ELINOR. Which is a fine way of saying you have a license for transgression that your wife has not.

CLAYTON. If you will—yes.

ELINOR. [*After a defiant pause.*] You're mistaken.

[DE LOTA *enters in wrap and carrying his hat.*

DE LOTA. Ready?

ELINOR. Yes. [*To* CLAYTON.] You'll go up to Dick occasionally?

CLAYTON. Certainly.

ELINOR. [*Calls.*] Good night, Mr. Burrill—good night. [*To* MRS. SEELIG *and* VEDAH.] I feel awfully selfish.

[MRS. SEELIG, VEDAH *and* BURRILL *come from music room.*

MRS. SEELIG. Good night.

VEDAH. Lovely time at dinner.

[ELINOR *and* DE LOTA *start out.*

CLAYTON. [*Getting the libretto from table.*] Here—isn't this your libretto?

ELINOR. Thank you. [*Takes it and goes out with* DE LOTA.] [*Sound of front door closing.*]

[MRS. SEELIG, VEDAH *and* BURRILL *are with* CLAYTON.

MRS. SEELIG. Now, if Papa doesn't come for us—you have us both on your hands.

DICK. [*Coming down the stairs and calling.*] Mama—Mama.

CLAYTON. Mama's gone, Dick. Don't let him call that way, Miss Doane.

[DICK *and* MISS DOANE, *the governess, appear in hallway.*

DICK. I want Mama.

MRS. SEELIG. Here's Auntie Seelig, my dear—won't she do?

[MISS DOANE *and* DICK *enter.*

CLAYTON. It's much after his bed time.
MISS DOANE. I don't think he's well, Mr. Clayton.
DICK. My throat hurts.
CLAYTON. Throat *hurts?*
MISS DOANE. He complained at supper. I didn't tell Mrs. Clayton because she's so easily alarmed.
CLAYTON. [*Taking* DICK *to the lamp.*] Let me see your throat, Dick. Open your mouth. [*To* BURRILL.] You know anything about throats?
BURRILL. Not inside.
VEDAH. Mama does.
MRS. SEELIG. Papa Seelig's coming in a few minutes, Dick—he'll cure your throat. [*To* CLAYTON *as she takes the boy's face in her hands.*] Feverish.
CLAYTON. [*To* MISS DOANE.] Let him wait then and see the Doctor.
MRS. SEELIG. Doctor can see him better in the nursery. Come Dick—Auntie Seelig will tell you a pretty story while Miss Doane gets you to bed.
DICK. [*To* CLAYTON.] Carry me.
CLAYTON. [*Laughing.*] Carry you? You're taking advantage of all this sympathy. [*Picks him up.*] Excuse me—[*To* BURRILL *and* VEDAH.]
MRS. SEELIG. What is a father for—with his magazines and newspapers—if he can't carry a little boy upstairs, eh?
 [*Goes with* MISS DOANE *after* CLAYTON *who carries* DICK *upstairs.*]
VEDAH. Looks sick, doesn't he?
BURRILL. [*Nodding.*] Poor kid.
VEDAH. He wants his mother. If Papa says he's ill I can go to Mrs. Clayton's box and let her know.
BURRILL. Yes.
VEDAH. Have you noticed the disposition of our two parties?

Burrill. Disposition?

Vedah. Mr. De Lota escorts Mrs. Clayton.

Burrill. *Mr.* Clayton doesn't care for the opera.

Vedah. Some of my friends have been good enough to comment on the frequency of Mr. De Lota's calls.

Burrill. [*Pause.*] Do you care?

Vedah. A woman's natural—pride.

Burrill. But—heartaches? [Vedah *shakes head.*] Does Mrs. Clayton know of your engagement?

Vedah. No. [*Pause.*] Have you done what I asked you?

Burrill. What?

Vedah. A letter to Paris.

Burrill. There's none to whom I could write—on such a subject.

Vedah. Your model friend—she is still there?

Burrill. I suppose so.

Vedah. Why not a line to her?

Burrill. [*Evasively.*] She owes me nothing.

Vedah. Well—?

Burrill. She'd probably take alarm and forward the letter to the man himself.

Vedah. Why " forward "—has he left the country?

Burrill. [*Quickly recovering.*] Probably—or perhaps not—but—either way—nothing accomplished.

Vedah. Either way nothing lost. Won't you try?

Burrill. [*Disturbed.*] It isn't a manly thing to do—even against a *rival*.

Vedah. [*Smiling.*] Thank you.

Burrill. Why?

Vedah. Rival.

Burrill. Well?

Vedah. So far you've said only that you loved me.

Burrill. You don't resent—rival?

VEDAH. Does any woman?

BURRILL. [*With quick look about.*] You know, if there weren't so many doors here—[*Approaches her.*]

VEDAH. [*Retreating.*] No—

[CLAYTON *re-appears on stairs.*

BURRILL. [*Changing the subject.*] And all originals. [*Indicates the framed sketches.*]

VEDAH. So wonderful to have them, isn't it?

[*Enter* CLAYTON.

CLAYTON. Boy's certainly not himself.

VEDAH. Poor child.

[SUTTON *enters.*

SUTTON. [*Announcing.*] Dr. Seelig.

[*Enter* SEELIG. *He is in evening dress and wears a cloak.*

SEELIG. Good evening Frank. [*Shakes hands with* CLAYTON.] Mr. Burrill.

BURRILL. Doctor.

SEELIG. [*To* VEDAH.] Sorry to be late. Where's Mama?

CLAYTON. With Dick—complains of his throat. Have you time to look at him?

VEDAH. Certainly.

SEELIG. What is more important? Go up?

CLAYTON. [*Nodding.*] The nursery. [SUTTON *takes* SEELIG'S *cloak and hat.*]

SEELIG. Get ready, my dear. [*Goes into hall and upstairs with* CLAYTON.]

VEDAH. [*Resuming the interrupted talk with* BURRILL.] But write to that girl.

BURRILL. [*Smiling.*] I did say I loved you.

VEDAH. A month ago.

BURRILL. Yes.

VEDAH. And now?

BURRILL. There isn't any stronger word or I'd use it.

VEDAH. [*Seriously.*] It isn't a thing a man says to a girl—betrothed to another man—is it?

BURRILL. Not generally.

VEDAH. That is another proof that you recognize Mr. De Lota as that man of the court room. You must—*do something.*

BURRILL. [*Easily.*] Does it really matter?

VEDAH. Matter? Why—we're engaged—aren't we—he and I?

BURRILL. I've said *I* love you.

VEDAH. Yes.

BURRILL. And you've listened to it—because—you love me.

VEDAH. [*Pause.*] Well?

BURRILL. [*Shaking head.*] Not *Mr. De Lota.* I shall marry you—so what difference does it make what he did in Paris?

VEDAH. I know my father. Mr. De Lota is of our faith, there would have to be good reason for breaking with him now.

[CLAYTON *comes downstairs with* MRS. SEELIG.

BURRILL. Breaking the engagement—would mean no distress to you?

VEDAH. [*In half coquetry.*] Why have I listened to you?

[*Enter* MRS. SEELIG *and* CLAYTON.

MRS. SEELIG. [*Getting her wrap.*] Not ready?

VEDAH. Where's Papa?

MRS. SEELIG. We are to send the car back to him. He wants to wait a while with Dick.

VEDAH. Excuse me. [*Goes to hall.*]

CLAYTON. [*To* MRS. SEELIG.] Can I help you?

MRS. SEELIG. It's very easy, this cloak.

[CLAYTON *assists* VEDAH *with her wrap.*

BURRILL. Allow me. [*Holds cloak for* MRS. SEELIG.]

MRS. SEELIG. [*To* CLAYTON *as she goes.*] I won't say anything to Elinor until Doctor comes.

VEDAH. Good night. [*Gives hand to* BURRILL *and goes out with* MRS. SEELIG.]

[CLAYTON *and* BURRILL *come down to the fireplace.*]

CLAYTON. Wonderful man with children, this Seelig.

BURRILL. I thought principally surgical cases?

CLAYTON. He's at the head of the hospital for crippled children but great in diagnosis—medicine—anything.

BURRILL. Heidelberg, Miss Vedah tells me.

CLAYTON. [*Getting a cigar.*] Postgraduate yes—but New York family. *Father* left him ten millions.

BURRILL. Might have struggled through with that.

CLAYTON. His heart makes him a doctor. If ever I go to Heaven and that old Jew isn't there I'll ask for a rain check.

BURRILL. [*Lights cigarette.*] I understand they receive Jews.

CLAYTON. Heaven? [BURRILL *nods.*] Yes—very carelessly managed. Sit down. Judge Hoover will be here presently—he tells me you're acquainted. [*He sits as* BURRILL *takes a chair.*]

BURRILL. [*Nodding.*] We meet at the Club.

CLAYTON. Mrs. Clayton's father.

BURRILL. I know.

CLAYTON. I'd have had Judge to dinner but— [*Pause.*] How long you been in the Club?

BURRILL. Two years only.

CLAYTON. Perhaps you know?

BURRILL. What?

CLAYTON. The way Hoover's resisted the admission of Jews? He hates 'em.

BURRILL. No.
CLAYTON. Blackballed Seelig. What rot, eh?
BURRILL. Foolish antipathy.
CLAYTON. I *love* 'em—not the cheap ones. I hate cheap *Yankees* and cheap *cattle* of all kinds—but a classy Jew with education and culture—
BURRILL. I agree with you.
CLAYTON. While we think in vulgar integers—they think in compound fractions.
BURRILL. True.
CLAYTON. Damn it—[*Looks about in playful caution.*] *I'm* so wrong that I like their *noses*.
BURRILL. [*Laughing.*] Not all of them.
CLAYTON. Yes, all of them. Dismiss your prejudice for a while. See how insignificant our average Scandinavian and North Europe noses become. [BURRILL *nods.*] But—don't tell father-in-law Hoover you like 'em.
BURRILL. [*Laughs.*] I won't. [*Seeing* SEELIG *who reappears on the stairs.*] The Doctor.

[CLAYTON *and* BURRILL *rise.* SEELIG *enters.*
SEELIG. Don't disturb yourselves, gentlemen.
CLAYTON. How do you find him?
SEELIG. [*Pause.*] I'll look at him again when he's quiet. I hope some of the trouble may be only excitement.
CLAYTON. Cigar?
SEELIG. [*Shakes head.*] Thank you.
CLAYTON. [*Standing by the fire.*] His mother tells me a singular thing. She was holding Dick's hand as he napped on her bed this afternoon—*babies* him a good deal. She was reading—to herself—an old book of Stockton's—some treasure trove—men carrying sacks of gold from cave to ship. Dick suddenly waked—sat up and said: "Where—where's all that money?" Elinor said, "What money?"

Dick said "that gold those—those men had!" *Reading to herself!*

SEELIG. [*Easily.*] Yes. [*Pause.*] The connection between mother and child is more subtle, more enduring than our physiologies even suggest.

[SEELIG *and* BURRILL *sit.*

CLAYTON. Elinor invited the Underwoods to the opera—or I don't think she would have gone herself.

SEELIG. Courtlandt Underwoods?

CLAYTON. Yes.

SEELIG. Mrs. Underwood's suddenly ill. That's where I was delayed this evening.

CLAYTON. Too ill to go out?

SEELIG. Oh yes.

CLAYTON. [*Thoughtfully.*] —M'm.

SEELIG. [*To* BURRILL.] Doesn't the opera attract you?

BURRILL. Yes, but—more important business here.

CLAYTON. Those architects have sued us.

SEELIG. Sued you?

CLAYTON. [*Nodding.*] Libel. My editor insinuated graft in the sculpture awards and they jumped us.

SEELIG. [*Laughing.*] Well. [*Looks to* BURRILL.] You insurgent artists are getting prompt action.

BURRILL. Yes—I feel a little guilty at involving Mr. Clayton.

CLAYTON. [*Reassuringly.*] We'll take care of that. [*To* SEELIG.] The Judge is coming to confer with us—Judge Hoover. [SEELIG *nods.* HOOVER *appears in hall.*]. Ah—here he is.

HOOVER. [*Removing his overcoat.*] Hello, Frank.

CLAYTON. Waiting for you. [*Meets* HOOVER *who comes into room.* SEELIG *rises.*] Dr. Seelig, you know.

HOOVER. Good evening.

SEELIG. Judge.
HOOVER. How are you, Burrill?
BURRILL. Good evening—[*Shake hands.*]

[*Enter* SUTTON.
SUTTON. Automobile for Dr. Seelig.
SEELIG. Tell him to wait, please. [SUTTON *goes.*
CLAYTON. [*Answering* HOOVER'*s look.*] Doctor's been good enough to stay and see Dick.
HOOVER. [*Anxiously.*] Boy sick?
SEELIG. These sudden fevers; can't tell immediately.
HOOVER. [*To* BURRILL.] Poor little Dick—when he's ill it gets me right in the stomach. Man's an idiot to have grandchildren.
SEELIG. Still a pardonable weakness.
HOOVER. [*To* BURRILL.] I did a stupid thing. Left the copies of those letters you sent me—the photographs—all at my office.
BURRILL. Originals are at my studio—only two blocks.
[*Starts out.*
CLAYTON. [*To* HOOVER.] Do we need them?
HOOVER. Better have them.
BURRILL. Won't be five minutes. [*Goes out.*
HOOVER. Doctor, may Dick see his grandfather?
[MISS DOANE *appears down the stairs.*
SEELIG. I'm waiting for him to get quiet, but—
[MISS DOANE *enters.*
HOOVER. No, you're the boss.
MISS DOANE. Doctor.
SEELIG. Ready?
[MISS DOANE *nods.* SEELIG *goes with her and upstairs.*
HOOVER. [*Alone with* CLAYTON.] Nearly scared me out of a year's growth.
CLAYTON. Dick?

HOOVER. Seelig. I feared you'd asked him to sit in this conference.

CLAYTON. [*Shaking head.*] I know your prejudice too well for that.

HOOVER. Not him expressly—but the whole breed—and it isn't prejudice. Observation and experience.

CLAYTON. I'll chance 'em.

HOOVER. *Chance* is the word. This libel suit's a proof of it. [*Gets a cigarette.*]

CLAYTON. An Irishman wrote the editorial.

HOOVER. [*Nods.*] On information furnished by a Jew. Wasn't it?

CLAYTON. De Lota! Yes—but De Lota's pretty cautious.

HOOVER. [*Shaking head in disapproval.*] Bad lot—I know him. He'll get in some nasty scandal before he finishes and it'll react on your business.

CLAYTON. Why do you say that?

HOOVER. A rounder—stamping ground the Great White Way.

CLAYTON. His contract's the Great White Way—he does art and music for us.

HOOVER. I passed his side street hotel on my way here. De Lota sneaking in with a girl.

CLAYTON. [*Easily.*] Guess you're mistaken.

HOOVER. I called him.

CLAYTON. His hotel? [HOOVER *nods.*] De Lota stops at the Ducal Apartments.

HOOVER. [*Nods.*] Ducal Apartments?

CLAYTON. That's a bachelor place—women not admitted.

HOOVER. Not *admitted* nor *permitted after eleven o'clock.*

CLAYTON. I'd hate to know as much about this town as you do.

HOOVER. Wait till you're my age.

CLAYTON. [*After a disarming pause.*] What kind of a girl?

HOOVER. Didn't get her number—she scooted ahead.

CLAYTON. You spoke to him?

HOOVER. *Called* to him.

CLAYTON. Called?

HOOVER. Yes— I was forty feet away.

CLAYTON. Had your nerve with you.

HOOVER. The girl dropped something—I thought it was a fan.

CLAYTON. Well?

HOOVER. 'Twasn't—but that's why I called De Lota.

CLAYTON. How do you know it wasn't?

HOOVER. I picked it up.

CLAYTON. What was it?

HOOVER. A libretto.

CLAYTON. What libretto?

HOOVER. Don't know— but grand opera—I remember that and libretto.

CLAYTON. You threw it away?

HOOVER. No—kept it.

CLAYTON. Where is it?

HOOVER. Overcoat pocket.

CLAYTON. [*Pause.*] I'd like to see it. Think I could have some fun with De Lota.

HOOVER. [*Going up to hallway.*] My idea too—fun and word of caution. [*Gets coat and returns feeling in pocket for libretto.*]

CLAYTON. Caution—naturally.

HOOVER. Here it is. [*Reads.*] Aïda.

CLAYTON. [*Taking libretto savagely.*] Aïda—let me see it.

HOOVER. What's the matter? [*Puts coat on a chair.*]

CLAYTON. [*In sudden anger, throws book.*] The dog! Damn him—damn both of them!

HOOVER. What is it? See here—Who's with Dick?

CLAYTON. Not his mother—no! [*Points to libretto on the floor.*] Marked. I did that myself, not an hour ago, and gave it to her.

HOOVER. To Elinor?

CLAYTON. [*Calling as he rushes to the hall.*] Sutton! Sutton!

HOOVER. Hold on, Frank—there's some mistake.

CLAYTON. [*Gets overcoat and hat.*] Get me a cab—never mind— I'll take Seelig's machine. [*Disappears.*] Here! Doctor Seelig says to take me to—[*He goes out. Door bangs.*] [SUTTON *enters from dining room.*

SUTTON. Is master Dick in danger, sir?

HOOVER. [*Nervously.*] I don't know, Sutton. Where's his mother?

SUTTON. Opera, sir.

HOOVER. With whom?

SUTTON. Mr. De Lota.

HOOVER. That'll do. [SUTTON *goes.*]

[*Enter* SEELIG *from upstairs.*

HOOVER. Doctor Seelig.

SEELIG. Judge Hoover.

HOOVER. Mr. Clayton was summoned hurriedly—he took your automobile.

SEELIG. I'm glad it could be of service.

HOOVER. I'll get *you* a cab. [*Goes to telephone.*]

SEELIG. I'm not going, thank you—simply sending a prescription. [*Starts toward push button.*]

HOOVER. Perhaps you'd—better go—Doctor Seelig.

SEELIG. [*Stopping.*] Why so, Judge? I've a very sick little patient upstairs.

HOOVER. Your pardon! But— [*Pause.*] Mr. Clayton's

just had some disturbing news—. The—I think the family would rather be left to themselves this evening.

SEELIG. I shan't intrude past professional requirement—believe me. [*Rings.*]

HOOVER. I *do* believe you! Doctor. [*Nervously getting his coat from the chair.*] You and I are not especially intimate—but in your own sphere of usefulness I respect you.

SEELIG. Thank you.

HOOVER. A physician is not unlike a lawyer in his relations to his client. [SEELIG *nods.*] I ask you to treat sacredly and with discretion—any matter that comes to your knowledge *here—tonight.*

SEELIG. My obligation to do that, Judge Hoover—has a firmer anchorage than even your request.

HOOVER. I know it—excuse me. Clayton's news—bears on me, too, a little.

[*Enter* SUTTON *in response to* SEELIG's *ring.*]

HOOVER. Sutton—Mr. Burrill will return. Say that important business has called me away.

SUTTON. Yes, sir.

HOOVER. And we'll make another appointment.

[*Quickly goes out.*]

SEELIG. Sutton—

SUTTON. Yes, sir [*Returns.*]

SEELIG. Is there someone who can take this prescription to the druggist and wait for it?

SUTTON. Yes, sir.

SEELIG. And go quickly?

SUTTON. Yes, sir.

SEELIG. Frazer's.

[SUTTON *nods and leaves.*]

SEELIG. [*At 'phone.*] Bryant 6151. [*Pause—regards watch.*] Hello—Frazer's? [*Pause.*] Doctor Seelig. I'm sending a prescription by messenger—from Mr. Frank

Clayton's. Will you please fill it as promptly as possible? [*Pause.*] Thank you. [*Hangs up 'phone.*]

[BURRILL *and* SUTTON *appear in hall.* BURRILL *carries a package of papers.*]

SUTTON. Mr. Clayton and Judge Hoover have been called away. Judge Hoover said he'd make another appointment. [SUTTON *and* BURRILL *enter.*]

BURRILL. Oh—[*Pause.*] Well—I'll leave this envelope for them—they may care to see it when they come in. [*Seeing* SEELIG.] How's the boy, Doctor?

SEELIG. Quite ill—poor baby.

BURRILL. Too bad—[*To* SUTTON.] I'll speak with the Doctor a moment. SUTTON *bows—and goes out.*]

BURRILL. You have a minute or two?

SEELIG. [*Still seated at 'phone table.*] I've sent for some medicine—and am free until it comes.

BURRILL. [*Approaching.*] I want to thank you, Doctor, for your interest in my work.

SEELIG. It's been a pleasure, Mr. Burrill.

BURRILL. It's been a lesson to me.

SEELIG. Lesson?

BURRILL. [*Nodding.*] I'm reprehensibly ignorant on most subjects, especially religion and—well—your interest in sculpture—your toleration of it surprised me.

SEELIG. Why?

BURRILL. I'd always thought there was something in your tenets that forbade any graven image.

SEELIG. Only as objects of idolatry I think. The words are: "Nor bow down and worship them." As works of art I don't know any prohibition. My dear old father was a very orthodox believer—closed his office on Saturday and all that—but he was a liberal patron of the arts. In fact, I don't know a Jew among a fairly extensive circle—that feels as you—as you feared, Mr. Burrill.

BURRILL. You are not so orthodox as your father then?
SEELIG. Not orthodox at all.
BURRILL. I got a contrary impression.
SEELIG. From Judge Hoover?
BURRILL. From Miss Vedah.
SEELIG. Vedah?
BURRILL. Yes. It is of her I wish to speak.
SEELIG. Ah!
BURRILL. I wouldn't speak of her—if—if I didn't think a mistake was being made, Dr. Seelig.
SEELIG. A mistake!
BURRILL. Yes—I mean that my own feelings are not my sole guide. I think that Miss Vedah—likes me.
SEELIG. I'm glad you see it. I have cautioned her myself—and now perhaps you will aid me.
BURRILL. I speak to you about it as a matter of honor. You—you've been so ready to invite me to your house and all that—and—
SEELIG. And to tell you early of Vedah's engagement?
BURRILL. Yes— so my duty is to be a trifle old fashioned, if you will, and to tell you that—I mean to increase her—regard for me—all I can.
SEELIG. Her regard? Only that?
BURRILL. I've no right to speak for her—so—
SEELIG. Has Vedah said more?
BURRILL. *I've* said more. She knows that I *love* her.
SEELIG. You told her so?
BURRILL. Yes.
SEELIG. Then this caution to me is somewhat late, isn't it?
BURRILL. But unavoidably. If I didn't think she cared more for me than for—the man to whom she's engaged, I don't think I'd have spoken.
SEELIG. You mean to me?
BURRILL. To either of you.

SEELIG. Why not *first* to me?

BURRILL. Until I was sure there was no need to distress you, as I felt you would be, as I feel you are. [*Walks away as having said all that is possible.*]

SEELIG. [*Pause, slowly rises and approaches* BURRILL.] In asking your patient understanding, Mr. Burrill—I am fortunate that you are a sculptor.

BURRILL. How so, Doctor?

SEELIG. Most sculptors think in large symbols. The little span of human life takes its true proportion.

BURRILL. This life is all *I'm* sure of. I fear its rather important to me.

SEELIG. It's all any of us is sure of. [*Pause.*] I'm not a religionist, Mr. Burrill—but—[*Pause.*] It has been wisely written, " Of all factors that make races and individuals what they are the most potent is religion." It would be a very sorry world without it.

BURRILL. There can be more than one religion, however, can't there?

SEELIG. There should be. Even to grind corn there must be two millstones. And for the world to grow in religion there must be more than one idea. [*Pause.*] The belief in one God is the trust given to the Jew—the precious idea of which every Jewish woman is custodian and which to transmit—the Jew suffers and persists. You see, Mr. Burrill, that there is something here to think of.

BURRILL. Yes.

SEELIG. The Christian faith itself needs our testimony. It is built upon our foundation—and whenever a daughter quits us the religious welfare of the whole world is the loser.

BURRILL. I don't see that.

SEELIG. Pardon the pride, which our proverb says " Goes often before a fall " and let me call your recollection to the nobility of this trust which a Jewish girl abandons if she marries elsewhere. [BURRILL *nods*.] [*A pause.*] When Egypt worshiped Isis and Osiris and Thoth, Israel proclaimed the one God. When India knelt to Vishnu and Siva and Kali, Israel prayed only to Jehovah and down past Greece and Rome, with their numerous divinities from Jove to Saturn, Judah looked up to one God. What a legacy—what a birthright! How small our personal desires grow in comparison. As a sculptor, who writes in bronze that all time may read, what message can you leave if one so grand as this fails of your respect?

BURRILL. It has my respect sir.

SEELIG. I was sure of it. Is it too much to ask that a girl shall have time to think of this?

BURRILL. No, sir! I shall say nothing to her more than I have said, which is I love her and I know she loves me.

[SEELIG *bows slowly*, BURRILL *respectfully acknowledges the bow.*]

[ELINOR *enters excitedly, sees* BURRILL *and* SEELIG *and quickly passes to the music room.* HOOVER *comes in.*]

HOOVER. [*Nervously.*] Mr. Burrill—you will have to excuse Mr. and Mrs. Clayton tonight?

BURRILL. I know—good night. [*Goes quickly out.*]

[HOOVER *turns helplessly toward* SEELIG, *who with a gesture of comprehension, goes upstairs. As* SEELIG *goes,* ELINOR *enters by the other arch.*]

ELINOR. Don't leave me, father. [*She walks excitedly.*]

HOOVER. I won't. But I'm not only your father—I'm your attorney—a counsellor. Let me have the truth, Elinor. The door was locked?

ELINOR. [*Sitting.*] De Lota locked it in sheer playfulness. I was begging him to open it when Frank came.

HOOVER. But why there at all? Why in De Lota's rooms?

ELINOR. Just plain madness. Twice at dinner the conversation got onto Mr. Burrill's sculpture. Frank has had an affair with Burrill's model. [*Rises and walks; throws her cloak onto the table.*]

HOOVER. When? Not since the trouble of Atlantic City?

ELINOR. This year in Paris—I've made him almost admit it. De Lota introduced them. Tonight when we found the Underwoods couldn't go—and we were alone for the evening, De Lota and I—he proposed seeing some Japanese carvings he has in his rooms.

HOOVER. But, Elinor—you're not an infant. A proposal of that kind is only a mask for lawlessness.

ELINOR. I *am* lawless. *He* claims the right to follow *his* fancy and does follow it—my right is equal. He introduced me to this very woman on the Boulevard—but I didn't strike her, did I?

HOOVER. Did Frank strike De Lota?

ELINOR. Like a cheap bully. [*The front door is slammed violently.* CLAYTON *enters, pale with excitement.*]

CLAYTON. You came *here*, did you?

ELINOR. Why shouldn't I? You haven't made it such a sanctified temple that I'm unworthy to enter it.

CLAYTON. [*To* HOOVER.] She can't stay.

HOOVER. [*Going to* CLAYTON.] See here, Frank. You're in no state of mind to make any important decision.

CLAYTON. The facts make the decision—

HOOVER. You haven't got the facts?

CLAYTON. I've got all I can stand and we won't vulgarly discuss them. I decline to live with an adulteress.

ELINOR. I'm not that—but I am an indignant and cruelly neglected woman.

CLAYTON. She's your daughter. Now take her from my house or—I'll have the servants do it!

[*Strides into the music room.*

ELINOR. [*Impetuously.*] Coward! His house—

HOOVER. Elinor—that's not the way.

ELINOR. I haven't worked in his office—but every step in his success we consulted and agreed upon. *His house!* You know that every investment—

HOOVER. He doesn't mean it. He's excited beyond control—any husband would be.

ELINOR. In every tight place it was *your* legal advice that—

HOOVER. We can't go into that now, my dear. Humor him—avoid a scene before the servants. I'll take you to a hotel and—

ELINOR. Hotel! The cruelty of it—turned like a common woman onto the street. [*Sinks overwhelmed into a chair.*]

HOOVER. Only a day or two. If things were only as you say at De Lota's we can get Frank to believe us—

ELINOR. After what I've forgiven him! Oh, dad—

HOOVER. Don't—don't! Change your gown and we'll go. Tomorrow will put another color on everything.
    [*Helps her up and leads her protesting toward the hall.*]

ELINOR. [*Resentfully.*] The injustice of it—! The cruelty—! The—

    [SEELIG *comes downstairs and meets* HOOVER *and* ELINOR *in the doorway.*]

SEELIG. Pardon—

HOOVER. [*Trying to pass.*] Mrs. Clayton isn't well.

    [SEELIG *enters.*]

SEELIG. [*Taking* ELINOR's *hand.*] I see—but come from the hall. Dick will hear you.

ELINOR. Dick?

SEELIG. Yes.

Elinor. Dick's ill—? I'll go to him.

Seelig. [*Restraining* Elinor.] One moment—[*To* Hoover.] *You* go to him.

Hoover. The situation here, Doctor—

Seelig. I think, Judge Hoover, I comprehend the situation here, please go. [Hoover *goes upstairs.*]

Elinor. [*As* Seelig *brings her further into the room.*] I can't *leave* without seeing my boy.

Seelig. Leave! [*Slowly.*] No—no—but you must be calm when you go to him. There must be no excitement whatever.

Elinor. [*Hysterically.*] I can't be calm and go away from him—if he's ill. You know the boy, Doctor. How much we are to each other—all his life—I've never neglected him.

Seelig. I know.

Elinor. It's too much to bear—[*Falls weeping into the chair at fireplace.*]

[Clayton *enters*

Clayton. [*With suppression.*] If there's any man, Doctor, your people should have run straight with—I'm the man.

Seelig. My people?

Clayton. [*Pointing to* Elinor.] Locked in Ben De Lota's rooms.

Seelig. My people! [*Pause.*] A Jew!

Clayton. [*Vehemently.*] A Jew.

Seelig. [*Pause.*] There was another Jew—if one of *His* people may quote Him—[*Puts hand on* Elinor's *head.*] "Are *you* to cast the first stone?"

Clayton. I'm no hypocrite—I never subscribed to his code—and I'll not begin the living hell—of life with a dishonored woman.

ELINOR. [*Rising defiantly.*] I'm not dishonored. I only *claim* the right you *exercise* for yourself to go where life interests me. If it's honorable and moral for *you*—it's equally honorable and equally moral for me.

CLAYTON. Every right you may possibly claim you have fully earned by your visit to Ben De Lota's room. I'm going to make your equality complete. From now on, you'll protect yourself and you'll earn the substance your vanity squanders.

ELINOR. Ah!—

SEELIG. [*Interrupting* ELINOR's *outburst.*] One moment—don't speak, my child. [*Pause. Calms* ELINOR *to her chair.*] Your difference must wait. Just now Mrs. Clayton must be composed.

CLAYTON. [*Explosively.*] We're past the consideration of her nerves. Just now Mrs. Clayton must take what she needs for the night and leave—her trunks will follow her. [*Goes to the push button and rings.*]

SEELIG. [*In masterful calm.*] No Frank—she shall not leave.

CLAYTON. She'll not—

SEELIG. She shall not.

CLAYTON. [*Angrily.*] What have *you* got to do with it?

SEELIG. Every thing! There's a little *boy* upstairs—no one shall move him until I give permission, and his life for the next few days will depend on the mother that gave it him.

[*Enter* SUTTON.]

CLAYTON. [*Pause.*] SUTTON— [*Pause—*SEELIG *looks sharply and steadily at* CLAYTON.] pack my valise—and send it to the Club.

SUTTON. Yes, sir. [*Goes out.*

Clayton. [*Leaving the room.*] Good night, Doctor Seelig.

SEELIG. [*Quietly.*] Good night.
  [ELINOR *still seated turns weeping to* SEELIG *who embraces her paternally.*
    Curtain.

ACT III

[*SCENE: Library in house of* DOCTOR SEELIG. *Door at back lets into Drawing Room which formed the first act. Another door to left lets into the hallway. Large diamond paned and leaded window with seat at right. Mantel and fireplace are at back. Over mantel is picture of Judith. Other pictures are heavily framed on wall. Book-cases height of mantel are at all walls. The ceiling is carved and heavily beamed. Near window is library table with lamp. In front of table and masking it is heavy sofa. Big easy chairs flank and half face the fire. A second table has a telephone. On mantel are* DE LOTA'S *two vases. Other ornaments complete shelf furniture. General tone of scene and carpet is red and gold.*
  At Rise of Curtain BURRILL *is discovered waiting.*
    [HOLLAND *enters.*
HOLLAND. Miss Seelig will be down immediately.
BURRILL. Thank you.   [*Exit* HOLLAND.
    [BURRILL *scans the book shelves.*
      [VEDAH *enters.*
VEDAH. Julian! [*Extends both hands.*]
BURRILL. My sweetheart! [*Kisses her.*]
VEDAH. Together after all the talk and tears and family councils.
BURRILL. Have there been tears?
VEDAH. [*Nodding.*] Some.

BURRILL. You poor dear.

VEDAH. I've tried so hard not to care for you.

BURRILL. Have you? [*They sit together on the sofa.*]

VEDAH. Yes. Read the persecutions of my ancestry and blamed it all on yours and then said, with Mercutio, "A plague on both your houses."

BURRILL. I hope you are as incurably smitten as Mercutio was when he said that.

VEDAH. I think I must be. Wasn't there something about a church door?

BURRILL. You angel!

VEDAH. Our critics write that the vice of our race is display.

BURRILL. Well?

VEDAH. And I fear it's true. I have a great *envie* to have the noted American sculptor in our box and all the opera glasses saying, "Vedah Seelig! She's caught him at last."

BURRILL. Have you manœuvred greatly?

VEDAH. Shamelessly—not even introduced to you.

BURRILL. I know it—but we've met, haven't we? [*Kisses her.*]

VEDAH. [*Resisting tardily.*] That isn't being done, you know, until the engagement is announced.

BURRILL. How does one tell?

VEDAH. I suppose—one doesn't *tell?*

BURRILL. What have you been doing since I saw you?

VEDAH. Home mostly. You know Mrs. Clayton is visiting us?

BURRILL. Mrs. Clayton?

VEDAH. And little Dick. He has the room that was my nursery. I've spent a lot of time with Dick.

BURRILL. And what operas—what parties?

VEDAH. Twice to the opera.

BURRILL. With—?
VEDAH. Mama. Then once to the theater.
BURRILL. With—?
VEDAH. Mama and papa.
BURRILL. No suitors? [VEDAH *shakes her head.*] Not even one?
VEDAH. You mean have I seen Mr. De Lota?
BURRILL. Well?
VEDAH. He is out of the city.
BURRILL. Oh.

[MRS. SEELIG *enters.*

MRS. SEELIG. Vedah! [BURRILL *and* VEDAH *rise.*
VEDAH. Mama.
MRS. SEELIG. Mr. Burrill. [*Gives hand.*]
BURRILL. Mrs. Seelig.
MRS. SEELIG. You didn't tell me Mr. Burrill had called.
VEDAH. Did you wish to know?
MRS. SEELIG. Of course. [*She goes to the telephone.*] Give me 2500 Plaza, please. [*Pause.*] I want to speak to Doctor Seelig if he's there. [*Pause.*] Mrs. Seelig.
VEDAH. Why do you want him, Mama?
MRS. SEELIG. You'll see in good time.
VEDAH. [*To* BURRILL.] A girl never grows up in her mother's mind.
MRS. SEELIG. Yes. That you, Samuel? [*Pause.*] Will you be home soon? [*Pause.*] Well, nothing important—except—[*Pause.*] Mr. Burrill is here—and—I thought I'd ask him to wait for you—[*Pause.*] No— [*Pause.*] No—well—I think it much better for you to do it yourself— [BURRILL *and* VEDAH *quickly exchange glances and* BURRILL *comically interests himself in the books.*] Perhaps—but are you coming? [*Pause.*] Thank you. [*Hangs up 'phone.*]
VEDAH. What is it?

Mrs. Seelig. You know— [*To* Burrill.] Sit down, Mr. Burrill— [Mrs. Seelig *and* Vedah *sit together.*] Vedah's father and I have had a good many talks about— about you and Vedah.

Burrill. Yes?

Mrs. Seelig. We haven't always agreed.

Burrill. I'm sorry to be the cause of any difference.

Mrs. Seelig. It's Doctor's fault. I've always said to him, don't invite any men to your house in whom you wouldn't be willing to see your daughter interested.

Vedah. But Mama, Papa didn't invite Mr. Burrill.

Mrs. Seelig. I know, but Papa was *with* you. That was the time for him to have been firm. And not go locking the stable after—

Vedah. Oh, Mama, don't make me into a stolen horse.

Burrill. No—see what I'd be.

Mrs. Seelig. [*To* Vedah.] You'd better listen.

Burrill. Pardon.

Mrs. Seelig. Vedah's our only child, Mr. Burrill, and my first wish is to see her happy—but—

Vedah. Mama means that any unhappiness of mine wouldn't matter if she had another daughter.

Mrs. Seelig. Mr. Burrill understands me, I'm sure.

Burrill. I do, Mrs. Seelig.

Mrs. Seelig. But Doctor and I agree that Vedah should *think* calmly.

Vedah. That's expecting a good deal.

Mrs. Seelig. The Doctor is—going to—well, not let you see so much of each other, and I want to prepare you, Mr. Burrill, for his talk with you.

[*Enter* Holland.

Holland. Mr. De Lota and Judge Hoover.

Mrs. Seelig. Judge Hoover! Excuse me. [*Follows* Holland *out.*]

BURRILL. Mr. De Lota?

VEDAH. Yes. And now with Papa going to talk—you haven't informed yourself about that Paris affair.

BURRILL. I wouldn't talk that no matter what I knew.

VEDAH. It's on my mind all the time.

[*Enter* MRS. SEELIG.

MRS. SEELIG. You go to the living room— [VEDAH *and* BURRILL *start out.*] I'll join you. [VEDAH *and* BURRILL *go to drawing room.*] Come in, gentlemen.

[*Enter* HOOVER *and* DE LOTA *from the hall.*

HOOVER. Some years since we met, Mrs. Seelig.

MRS. SEELIG. Yes— [*To* DE LOTA.] *You've* been away, Benjamin?

DE LOTA. [*Nods.*] How is Mrs. Clayton's son?

MRS. SEELIG. Doctor says he may go out in a day or two.

DE LOTA. [*To* HOOVER *in tone of congratulation.*] Ah!

HOOVER. It's been very good of you, Mrs. Seelig, to have him and his mother here.

MRS. SEELIG. A change of surroundings—and Dick's always called me Auntie. [ELINOR *enters by the door from hall.*]

ELINOR. Father!

HOOVER. My dear. [*Kisses her.*]

MRS. SEELIG. We shall see *you* later, Mr. De Lota?

DE LOTA. Oh—yes—yes.

[MRS. SEELIG *goes into the drawing room closing the door after her.*

ELINOR. You two come—here *together.*

HOOVER. I *brought* Mr. De Lota—yes.

ELINOR. Why?

HOOVER. Sit down, my dear. It's going to take more than a minute. [ELINOR *sits.*] And you— [DE LOTA *sits.*] When have you heard from Frank?

ELINOR. [*Anxiously rising.*] Don't they know where he is?

HOOVER. Good Heavens, Elinor—don't answer my question by asking another.

ELINOR. But don't they?

HOOVER. Don't *who* know where he is?

ELINOR. Anybody.

HOOVER. Hundreds I suppose—but have *you* heard from him?

ELINOR. No.

HOOVER. Doesn't he ask after little Dick?

ELINOR. He 'phones Doctor Seelig every day.

HOOVER. But you?

ELINOR. No. [*Pause.*]

HOOVER. Frank has instructed Colonel Emory to begin suit.

ELINOR. You mean?

HOOVER. Divorce.

ELINOR. Oh!

HOOVER. You expected it, didn't you?

ELINOR. Not after his conduct with this second woman—this sculptor model in Paris.

HOOVER. That wasn't condoned, eh?

ELINOR. Not after I discovered it.

HOOVER. What—what proof have you of *that* affair?

ELINOR. He *admitted* it.

HOOVER. [*Quickly.*] He did?

ELINOR. Almost.

HOOVER. I fear " almost " won't go in court.

ELINOR. And—Mr. De Lota *knows* it. He told me so.

DE LOTA. [*As* HOOVER *turns to him.*] My opinion.

HOOVER. You *told* Mrs. Clayton that, did you?

DE LOTA. My opinion—yes.

Hoover. Have you and she met since—Clayton and I —came to your hotel?

De Lota. No.

Hoover. Communicated? [De Lota *shakes head.*] Oh—then you told her—this opinion of yours with an idea of its influence upon *her?*

De Lota. I answered her questions.

Hoover. And a damn fine mess you've made of it.

De Lota. Perhaps Judge Hoover, we'd better get to the purpose of our call.

Hoover. Perhaps. [*To* Elinor.] I don't need to tell you, Elinor, that this thing's awkward for *me.*

Elinor. I know.

Hoover. The other side can subpœna me—and my testimony can't help you—[*Pause.*] If we go about it rightly, however, Colonel Emory thinks Frank can be persuaded to let you get the decree.

Elinor. No.

Hoover. No?

Elinor. The reason for not getting a divorce two years ago is much greater now.

Hoover. You mean—?

Elinor. I mean Dick.

Hoover. It's better for Dick to have the blame fixed on his father than upon you.

Elinor. I'm not guilty.

Hoover. My dear Elinor, I'm your father—and—and I believe you—but [*Pause.*] I'm an attorney and I have been a Judge. The case is against you.

Elinor. [*To* De Lota.] *You* know I'm not a guilty woman.

De Lota. I do—but your father is right. We must face the situation as it is. I love you, Elinor. [*Comes to her.*]

Elinor. [*Recoiling.*] Don't say that to me.

HOOVER. My dear, I've brought Mr. De Lota here that, unpleasant as it is, he *might* say it—in my hearing.

ELINOR. You?

HOOVER. Yes. If we can't arrange it as Colonel Emory proposes—[*Pause.*] Mr. De Lota's willing to marry you.

ELINOR. Oh! [*Covers her face in revulsion.*]

HOOVER. [*Soothing her.*] Don't—don't do that. It isn't what any of us hoped for some years ago—but it's a devilish sight better, my dear, than it all looked last month.

ELINOR. There can't be such injustice in the world—that he may go unscathed and little Dick and I—no—no—I can't live and have it come to that. I won't consent to any such arrangement of it all.

HOOVER. It's little Dick I'm asking you to think of.

ELINOR. He's all I am thinking of. He's like his father—it's his father's name he'll carry through his life and I'm not going even to *propose* to blacken it.

HOOVER. What are you going to do?

ELINOR. Defend myself—defend my boy's mother.

HOOVER. Against the boy's father?

ELINOR. Yes.

HOOVER. And if the court gives Clayton a decree of divorce?

ELINOR. Then I shall *live*—live so that he'll see some day he was mistaken.

HOOVER. There's one point we mustn't overlook. Dick's how old?

ELINOR. He's seven.

HOOVER. The court may award his custody to Clayton.

ELINOR. [*Greatly agitated.*] Oh no! Father! They won't—they can't do that.

HOOVER. I don't know.

ELINOR. You can think—arrange some way to avoid that.

HOOVER. I have thought of one way—you won't listen. If we can persuade Clayton to be the defendant, that settles it. If we fight him as you propose, his anger may lead him to take the boy.

ELINOR. Divorce!

DE LOTA. And no certainty it can be kept quiet.

ELINOR. You mean the papers?

DE LOTA. Yes. If Mr. Clayton lets you get the decree—only the Chardenet girl will be named.

[ELINOR *rings push button by fireplace.*

HOOVER. What are you doing?

ELINOR. Tell Mrs. Seelig—

DE LOTA. No—no—

HOOVER. Why?

ELINOR. Because Doctor Seelig has told her nothing.

[*Enter* HOLLAND.

HOOVER. One minute.

HOLLAND. [*Going.*] Yes, sir.

ELINOR. Holland—ask Mrs. Seelig to come here.

[HOLLAND *goes.*

HOOVER. Wait 'till Frank decides.

ELINOR. *I've* decided.

HOOVER. But you may reconsider.

DE LOTA. Yes—why tell her now?

ELINOR. She has a right to know.

HOOVER. What right?

ELINOR. A wife's right—a mother's right. The right of a woman who has taken an outcast into her home.

HOOVER. You were not an outcast, Elinor—you could have come to me.

ELINOR. In your club?

HOOVER. I'd have gone to a hotel.

DE LOTA. I beg of you, Elinor—wait—or at least don't tell *everything*. My position in this house is—peculiar.

HOOVER. *Your* position?
DE LOTA. Yes—a tacit engagement to—Vedah.
ELINOR. Oh! How vile it all makes me.
DE LOTA. The more reason to be careful.
[*Enter* MRS. SEELIG.]
MRS. SEELIG. My dear?
HOOVER. [*Cautioning.*] Elinor!
MRS. SEELIG. What is it? [*Starts to* ELINOR.]
ELINOR. Wait—[*Pause.*]—until I tell you—[*Pause.*]—doctor told you only that it would be good for Dick to come here? Nothing more?
MRS. SEELIG. Nothing.
ELINOR. Not—my trouble—with Frank?
MRS. SEELIG. No—and don't you tell it, my dear, if it agitates you. Besides, Frank has lots to worry him. We mustn't judge too quickly.
ELINOR. He wants a divorce.
MRS. SEELIG. *He* does?
ELINOR. [*Nodding.*] He's already gone to a lawyer about it—father has just told me.
MRS. SEELIG. Because [*Looks at* HOOVER *who nods toward* DE LOTA.] Frank's jealous—of Benjamin? [*To* ELINOR.]
ELINOR. I had no idea Vedah was engaged to him. Oh, it's too—too horrible.
MRS. SEELIG. What ideas men *can* get in their heads.
ELINOR. No, I'm to blame, Mrs. Seelig. I deserve it all—I did go to his rooms—the Doctor knows.
MRS. SEELIG. Your rooms—[DE LOTA *nods.*] Together?
DE LOTA. Yes.
MRS. SEELIG. But, my dear Elinor—
ELINOR. The Doctor believes me—I was crazy—rebellious—vengeful—striking back—bitterly resentful of deceit Frank had been newly guilty of. I went as much in the

name of all women despitefully treated as I did in assertion of my own freedom. And then—I came to my senses. I'm not guilty or I wouldn't be in your home—

MRS. SEELIG. My dear! [*Takes* ELINOR *in her arms.*]

[*Enter* SEELIG.]

MRS. SEELIG. [*Quietly.*] She's just told me.

SEELIG. [*To* HOOVER.] Col. Emery called on me this afternoon.

HOOVER. Then you know?

SEELIG. Yes.

HOOVER. Naturally somewhat of a shock. [*Indicates* ELINOR.]

SEELIG. Yes.

HOOVER. We haven't any right to expect less from Clayton.

ELINOR. No right? Did I divorce him two years ago when he was *guilty*—really guilty? Did I?

HOOVER. No! You made a scene with the woman and got a rotten lot of newspaper notoriety—but the offense you condoned.

MRS. SEELIG. And a man that's been forgiven all that shouldn't talk about divorce if his poor wife loses her head for a minute. It's unbearable the privileges these men claim—and the double standard of morality they set up.

SEELIG. These men?

MRS. SEELIG. All of them. And that woman dramatist with her play was right. It is " a man's world."

SEELIG. It's a pretty wise world, my dear.

ELINOR. You think I should be made to suffer?

SEELIG. I think you do suffer.

ELINOR. That my offense is less forgivable than Frank's was?

SEELIG. [*Pause.*] You have my pity, Elinor, and shall have my help but I can't lie to you.

ELINOR. That I'm more guilty than he?

MRS. SEELIG. [*Pause.*] Don't ask that of a Jew, my dear—however liberal in his religion he pretends to be. My father was an orthodox Rabbi—I know.

SEELIG. What do you know?

MRS. SEELIG. Our ancient law—from which all your ideas come. A man's past was his own. *He* was not forbidden as many wives as he wanted, but if a poor girl had made a mistake and concealed it from these lords of creation, she was stoned to death unless she was the daughter of a priest—in which case she was to be burnt alive. It's always been a man's world.

SEELIG. Elinor. [*Pause.*] Do you hear that rattle of the railroad?

ELINOR. Yes.

SEELIG. All over this great land thousands of trains run every day starting and arriving in punctual agreement because this is *a woman's world*. The great steamships, dependable almost as the sun—a million factories in civilization—the countless looms and lathes of industry—the legions of labor that weave the riches of the world—all—all move by the mainspring of man's faith in woman—man's *faith*.

ELINOR. I want *him* to have faith in me.

SEELIG. This old world hangs together by love.

MRS. SEELIG. Not man's love for woman.

SEELIG. No—nor woman's love for man, but by the love of both—for the children.

ELINOR. Dick!

SEELIG. Men work for the children because they believe the children are—their own—*believe*. Every mother *knows* she is the mother of her son or daughter. Let her be however wicked, no power on earth can shake that knowledge. Every father believes he is a father only by his faith in the woman. Let him be however virtuous, no power on earth can strengthen in him a conviction greater than that faith. There is a double standard of morality because upon the golden basis of woman's virtue rests the welfare of the world.

ELINOR. Have I—lost *everything?*

SEELIG. Frank must be convinced of your love and your loyalty.

ELINOR. I *do* love him.

SEELIG. Of course. [*To* DE LOTA.] Why are you here?

DE LOTA. To—do anything that is in my power—to assure Mrs. Clayton that she will have my protection if—it comes to the worst.

SEELIG. Well—that's where it would be.

DE LOTA. And there must be some things *you* want to say to me?

SEELIG. There are.

HOOVER. [*To* SEELIG.] Clayton's always had great respect for your opinion, Dr. Seelig.

SEELIG. I'll see Clayton, of course. [*To* MRS. SEELIG.] You 'phoned me that Mr. Burrill—

MRS. SEELIG. He's there. [*Indicates living room.*]

SEELIG. Have you seen your grandson, Judge Hoover?

HOOVER. No.

ELINOR. You must—Dick's asked for you—[*Rises.*] Come.

SEELIG. On your way out I'll see you again.

[HOOVER *and* ELINOR *go out.*

SEELIG. [*To* MRS. SEELIG.] You entertain Mr. Burrill a moment.

MRS. SEELIG. He doesn't lack entertainment.

SEELIG. What?

MRS. SEELIG. Vedah's with him.

SEELIG. [*Starting to door.*] I thought we'd agreed about that?

MRS. SEELIG. Doesn't this trouble make a difference?

SEELIG. It can't affect our decision concerning Burrill.

MRS. SEELIG. Not before Vedah. [SEELIG *goes to living room.*]

DE LOTA. Perhaps the trouble can be fixed, Mrs. Seelig —if the doctor talks to Clayton.

MRS. SEELIG. It can't be " fixed " as you call it, with me.

DE LOTA. You won't tell Vedah?

MRS. SEELIG. I won't have to tell Vedah, she loves this artist.

DE LOTA. But to marry a Christian!

MRS. SEELIG. When she might have you.

DE LOTA. It's taught me something.

MRS. SEELIG. No doubt. But, I won't sacrifice my girl to finish your education.

[*Re-enter* SEELIG *with* BURRILL.

SEELIG. Mr. Burrill is going. He first wishes to speak with Mr. De Lota.

MRS. SEELIG. Why?

SEELIG. Sarah!

MRS. SEELIG. Pardon.

BURRILL. A business matter, Mrs. Seelig. If you are leaving, Mr. De Lota, I'll walk with you—if you permit.

DE LOTA. I have some business with Dr. Seelig.

BURRILL. Could you spare *us* a few minutes?

SEELIG. Well? De Lota?

DE LOTA. With pleasure.

SEELIG. [*Going.*] Sarah.

MRS. SEELIG. [*In undertone.*] You told him?

[SEELIG *nods. Goes out with* MRS. SEELIG.

DE LOTA. Well?

BURRILL. I'm going to give you a chance to retire from this, Mr. De Lota, without exposure.

DE LOTA. Good of you.

BURRILL. Miss Seelig believes that you have served time in a penitentiary.

DE LOTA. You told her that?

BURRILL. I hadn't met you when I told Miss Seelig that the man who got an engagement in Antoine's Theater for Mimi Chardenet had been in prison. Then you came into the room and told the rest yourself.

DE LOTA. Miss Seelig's belief is based on those two remarks?

BURRILL. Yes.

DE LOTA. Reinforced, I suppose by your own opinion.

BURRILL. I have tried to conceal my opinion.

DE LOTA. What is your opinion, Mr. Burrill?

BURRILL. That I saw you sentenced in the Cour d'Assizes to a year's imprisonment.

DE LOTA. And you threaten to say so?

BURRILL. I hope I'm a little cleaner than that, I threaten nothing.

DE LOTA. What is it you're doing?

BURRILL. I foresee trouble—I inform you of it.

DE LOTA. You mean you foresee Miss Seelig asking me a question?

BURRILL. Yes! I foresee your answer failing to satisfy. I foresee her doubt grow deeper—I foresee her going to her father with that doubt.

DE LOTA. And then?

BURRILL. I foresee Doctor Seelig asking what *I* know.

DE LOTA. Ah! Now we have it. Disguised, but still the threat. You tell Doctor Seelig your belief.

BURRILL. I shall decline to express my belief.

De Lota. Same thing, isn't it? Your reluctance and your shrugs being quite as convincing.

Burrill. You can hardly ask me to lie for you.

De Lota. Miss Vedah may believe me.

Burrill. No, she has asked me more than once to write to Paris.

De Lota. It would make this bluff of fair play very convincing if you did write to persons whose names I can furnish you.

Burrill. You mean arrange a deception.

De Lota. I mean *write*—show Miss Seelig your letters. *Wait*—show her the answers.

Burrill. You make it pretty hard to keep still, believe me.

De Lota. You think I'm unworthy to marry this girl.

Burrill. I know you are.

De Lota. [*Pause.*] I'm going to tell you the truth about that Paris affair.

Burrill. I don't care to hear it.

De Lota. You don't want the truth?

Burrill. I don't want your confidence. I won't be bound by it.

De Lota. You're *a man's* man, Burrill—you fight in the open. Your part in this architect's row shows that. Now, in fair play— [*Telephone rings.*]

Burrill. Someone will come to answer that. Our interview's at an end.

De Lota. Wait. [*Goes quickly to telephone and takes receiver from its hook.*] They may not come. [*Pause.*] I have served a year in a French prison. Captain Dreyfus served even longer for the same prejudice.

Burrill. Your crime was proven.

De Lota. I'm as good as you, Mr. Burrill, or any

bachelor that spends his several years in Paris. That imprisonment was a decoration.

BURRILL. Rot!

DE LOTA. I'm not a male *ingenue*. Doctor Seelig knows I've had my wild oats and I'll make a clean breast of it—my sufferings for my race will not be held against me. Vedah Seelig is a Jewess, remember, and—

BURRILL. Be still, she's a clean, high-minded girl—she'll forgive adultery in you no quicker than she'd forgive it anywhere.

DE LOTA. You think so?

BURRILL. I do.

DE LOTA. And that belief determines you to bring it to her knowledge?

BURRILL. It is already brought to her knowledge. You did that.

DE LOTA. And you make the consequence as sinister as if it had been planned?

BURRILL. I won't conspire to hoodwink a girl into marrying you.   [*Enter* SEELIG.]   [*Pause.*

SEELIG. That 'phone rang?

DE LOTA. Yes—I was going to answer it.

SEELIG. I answered it—on the branch—upstairs. I heard what you were saying.

BURRILL. Through that?

SEELIG. Yes.   [SEELIG *replaces receiver on 'phone.*

DE LOTA. I was telling Mr. Burrill a story—for a magazine.

SEELIG. [*To* BURRILL.] Is that true?

BURRILL. I can't answer you.

SEELIG. In prison!

DE LOTA. The man I was quoting.

SEELIG. Why should a man in a story say: " Vedah

Seelig is a Jewess, remember." Why should Mr. Burrill interrupt you to defend her?

BURRILL. Good day, Doctor. [BURRILL *goes.*

SEELIG. Your confession—just now—[*Indicates 'phone.*]

DE LOTA. At that time in Paris, with public hatred at a white heat, an obsolete law was dug up to persecute a foreigner and a Jew.

SEELIG. What law?

DE LOTA. Imprisoning a man on the complaint of a woman's husband.

SEELIG. We are fortunate to learn it.

DE LOTA. There are some Jews I'd expect to condemn me—apostates, renegades, that join the wolves, but not you. That imprisonment was my share of the hatred the race sustains. You're big enough to see that and dismiss it. As for the offense itself—well—you know men, Doctor Seelig. You're a physician—not a Rabbi.

SEELIG. Clayton's home was not your first adventure?

DE LOTA. I didn't know this man in Paris.

SEELIG. You knew Clayton?

DE LOTA. Yes.

SEELIG. That's enough.

DE LOTA. And Mrs. Clayton?

SEELIG. What of her?

DE LOTA. You brought her *here.*

SEELIG. Well?

DE LOTA. You excuse her and condemn me?

SEELIG. [*Pause.*] There is a cynical maxim that every country has the kind of Jews it deserves. This generous New York deserves the best. A Jew has destroyed the home of a benefactor, a Jew intimate in my own home approved by me and mine. I shall do what I can to repair that destruction.

DE LOTA. There's some extenuation.

SEELIG. What?

DE LOTA. This engagement to Vedah is not the first time I have believed I was in love. There was one other —when I was much younger. The father of the Christian girl was a Jew-baiter.

SEELIG. Well?

DE LOTA. I was thrown over—not because I wasn't a man—not because I hadn't ability—nor ambition—nor strength—nor promise of success but—I was a Jew.

SEELIG. You will pay that price—the price of being a Jew—almost every day of your life.

DE LOTA. I know—in money—in opportunity—in sensibilities—yes; but that time I paid it—with all those and —more. [*Pause.*] Consider then the temptation when that woman who had thrown me over and married her Christian found that she still could listen to the Jew.

SEELIG. [*Pause.*] This would be a proud moment for me, Benjamin, if one of my own people had told me that story just as you have told it except—that his revenge had been to protect this Christian woman from herself.

[*Noise at door.* CLAYTON *enters violently.*]

CLAYTON. [*To* HOLLAND *who restrains him.*] Don't put your hand on my arm. [*Seeing* DE LOTA.] I thought so.

SEELIG. [*Interposing.*] Thought what?

CLAYTON. I called you on the 'phone—I heard that dog's voice.

SEELIG. One moment—[*To* DE LOTA, *who confronts* CLAYTON] Go. [DE LOTA *starts out.*]

CLAYTON. He came here to see *her.*

DE LOTA. [*Angrily returning.*] Yes. To see her!

SEELIG. [*Loudly and again interposing.*] I said go.

[DE LOTA *sullenly goes.*]

CLAYTON. And you stand for it. Your house.

SEELIG. Judge Hoover was with Mrs. Clayton—also Mrs. Seelig—then I.

CLAYTON. And my boy. Where was Dick?

SEELIG. In his room.

CLAYTON. Well, I *want* him. *He* shan't be corrupted by their damned assignations.

SEELIG. His first call, Frank, and his last.

CLAYTON. That part of it doesn't interest me.

SEELIG. And your threatened divorce was the reason.

CLAYTON. I thought they'd get together on that. Well —I want Dick. [*Pause.*] Send for him, please.

SEELIG. In a minute. He'll be glad to see you—but you mustn't say anything before him you'll regret.

CLAYTON. I promise. I just want him, that's all.

SEELIG. He's with his mother, you know.

CLAYTON. Well?

SEELIG. And Judge Hoover is also with Elinor.

CLAYTON. What of it?

SEELIG. Nothing—except—well, the boy. There mustn't be a dispute, Frank.

CLAYTON. Say that to *them*.

SEELIG. And you can't treat Mrs. Clayton as though she were a guilty woman.

CLAYTON. Why can't I?

SEELIG. Because in the *first* place she isn't guilty.

CLAYTON. Isn't?

SEELIG. No.

CLAYTON. She fools you, Seelig.

SEELIG. The physician who takes a woman through the sacred crises of her life—mental as well as physical—can't be deceived, Frank, and in the *second* place you have forfeited the right to judge her—you came into court yourself unclean.

CLAYTON. And therefore can't resent adultery.

SEELIG. Her defiant visit to De Lota's rooms wasn't adultery.

CLAYTON. Damnation! when a woman's gone that far, the specific degrees of her behavior aren't important.

SEELIG. They're very important, especially when they show recovery. A woman who stops at the edge of the precipice instead of taking the headlong plunge, mustn't be thrown into the gulf—and that by the man she herself had already rescued—by the man whose brutality forced her into the peril.

CLAYTON. Brutality!

SEELIG. A word ill chosen—I meant bestiality—who are you to pass sentence upon her?

CLAYTON. Unfortunately the man who married her.

SEELIG. Why! Dismiss the moral view of marriage. Consider it only as our modern and manly and commercial mind is organized to consider it—a civil covenant—no more.

CLAYTON. What then?

SEELIG. Why, even then your position is that of a thief—a confessed embezzler—complaining in his hypocrisy of what?—that his partner's books appear inaccurate. That is the proportion. On the sacred side of the relation you are doubly guilty—guilty of your immoral conduct—guilty of your base example and guilty of goading a good woman into desperate things. For God's sake, Frank Clayton, cleanse your mind of its masculine conceit, prejudice, selfishness and partiality—recognize your own destructive work—admit it—regret it, undo it, and ask a good woman's forgiveness. [CLAYTON *laughs ironically.*

[HOOVER *and* ELINOR *enter. Her appearance stills* CLAYTON, *as he turns and sees her.*

ELINOR. Frank? [*Extends her hand pleadingly.*]

CLAYTON. Well?

ELINOR. I'm in the dust—forgive me.

SEELIG. [*In undertone.*] Judge—
[*Starts out*, HOOVER *following.*]
CLAYTON. [*Checking them.*] No—none of that. Let's not contrive any interview of repentance.

ELINOR. You—you're not going to drag the—the whole story into the courts.

CLAYTON. I'm going to—[*Pause.*] do only what is necessary.

ELINOR. [*Sits—speaks with effort at control.*] *As we forgive*—those that trespass against *us*—

CLAYTON. It's too late to adjust matters with a few appropriate quotations.

HOOVER. You won't waive any right by a reasonable delay.

SEELIG. None—so for pity's sake, Frank, tell Colonel Emory to wait.

CLAYTON. I've retained my own counsel—I don't ask other advice.

ELINOR. [*Brokenly.*] Why—why do you come to *see* me?

CLAYTON. I don't! I came because your friend Mr. De Lota was here *with* you.

ELINOR. Frank!

HOOVER. *I* brought De Lota.

CLAYTON. [*Explosively.*] I don't object. [*Then with fateful control.*] I'm just going to take Dick out of the muck, that's all.

ELINOR. Dick!

HOOVER. [*Bristling.*] The law prescribes the only way that—

ELINOR. [*Quickly interposing.*] Father—don't—don't. We mustn't talk of law and its wrangle over Dick. Frank's perfectly right. If I were meeting Mr. De Lota after the terrible mistake of that night Dick shouldn't be in my care at all. [*Turns to* CLAYTON.] It—it was on account of the suit—that's all. If you let Colonel Emory do that cruel thing without believing me. Father brought him—Dick wasn't here. I said that I wouldn't bring up my jealousy of that woman in Paris—nothing to blacken the name of Dick's *father*—didn't I? [*Turns to* HOOVER.]

HOOVER. She did.

ELINOR. [*Again to* CLAYTON.] You must see Dick—but leave him here, Frank, until you know the very truth —about—it all. You get him, father—

HOOVER. [*Going.*] Of course. I've seen fifty cases that looked worse than this smoothed out by a little patience.

ELINOR. [*Anxiously.*] Get Dick.

CLAYTON. You saw De Lota?

ELINOR. With father.

HOOVER. [*Turning.*] De Lota's statement to me, Frank, was identical with Elinor's.

CLAYTON. Never mind.

HOOVER. [*Coming back.*] I've got to mind—you're not informed. Elinor and De Lota were friends before you ever came to New York. [ELINOR *tries to silence* HOOVER.]

CLAYTON. Friends?

ELINOR. [*Pause, and as* CLAYTON *glares at her.*] Yes. [*To* HOOVER.] Get Dick. Go—don't say any more.

[HOOVER *goes.*

CLAYTON. [*Accusingly.*] I introduced De Lota to you only a year ago.

ELINOR. I know, but—

CLAYTON. Why pretend you were not acquainted?

ELINOR. I—I was considering his feelings.

CLAYTON. What do you mean by *that?*

ELINOR. Before I knew you—we were engaged.

CLAYTON. Engaged!

ELINOR. He and I. Father objected on account of De

Lota's race—and—Father forbade me ever to speak of it in his hearing. When you and I met I was still over-sensitive about it and—

CLAYTON. [*Furiously.*] No, by God! It won't do. You can't square it. I see it now. I've been a dupe for years and years.

ELINOR. I never saw him again until you brought him home.

CLAYTON. Don't, I'm through with it. [*Going.*]

ELINOR. *Frank*—don't go—wait! See Dick!

CLAYTON. [*Turning.*] Dick.

ELINOR. You must see your boy.

CLAYTON. *My* boy! How do I *know* he's my boy?

[ELINOR *and* SEELIG *both exclaim.*

ELINOR. Oh!

SEELIG. Frank!

CLAYTON. You've lived a lie about that blackguard all along until I trap you in his room.

ELINOR. But Dick—our baby Dick. For God's sake, Frank, don't say a thing like that.

CLAYTON. Why not, if it's here—here—[*Striking forehead.*] And hell itself can't burn it out.

SEELIG. [*At the door.*] Frank—it's the boy.

CLAYTON. No—no!

[*Turns and goes rapidly out by the other door.*
[*Enter* DICK.

ELINOR. [*To* SEELIG.] What have I done? I didn't know—I didn't know.

DICK. [*To* ELINOR.] Where's Papa?

ELINOR. [*With a heartbroken cry.*] Ah! [*Kneels and takes* DICK *in her arms.*] My boy—my boy—[*Brushes back his hair.*] Our baby—boy. [*Kisses and embraces him hysterically, sobbing.*]

Curtain.

ACT IV

[*SCENE: Same as Act II, the Lounging Room at Clayton's. A large couch is drawn up in front of fire. The room is lighted only by the lamp on the small table and a candlelabrum near the telephone. The pictures on the wall are awry, and there is a look of general desolation about the place. A window is open at left side of room and the sound of church bells comes in.*

DISCOVERED: CLAYTON on couch near fire—steamer rug over him—he in dressing gown and slippers. His shoes are on floor.]

[*Enter* SUTTON *from dining room carrying tray.*]

SUTTON. I beg pardon, sir.

CLAYTON. Well?

SUTTON. I've a bowl of bouillon and some toast—I thought maybe you'd try it, sir.

CLAYTON. [*Indifferently.*] Thank you, Sutton.

SUTTON. [*Putting tray on table at head of the couch.*] Shall I put it nearer? [CLAYTON *shakes head.*] If you'd rather have a milk punch, sir?

CLAYTON. No.

SUTTON. Or an egg-nogg—[CLAYTON *shakes head.*]

CLAYTON. You might shut that window.

SUTTON. Yes, sir. [*Going to the window.*]

CLAYTON. Those damn bells—

SUTTON. Yes, sir. [*Closes window.*]

CLAYTON. When did Doctor Seelig say he'd come?

SUTTON. As soon as possible.

CLAYTON. And it's been three hours.

SUTTON. Nearly three hours, yes, sir. There's the door —may be Doctor now. [*Goes to hall.*]

[CLAYTON *re-arranges pillow and lies down again.*
[HOOVER'S *voice is heard outside.*
SUTTON. [*Also outside.*] He's lying down—in the smoking room.

[*Enter* SUTTON.

[HOOVER *and* ELINOR *appear in hallway.*
SUTTON. [*Leaning over the back of the couch.*] Pardon, sir—Judge Hoover!
CLAYTON. [*Shaking head.*] No—
SUTTON. And Mrs. Clayton, sir.
CLAYTON. [*Sitting up.*] Here?
HOOVER. [*Entering.*] I don't want to intrude, Frank, but—it seems necessary. Come in, Elinor!

[SUTTON *goes.* ELINOR *comes down to the couch.*

CLAYTON. You'll have to see my attorney. I'm not able to talk any business.
ELINOR. [*Tenderly.*] You're ill, Frank?
CLAYTON. [*Coldly.*] Resting a minute—
ELINOR. I'm sorry to disturb you, but—it's for Dick. [*Pause.*] [CLAYTON *motions slightly to a chair which* HOOVER *places*—ELINOR *sits.*] You know that to-morrow is—a holiday? [CLAYTON *nods.*] Dick's eager about it—
CLAYTON. [*Complainingly to* HOOVER.] This isn't necessary, is it?
ELINOR. Dick's talked for days about his tree and hanging up his stocking by the big fireplace at home. Our difference, Frank, mustn't put a blight on the boy's Christmas.
CLAYTON. [*In undertone.*] My God! What drivel!
ELINOR. Drivel when I repeat it—if you will—but not as little Dick talks it day after day. His love for you isn't drivel.

CLAYTON. [*To* HOOVER.] You promised Emory to begin suit if I'd keep quiet.

HOOVER. Yes.

CLAYTON. Nearly a month ago.

HOOVER. I know—but—[*Turns to* ELINOR.]

ELINOR. *I* refuse. There's nothing left me to live for but my baby and his happiness. I won't—I won't bring an accusation against his father—[CLAYTON *moves away wearily to mantel*—ELINOR *rises*.] You *are* his father and only your wish to crush me makes you pretend to doubt it. I've forfeited your love, I know—I'm not here to plead against that—but to avoid any scar I can for the boy's heart. I want you to let Dick come here to-morrow—[CLAYTON *moves impatiently*.] Not with *me*—with Miss Doane. I want you to see him—and take him in your arms—

CLAYTON. [*Shakes head.*] No—

HOOVER. [*With some indignation.*] Whatever he is—he's a child, and for seven years this was his home.

CLAYTON. There'll be other anniversaries. He may as well learn now.

ELINOR. No—not now. When he's old enough to understand I'll *tell* him—the truth.

CLAYTON. What is the truth?

ELINOR. That his mother—was a foolish woman who thought her husband didn't understand her. That his father punished her out of all proportion to her offense, but only as *women* must expect punishment.

CLAYTON. [*Sneering.*] I know—because *men* are brutes.

ELINOR. Because—God has put into woman's keeping a trust—of which no one—neither husbands nor fathers tell them truly—about which the world in its vain disputes of equality misleads them—of which they learn only through their own suffering.

CLAYTON. [*Leaving* ELINOR *and going to* HOOVER.] This kind of thing is—what I try to escape.

ELINOR. [*Following.*] Let Dick spend his Christmas morning here. [CLAYTON *shakes head.*] You used to ask after him every day until you took this cruel pose of pretending that he's not *your* boy.

CLAYTON. [*To* HOOVER.] Please—

ELINOR. I couldn't tell you in Doctor Seelig's presence plainly enough. You know Father's insane antipathy to—[*Pause.*] to *those people.* Any word—the most sacred—any name—the most honored—by scornful repetition becomes a reproach, and I had grown fearful of ridicule about my former friendship for—Ben De Lota. That was my sole reason for silence.

CLAYTON. [*Wearily.*] My God!

HOOVER. Elinor, Frank! [*Indicates hall.*]

BURRILL. [*Outside.*] Is he too ill to be seen a moment?

HOOVER. [*Peering cautiously into hall.*] Woman, too.
[*Enter* SUTTON.

SUTTON. Mr. Burrill, sir.

CLAYTON. I said no one but Doctor Seelig.

SUTTON. Miss Seelig, Doctor's daughter, is with Mr. Burrill.

ELINOR. Father! [*Going quickly out by dining room door.*]

HOOVER. [*Following.*] I want a word, Frank, when they're gone.

CLAYTON. But not with *her.*

HOOVER. No—she'll go. [HOOVER *leaves.*

CLAYTON. My coat! [SUTTON *gets* CLAYTON's *coat and waistcoat from the table—*CLAYTON *takes them and nods for* SUTTON *to go.*] [SUTTON *goes.*

[CLAYTON *feebly unbuttons his dressing gown, pauses, wearily throws coat and*

waistcoat to a chair from which they slip to the floor. CLAYTON *sits on the couch.*
[BURRILL *and* VEDAH *enter.*]

BURRILL. Sorry to disturb you, Mr. Clayton.

VEDAH. And your man says you're not well.

CLAYTON. Nothing! Won't you be seated? [VEDAH *takes chair* BURRILL *places for her.*]

BURRILL. I'm—[*Pause.*] That is, we're—well, I wanted to thank you for my contract on the court-house sculpture.

CLAYTON. They gave it to you, did they?

BURRILL. Yes. The finished marble must be up in a year. Material—workmen—studio—everything's cheaper on the other side—

CLAYTON. I know.

BURRILL. So I'm sailing day after to-morrow—unless you need me here in the architect's libel suit!

CLAYTON. They've withdrawn that.

BURRILL. They have? [CLAYTON *nods.* BURRILL *turns eagerly to* VEDAH.] Then we go—

VEDAH. Yes!

BURRILL. Vedah and I have been married.

CLAYTON. Married?

BURRILL. Half an hour ago.

VEDAH. Yes. [*Rises and stands by* BURRILL.]

BURRILL. [*Taking* VEDAH's *hand.*] I'm the happiest man alive.

CLAYTON. [*Moodily.*] Half an hour? Ah, yes. [*With an effort rises and goes to them.*] Well, I congratulate you both.

VEDAH. Papa and Mama don't know it yet. [BURRILL *goes to the fireplace.*]

CLAYTON. An elopement?

VEDAH. Is it? If we didn't leave the city?

[*Enter* SUTTON.]

SUTTON. Mrs. Seelig, sir.

[VEDAH *anxiously goes to* BURRILL.
[*Enter* MRS. SEELIG.

[SUTTON *goes out.*

MRS. SEELIG. Vedah. [*Sees* BURRILL.] You know your father's wishes.

BURRILL. We've been married, Mrs. Seelig.

MRS. SEELIG. Vedah!

VEDAH. Yes, Mama.

MRS. SEELIG. When?

VEDAH. At five o'clock.

MRS. SEELIG. How? Who married you?

BURRILL. A Justice of the Peace.

MRS. SEELIG. Frank! [*Turns to* CLAYTON.]

VEDAH. [*Going to her mother.*] Remember your parents objected to Papa.

MRS. SEELIG. [*To* CLAYTON.] My father was a Rabbi—Doctor Seelig's ideas were advanced—even his own people thought so.

VEDAH. No couple could be happier than you have been.

MRS. SEELIG. Is *this* happiness—my only daughter runs away—why? To-day? Why secretly?

BURRILL. I'm sailing for Paris.

VEDAH. [*Returning to* BURRILL.] To be gone a year.

BURRILL. The separation was impossible.

MRS. SEELIG. Couldn't you have trusted Vedah that long?

VEDAH. It was *I*, Mama.

MRS. SEELIG. You?

VEDAH. To risk a sculptor in Paris? Oh no!

MRS. SEELIG. Well, go home and tell your poor father.

VEDAH. I want you with us, Mama.

BURRILL. I'm willing to tell the Doctor alone.

VEDAH. [*In alarm.*] No.

MRS. SEELIG. Very well, wait for me and we'll meet Papa together.

VEDAH. [*To* CLAYTON.] Good-bye!

[*They shake hands.*

CLAYTON. Good-bye. [*Shakes hands with* BURRILL.] Bon voyage.

BURRILL. Thank you. [*Starts out with* VEDAH.]

MRS. SEELIG. [*Impulsively.*] Vedah! [VEDAH *turns,* MRS. SEELIG *embraces and kisses her.*]

BURRILL. Thank you, Mrs. Seelig. [*Goes out with* VEDAH.]

MRS. SEELIG. [*Sighing and turning to* CLAYTON *who is at the fireplace.*] I left Elinor—waiting for Judge Hoover. When I go back I want to carry her some comfort.

CLAYTON. Your arrival will do that, Mrs. Seelig.

MRS. SEELIG. I hope so. This is Christmas Eve, you know.

CLAYTON. Yes.

MRS. SEELIG. Little Dick has always found his stocking—in there. [*Indicates the music room.*]

CLAYTON. Mrs. Clayton mustn't use Dick to break down my decision.

MRS. SEELIG. I bought a little tree—[*Indicates its height.*] I caught the Christian shopkeeper smiling—but no matter. I had Sutton take it in at the tradesman's entrance. [CLAYTON *turns away.*] I know. You think that is more indelicacy characteristic of the race—but Vedah is going with that young man—my own heart is alive to the suffering around us. *Yours?*—yes! it comes soon enough to us all—but Frank!—that little boy who is—

CLAYTON. Please! Mrs. Seelig, the doctor's ordered me to avoid all excitement. [*Sits wearily on couch.*]

MRS. SEELIG. [*Sympathetically.*] He didn't tell *us*.

CLAYTON. Not Doctor Seelig.

MRS. SEELIG. Oh!

CLAYTON. A specialist—but he doesn't help me. Sutton phoned and I'm waiting for Doctor Seelig now.

MRS. SEELIG. Now? I can't meet him here. But that tree's in the house and you must let us bring Dick over.

[*Enter* HOOVER.

HOOVER. Pardon.

MRS. SEELIG. I'm going—Good night. [*She goes.*

CLAYTON. [*Pause.*] Where is—?

HOOVER. Elinor? [CLAYTON nods.] She left immediately. [CLAYTON *lies down on couch.*] She's—not—a bad woman, Frank! What she said about my opposition was true—but we all learn. I didn't know the hearts those people had in 'em—[*Pause.*] And her girlish affair with De Lota was—well, you know Elinor's craze for music. That's the explanation—attraction was mostly artistic.

[*Enter* SUTTON.

SUTTON. Doctor Seelig.

CLAYTON. You'll have to excuse me, Judge.

HOOVER. Sorry to see you—ill, old man.

[*Enter* SEELIG.

SEELIG. Good evening.

HOOVER. Good evening, Doctor. [*Going, extends hand.*] I wish you—[*Pause.*] the compliments of the season.

SEELIG. The same to you, Judge.

[HOOVER *goes.*] [SUTTON *takes* SEELIG'S *hat and coat.*

SEELIG. Well, Frank—under the weather? [*Leans over back of couch.*]

CLAYTON. Pretty rotten.

SEELIG. Need a little air in here.

CLAYTON. I couldn't stand the damned bells.

SEELIG. Better stand them a minute.
[*Opens window. The sound of church bells is heard.*]

CLAYTON. " Peace on earth, good will to men."

SEELIG. How long have you been this way? [*Taking* CLAYTON'S *pulse.*]

CLAYTON. Been here—since last night.

SEELIG. Drinking?

CLAYTON. Very little.

SEELIG. Pain anywhere?

CLAYTON. Some—back of my neck near the shoulders.

SEELIG. Headache? [CLAYTON *shakes head.*] No other pains? [CLAYTON *shakes head.*] What kept you in the house?

CLAYTON. I feel all in—rotten tired.

SEELIG. I'd have come earlier, Frank, but a long list. Then there was an accident to a little chap on Third Avenue—they brought him to the hospital—smaller than your boy. We operate on him at eight-thirty. [*Regards watch.*] When I got away from that the police stopped us at every cross street. Wonderful sight on the Avenue—people seem to have money. I think a prosperity Christmas.

[*Picks up the coat and waistcoat from the floor—folds them. Straightens pictures on wall.*]

CLAYTON. Can't we have that window closed now? [*Pause*—SEELIG *closes the window, shutting out the sound of the bells.*] Ha! " Glad tidings of great joy."

SEELIG. Comes only once a year.

CLAYTON. You any respect for the whole business—that Christ fabrication?

SEELIG. [*Going to fireplace.*] You mean the Church idea—the creeds?

CLAYTON. Yes.

SEELIG. [*Pause.*] I've outgrown the one my own mother started me in, but I take off my hat to the man.

CLAYTON. Why!

SEELIG. Oh, He knew—He'd worked it all out.

CLAYTON. Worked what out?

SEELIG. This thing we call Life. He knew the essence of it.

CLAYTON. I don't see that.

SEELIG. "As a man thinketh"—that was His answer.

CLAYTON. What does that answer?

SEELIG. Everything. When I felt your pulse there and let go your hand you carried it back to the couch—so.

CLAYTON. Expect me to keep it out there like a hat-rack?

SEELIG. I'd hoped you would drop it a little.

CLAYTON. Why?

SEELIG. Hoped you'd relax. Let's try it now. [*Lifts* CLAYTON'S *hand.*] Don't tense those muscles—put your weight on me. [*Drops hand.*] There!

CLAYTON. Well, what does that do?

SEELIG. That's the only part of your body that's relaxed—Now a deep breath and let go. Don't hold yourself up from the couch. So! [CLAYTON *does as told and perceptibly relaxes.*]

CLAYTON. Nerves, I know.

SEELIG. [*Tapping his own forehead.*] It's this. Why, I have patients—business men—who are always tied up like a wet fishing line—sleep that way. Do you know why that wrinkle is between your eyes?

CLAYTON. I'm sick, that's why.

SEELIG. Because the wrinkle's in your mind. That coat I took from the floor said mental wrinkles, "As a man thinketh," my dear Frank. [*Pause.*] What is it now—come?

CLAYTON. You don't have to ask, do you?

SEELIG. I do ask.

CLAYTON. Just to keep my mind on it, I suppose?

SEELIG. No—I want to hear you talk about it.

CLAYTON. My mind will be all right, I'll be all right, when that damned dog is dead in hell!

SEELIG. [*Pause.*] You hate him pretty bitterly, don't you?

CLAYTON. I hate him the best I know how.

SEELIG. You know what good hating does to the hater?

CLAYTON. You mean to me?

SEELIG. [*Nodding.*] To everybody. Kills him.

CLAYTON. Kills him? [SEELIG *nods.*

SEELIG. [*Pause.*] Hate generates one of the deadliest poisons in nature. I've had trouble in my time saving a baby that had nursed milk from the breast of an angry woman. You've heard of the bite of a blue gum negro being poison.

CLAYTON. Knew a man who lost his thumb that way.

SEELIG. Well, it is no more poisonous than the bite of a red gum negro, or the bite of a red gum white man, if either of them gets angry enough, the blue gum negro is just a little nearer the animal and gets mad quicker, that's all. Now, you lie here with this grouch of yours and you generate constantly an internal poison. I haven't any medicines that can beat that.

CLAYTON. When I get so much of it in me that I shoot that cur, as I shall some day, they'll call it murder.

SEELIG. [*Pause.*] I used to get pretty angry when I was younger, but I think it was more to show off.

CLAYTON. You mean I do this to " show off!"

SEELIG. I mean you are influenced by public opinion. If you and he were the only creatures left in the world you'd admit he didn't do much more than you'd have done in his place.

CLAYTON. You mean I'd go into another man's home and ruin it?

SEELIG. This man didn't come into your home and ruin it. He meets an old sweetheart, meets her when she thinks she is being neglected.

CLAYTON. [*Sitting up.*] Neglected? Why, she had this house and our summer place at Newport—a forty-five horse-power limousine—she had—

SEELIG. See here, Frank, you were neglecting her. He did what nine men out of ten would do. He knows the price that's being paid, and I know, that he'd walk around the Belt Line to-night in the snow, barefooted, to have the record closed.

CLAYTON. Suppose you think I ought to hunt him up and shake hands with him?

SEELIG. No—don't think you should ever see him again, even mentally; but it doesn't need murder to acquire that attitude. I want you to be big enough to dismiss it. That's why I quote this carpenter-prophet of Nazareth—a truth that took me a post-graduate course to learn and twenty-five years to demonstrate—He found out by himself. He said in one of his first sermons: "*Forgive,* and ye shall be forgiven; *give* and it shall be given unto you, good measure pressed down, shaken together and running over shall men give unto your bosom."

CLAYTON. Oh that religious elation—

SEELIG. It wasn't religion He was preaching, but a good working rule of life. This precept of good-will—people regard the words "Good-will" as interchangeable with "Peace," but will is active, good-will is a constructive force. I've seen sick people get well merely through two or three hearty good wishers rooting for them. I've figured it out that there's an influence circulating through all men when they'll permit it, just as the current through that lamp goes through all other lamps in this house. Stop it in the man by avarice or cupidity, divert it by envy, *turn it back* by hate, and something goes wrong with the machinery. " Give and it shall be given unto you."

CLAYTON. You take Him too literally, Doctor.

SEELIG. The mistake is not taking Him *literally enough.* I've cured many taking that sermon literally. [*Sits beside* CLAYTON *on his couch.*] I find what is on the patient's mind. Generally some hate or fear—sometimes regret or remorse—then I try to show the patient that yesterday is yesterday, that his past life doesn't concern him any more than last year's snow. If I can get a man looking ahead—hopeful—anxious to get on the job—why he's cured.

CLAYTON. [*Doggedly.*] I'll look ahead when I get even with this fellow.

SEELIG. Well, say you've got even—that you've dealt him some deadly blow, irreparably injured him or his happiness! What then? My dear Frank, there is nothing so disappointing as a satisfied revenge.

CLAYTON. I can't forget it.

SEELIG. Yes you can.

CLAYTON. It's here on my mind. [*Covers his eyes and forehead.*]

SEELIG. Because your mind is empty. Work is the answer to your condition.

CLAYTON. [*Shaking his head.*] Too late for that now.

SEELIG. Nonsense! Take this parable of the eleventh hour. The men in that were kicking because those who had worked one hour got as much as those who had put in a full day. Remember what the Nazarene proposed to pay.

CLAYTON. What?

SEELIG. Peace of mind. A sharehold in what He called the Kingdom of Heaven. The eleventh hour men worked only one hour, but they worked—*the last hour.* You get that peace of mind, whenever—you work, whenever you *do* something—and the splendid thing is, it's *never too late to do it.* [*Rises vigorously—stands at mantel.*]

CLAYTON. [*Wearily.*] Good God, Doctor, a man can't get up and work at something he doesn't care for in order to forget something he's thinking of all the time. It's well enough for you—always called in by some poor devil who thinks you can help him. Give me your job and your equipment for it and I'll talk hope and clean living myself.

SEELIG. [*Half sadly.*] I know that attitude. It's always the next pasture that seems the greenest. If I have any regret it is that instead of being a physician I wasn't a priest. I think most diseases are not physical so much as they are mental or spiritual.

CLAYTON. Well, I'd like to do that kind of thing myself.

SEELIG. You can do it.

CLAYTON. I can?

SEELIG. Yes—only you have to *begin.*

CLAYTON. You mean with myself?

SEELIG. I mean with the work that's nearest to you, Frank. If I wanted you to walk around Central Park you would have to get up, you would have to walk to the door; you would have to go down the steps; you would have to *walk* to Central Park. In other words, you would have to cover the ground that is nearest to you. Now, in the work you say you would like to do, you've also got to cover the ground that's nearest you. Suppose you *were* going to *save* somebody and you had your choice—whom would you save? Why, the people dearest to you. You would save—little Dick—eh?

CLAYTON. [*In pain.*] Don't talk of Dick.

SEELIG. I've got to talk of him. The boy isn't getting a father's care.

CLAYTON. You advised me not to take him.

SEELIG. I still advise that. He *is* getting a mother's care, but he needs a father's also. Now suppose you could save little Dick. The next dearest person to you would be his mother, wouldn't she?

CLAYTON. She's made her bed.

SEELIG. Yes, but after you've made beds there's something more to do than lie in them. After a reasonable time you are to get up and get *out* of them.

CLAYTON. She's all right—free to do as she likes.

SEELIG. No, she isn't. She's a slave to her remorse—she's looking back. *She* can't realize that yesterday is yesterday and that a dead yesterday is just as dead as Babylon. Now, you want work to do—why not do that?

CLAYTON. Overlook what she's done?

SEELIG. Yes—overlook what she's done. She wasn't perfect—nobody is. She makes one mistake—with you it's final. You don't judge anyone else that way. I've seen you throwing little Dick the baseball teaching him to hold it and not to break his chubby fingers—standing two yards from him—drop and drop and drop it. You didn't get tired—you were developing the boy. Now the assumption is that Elinor came to you with her character fully developed; but my dear old friend, character never stops developing if we are in the right line. There's still the perfecting of a fine woman. You want something to do—do that.

CLAYTON. All right—Tell her.—[*Pause.*] I forgive her [*Pause.*] but that I'm through with it just the same.

SEELIG. I'll not carry lies to her. If you forgive her you'll go where she is—you'll go looking forward and not backward—[CLAYTON *shakes head, pause*—SEELIG *regards watch.*] I hate to leave you in this mood, Frank.

CLAYTON. I'll—be all right.

SEELIG. Why not get in the machine and take a run through the Park—only a half hour—because I must get back to the hospital.

CLAYTON. [*Pause.*] You won't try any snap judgment on me—no driving up to your door and making a scene of it?

SEELIG. Chauffeur will take your order.

> [*Pause.* CLAYTON *begins to put on his shoes.* SEELIG *goes to the telephone.*

CLAYTON. What are you doing?

SEELIG. I can't be home to dinner. [*'Phones.*] Yes—operator. Give me 319 Plaza—Plaza—yes.

CLAYTON. I think—[*Pause.*] Mrs. Seelig was here; just before you came—

SEELIG. Yes?

CLAYTON. [*Pause.*] They *expect* you at dinner.

SEELIG. [*'Phoning.*] Holland? [*Pause.*] This is Doctor—I'll speak to Mrs. Seelig—[*Speaks to* CLAYTON.] What did she want?

CLAYTON. Oh—Dick's Christmas principally.

SEELIG. That reminds me—I told Dick I'd see *you* [*'Phones.*] Hello?—yes Sarah? I can't get home to dinner dear—[*Pause.*] No—impossible. [*Pause.*] I'm at Frank Clayton's—[*Pause.*] Nothing—that is, nothing serious. He's going out with me—just to get the air, that's all. What's that? [*Pause.*] Yes, I'll speak to her.

CLAYTON. Speak to whom?

SEELIG. [*Speaking to* CLAYTON.] Mrs. Seelig wants to know if I won't speak to your wife. [*'Phones.*] Hello—that you, Elinor? [*Pause.*] Yes—he's all right—perfectly. [*Pause.*] Not yet, but we're going out—in the car—I'll give it to him.

CLAYTON. Give what?

SEELIG. Just a minute. [*Turns to* CLAYTON *who is put-*

ting on his coat.] It was a Christmas gift—from little Dick —he asked me to bring it here.

CLAYTON. What is it?

[SEELIG *takes small package from his pocket and hands it to* CLAYTON. *As* CLAYTON *opens package* SEELIG *turns attention to 'phone again.*]

SEELIG. Yes, I'm still here—yes. [*Listens in silence as* CLAYTON *undoes the package which contains a photograph in a leather case.* CLAYTON *bends over it, deeply moved.*] Yes—yes—very well—thank you—good night.

CLAYTON. [*Quickly.*] Wait.

SEELIG. [*Startled by loudness of* CLAYTON'S *call.*] Wait. [*Laughs and explains.*] I said wait a minute.

CLAYTON. She at that 'phone?

SEELIG. Yes.

CLAYTON. [*Angrily.*] Let me have it—there are a few things I want to say to her.

SEELIG. [*Protesting.*] Not in that mood, Frank.

CLAYTON. It's all a frame up to torture me. [*Takes 'phone speaks angrily.*] Hello! [*Anger goes from his face—whole manner changes—tone becomes gentle and affectionate.*] Dick, that you, Dick? [*Pause.*] Yes, I hear you—[*Pause.*] I got it, my boy, thank you—[*Pause.*] You bet I like it—[*Pause.*] The *tree?* [*Pause.*] Yes, by the big fireplace—[*Pause.*] To-night? Well—[*Pause.*] Then—[*Pause and effort.*] Tell her to *come—with you!*

[*Drops 'phone on table, receiver hanging towards the floor. Sinks into chair face down on elbow sobbing.* SEELIG *walks to 'phone, hangs up receiver.* CLAYTON *reaches out his right hand blindly.* SEELIG *takes it—holds it reassuringly and firmly. Gives* CLAYTON *a tonic slap on back and helps him rise.* CLAYTON *walks back to chair facing the fire.*

SEELIG. [*Solemnly.*] Frank! There is one moment in a woman's life—dazed by chloroform—wrung with pain—when her physician hears her speak the name of the man for whom she suffers. [*Pause.*]. Every vestige of that doubt you uttered in my library must be effaced from your heart. [*Rings push button.*]

CLAYTON. I didn't—*invent* the doubt.

SEELIG. I know.

CLAYTON. I think—[*Pause.*] I *hope* to God I'll get rid of it—in time.

SEELIG. It mustn't mar this reunion. [*Pause.*] When I started for this house—I hoped—for what has occurred. [*Indicates 'phone.*] I didn't know just how it would come about—but—I knew—that doubt had to be removed.

CLAYTON. I don't want to think of it.

[*Enter* SUTTON.

SEELIG. [*To* SUTTON.] A gentleman is outside in a cab, just behind my car? Ask him to come in.

[SUTTON *goes.*

CLAYTON. [*Quickly turning.*] Who is it? [*Pause.*] Who?

SEELIG. I want you to be calm Frank.

CLAYTON. *Who?*

SEELIG. [*Calmly.*] The one you hate.

CLAYTON. No! By God, no!

[*Starts toward the hall.*

SEELIG. [*Interposing and catching him.*] Frank—if you had to go under the knife you'd trust me as a surgeon, wouldn't you?

CLAYTON. [*Struggling to free himself.*] You're bungling this job.

SEELIG. [*Still holding* CLAYTON.] I'm not bungling it.

[*Enter* DE LOTA.]

CLAYTON. Don't come in here.

DE LOTA. Mr. Clayton—

SEELIG. [*Between the two men.*] Speak only when I bid you—[*Pause. To* CLAYTON.] Now listen! [*To* DE LOTA.] Before Mr. Clayton introduced you to Mrs. Clayton a year ago—when had you last seen her?

DE LOTA. About eight years before.

SEELIG. That is nine years *ago*.

DE LOTA. Nine years ago.

CLAYTON. What's one *lie* more or less.

SEELIG. Where were you *eight years* ago?

DE LOTA. In France.

SEELIG. [*Sternly.*] Where!

DE LOTA. [*Pause.*] The prison *de La Santé,* in Paris.

SEELIG. For how long a term?

DE LOTA. One year.

SEELIG. I asked you to bring your prison paper of discharge. [DE LOTA *hands paper to* SEELIG. SEELIG *regards paper and displays it to* CLAYTON.] You read French—numerals at least. The date is there.

CLAYTON. [*After a glance.*] Well?

SEELIG. Also Mr. Burrill was in the court-room when Mr. De Lota was sentenced. [*Pause.*] To show this paper, to admit in your hearing—this fact has not been an easy thing for Benjamin De Lota to do. He does it at my urging—the appeal of one *Jew*—to another *Jew*. He is going—he lives by writing criticism. His signature to an article has a money value—and despite these personal mistakes, I believe his influence in print is wholesome. He leaves your magazines. Of course, he can't expect their recommendation, but I have *promised* him—*your silence.*

CLAYTON. [*Pause.*] I shan't—[*Pause.*] Interfere.

[SEELIG *turns*—DE LOTA *goes.*

SEELIG. [*Hand on* CLAYTON'*s shoulder.*] I'm proud of you—[*Pause.*] Now forgive an old practitioner who knew he had to cauterize quickly.

CLAYTON. You're—a friend all right. [*Pause.*] Prison!

SEELIG. That year.

CLAYTON. And I made that rotten accusation. What a brute I've been!

SEELIG. My dear Frank, that also is yesterday. [*Pause and change of manner.*] Dick is coming to-night?

CLAYTON. Yes.

SEELIG. And his mother—[CLAYTON *nods.*] I'll leave you alone.

CLAYTON. I'd rather you were here.

SEELIG. I'll wait as long as I can. [*Consults watch.*]

CLAYTON. [*Seated on couch.*] There's some troubling news for you.

SEELIG. For me?

CLAYTON. [*Nodding.*] I'd like to cushion it if I could.

SEELIG. You mean *bad* news!

CLAYTON. Depends.

SEELIG. [*Pause.*] Well—

CLAYTON. [*Carefully.*] You know—Vedah—rather fancied Burrill, don't you?

SEELIG. Yes.

CLAYTON. Burrill is sailing in a day or two—and—

SEELIG. [*Pause.*] Well?

CLAYTON. Well—they've been—[*Pause.*]

SEELIG. [*Calmly.*] Married?

CLAYTON. To-day. [SEELIG *nods ruminatively.*
[*Enter* DICK. MRS. SEELIG *and* ELINOR *appear in arch.*

DICK. [*Running to* CLAYTON.] Papa!

CLAYTON. Why, Dick boy!
 [*Embraces him.* ELINOR *goes into the music room.* MRS. SEELIG *comes down.*

DICK. [*To* SEELIG.] Did you give it to him?
SEELIG. [*Still brooding.*] Yes.
DICK. [*To* CLAYTON.] You like it?
CLAYTON. You bet I liked it. [DICK *laughs*—CLAYTON *leading* DICK *toward the music room speaks to* MRS. SEELIG.] I told the Doctor.
MRS. SEELIG. You mean—?
CLAYTON. Vedah and Burrill.
[*Goes with* DICK *into music room.*
MRS. SEELIG. [*Coming to* SEELIG'S *side.*] Samuel.
SEELIG. [*Pause.*] You knew it?
MRS. SEELIG. I had no idea of it—but he has to cross the ocean. They love each other—Vedah was almost broken-hearted. We wanted Vedah to sacrifice her life to teach the idea of one God—but Samuel—[*Pause. Puts hand on* SEELIG'S *arm.*]
SEELIG. Well?
MRS. SEELIG. The one God was wiser than my father, who was a Rabbi. He may be wiser than we are. [*Pause*—SEELIG *gently lifts her hand and kisses it. Pause.*] Samuel—they're at home. Come forgive them and let's be happy at dinner. [SEELIG *shakes head.*] You mean you won't forgive them?
SEELIG. [*Pause.*] I mean *only* that I can't come to dinner. There is a surgery case at the hospital.
MRS. SEELIG. [*Pleading.*] Let someone else.
SEELIG. [*Shaking head.*] Too important.
MRS. SEELIG. Who is it?
SEELIG. A little boy from the East Side. I don't remember his name, but the appointment is for eight thirty. [MRS. SEELIG *leaves his side.*]

[ELINOR *enters,* CLAYTON *and* DICK *appear in doorway after her.* ELINOR *comes down to* SEELIG.

SEELIG. It's all right?
> [ELINOR *nods yes—takes* SEELIG's *face in both hands and kisses him.*

DICK. [*To* CLAYTON *in childish treble.*] She kissed him—

Curtain.

THE RETURN OF PETER GRIMM

A Play in Three Acts

By
DAVID BELASCO

DAVID BELASCO was born in San Francisco, July 25, 1859. He received his early education under a Catholic priest at Vancouver, B. C., and graduated from Lincoln College, California, in 1875. He was stage manager of the Baldwin Theatre, San Francisco, in 1878, and later stage manager of the Grand Opera House and the Metropolitan Theatre in the same city. During these years, besides his original work, he was engaged in dramatizing novels and adapting foreign plays. In 1880 he took charge of production for Mallory Brothers at the Madison Square Theatre, New York City. In 1887 he went to Charles Frohman. From 1902 he was manager and proprietor of the Republic Theatre, and from 1908 of the Belasco Theatre. Among his plays are *May Blossoms* (1884), *Lord Chumley* (1887), *The Heart of Maryland* (1895), *Madame Butterfly* (1900), *Mme. du Barry* (1901), *The Girl of the Golden West* (1905), *The Return of Peter Grimm* (1911).

The Return of Peter Grimm was first produced at the Belasco Theatre, New York, October 17, 1911, with David Warfield as the leading character. It is to be revived in 1920 with Mr. Warfield again as Peter Grimm.

For the courteous permission to print this play for the first time, the present editor desires to express his personal thanks to the author.

[Copyrighted]

"Only one thing really counts—only one thing—love. It is the only thing that tells in the long run: nothing else endures to the end."

CHARACTERS

PETER GRIMM
FREDERIK, his nephew
JAMES HARTMAN
ANDREW MACPHERSON
REV. HENRY BATHOLOMMEY
COLONEL TOM LAWTON
WILLIAM
CATHERINE
MRS. BATHOLOMMEY
MARTA
THE CLOWN

SYNOPSIS

The scene of the play is laid in the living room of Peter Grimm's home at Grimm Manor, a small town in New York State, founded by early settlers from Holland.

The first act takes place at eleven o'clock in the morning on a fine spring day.

The second act passes ten days later, towards the close of a rainy afternoon.

The third act takes place at twenty minutes to twelve on the same night.

NOTE

The author does not advance any theory as to the probability of the return of the main character of this play. For *the many*, it may be said that Peter could exist only in the minds of the characters grouped about him—in their subconscious memories. For *the few*, his presence will embody the theory of the survival of the persistent personal energy. This character has, so far as possible, been treated to accord with either thought.

THE RETURN OF PETER GRIMM

ACT I

[*SCENE: The scene shows a comfortable living room in an old house. The furniture was brought to America by* PETER GRIMM'S *ancestors. The* GRIMMS *were, for the most part, frugal people, but two or three fine paintings have been inherited by* PETER. *A small old-fashioned piano stands near the open window, a few comfortable chairs, a desk with a hanging lamp above it and an arm-chair in front of it, a quaint old fireplace, a Dutch wall clock with weights, a sofa, hat rack, and mahogany flower pot holders, are set about the room; but the most treasured possession is a large family bible lying on a table. A door leads to a small office occupied by* PETER'S *secretary. Stairs lead to the sleeping-rooms above. Through the window, hot houses, beds of tulips and other flowers, shrubs and trees are seen. "* PETER GRIMM'S *Botanic Gardens" supply seeds, plants, shrubbery and trees to the wholesale, as well as retail trade, and the view suggests the importance of the industry. An old Dutch windmill, erected by a Colonial ancestor, gives a quaint touch to the picture. Although* PETER GRIMM *is a very wealthy man he lives as simply as his ancestors.*

DISCOVERED: As the curtain is raised, the room is empty; but CATHERINE *is heard singing in the dining room.* JAMES HARTMAN, PETER'S *secretary, opens his* door to listen, a small bundle of letters in his hand. He is a well set up young man, rather blunt in his manner and a trifle careless in his dress. After a pause, he goes back into the office, leaving the door ajar. Presently CATHERINE enters. In spite of her youth and girlish appearance, she is a good thrifty housekeeper. She wears a simple summer gown, and carries a bunch of gay tulips and an old silver pitcher from which she presently pours water into the Harlequin Delft vase on PETER GRIMM's desk. She peeps into the office, retreating with a smile on her lips as JAMES appears.]*

CATHERINE. Did I disturb you, James?
JAMES. [*On the threshold.*] No indeed.
CATHERINE. Do you like your new work?
JAMES. Anything to get back to the gardens, Catherine. I've always done outside work and I prefer it; but I would shovel dirt rather than work for any one else.
CATHERINE. [*Amused.*] James!
JAMES. It's true. When the train reached the Junction and a boy presented the passengers with the usual flower and the "compliments of Peter Grimm,"—it took me back to the time when that was my job; and when I saw the old sign, "Grimm's Botanic Gardens and Nurseries"—I wanted to jump off the train and run through the grounds. It seemed as though every tulip called "hello" to me.
CATHERINE. Too bad you left college! You had only one more year.
JAMES. Poor father! He's very much disappointed. Father has worked in the dirt in overalls—a gardener—all his life; and of course, he over-estimates an education. He's far more intelligent than most of our college professors.

CATHERINE. I understand why you came back. You simply *must* live where things grow: mustn't you, James? So must I. Have you seen our orchids?

JAMES. Orchids are pretty; but they're doing wonderful things with potatoes these days. I'd rather improve the breed of a squash than to have an orchid named after me. Wonderful discovery of Luther Burbank's—an edible cactus. Sometimes I feel bitter thinking what I might have done with vegetables, when I was wasting my time studying Greek.

CATHERINE. [*Changing suddenly.*] James: why don't you try to please Uncle Peter Grimm?

JAMES. I do; but he is always asking my opinion and when I give it, he blows up.

CATHERINE. [*Coaxingly.*] Don't be quite so blunt. Try to be like one of the family.

JAMES. I'm afraid I shall never be like one of *this* family.

CATHERINE. Why not? I'm no relation at all; and yet—

JAMES. [*Making a resolution.*] I'll do my best to agree with him. [*Offering his hand.*] It's a promise.

[*They shake hands.*]

CATHERINE. Thank you, James.

JAMES. [*Still holding her hand.*] It's good to be back, Catherine. It's good to see you again.

> [*He is still holding her hand when* FREDERIK GRIMM *enters. He is the son of* PETER GRIMM's *dead sister and has been educated by* PETER *to carry on his work. He is a graduate of Amsterdam College, and in appearance and manner, suggests the foreign student. He has managed to pull through college creditably, making a specialty of botany.* PETER *has*

given him the usual trip through Europe and FREDERIK *has come to his rich uncle to settle down and learn his business. He has been an inmate of the household for a few months. He poses as a most industrious young man, but is, at heart, a shirker.*

FREDERIK. Where's uncle?

JAMES. Good morning, Frederik. Your uncle's watching father spray the plum trees. The black knot's after them again.

FREDERIK. I can hardly keep my eyes open. Uncle wakes me up every morning at five—creaking down the old stairs. [*Eyeing* CATHERINE *admiringly.*] You're looking uncommonly pretty this morning, Kitty.

[CATHERINE *edges away and runs upstairs to her room.*

FREDERIK. Hartman!

JAMES. Yes?

FREDERIK. Miss Catherine and you and I are no longer children—our positions are altered: please remember that. I'm no longer a student home for the holidays from Amsterdam College. I'm here to learn the business which I am expected to carry on. Miss Catherine is a young lady now, and my uncle looks upon her as his daughter. You are here as my uncle's secretary. That's how we three stand in this house. Don't call me "Frederik" and hereafter be good enough to say: "Miss Grimm."

JAMES. [*Amiably.*] Very well.

FREDERIK. James: there's a good opportunity for a young man like you in our Florida house. I think that if I spoke for you—

JAMES. Why do you wish to ship me off to Florida?

FREDERIK. I don't understand you, Hartman. I don't wish to ship you off. I am merely thinking of your future. You seem to have changed since—

JAMES. We've all grown up, as you just said.
[JAMES *has laid some mail on the desk and is about to leave the room, when* FREDERIK *speaks again, but in a more friendly manner.*

FREDERIK. The old man's ageing: do you notice it?

JAMES. Your uncle's mellowing, yes; but that's only to be expected. He's changing foliage with the years.

FREDERIK. He's growing as old fashioned as his hats. In my opinion, this would be the time to sell.

JAMES. [*Astonished.*] Sell? Sell a business that has been in the family for—why, it's his religion!

FREDERIK. It's at the height of its prosperity. It would sell like that! [*Snapping his fingers.*] What was the last offer the old man refused from Hicks of Rochester?

JAMES. [*Noticing the sudden friendliness—looking at* FREDERIK, *half amused, half disgusted.*] Can't repeat correspondence, Mr. Grimm. [*Amazed.*] Good heavens! You surprise me! Would you sell your great, great grandfather? I learned to read by studying his obituary out in the peach orchard: "Johann Grimm of Holland, an upright settler." There isn't a day your uncle doesn't tell me that you are to carry on the work.

FREDERIK. So I was, but it's not my religion. [*Sarcastically.*] Every man can't be blessed like you with the soul of a market gardener—a peddler of turnips.

JAMES. [*Thinking—ignoring* FREDERIK.] He's a great old man—your uncle. It's a big name—Grimm—Peter Grimm. The old man knows his business—he certainly knows his business. [*Changing.*] God! It's an awful thought that a man must die and carry all that knowledge of orchids to the grave! I wonder if it doesn't all count somewhere. . . . I must attend to the mail.

[PETER GRIMM *enters from the gardens. He is a well preserved man of sixty, very simple and plain in his ways. He has not changed his style of dress in the past thirty years. His clothing, collar, tie, hat and shoes are all old fashioned. He is an estimable man, scrupulously honest, gentle and sympathetic; but occasionally he shows a flash of Dutch stubbornness.*

FREDERIK. I ran over from the office, Uncle Peter, to make a suggestion.

PETER. Yes?

FREDERIK. I suggest that we insert a full page out of your new tulip in our mid-summer floral almanac.

PETER. [*Who has hung up his hat on his own particular peg, affably assenting.*] A good idea!

FREDERIK. The public is expecting it.

PETER. You think so, my boy?

FREDERIK. Why, Uncle: you've no idea of the stir this tulip has created. People stop me in the street to speak of it.

PETER. Well, well: you surprise me. I didn't think it so extraordinary.

FREDERIK. I've had a busy morning, sir, in the packing house.

PETER. That's good. I'm glad to see you taking hold of things, Fritz. [*Humorously, touching* FREDERIK *affectionately on the shoulder.*] We mustn't waste time; for that's the stuff life's made of. [*Seriously.*] It's a great comfort to me, Frederik, to know that when I'm in my little private room with James, or when I've slipped out to the hot houses,—you are representing me in the offices—*young* Mr. Grimm. . . . James: are you ready for me?

JAMES. Yes, sir.

PETER. I'll attend to the mail in a moment. [*Missing* CATHERINE—*he calls, according to the household signal.*] Ou—oo! [*He is answered by* CATHERINE, *who immediately appears from her room and comes running downstairs.*] Catherine: I have news for you. I've named the new rose after you: " Katie—a hardy bloomer." It is as red as the ribbon in your hair.

CATHERINE. Thank you, Uncle Peter, thank you very much. And now you must have your cup of coffee.

PETER. That's a fine little housewife! A busy girl about the house: eh, Fritz? Is there anything you need to-day, Katie?

CATHERINE. No, Uncle Peter: I have everything I need, thank you.

PETER. Not everything—not everything my dear. [*Smiling at* FREDERIK. JAMES, *ignored, is standing in the background.*] Wait! Wait till I give you a husband. I have my plans. [*Looking from* FREDERIK *to* CATHERINE.] People don't always know what I'm doing, but I'm a great man for planning. Come Katie: tell me on this fine spring morning, what sort of husband would you prefer?

CATHERINE. [*Annoyed—with girlish impatience.*] You're always speaking of weddings, Uncle Peter. I don't know what's come over you of late.

PETER. It's nesting time . . . spring weddings are in the air; besides my grandmother's linen chest upstairs must be used again for you, [*Impulsively drawing* CATHERINE *to him*] my house fairy. [*Kisses her.*] There: I mustn't tease her. But I leave it to Fritz if I don't owe her a fine husband—this girl of mine. Look what she has done for *me*.

CATHERINE. Done for you? I do you the great favor to let *you* do everything for *me*.

PETER. Ah, but who lays out my linen? Who puts

flowers on my desk every day? Who gets up at dawn to eat breakfast with me? Who sees that I have my second cup of coffee? But better than all that—who brings youth into my old house?

CATHERINE. That's not much—youth.

PETER. No? We'll leave it to Fritz. [FREDERIK, *amused, listens in silence.*] What should I be now—a rough old fellow—a bachelor—without youth in my house, eh? God knows! Katie has softened me towards all the ladies —er—mellowed me as time has mellowed my old pictures. [*Points to a picture.*] And I was growing hard—hard and fussy.

CATHERINE. [*Laughing.*] Ah, Uncle Peter: have I made you take a liking to all the rest of the ladies?

PETER. Yes. It's just as it is when you have a pet: you like all that breed. You can only see *your* kind of kitten.

JAMES. [*Coming down a step, impressed by* PETER'S *remark—speaking earnestly.*] That's so, sir. [*The others are surprised.*] I hadn't thought of it in that way, but it's true. You study a girl for the first time, and presently you notice the same little traits in every one of them. It makes you feel differently towards all the rest.

PETER. [*Amused.*] Why, James, what do you know about girls? " Bachelor " is stamped all over you—you're positively labelled.

JAMES. [*Good naturedly.*] Perhaps.

[*Goes back to the office.*

PETER. Poor James! What a life before him! When a bachelor wants to order—three rib roast, who's to eat it? I never had a proper roast until Katie and Frederik came to make up my family; [*Rubbing his hands*] but the roasts are not big enough. [*Giving* FREDERIK *a knowing look.*] We must find a husband.

CATHERINE. You promised not to—

PETER. I want to see a long, long table with plenty of young people.

CATHERINE. I'll leave the room, Uncle.

PETER. With myself at the head, carving, carving, carving, watching the plates come back, and back, and back. [*As she is about to go.*] There, there: not another word of this to-day.

[*The 'phone rings.* JAMES *re-enters and answers it.*

JAMES. Hello! [*Turns.*] Rochester asks for Mr. Peter Grimm to the 'phone. Another message from Hicks' greenhouses.

PETER. Ask them to excuse me.

JAMES. [*Bluntly.*] You'll have to excuse him. [*Listens.*] No, no, the gardens are not in the market. You're only wasting your time.

PETER. Tc! Tc! James! Can't you say it politely?

[JAMES *listens in 'phone.*

FREDERIK. [*Aside to Peter.*] James is so painfully blunt. [*Then changing.*] Is it—er—a good offer? Is Hicks willing to make it worth while? [*Catching his Uncle's astonished eye—apologetically.*] Of course, I know you wouldn't think of—

CATHERINE. I should say not! My home? An offer? *Our* gardens? I should say not!

FREDERIK. Mere curiosity on my part, that's all.

PETER. Of course, I understand. Sell out? No indeed. We are thinking of the next generation.

FREDERIK. Certainly, sir.

PETER. We're the last of the family. The business—that's Peter Grimm. It will soon be Frederik Grimm. The love for the old gardens is in our blood.

FREDERIK. It is, sir.

[*Lays a fond hand on* PETER's *shoulder.*

PETER. [*Struck.*] I have an idea. We'll print the family history in our new floral almanac.

FREDERIK. [*Suppressing a yawn.*] Yes, yes, a very good idea.

PETER. Katie: read it to us and let us hear how it sounds.

CATHERINE. [*Reads.*] "In the Spring of 1709 there settled on Quassick Creek, New York State, Johann Grimm, aged twenty-two, husbandman and vine dresser, also Johanna, his wife."

PETER. Very interesting.

FREDERIK. Very interesting, indeed.

CATHERINE. "To him Queen Anne furnished one square, one rule, one compass, two whipping saws and several pieces. To him was born—"

PETER. [*Interrupting.*] You left out two augers.

CATHERINE. [*Reads.*] O, yes—" and two augers. To him was born a son—"

PETER. [*Who knows the history by heart, has listened, his eyes almost suffused—repeating each word to himself, as she reads. He has lived over each generation down to the present and nods in approval as she reaches this point.*] The foundation of our house. And here we are prosperous and flourishing—after seven generations. We'll print it, eh, Fritz?

FREDERIK. Certainly, sir. By all means let us print it.

PETER. And now we are depending upon you, Frederik, for the next line in the book. [*To* CATHERINE—*slyly—as she closes the book.*] If my sister could see Frederik, what a proud mother she would be!

JAMES. [*Turning from the 'phone to* PETER.] Old man Hicks himself has come to the 'phone. Says he *must* speak to Mr. Peter Grimm.

FREDERIK. Make short work of him, uncle.

PETER. [*At the 'phone.*] How are you, my old friend? . . . How are your plum trees? [*Listens.*] Bad, eh? Well, we can only pray and use Bordeaux Mixture. . . . No. . . . Nonsense! This business has been in my family for seven generations. Why sell? I'll see that it stays in the family seven generations longer! [*Echoing.*] Do I propose to live that long? N—no; but my plans will. [*Looks towards* FREDERIK *and* CATHERINE.] How? Never mind. Good morning.   [*Hangs up the receiver.*

JAMES. Sorry to disturb you, sir, but some of these letters are—

FREDERIK. I'm off.

PETER. [*Who has lifted a pot of tulips to set it in the sun—standing with the pot in his hands.*] And remember the saying: [*A twinkle in his upraised eyes*] " Thou, O God, sellest all good things at the price of labor."

[*Smells the tulips and sets them down.*

FREDERIK. [*Goes briskly towards the door.*] That's true, sir. I want to speak to you later, uncle—[*Turning, looking at* JAMES] on a private matter.

[*He goes off looking at his watch, as though he had a hard day's work before him.*

PETER. [*Looking after* FREDERIK.] Very capable young fellow, Frederik. I was a happy man, James, when I heard that he had won the prize for botany at Amsterdam College. I had to find out the little I know by experience.

JAMES. [*Impulsively.*] Yes, and I'll wager you've forgotten more than—

[*Catching a warning glance from* CATHERINE *he pauses.*

PETER. What?

JAMES. Nothing, sir. I—

CATHERINE. [*Tugging at* PETER'S *coat—speaking to him apart, as* JAMES *busies himself at the desk.*] Uncle Peter: I think you're unfair to James. We used to have him to dinner very often before he went away. Now that he's back, you treat him like a stranger.

PETER. [*Surprised.*] Eh? I didn't know that I— [*Petting* CATHERINE.] A good, unselfish girl. She thinks of everybody. [*Aloud.*] James, will you have dinner with us to-day?

JAMES. [*Pleased and surprised.*] Thank you, sir: yes, sir.

PETER. It's a roast goose,—cooked sweet, James. [*Smacks his lips.*] Fresh green herbs in the dressing and a Figaro pudding. Marta brought over that pudding receipt from Holland. [MARTA, *an old family servant, has entered with the air of having forgotten to wind the clock. She smiles happily at* PETER's *allusion to her puddings, attends to the old clock, and passes off with* CATHERINE. PETER *sits at the desk, glancing over the mail.*] Katie's blossoming like a rose. Have you noticed how she's coming out lately, James?

JAMES. Yes, sir.

PETER. You've noticed it, too?

[*Picks up another letter, looking over it.*]

JAMES. Yes, sir.

PETER. [*Pausing, taking off his eyeglasses and holding them on his thumb. Philosophically.*] How prettily nature accomplishes her will—making a girl doubly beautiful that a young man may yield his freedom the more easily. Wonderful! [*During the following, he glances over letters.*] A young girl is like a violet sheltered under a bush, James; and that is as it should be, isn't it?

JAMES. No sir, *I* don't think so.

PETER. [*Surprised.*] What?

JAMES. I believe people should think for themselves— not be. . . .

PETER. Go on.

James.—er—

Peter. Well?

James. [*Remembering his promise to* Catherine.] Nothing.

Peter. Go on, James.

James. I mean swallowed up.

Peter. Swallowed up? Explain yourself, James.

James. I shouldn't have mentioned it.

Peter. Certainly, certainly. Don't be afraid to express an honest opinion.

James. I only meant that you can't shape another's life. We are all free beings and—

Peter. Free? Of course Katie's free—to a certain extent. Do you mean to tell me that any young girl should be freer? Nonsense! She should be happy that I am here to think for her—*I! We* must think for people who can't think for themselves; and a young girl can't. [*Signing an answer to a letter after hastily glancing over it.*] You have extraordinary ideas, James.

James. Excuse me, sir; you asked my opinion. I only meant that we can't think for others—any more than we can eat or sleep for them.

Peter. [*As though accepting the explanation.*] O . . . I see what you mean.

James. Of course, every happy being is bound by its nature to lead its own life—that it may be a free being. Evidently I didn't make my meaning clear.

[*Giving* Peter *another letter to sign.*

Peter. Free? Happy? James, you talk like an anarchist! You surprise me, sir. Where do you get these extraordinary ideas?

James. By reading the modern books and magazines, sir, and of course—

Peter. I thought so. [*Pointing to his books.*] Read

Heine. Cultivate sentiment. [*Signing the letter.*] Happy? Has it ever occurred to you that Katie is not happy?

JAMES. No, sir; I can't truthfully say that it has.

PETER. I imagine not. These are the happiest hours of her life. Young . . . in love . . . soon to be married.

JAMES. [*After a long pause.*] Is it settled, sir?

PETER. No; but I'll soon settle it. Anyone can see how she feels towards Frederik.

JAMES. [*After a shorter pause.*] Isn't she very young to marry, sir?

PETER. Not when she marries into the family; not when *I* am in the house, [*Touching his chest*] to guard her—to watch over her. Leave it to *me*. [*Enthusiastically.*] Sit here, James. Take one of Frederik's cigars. [JAMES *politely thanks him, but doesn't take one.*] It's a pleasure to talk to someone who's interested; and you *are* interested, James?

JAMES. Yes, sir: I'm much more interested than you might think.

PETER. Good. We'll take up the mail in a minute. Now: in order to carry out my plans—

CATHERINE. [*Sticking her head in the door.*] Ready for coffee?

PETER. Er—a little later. Close the door, dear. [*She disappears, closing the door.*] In order to carry out my plans, I have had to use great diplomacy. I made up my mind to keep Katie in the family; being a rich man—everybody knows it—I've had to guard against fortune hunters. However I think I've done away with them, for the whole town understands that Katie hasn't a penny—doesn't it, James?

JAMES. Yes, sir.

PETER. Yes, I think I've made that very clear. My

dream was to bring Catherine up to keep her in the family and it has been fulfilled. My plans have turned out beautifully for she is satisfied and happy.

JAMES. But did you want her to be happy simply because *you* are happy, sir? Don't you want her to be happy because *she* is happy?

PETER. If she's happy, why should I care?
[*Picks up the last letter.*]

JAMES. *If* she's happy.

PETER. [*Losing his temper.*] What do you mean? That's the second time you've said that. Why do you harp on—

JAMES. [*Rising.*] Excuse me, sir.

PETER. [*Angrily.*] Sit down. What do you know?

JAMES. Nothing, sir. . . .

PETER. You must know something to speak in this manner.

JAMES. No, I don't. You're a great expert in your line, Mr. Grimm, and I have the greatest respect for your opinion; but you can't mate people as you graft tulips. And more than once, I've—I've caught her crying and I've thought perhaps. . . .

PETER. [*Pooh-poohing.*] Crying? Of course! Was there ever a girl who didn't cry? . . . You amuse me . . . with your ideas of life. . . . Ha! Haven't I asked her why she was crying—and hasn't she always said: "I don't know why—it's nothing." They love to cry. [*Signs the last letter.*] But that's what they all cry over—nothing. James: do you know how I happened to meet Katie? She was prescribed for me by Doctor MacPherson.

JAMES. [*Taking the letter.*] Prescribed?

PETER. As an antidote. I was growing to be a fussy old bachelor with queer notions. You are young, but see that you don't need the Doctor, James. Do you know how

I was cured? I'll tell you. One day when I had business in the city, the Doctor went with me, and before I knew what he was at—he had marched me into a home for babies. . . . Katie was nearest the door—the first one. Pinned over her crib was her name: "Catherine Staats, aged three months." She held out her little arms . . . so friendless—so pitiful—so alone—and I was done for. We brought her back home, the Doctor, a nurse and I. The first time I carried her up those stairs—all my fine bachelor's ideas went out of my head. I knew then that my theories were all humbug. I had missed the child in the house who was to teach me everything. I had missed many children in my house. From that day I watched over her life. [*Rising, pointing towards the head of the stairs.*] James: I was born in this house—in the little room where I sleep; and her children shall one day play in the room in which I was born. . . . That's very pretty, eh? [*Wipes his eyes, sentimentally.*] I've always seen it that way.

JAMES. [*Coolly.*] Yes; it's *very* pretty if it turns out well.

PETER. How can it turn out otherwise?

JAMES. To me, sir, it's not a question of sentiment—of where her children shall play, so long as they play happily.

PETER. What? Her children can play anywhere—in China if they want to? Are you in your senses? A fine reward for giving a child all your affection—to live to see *her* children playing in China. No, sir! I propose to keep my household together, by your leave. [*Banging his clenched fist on the desk.*] It's my plan. [*Cleans his pipe, looking at* JAMES *from time to time.* JAMES *posts the letters in a mail box outside the door.* PETER *goes to the window, calling off.*] Otto! Run to the office and tell Mr. Frederik he may come in now. [*The voice of a gruff Dutchman:* "*Het is pastoor's dag.*" *It is the pastor's day.*] Ah, yes; I had forgotten. It's William's day to take the flowers to the Pastor. [*A knock is heard and as* PETER *calls* "*Come in,*" WILLIAM, *a delicate child of eight, stands timidly in the doorway of the dining room, hat in hand.*] How are you to-day, William? [*Pats* WILLIAM *on the shoulder.*]

WILLIAM. The Doctor says I'm well now.

PETER. Good! Then you shall take flowers to the church. [*Calls off.*] A big armful, Otto! [MARTA *has entered with a neatly folded clean handkerchief, which she tucks into* WILLIAM's *breast pocket. In a low voice to* JAMES.] There's your example of freedom! William's mother, old Marta's spoiled child, was free. You remember Annamarie, James?—let to come and go as she pleased. God knows where she is now . . . and here is William with the poor old grandmother. . . . Run along with the flowers, William. [*Gives* WILLIAM *some pennies as he goes.*] How he shoots up, eh, Marta?

MARTA. [*With the hopeless sorrow of the old, as she passes off.*] Poor child . . . poor child.

PETER. Give Katie more freedom, eh? O no! I shall guard her as I would guard my own, for she is as dear to me as though she were mine, and by marriage, please God, she shall be a Grimm in *name*.

JAMES. Mr. Grimm: I—I wish you would transfer me to your branch house in Florida.

PETER. What? You who were so glad to come back! James: you need a holiday. Close your desk. Go out and busy yourself with those pet vegetables of yours. Change your ideas, then come back sane and sensible and attend to your work. [*Giving a last shot at* JAMES *as he passes into the office and* FREDERIK *re-enters.*] You don't know what you want!

FREDERIK. [*Looking after* JAMES.] Uncle Peter: when I came in this morning, I made up my mind to speak to you of James.

PETER. James?

FREDERIK. Yes. I've wondered lately if . . . it seems to me that James is interested in Catherine.

PETER. James? Impossible.

FREDERIK. I'm not so sure.

PETER. [*Good naturedly.*] James? James Hartman?

FREDERIK. When I look back and remember him as a barefoot boy living in a shack behind our hot houses—and see him now—in here with you—

PETER. All the more credit, Frederik.

FREDERIK. Yes; but these are the sort of fellows that dream of getting into the firm. And there are more ways than one.

PETER. Do you mean to say—He wouldn't presume to think of such a thing.

FREDERIK. O, wouldn't he! The class to which he belongs presumes to think of anything. I believe he has been making love to Catherine.

PETER. [*After a slight pause, goes to the dining room door and calls.*] Katie! Katie!

FREDERIK. [*Hastily.*] Don't say that I mentioned it.

[CATHERINE *enters.*

PETER. Katie: I wish to ask you a question. I—[*He laughs.*] O, it's absurd. No, no, never mind.

CATHERINE. What is it?

PETER. I can't ask you. It's really too absurd.

CATHERINE. [*Her curiosity aroused.*] What is it, Uncle? . . . Tell me . . . tell me. . . .

PETER. Has James ever—

CATHERINE. [*Taken back and rather frightened—quickly.*] No. . . .

PETER. What? . . . How did you know what I . . . [FREDERIK *gives her a shrewd glance; but* PETER *suspecting nothing, continues.*] I meant . . . has James shown any special interest in you?

CATHERINE. [*As though accepting the explanation.*] Oh. . . . [*Flurried.*] Why, Uncle Peter! . . . Uncle Peter! . . . whatever put that notion into your head?

PETER. It's all nonsense, of course, but—

CATHERINE. I've always known James. . . . We went to school together. . . . James has shown no interest he ought not to have shown, Uncle Peter,—if that's what you mean. He has always been very respectful in a perfectly friendly way.

PETER. [*Convinced.*] Respectful in a perfectly friendly way. [*To* FREDERIK.] You can't say more than that. Thank you, dear, that's all I wanted. Run along. [*Glad to escape,* CATHERINE *leaves the room.*] He was only respectful in a perfectly friendly way. [*Slaps* FREDERIK *on the back.*] You're satisfied now, I hope?

FREDERIK. No, I am not. If she hasn't noticed what he has in mind,—I have. When I came into this room a few moments ago—it was as plain as day. He's trying to make love to her under our very eyes. I saw him. I wish you would ask him to stay in his office and attend to his own business.

[JAMES *now re-enters on his way to the gardens.*

PETER. James: it has occurred to me—that—[JAMES *pauses.*] What was your reason for wanting to give up your position? Had it anything to do with my little girl?

JAMES. Yes, sir.

PETER. You mean that—you—you love her?

JAMES. [*In a low voice.*] Yes, sir.

PETER. O-oh!

[Frederik *gives* Peter *a glance as though to say:* " *Now, do you believe it?* "]

James. But she doesn't know it, of course; she never would have known it. I never meant to say a word to her. I understand, sir.

Peter. James! Come here . . . here! . . . [*Bringing* James *up before him at the desk.*] Get your money at the office. You may have that position in Florida. Good-bye, James.

James. I'm very sorry that . . . Good-bye, sir.

Frederik. You are not to tell her that you're going. You're not to bid her good-bye.

Peter. [*To* Frederik.] Sh! Let me attend to—

James. [*Ignoring* Frederik.] I'm sorry, Mr. Grimm, that— [*His voice falters.*]

Peter. [*Rising.*] James: I'm sorry too. You've grown up here and—Tc! Tc! Good fortune to you—James. Get this notion out of your head, and perhaps one day you'll come back to us. We shall see.

[*Shakes hands with* James, *who leaves the room, too much overcome to speak.*

Dr. MacPherson. [*Who has entered, saying carelessly to* James *as he passes him.*] Hy're you, Jim? Glad Jim's back. One of the finest lads I ever brought into this world.

[*The Doctor is a man of about* Peter's *age, but more powerfully built. He has the bent shoulders of the student and his face is exceedingly intellectual. He is the rare type of doctor that forgets to make out bills. He has a grizzled grey beard, and his hair is touched with grey. He wears silver-rimmed spectacles. His substantial but unpressed clothing is made by the village tailor.*

PETER. Good morning, Andrew.

FREDERIK. Good morning, Doctor.

DR. MACPHERSON. [*Casts a quick, professional glance at* PETER.] Peter: I've come over to have a serious word with you. Been on my mind all night. [*Brings down a chair and sits opposite* PETER.] I—er—Frederik. . . . [FREDERIK, *who is not a favorite of the Doctor's, takes the hint and leaves the room.*] Peter: have you provided for everybody in this house?

PETER. What? Have I—

DR. MACPHERSON. You're a terrible man for planning, Peter; but what have you done? [*Casually.*] Were you to die,—say to-morrow,—how would it be with—[*Making a gesture to include the household*]—the rest of them?

PETER. What do you mean? If I were to die to-morrow. . . .

DR. MACPHERSON. You won't. Don't worry. Good for a long time yet, but everyone must come to it—sooner or later. I mean—what would Katie's position be in this house? I know you've set your heart upon her marrying Frederik, and all that sort of nonsense, but will it work? I've always thought 'twas a pity Frederik wasn't James and James wasn't Frederik.

PETER. What!

DR. MACPHERSON. O, it's all very well if she *wants* Frederik, but supposing she does not. Peter: if you mean to do something for her—do it *now*.

PETER. Now? You mean that I—You mean that I might . . . die?

DR. MACPHERSON. All can and do.

PETER. [*Studying the* DOCTOR'S *face.*] You think . . .

DR. MACPHERSON. The machinery is wearing out, Peter. Thought I should tell you. No cause for apprehension, but—

PETER. Then why tell me?

DR. MACPHERSON. When I cured you of that cold—wet flower beds—two days ago, I made a discovery. [*Seeing* CATHERINE *enter, he pauses. She is followed by* MARTA, *carrying a tray containing coffee and a plate of waffles.*] Coffee! I told you not to touch coffee, Peter. It's rank poison.

CATHERINE. Wouldn't you like a cup, Doctor?

PETER. Yes, he'll take a cup. He won't prescribe it, but he'll drink it.

DR. MACPHERSON. [*Horrified.*] And hot waffles between meals!

PETER. Yes, he'll take hot waffles too. [MARTA *goes to get another plate and more waffles and* CATHERINE *follows her.*] Now Andrew: you can't tell me that I'm sick—I won't have it. Every day we hear of some old boy one hundred years of age who was given up by the doctors at twenty. No sir! I'm going to live to see children in my house,—Katie's babies creeping on my old floor; playing with my old watch dog, Toby. I've promised myself a long line of rosy Grimms.

DR. MACPHERSON. My God, Peter! That dog is fifteen years old now. Do you expect nothing to change in your house? Man: you're a home worshiper. However, I—I see no reason why—[*Lying*] you shouldn't reach a ripe old age. [*Markedly, though feigning to treat the subject lightly.*] Er—Peter: I should like to make a compact with you . . . that whoever *does* go first,—and you're quite likely to outlive me,—is to come back and let the other fellow know . . . and settle the question. Splendid test between old neighbors—real contribution to science.

PETER. Make a compact to—Stuff and nonsense!

DR. MACPHERSON. Don't be too sure of that.

PETER. No, Andrew, positively no. I refuse. Don't

count upon *me* for any assistance in your spook tests.

DR. MACPHERSON. And how many times do you think *you've* been a spook yourself? You can't tell me that man is perfect; that he doesn't live more than one life; that the soul doesn't go on and on. Pshaw! The persistent personal energy *must* continue, or what *is* God?

[CATHERINE *has re-entered with another cup, saucer and plate which she sets on the table, and pours out the coffee.*

CATHERINE. [*Interested.*] Were you speaking of—of ghosts, Doctor?

PETER. Yes, he has begun again. [*To* CATHERINE.] You're just in time to hear it. [*To* MACPHERSON.] Andrew: I'll stay behind, contented in *this* life; knowing what I have here on earth and you shall die and return with your —Ha!—persistent personal whatever-it-is, and keep the spook compact. Every time a knock sounds or a chair squeaks, or the door bangs, I shall say: "Sh! There's the Doctor!"

CATHERINE. [*Noticing a book, which the Doctor has taken from his pocket, and reading the title.*] "Are the Dead Alive?"

DR. MACPHERSON. I'm in earnest, Peter. *I'll* promise and I want *you* to promise, too. Understand that I am not a so-called spiritist. I am merely a seeker after truth.

[*Puts more sugar in his coffee.*

PETER. That's what they *all* are—seekers after truth. Rubbish! Do you really believe in such stuff?

DR. MACPHERSON. I know that the dead are alive. They're here—here—near us—close at hand. [PETER, *in derision, lifts the table cloth and peeps under the table— then taking the lid off the sugar bowl, peers into it.*] Some of the greatest scientists of the day are of the same opinion.

PETER. Bah! Dreamers! They accomplish nothing in the world. They waste their lives dreaming of the world to come.

DR. MACPHERSON. You can't call Sir Charles Crookes, the inventor of Crookes Tubes,—a waster: no, nor Sir Oliver Lodge, the great biologist; nor Curie, the discoverer of radium; nor Doctor Lombroso, the founder of Science of Criminology; nor Doctor Maxwell, de Vesme, Richet, Professor James of Harvard, nor Professor Hyslop. Instead of laughing at ghosts, the scientific men of to-day are trying to lay hold of them. The frauds and cheats are being crowded from the field. Science is only just peeping through the half opened door which was shut until a few years ago.

PETER. If ever I see a ghost, I shall lay violent hands upon it and take it to the police station. That's the proper place for frauds.

DR. MACPHERSON. I'm sorry, Peter, very sorry, to see that you, like too many others, make a jest of the most important thing in life. Hyslop is right: man will spend millions to discover the North Pole but not a penny to discover his immortal destiny.

PETER. [*Stubbornly.*] I don't believe in spook mediums and never shall believe in them.

DR. MACPHERSON. Probably most professional mediums cheat—perhaps every one of them; but some of them are capable of real demonstrations at times.

PETER. Once a swindler, always a swindler. Besides, why can't my old friends come straight back to me and say: "Peter Grimm; here I am!" When they do—if they do— I shall be the first man to take off my hat to them and hold out my hand in welcome.

DR. MACPHERSON. You ask me why? Why can't a telegram travel on a fence instead of on a wire? Your friends *could* come back to you if you could put yourself in a receptive condition; but if you cannot, you must depend upon a medium—a sensitive.

PETER. A what? [*To* CATHERINE.] Something new, eh? He has the names for them. Yesterday it was "apports,"—flowers falling down from nowhere—hitting one on the nose. He talks like a medium's parrot. He has only to close his eyes and along comes the parade. Spooks! Spooky spooks! And now he wants me to settle my worldly affairs and join in the procession.

CATHERINE. [*Puzzled.*] Settle your worldly affairs? What do you mean, Uncle Peter?

PETER. [*Evasively.*] Just some more of his nonsense. Doctor: you've seen a good many cross to the other world: tell me?—did you ever see one of them come back—one?

DR. MACPHERSON. No.

PETER. [*Sipping his coffee.*] Never have, eh? And never will. Take another cup of poison, Andrew.

[*The Doctor gives his cup to* CATHERINE, *who fills it.* PETER *passes the waffles to the Doctor, at the same time winking at* CATHERINE *as the Doctor helps himself.*

DR. MACPHERSON. There was not perhaps the intimate bond between the doctor and patients to bring them back. But in my own family, I know of a case.

PETER. [*Apart to* CATHERINE.] He's off again.

CATHERINE. [*Eager to listen.*] Please don't interrupt, Uncle. I love to hear him tell of—

DR. MACPHERSON. I know of a return such as you mention. A distant cousin died in London and she was seen almost instantly in New York.

PETER. She must have travelled on a biplane, Andrew.

DR. MACPHERSON. If my voice can be heard from San

Francisco over the telephone, why cannot a soul, with a God-given force behind it, dart over the entire universe? Is Thomas Edison greater than God?

CATHERINE. [*Shocked.*] Doctor?

DR. MACPHERSON. And they can't tuck it *all* on telepathy. Telepathy cannot explain the case of a spirit message giving the contents of a sealed letter known only to the person that died. Here's another interesting case.

PETER. This is better than "Puss in Boots," isn't it, Katie? More—er—flibbertigibberty. Katie always loved fairy stories.

CATHERINE. [*Listening eagerly.*] Uncle, please.

DR. MACPHERSON. [*Ignoring* PETER, *speaking directly to* CATHERINE, *who is all attention.*] An officer on the Polar vessel, the Jeanette, sent to the Arctic regions by the New York *Herald*, appeared at his wife's bedside. *She* was in Brooklyn—*he* was on the Polar Sea. He said to her, "Count." She distinctly heard a ship's bell and the word "count" again. She had counted six when her husband's voice said: "Six bells—and the Jeanette is lost." The ship was really lost at the time she saw the vision.

PETER. A bad dream. "Six bells and the"—Ha! Ha! Spirit messages! Suet pudding has brought me messages from the North Pole and I receive messages from Kingdom come after I've eaten a piece of mince pie.

DR. MACPHERSON. There have been seventeen thousand other cases found to be worth investigation by the London Society of Psychical Research.

PETER. [*Changing.*] Supposing, Andrew, that I did "cross over"—I believe that's what *you* call dying,—that I did want to come back to see how you and little Katie and Frederik were getting on, how do you think I could manage to do it?

DR. MACPHERSON. When we hypnotize a subject, Peter,

Act I] THE RETURN OF PETER GRIMM 129

our thoughts take possession of them. As we enter their bodies, we take the place of a something that leaves them—a shadow self. This self can be sent out of the room—even to a long distance. This self leaves us entirely after death on the first, second or third day, or so I believe. This is the force which you would employ to come back to earth—the astral envelope.

PETER. Yes, but what proof have you, Doctor, that I've got an—an astral envelope?

DR. MACPHERSON. [*Easily.*] De Rochas has actually photographed it by radio photography.

PETER. Ha! Ha! Ha! Ho! Ho!

DR. MACPHERSON. Mind you—they couldn't *see* it when they photographed it.

PETER. I imagine not. See it? Ho! Ho!

DR. MACPHERSON. It stood a few feet away from the sleeper and was located by striking at the air and watching for the corresponding portion of the sleeper's body to recoil. By pricking a certain part of the shadow self with a pin, the cheek of the patient could be made to bleed. The camera was focussed on this part of the shadow self for fifteen minutes. The result was the profile of a head.

PETER. [*After a pause.*] . . . You believe that?

DR. MACPHERSON. The experiment has been repeated again and again. Nobody acquainted with the subject denies it now.

PETER. Spook pictures taken by professional mediums.
[*Turning away from the table as though he had heard enough.*]

DR. MACPHERSON. De Rochas, who took the pictures of which I speak, is a lawyer of standing; and the room was full of scientists who saw the pictures taken.

PETER. Hypnotized—all of them. Humbug, Andrew!

DR. MACPHERSON. Under these conditions it is quite

impossible to hypnotize a room full of people. Perhaps you think the camera was hypnotized? In similar circumstances, says Lombroso, an unnatural current of cold air went through the room and lowered the thermometer several degrees. Can you hypnotize a thermometer?

CATHERINE. [*Impressed.*] That's wonderful, Doctor!

PETER. Yes, it's a very pretty fairy story; but it would sound better set to shivery music. [*Sings.*] Tol! Dol! Dol! Dol! [*Rising to get his pipe and tobacco.*] No, sir! I refuse to agree to your compact. You cannot pick the lock of heaven's gate. We don't come back. God did enough for us when he gave us life and strength to work and the work to do. He owes us no explanation. I believe in the old fashioned paradise with a locked gate. [*He fills his pipe and lights it.*] No bogies for me.

DR. MACPHERSON. [*Rising.*] Peter: I console myself with the thought that men have scoffed at the laws of gravitation, at vaccination, magnetism, daguerreotypes, steamboats, cars, telephone, wireless telegraphy, and lighting by gas. [*Showing feeling.*] I'm *very* much disappointed that you refuse my request.

PETER. [*Laying down his pipe on the table.*] Since you take it so seriously—here—[*Offers his hand*] I'll agree. I know you're an old fool—and I'm another. Now then—[*Shakes hands*] it's settled. Whichever one shall go first—[*He bursts into laughter—then controlling himself.*] If I *do* come back, I'll apologize, Andrew.

DR. MACPHERSON. Do you mean it?

PETER. I'll apologize. Wait: [*Taking the keys from the sideboard*] let us seal the compact in a glass of my famous plum brandy.

DR. MACPHERSON. Good!

PETER. [*As he passes off.*] We'll drink to spooks.

CATHERINE. You really do believe, Doctor, that the dead can come back, don't you?

DR. MACPHERSON. Of course I do, and why not?

CATHERINE. Do you believe that you could come back here into this room and I could see you?

DR. MACPHERSON. You might not see me; but I could come back to this room.

CATHERINE. Could you talk to me?

DR. MACPHERSON. Yes.

CATHERINE. And could I hear you?

DR. MACPHERSON. I believe so. That's what we're trying to make possible.

> [CATHERINE, *still wondering, passes off with the tray. From the cellar,* PETER *can be heard singing lustily.*

PETER. " If you want a bite that's good to eat,
> (Tra, la, ritte, ra, la, la, la!)
> Try out a goose that's fat and sweet,
> (Tra, la, ritte, ra, la, la, la!) "

> [*During the song* MRS. BATHOLOMMEY *has given a quick tap on the door and entered. She is about forty years of age. Her faded brown hair is streaked with grey. She wears a plain black alpaca costume.*

MRS. BATHOLOMMEY. [*Agitated.*] Good morning, Doctor. Fortunate that I found you alone.

DR. MACPHERSON. [*Drily.*] Hy're you, Mrs. Batholommey? [*The* REV. HENRY BATHOLOMMEY *now enters. He is a man of about forty-five, wearing the frock coat, high waistcoat and square topped hat of a minister of the Dutch Reformed Church.*] Hy're, Henry?

> [*The* REV. BATHOLOMMEY *bows.* WILLIAM *has returned from his errand and entered the room,—a picture book under his arm.*

He sits up by the window absorbed in the pictures—unnoticed by the others.

Mrs. Batholommey. [*Closing the door left open by* Peter—*shutting out the sound of his voice.*] Well, Doctor. . . . [*She pauses for a moment to catch her breath and wipe her eyes.*] I suppose you've told him he's got to die.

Dr. MacPherson. [*Eyeing* Mrs. Batholommey *with disfavor.*] Who's got to die?

Mrs. Batholommey. Why, Mr. Grimm, of course.

Dr. MacPherson. [*Amazed.*] Does the whole damned town know about it?

Mrs. Batholommey. Oh!

Rev. Batholommey. Easy, Doctor. You consulted Mr. Grimm's lawyer and *his* wife told *my* wife.

Dr. MacPherson. He gabbed, eh? Hang the professional man who tells things to his wife.

Mrs. Batholommey. Doctor!

Rev. Batholommey. [*With solicitude.*] I greatly grieve to hear that Mr. Grimm has an incurable malady. His heart, I understand. [*Shakes his head.*]

Dr. MacPherson. He's not to be told. Is that clear? He may die in twenty minutes—may outlive us all—probably will.

Mrs. Batholommey. [*Pointing to* Rev. Mr. Batholommey.] It seems to me, Doctor, that if *you* can't do any more, it's *his* turn. It's a wonder you Doctors don't baptize the babies.

Rev. Batholommey. Rose!

Mrs. Batholommey. At the last minute, he'll want to make a will—and you know he hasn't made one. He'll want to remember the church and his charities and his friends; and if he dies before he can carry out his intentions, the minister will be blamed as usual. It's not fair.

Rev. Batholommey. Sh! Sh! My dear! These private matters—

Dr. MacPherson. I'll trouble you, Mistress Batholommey, to attend to your own affairs. Did you never hear the story of a lady who flattened her nose—sticking it into other people's business?

Rev. Batholommey. Doctor! Doctor! I can't have that!

Mrs. Batholommey. Let him talk, Henry. No one in this town pays any attention to Dr. MacPherson since he took up with spiritualism.

Rev. Batholommey. Rose!

[*He motions her to be silent, as* Peter, *coming up the stairs from the cellar, is heard singing.*]

Peter. "Drop in the fat some apples red,
(Tra, la, ritta, ra, la, la, la!)
Then spread it on a piece of bread,
(Tra, la, ritta, ra, la, la, la!)"

[*He opens the door, carrying a big jug in his hand. Hailing the* Batholommeys *cheerfully.*] Good morning, good people.

[*He puts the jug on the sideboard and hangs up the key. The* Batholommeys *look sadly at* Peter. Mrs. Batholommey *in the foreground tries to smile pleasantly, but can only assume the peculiarly pained expression of a person about to break terrible news.*]

Rev. Batholommey. [*Rising to the occasion—warmly grasping* Peter's *hand.*] Ah, my good friend! Many thanks for the flowers William brought us and the noble cheque you sent me. We're still enjoying the vegetables you generously provided. I *did* relish the squash.

PETER. [*Catching a glimpse of* MRS. BATHOLOMMEY'*s gloomy expression.*] Anything distressing you this morning, Mrs. Batholommey?

MRS. BATHOLOMMEY. No, no . . . I hope *you're* feeling well—er—I don't mean that—I—

REV. BATHOLOMMEY. [*Cheerily.*] Of course, she does; and why not, why not, dear friend?

PETER. Will you have a glass of my plum brandy?

MRS. BATHOLOMMEY. [*Stiffly.*] No, thank you. As you know, I belong to the W. C. T. U.

PETER. Pastor?

REV. BATHOLOMMEY. [*Tolerantly.*] No, thank you. I am also opposed to er—

PETER. We're going to drink to spooks—the Doctor and I.

MRS. BATHOLOMMEY. [*With a startled cry.*] Oh, how can you! [*Lifts her handkerchief to her eyes.*] And at a time like this. The very idea—you of all people!

PETER. [*Coming down with two glasses—handing one to the Doctor.*] You seem greatly upset, Mrs. Batholommey. Something must have happened.

REV. BATHOLOMMEY. Nothing, nothing, I assure you. My wife is a trifle nervous to-day. We must all keep up our spirits, Mr. Grimm.

PETER. Of course. Why not? [*Looking at* MRS. BATHOLOMMEY—*struck.*] I know why you're crying. You've been to a church wedding. [*To the Doctor, lifting his glass.*] To astral envelopes, Andrew. [*They drink.*]

MRS. BATHOLOMMEY. [*With sad resignation.*] You were always kind to us, dear Mr. Grimm. There never *was* a kinder, better, sweeter man than you *were.*

PETER. Than I *was?*

REV. BATHOLOMMEY. Rose, my dear!

MRS. BATHOLOMMEY. What *will* become of William? [*Weeps.*]

Peter. William? Why should you worry over William? I am looking after him. I don't understand—

Mrs. Batholommey. [*Seeing that she has gone too far.*] I only meant—it's too bad he had such an M—

Peter. An M—?

Mrs. Batholommey. [*In pantomime—mouthing the word so that* William *cannot hear.*] Mother. . . . Annamarie.

Peter. O. . . .

Mrs. Batholommey. She ought to have told you or Mr. Batholommey who the F—was.

Peter. F—?

Mrs. Batholommey. [*In pantomime as before.*] Father.

Peter. O. . . . [*Spelling out the word.*] S-c-o-u-n-d-r-e-l—whoever he is! [*Calls.*] William: [William *looks up from his book.*] You're very contented here with me, are you not?

William. Yes, sir.

Peter. And you want to stay here?

William. Yes, sir. [*At that moment a country circus band—playing a typical parade march—blares out as it comes up some distant street.*] There's a circus in town.

Peter. A circus?

William. Yes, sir. The parade has started. [*Opens the window and looks out towards left.*] Here it comes—

Peter. [*Hurrying to the door.*] Where? Where?

William. [*Pointing.*] There!

Peter. [*As delighted as* William.] You're right. It's coming this way! Here come the chariots.

[*Gestures to the* Batholommeys *to join him at the window. The music sounds nearer and nearer—the parade is supposed to be passing,* William *gives a cry of delight as a* Clown *appears at the window with handbills under his arm.*

The Clown. [*As he throws the handbills into the room.*] Billy Miller's big show and monster circus is in town this afternoon. Only one ring. No confusion. [*Seeing* William.] Circus day comes but once a year, little sir. Come early and see the wild animals and hear the lions roar-r-r! Mind! [*Holding up his finger to* William.] I shall expect to see *you*. Wonderful troupe of trained mice in the side show. [*Sings.*]

"Uncle Rat has gone to town,
   Ha! Hm!
 Uncle Rat has gone to town,
   To buy Miss Mouse—"

[*Ends the song abruptly.*] Ha! Ha! Ha! Ha!

[*The* Clown *disappears repeating "Billy Miller's big show," etc., until his voice is lost and the voices of shouting children are heard as they run after him.*

Peter. [*Putting his hand in his pocket.*] We'll go. You may buy the tickets, William—two front seats.

[Frederik *re-enters with a floral catalogue.*

Mrs. Batholommey. [*Apart to* Rev. Batholommey—*looking at* Peter.] Somebody ought to tell him.

William. [*Getting the money from* Peter.] I'm going! I'm going! [*Dances.*] Oh, Mr. Grimm: there ain't anyone else like you in the world. When the *other boys* laugh at your funny old hat, *I* never do.

[*Pointing to* Peter's *hat on the peg.*

Peter. My hat? They laugh at my hat?

William. We'll have such a good time at the circus. It's too bad you've got to die, Mr. Grimm.

[*There is a pause.* Peter *stops short, looking at* William. *The others are startled,*

> *but stand motionless, watching the effect of* WILLIAM's *revelation.* FREDERIK *doesn't know what to make of it. There is an ominous silence in the room. Then* MRS. BATHOLOMMEY, *whose smile has been frozen on her face, takes* WILLIAM's *hand and is about to draw him away, when* PETER *lays his hand on* WILLIAM's *shoulder.* MRS. BATHOLOMMEY *steps back.*

PETER. [*Kindly.*] Yes, William, most people have to. . . . What made you think of it just then?

WILLIAM. [*Points to the Doctor.*] He said so. Perhaps in twenty minutes.

REV. BATHOLOMMEY. [*Quietly, but very sternly.*] William!

> [WILLIAM *now understands that he should not have repeated what he heard.*

PETER. Don't frighten the boy. Only children tell the truth. Tell me, William—you heard the Doctor say that? [WILLIAM *is silent. He keeps his eyes on the clergyman, who is looking at him warningly. The tears run down his cheeks—he puts his fingers to his lips—afraid to speak.*] Don't be frightened. You heard the Doctor say that?

WILLIAM. [*His voice trembling.*] Y-es sir.

PETER. [*Looks around the room—beginning to understand.*] . . . What did you mean, Andrew?

DR. MACPHERSON. I'll tell you, Peter, when we're alone.

PETER. But . . . [MRS. BATHOLOMMEY *shakes her finger threateningly at* WILLIAM, *who whimpers.*] Never mind. It popped out, didn't it, William? Get the circus tickets and we'll have a fine time just the same.

> [WILLIAM *goes to buy the tickets.*

REV. BATHOLOMMEY. I—er—good morning, dear friend. [*Takes* PETER's *hand.*] Any time you 'phone for me—

day or night—I'll run over instantly. God bless you, sir. I've never come to you for any worthy charity and been turned away—never.

Mrs. Batholommey. [*Suddenly overcome.*] Good-bye, Mr. Grimm. [*In tears, she follows her husband. The Doctor and* Peter *look at each other.*]

Dr. MacPherson. [*Cigar in mouth—very abruptly.*] It's cardiac valvular—a little valve—[*Tapping heart*]—in here. [*Slaps* Peter *on the shoulder.*] There's my 'phone. [*As a bell is heard faintly, but persistently, ringing across the street.*] I'll be back.

[*Catches up his hat to hasten off.*]

Peter. Just a minute.

Dr. MacPherson. [*Turning.*] Don't fret yourself, Peter. You're not to imagine you're worse than you are. [*Angrily.*] Don't funk!

Peter. [*Calmly.*] That wasn't my reason for detaining you, Andrew. [*With a twinkle in his eye.*

Dr. MacPherson. Yes?

Peter. That if there is anything in that ghost business of yours, I won't forget to come back and apologize for my want of faith. [*The Doctor goes home.* Frederik *stands looking at his Uncle. There is a long pause.* Peter *throws up both hands.*] Rubbish! Doctors are very often wrong. It's all guess work, eh, Fritz?

Frederik. [*Thinking of his future in case of* Peter's *death.*] Yes, sir.

Peter. However, to be on the safe side, I'll take that nip of plum brandy. [*Then thinking aloud.*] Not yet. . . . Not yet. . . . I'm not ready to die yet. I have so much to live for . . . . When I'm older. . . . When I'm a little old leaf ready to curl up, eh, Fritz? [*He drains his glass, goes up to the peg, takes down his hat, looks at it as though remembering* William's *words, then puts it back on peg. He shows no sign of taking* DR. MAC-PHERSON'S *verdict to heart—in fact, he doesn't believe it.*] Frederik: get me some small change for the circus—enough for William and me.

FREDERIK. Are you going . . . after all. . . . And with that child?

PETER. Why not?

FREDERIK. [*Suddenly showing feeling.*] That little tattler? A child that listens to everything and just told you. . . . He shouldn't be allowed in this part of the house. He should be sent away.

PETER. [*Astonished.*] Why do you dislike him, Frederik? He's a fine little fellow. You surprise me, my boy. . . . [CATHERINE *enters and goes to the piano, running her hands softly over the keys—playing no melody in particular.* PETER *sits in his big chair at the table and picks up his pipe.* FREDERIK, *with an inscrutable face, now strikes a match and holds it to his uncle's pipe.* PETER *thoughtfully takes one or two puffs; then speaking so as not to be heard by* CATHERINE.] Frederik: I want to think that after I'm gone, everything will be the same here. . . . just as it is now.

FREDERIK. Yes, sir. [*Sitting near* PETER.

PETER. Just as it is. . . .

[FREDERIK *nods assent.* PETER *smokes. The room is very cheerful. The bright midday sunshine creeps through the windows, —almost causing a haze in the room— and resting on the pots and vases and bright flowers on the tables.*

CATHERINE. [*Singing.*] "The bird so free in the heavens—"

PETER. [*Looking up—still in thought—seeming not to hear the song.*] And my charities attended to.

[FREDERIK *nods assent.*

CATHERINE. " Is but the slave of the nest;
　　　　　For all must toil as God wills it,—
　　　　　Must laugh and toil and rest."

PETER. [*Who has been thinking.*] Just as though I were here. . . .

CATHERINE. " The rose must blow in the garden;"

PETER. William too. Don't forget *him,* Frederik.

FREDERIK. No, Uncle.

CATHERINE. " The bee must gather its store;
　　　　　The cat must watch the mouse-hole,
　　　　　The dog must guard the door."

PETER. [*As though he had a weight off his mind.*] We won't speak of this again. It's understood.

　　　　　[*Smokes, listening with pleasure as* CATHER-
　　　　　INE *finishes the song.*

CATHERINE. [*Repeats the chorus.*]
　　　　　" The cat must watch the mouse-hole,
　　　　　The dog must guard the door.
　　　　　La la, La la," etc.

　　　　　[*At the close of the song,* PETER *puts down
　　　　　his pipe and beckons to* CATHERINE.

PETER. Give me the book.

　　　　　[CATHERINE *brings the bible to* PETER *as
　　　　　the garden bell rings outside.*

FREDERIK. Noon.

PETER. [*Opening the book at the history of the family—points to the closely written page.*] Under my name I want to see this written: " Married: Catherine and Frederik." I want to see you settled, Katie—[*Smiling.*]—settled happily for life. [*He takes her hand and draws* FREDERIK *towards his chair.* CATHERINE, *embarrassed, plays with a rose in her belt.*] Will you? . . .

CATHERINE. I . . . I don't know. . . .

PETER. [*Taking the rose and her hand in his own.*] *I* know for you, my dear. Make me happy.

CATHERINE. There's nothing I wouldn't do to make *you* happy, uncle, but—

FREDERIK. You know that I love you, Kitty.

PETER. Yes, yes, yes. *That's* all understood. He has always loved you. Everybody knows it.

CATHERINE. Uncle. . . .

PETER. Make it a June wedding. We have ten days yet.
> [*Slipping her hand in* FREDERIK's, *taking the rose and tapping their clasped hands with the flower as he speaks.*]

FREDERIK. Say yes, Kitty.

CATHERINE. [*Nervously.*] I couldn't in ten days. . . .

FREDERIK. But—

PETER. [*To* FREDERIK.] Who is arranging this marriage, you or I? Say a month, then, Katie. . . . Promise me.

CATHERINE. [*Her lips set.*] If you have set your heart on it, I will, Uncle Peter. . . . I will . . . I promise.

PETER. [*Takes a ring off his hand.*] The wedding ring—my dear mother's. [*Gives it to* CATHERINE.] You've made me very happy, my dear.
> [*He kisses* CATHERINE. *Then releasing her, he nods to* FREDERIK *to follow his example.* PETER *turns his back to the young couple and smokes.*]

FREDERIK. Catherine. . . .
> [*Dreading his embrace, she retreats towards* PETER *and as she touches him, his pipe falls to the floor. She looks at him, startled.* FREDERIK, *struck, looking intently at* PETER, *who sits motionless.*]

CATHERINE. Uncle Peter. . . . Uncle! What is it? What's the matter? [*Runs to the door—calling across the street.*] Doctor! There he is—just going out. [*Calls.*] Come back. Come back, Doctor. [*To* FREDERIK.] I felt it. I felt something strange a minute ago. I felt it.

FREDERIK. [*Taking* PETER's *hand.*] Uncle Peter!

CATHERINE. [*Coming back to* PETER *and looking at him transfixed.* Uncle Peter! Answer me! . . . It's Katie!

[*The Doctor enters hurriedly.*

DR. MACPHERSON. Is it . . . Peter?

> [*He goes quickly to* PETER *and listens to his heart.* CATHERINE *and* FREDERIK *on either side of him. The Doctor with tender sympathy takes* CATHERINE *in his arms.*

WILLIAM. [*Rushes in with two tickets in his hand, leaving the door open. The circus music is faintly heard.*] Mr. Grimm!

DR. MACPHERSON. Sh! [*A pause, as though breaking the news to them all.*] He's gone.

FREDERIK. [*Questioningly—dazed.*] Dead?

[CATHERINE *is overcome.*

WILLIAM. [*At* PETER's *side—holding up the circus tickets.*] He can't be dead. . . . I've got his ticket to the circus.

Curtain.

ACT II

[*SCENE: The second act takes place ten days later, towards the close of a rainy afternoon. A fire is burning in the grate and a basket of hickory wood stands beside the hearth.* PETER's *hat is no longer on the*

peg. His pipes and jar of tobacco are missing. *A
number of wedding presents are set on a table, some
unopened. The interior of the room, with its snapping
fire, forms a pleasant contrast to the gloomy exterior.
The day is fading into dusk.*

MRS. BATHOLOMMEY *is at the piano, playing the
wedding march from " Lohengrin." Four little girls
are grouped about her, singing the words to the air.*

> " Faithful and true:
> We lead ye forth,
> Where love triumphant
> Shall lighten the way."

> " Bright star of love,
> Flower of the earth,
> Shine on ye both
> On Love's perfect day."

MRS. BATHOLOMMEY. That's better. Children: remember that this is to be a very *quiet* wedding. You're to be here at noon to-morrow. You're not to speak as you enter the room and take your places near the piano. Miss Staats will come down from her room, at least I suppose she will —and will stand. . . . [*Thinks.*] I don't know where —but you're to stop when *I* look at you. Watch me as though I were about to be married. [*She takes her place at the foot of the stairs and the children repeat the song until she has marched across the room and stationed herself in some appropriate corner. As* FREDERIK *appears from the hall, where he leaves his rain coat and umbrella,* MRS. BATHOLOMMEY *motions the children to silence.*] That will do, dears, thank you. Hurry home between showers. [*The children go as she explains to* FREDERIK.] My Sunday

School scholars. . . . I thought your dear uncle would like a song at the wedding. I know how bright and cheery he would have been—poor man. Dear, noble, charitable soul!

FREDERIK. [*In a low voice.*] Where's Catherine?

MRS. BATHOLOMMEY. [*Taking up her fancy work, seating herself.*] Upstairs.

FREDERIK. With that sick child? Tc!

MRS. BATHOLOMMEY. Catherine finds it a pleasure to sit beside the little fellow. William is very much better.

FREDERIK. [*Taking a telegram from his pocket-book.*] Well, we shall soon be off to Europe. I've just had a telegram—a cabin has been reserved for me on the Imperator. To-morrow, thank God, we shall take the afternoon train to New York.

MRS. BATHOLOMMEY. I must confess that I'm very glad. Of course, I'm happy to stay and chaperone Catherine; but poor Mr. Batholommey has been alone at the parsonage for ten days . . . ever since your dear uncle . . . [*Pauses, unwinding yarn, then unburdening her mind.*] I didn't think at first that Catherine could persuade herself to marry you.

FREDERIK. [*Sharply.*] I don't understand you, Mrs. Batholommey.

MRS. BATHOLOMMEY. I mean she seemed so averse to—to an immediate marriage; but of course it was your uncle's last request, and that influenced her more than anything else. So it's to be a June wedding, after all: he has his wish. You'll be married in ten days from the time he left us. [*Remembering.*] Some more letters marked personal came for him while you were out. I put them in the drawer—[*Points to desk*]—with the rest. It seems odd to think the postman brings your uncle's letters regularly, yet *he* is not here.

FREDERIK. [*Looking towards the office door.*] Did Hartman come?

MRS. BATHOLOMMEY. Yes. He seemed rather surprised that you'd sent for him.

FREDERIK. Did you—er—tell him that we intend to leave to-morrow?

MRS. BATHOLOMMEY. I spoke of your wedding trip,—yes.

FREDERIK. Did he seem inclined to stay?

MRS. BATHOLOMMEY. He didn't say. He seemed very much agitated. [MARTA *enters, carying a night lamp.*] We'll pack Miss Catherine's things to-night, Marta. [*She notices the lamp.*] The night lamp for William? [*Looks up towards the door of his room.*] Go in very quietly. He's asleep, I think. [MARTA *goes up the stairs and into* WILLIAM's *room.*] By the way, Mr. Batholommey was very much excited when he heard that your uncle had left a personal memorandum concerning *us*. We're anxious to hear it read. [FREDERIK, *paying no attention to her words, is glancing at the wedding presents.*] We're anxious to hear it read.

JAMES. [*Entering.*] Did you wish to see me?

FREDERIK. [*Offering his hand to* JAMES.] How do you do, Hartman? I'm very glad you consented to come back. My uncle never went into his office again after you left. There is some private correspondence concerning matters of which I know nothing: it lies on your old desk. . . . I'm anxious to settle everything to-night.

[MRS. BATHOLOMMEY *leaves the room.*]

JAMES. Very well.

FREDERIK. If you care to remain longer with the firm, I—er—

JAMES. No, thank you. As soon as my work is done to-night,—I'll go.

FREDERIK. I appreciate the fact that you came on my uncle's account. I have no ill feeling against you, Hartman.

JAMES. I'm not refusing to stay because of any ill feeling. I'm going because I know that you'll sell out before your uncle is cold in his grave. I don't care to stay to see the old place change hands.

FREDERIK. I? Sell out? My intention is to carry out every wish of my dear old uncle's.

JAMES. I hope so. I haven't forgotten that you wanted him to sell out to Hicks of Rochester on the very day he died.   [*Exit into the office.* CATHERINE *comes from* WILLIAM'S *room, simply dressed in white—no touch of mourning.* FREDERIK *goes to the foot of the stairs and calls softly.*

FREDERIK. Kitty! Here is our wedding license. I have the cabin on the Imperator. Everything is arranged.

CATHERINE. [*Coming down stairs.*] Yes. . . . I meant to speak to you—again.

FREDERIK. To-morrow's the day, dear.

CATHERINE. [*Very subdued.*] Yes. . . .

FREDERIK. A June wedding—just as Uncle Peter wished.

CATHERINE. [*As before.*] Yes. . . . Just as he wished. *Everything* is just as he . . . [*With a change of manner—earnestly—looking at* FREDERIK.] Frederik: I don't want to go away. I don't want to go to Europe. If only I could stay quietly here in—[*Tears in her voice as she looks around the room.*]—in my dear home.

FREDERIK. Why do you want to stay in this old cottage—with its candles and lamps and shadows? It's very gloomy, very depressing.

CATHERINE. I don't want to leave this house. . . . I don't want any home but this. [*Panic stricken.*] Don't take me away, Frederik. I know you've never really liked it at Grimm's Manor: are you sure you'll want to come back to live here?

FREDERIK. [*As though speaking to a child.*] Of course. I'll do anything you ask.

CATHERINE. I—I've always wanted to please . . . [*After a slight pause, finding it difficult to speak his name.*] Uncle Peter. . . . I felt that I owed everything to him. . . . If he had lived . . . if I could see *his* happiness at our marriage—it would make *me* happy; [*Pathetically*] but he's gone . . and . . . I'm afraid we're making a mistake. I don't feel towards you as I ought, Frederik. I've told you again and again; but I want to tell you once more: I'm willing to marry you . . . but I don't love you—I never shall.

FREDERIK. How do you know?

CATHERINE. I know. . . . I know. . . . It seems so disloyal to speak like this after I promised *him;* but—

FREDERIK. Yes, you *did* promise Uncle Peter you'd marry me, didn't you?

CATHERINE. Yes.

FREDERIK. And he died believing you?

CATHERINE. Yes.

FREDERIK. Then it all comes to this: are you going to live up to your promise?

CATHERINE. That's it. That's what makes me try to live up to it. [*Wiping her eyes.*] But you know how I feel. . . . You understand. . . .

FREDERIK. Perfectly: you don't quite know your own mind. . . . Very few young girls do, I suppose. I love you and in time you'll grow to care for me. [MARTA *re-enters from* WILLIAM'S *room, and closing the door, comes down the stairs and passes off.*] What *are* we to do with that child?

CATHERINE. He's to stay here, of course.

FREDERIK. The child should be sent to some institution. What claim has he on you—on any of us?

CATHERINE. Why do you dislike him?

FREDERIK. I don't, but—

CATHERINE. Yes, you do. I can't understand it. I remember how angry you were when you came back from college and found him living here. You never mention his mother's name, yet you played together as children. When Uncle tried to find Annamarie and bring her back, you were the only one to oppose it.

FREDERIK. William is an uncomfortable child to have in the house. He has a way of staring at people as though he had a perpetual question on his lips. It's most annoying.

CATHERINE. What question?

FREDERIK. As for his mother—I've never seen her since she left this house and I don't care to hear her name on your lips. Her reputation is—[*The rain starts pattering on the shingled roof.*] Tc! More rain. . . . the third day of it. [*Going to the window—calling.*] Otto! [*Angrily.*] Otto! See what the wind has done—those trellises. [*Bangs the window shut.*] That old gardener should have been laid off years ago. . . . By the way, his son James is here for a few hours—to straighten matters out. I must see how he's getting on. [*Taking her hand, drawing her towards the table with a change of manner.*] Have you seen all the wedding presents, Kitty? I'll be back in a few minutes.

> [*Pats her cheek and exit.* CATHERINE *stands over her wedding presents just as he left her—not looking at them—her eyes filled with tears. The door is suddenly opened and the Doctor enters, a tweed shawl over his shoulders, wearing a tweed cap. He has a book under his arm.*

Dr. MacPherson. How's William? [CATHERINE *tries to hide her tears, but he sees through her. He tosses his cap, coat and book on the sofa.*] What's the matter?

CATHERINE. Nothing. . . . I was only thinking. . . . I was hoping that those we love . . . and lose . . . *can't* see us here. I'm beginning to believe there's not much happiness in *this* world.

Dr. MacPherson. Why, you little snip. I've a notion to spank you. Talking like that with your life before you! Read this book, child: [*Gesturing towards the book on the sofa.*] it proves that the dead *do* see us; they *do* come back. [*Walks to the foot of the stairs—turns.*] Catherine: I understand that you've not a penny to your name—unless you marry Frederik; that he has inherited you along with the orchids and tulips. Don't let that influence you. If Peter's plans bind you—and you look as though they did —my door's open. Think it over. It's not too late. [*Goes half way up the stairs—then pauses.*] Don't let the neighbors' opinions and a few silver spoons—[*Pointing to the wedding presents*]—stand in the way of your future.

[*Exit into* WILLIAM's *room. The rain increases. The sky grows blacker—the room darker.* CATHERINE *gives a cry and stretches out her arms, not looking up.*]

CATHERINE. Uncle Peter! Uncle Peter! Why did you do it? Why did you ask it? Oh, dear! Oh, dear! If you could see me now. [*She stands rigid—her arms outstretched.* MARTA, *who has silently entered from the dining room with fresh candles, goes to* CATHERINE *suddenly buries her face on* MARTA's *broad breast, breaking into sobs; then recovering, wipes her eyes.*] There, there. . . . I mustn't cry . . . others have troubles too, haven't they?

MARTA. Others have troubles, too.

CATHERINE. I had hoped, Marta, that Annamarie would have heard of Uncle's loss and come back to us . . .

MARTA. If it had only brought us all together once more; but no message . . . nothing. . . . I cannot understand.

CATHERINE. She knows that our door is open.

> [*The rain beats against the window. A sharp double knock is heard at the door.* CATHERINE *starts as though suddenly brought to herself, hastily goes into the next room, taking the Doctor's book with her.* MARTA *has hurried towards the front door, when the* REV. MR. BATHOLOMMEY *and* COLONEL LAWTON *appear in the hall as though they had entered quickly, to escape the storm.* MARTA, *greeting them, passes off to tell* FREDERIK *of their presence. The* REV. MR. BATHOLOMMEY *wears a long black cloth rain-proof coat.* COLONEL LAWTON *is a tall man with a thin brown beard and moustache, about forty-eight. He is dressed in a Prince Albert coat, unpressed trousers, and a negligee shirt. He wears spectacles and has a way of throwing back his head and peering at people before answering them. The* REV. MR. BATHOLOMMEY *sets his umbrella in the hall and the* COLONEL *hangs his broad brimmed hat on the handle—as though to let it drip.*]

REV. BATHOLOMMEY. Brr! I believe it's raining icicles.

COLONEL LAWTON. [*Taking off his over-shoes.*] Gee Whillikins! What a day! Good thing the old windmill out yonder is tied up. Great weather for baptisms, Parson. [*There is a faint far-away rumble of thunder.* FREDERIK *enters.*] Well, here we are, Frederik, my boy—at the time you mentioned.

REV. BATHOLOMMEY. How are you, Frederik?

[COLONEL LAWTON *crosses to the fire, followed by the* REV. MR. BATHOLOMMEY.

FREDERIK. [*Who has gone to the desk for a paper lying under a paper weight.*] I sent for you to hear a memorandum left by my uncle. I only came across it yesterday.

[*There is a louder peal of thunder. A flash of lightning illuminates the room.*

COLONEL LAWTON. I must have drawn up ten wills for the old gentleman, but he always tore 'em up. May I have a drink of his plum brandy, Frederik?

FREDERIK. Help yourself, Pastor?

REV. BATHOLOMMEY. Er—er—

[COLONEL LAWTON *goes to the sideboard and fills two glasses. A heavy roll of thunder now ends in a sharp thunder clap.* MRS. BATHOLOMMEY, *who is entering the room, gives a cry and puts her hands over her face.* COLONEL LAWTON *bolts his whiskey. The* REV. MR. BATHOLOMMEY *takes a glass and stands with it in his hand.*

MRS. BATHOLOMMEY. [*Removing her hands in time to see the brandy.*] Why, Henry! What are you doing? Are your feet wet?

REV. BATHOLOMMEY. No, Rose, they're not. I want a drink and I'm going to take it. It's a bad night.

[*Drinks.*

COLONEL LAWTON. [*Throws a hickory log on the fire, which presently blazes up making the room much brighter.*] Go ahead, Frederik.

[*Sits.* REV. MR. BATHOLOMMEY *has drawn up a chair for his wife and now seats himself before the snapping hickory fire.*]

REV. BATHOLOMMEY. I knew that your uncle would remember his friends and his charities. He was so liberal! One might say of him that he was the very soul of generosity. He gave in such a free-handed princely fashion.

FREDERIK. [*Reading in a business-like manner.*] For Mrs. Batholommey—

MRS. BATHOLOMMEY. The dear man—to think that he remembered me! I knew he'd remember the church and Mr. Batholommey, of course; but to think that he'd remember me! He knew that my income was very limited. He was so thoughtful! His purse was always open.

FREDERIK. [*Eyes* MRS. BATHOLOMMEY *for a second, then continues.*] For Mr. Batholommey—[REV. MR. BATHOLOMMEY *nods solemnly*]—and the Colonel.

COLONEL LAWTON. [Taking out a cigar.] He knew that I did the best I could for him . . . [*His voice breaks*] the grand old man. [*Recovering.*] What'd he leave me? Mrs. B.—er?

[*Nods inquiringly at* MRS. BATHOLOMMEY, *who bows assent and he lights his cigar.*]

FREDERIK. [*Glancing at the paper.*] Mrs. Batholommey: he wishes you to have his miniature—with his affectionate regards.

MRS. BATHOLOMMEY. Dear old gentleman—and er—yes?

FREDERIK. To Mr. Batholommey—

MRS. BATHOLOMMEY. But—er—you didn't finish with me.

FREDERIK. You're finished.

MRS. BATHOLOMMEY. I'm finished?

FREDERIK. You may read it yourself if you like.

Rev. Batholommey. No, no, no. She'll take your word for it. [*Firmly.*] Rose!

Frederik. [*Reads.*] To Mr. Batholommey: my antique watch fob—with my profound respects. [*Continues.*] To Colonel Lawton—

Mrs. Batholommey. His watch fob? Is *that* what he left to *Henry?* Is that all? [*As* Frederik *nods.*] Well! If he had no wish to make *your* life easier, Henry, he should at least have left something for the church. Oh, won't the congregation have a crow to pick with you!

Frederik. [*Reading.*] To my life-long friend, Colonel Lawton: I leave my most cherished possession.

> [Colonel Lawton *has a look on his face as though he were saying: "Ah! It will be something worth while."*]

Mrs. Batholommey. [*Angrily.*] When the church members hear that—

Colonel Lawton. [*Chewing his cigar.*] I don't know why he was called upon to leave anything to the church—he gave it thousands; and only last month, he put in chimes. As *I* look at it, he wished to give you something he had *used*—something personal. Perhaps the miniature and the fob *ain't* worth three whoops in Hell,—it's the sentiment of the things that counts—[*Chewing the word with his cigar*] the sentiment. Drive on, Fred.

Frederik. To Colonel Lawton: my father's prayer book.

Colonel Lawton. [*Suddenly changing—dazed.*] His prayer book . . . me?

Mrs. Batholommey. [*Seeing* Frederik *lay down the paper and rise.*] Is that all?

Frederik. That's all.

Colonel Lawton [*Still dazed.*] A prayer book. . . . Me? Well, I'll be—[*Struck.*] Here, Parson, let's swap. You take the prayer book—I'll take the old fob.

Rev. Batholommey. [*Stiffly.*] Thank you. I already *have* a prayer book.

> [*Goes to the window and looks out—his back turned to the others—trying to control his feelings.*]

Mrs. Batholommey. [*Her voice trembling with vexation and disappointment.*] Well, all I can say is—I'm disappointed in your uncle.

Colonel Lawton. Is it for this you hauled us out in the rain, Frederik?

Mrs. Batholommey. [*Bitterly.*] I see now . . . he only gave to the church to show off.

Rev. Batholommey. Rose! . . . I myself am disappointed, but—

Mrs. Batholommey. He did! Or why didn't he *continue* his work? He was *not* a generous man. He was a hard, uncharitable, selfish old man.

Rev. Batholommey. [*Horrified.*] Rose, my dear!

Mrs. Batholommey. He was! If he were here, I'd say it to his face. The congregation sicked *you* after him. Now that he's gone and you'll get nothing more, they'll call you slow—slow and pokey. You'll see! You'll see to-morrow.

Rev. Batholommey. Sh!

Mrs. Batholommey. As for the Colonel, who spent half his time with Mr. Grimm, what is *his* reward? A watch fob! [*Prophetically.*] Henry: mark my words—this will be the end of *you*. It's only a question of a few weeks. One of these new football playing ministers just out of college, will take *your* place. It's not what you *preach* now that counts: it's what you coax out of the rich parishioner's pockets.

Rev. Batholommey. [*In a low voice.*] Mrs. Batholommey!

Mrs. Batholommey. Religion doesn't stand where it did, Henry,—there's no denying that. There was a time when people had to go to church—they weren't decent if they didn't. Now you have to wheedle 'em in. The church needs funds in these days when a college professor is openly saying that—[*Her voice breaks*] the Star of Bethlehem was a comet. [*Weeps.*

Rev. Batholommey. Control yourself. I must insist upon it, Mrs. Batholommey.

Mrs. Batholommey. [*Breaking down—almost breathlessly.*] Oh! If I said all the things I feel like saying about Peter Grimm—well—I shouldn't be fit to be a clergyman's wife. Not to leave his dear friends a—

Colonel Lawton. He *wasn't* liberal; but for God's sake, madam, pull yourself together and think what he ought to have done for me!—I've listened to his plans for twenty years. I've virtually given up my business for him, and what have I for it? Not a button! Not a button! A bible. Still I'm not complaining. Hang that chimney, Frederik, it's smoking.

[Colonel Lawton *stirs the fire—a log drops and the flame goes down. The room has gradually grown darker as the night approaches.*

Mrs. Batholommey. [*Turning on* Colonel Lawton.] Oh, you've feathered your nest, Colonel! You're a rich man.

Colonel Lawton. [*Enraged, raising his voice.*] What? I never came here that *you* weren't begging.

Frederik. [*Virtuously—laying down the paper.*] Well, I'm disgusted! When I think how much more I should have if he hadn't continually doled out money to every one of you!

Colonel Lawton. What?

FREDERIK. He was putty in your hands.

MRS. BATHOLOMMEY. Yes, you can afford to defend his memory—you've got the money.

FREDERIK. I don't defend his memory. He was a gullible old fossil, and the whole town knew it.

MRS. BATHOLOMMEY. *You* did at any rate. I've heard you flatter him by the hour.

FREDERIK. Of course. He liked flattery and I gave him what he wanted. Why not? I gave him plenty. The rest of you were at the same thing; and I had the pleasure of watching him give you the money that belonged to me—to *me*—my money. . . . What business had he to be generous with my money? [*The* COLONEL *strikes a match to light his cigar and as it flares up, the face of* FREDERIK *is seen—distorted with anger.*] I'll tell you this: had he lived much longer, there would have been nothing left for me. It's a fortunate thing for me that—

> [*He pauses, knowing that he has said too much.*
> [*The room is now very dark. The rain has subsided. Everything is quiet outside. There is not a sound, save the ticking of the clock.*

REV. BATHOLOMMEY. [*Solemnly—breaking the pause.*] Young man: it might have been better had Mr. Grimm given his *all* to charity—for he has left his money to an ingrate.

FREDERIK. [*Laughing derisively.*] Ha! ha!

MRS. BATHOLOMMEY. Sh! Someone's coming.

> [*All is quiet. The clock ticks in the dark. The door opens.*

FREDERIK. [*With a change of voice.*] Come in. [*Nobody enters.*] Where's a light? We've been sitting in the dark like owls. Come in.

> [*A pause. He strikes a match and holds it above his head. The light shows the open*

door. *A gust of wind blowing through the doorway, causes the light to flicker.*]

COLONEL LAWTON. I'll see who's . . . [*Looks out.*] No one.

MRS. BATHOLOMMEY. Someone *must* be there. Who opened the door? [*The wind puts out the match in* FREDERIK's *hand. The room is once more in semi-darkness.*] There . . . it closed again. . . .

[FREDERIK *strikes another match and holds it up. The door is seen to be closed.*

COLONEL LAWTON. [*Who is nearest to the door.*] I didn't touch it.

FREDERIK. [*Blowing out the match.*] I'll have the lamps brought in.

MRS. BATHOLOMMEY. Curious. . . .

REV. BATHOLOMMEY. It was the wind—a draught.

COLONEL LAWTON. [*Returning to his chair.*] Must have been.

CATHERINE. [*Entering with a lamp.*] Did someone call me?

[*Without pausing she sets the lamp on the table and turns up the wick.* PETER GRIMM *is seen standing in the room— half in shadow. He is as he was in life. The clothes he wears appear to be those he wore about his house in the first act. He carries his hat in his hand. He has the same kind smile, the same deferential manner, but his face is more spiritual and years younger. He is unseen by all.*

PETER. [*Whose eyes never leave* CATHERINE.] Yes. , . . I called you. . . . I've come back.

FREDERIK. [*To* CATHERINE.] No.

PETER. Don't be frightened, Katie. It's the most

natural thing in the world. You wanted me and I came.

FREDERIK. Why? What made you think someone called you?

CATHERINE. I'm so accustomed to hear Uncle Peter's voice in this room, that sometimes I forget he's not here. . . . I can't get over it! I was almost sure I heard him speak . . . but of course, as soon as I came in—I remembered . . . but someone must have called me.

FREDERIK. No.

> [PETER *stands looking at them, perplexed; not being able to comprehend as yet that he is not seen.*

CATHERINE. Isn't it curious . . to hear your name and turn and . . . [*Unconsciously, she looks in* PETER's *face*] no one there?

REV. BATHOLOMMEY. [*Kindly.*] Nerves. . . . Imagination.

FREDERIK. You need a complete change. [*Crossing to the door.*] For Heaven's sake, let's have more light or we shall all be hearing voices.

PETER. Strange . . . nobody seems to see me. . . . It's—it's extraordinary! Katie! . . . Katie! . . .

> [*His eyes have followed* CATHERINE, *who is now at the door.*

CATHERINE. [*Pausing.*] Perhaps it was the book I was reading that made me think I heard. . . . The Doctor lent it to me.

FREDERIK. [*Poo-poohing.*] O!

CATHERINE. [*Half to herself.*] If he *does* know, if he *can* see, he'll be comforted by the thought that I'm going to do everything he wanted.

> [*She passes out of the room.*

PETER. [*Showing that he does* not *want her to carry out*

Act II] THE RETURN OF PETER GRIMM 159

his wishes.] No, no, don't . . . Frederik! I want to speak to you.

[FREDERIK, *not glancing in* PETER'*s direction, lights a cigarette.*]

MRS. BATHOLOMMEY. Well, Frederik: I hope the old gentleman can see his mistake *now*.

PETER. I can see several mistakes. [REV. MR. BATHOLOMMEY *rises and goes towards the door, pausing in front of* PETER *to take out his watch.*] . . . Mr. Batholommey: I'm glad to see you in my house. . . . I'm very sorry that you can't see *me*. I wasn't pleased with my funeral sermon: it was very gloomy—very. I never was so depressed in my life.

MRS. BATHOLOMMEY. [*To* FREDERIK.] Do you know what I should like to say to your uncle?

PETER. I know.

REV. BATHOLOMMEY. I hope at least you'll care for the parish poor as your uncle did—and keep on with *some* of his charities.

PETER. [*Putting his hand on* REV. MR. BATHOLOMMEY'*s shoulder.*] That's all attended to. I arranged all that with Frederik. He must look after my charities.

FREDERIK. I might as well tell you now—you needn't look to me. It's Uncle Peter's fault if your charities are cut off.

REV. BATHOLOMMEY. [*Half doubtingly.*] It doesn't seem possible that he made no arrangements to continue his good works. [FREDERIK *remains stolid.* REV. MR. BATHOLOMMEY *puts back his watch after glancing at it.*] Just thirty minutes to make a call.

[*Goes to the hall to put on his over-shoes, coat, etc., leaving* PETER'*s hand extended in the air.*]

COLONEL LAWTON. [*Rising.*] I must be toddling.

[*Pauses.*] It's queer, Frederik, how things turn out in this world. [*He stands thinking matters over—cigar in mouth, his hand on his chin.*

PETER. [*Slipping his hand through* COLONEL LAWTON's *arm. They seem to look each other in the eye.*] You were perfectly right about it, Thomas: I *should* have made a will . . . I—suppose it *is* a little too late, isn't it? . . . It would be—er—unusual to do it now, wouldn't it?

[COLONEL LAWTON, *who has heard nothing —seen nothing—moves away as though* PETER *had never held his arm—and goes up into the hall for his cape and overshoes.*

COLONEL LAWTON. [*Noticing an old gold headed walking stick in the hall.*] O, cr—what are you going to do with all the old man's family relics, Frederik?

FREDERIK. The junk, you mean? I shall lay it on some scrap heap, I suppose. It's not worth a penny.

COLONEL LAWTON. I'm not so sure of that. They say there's a lot of money paid for this sort of trash.

FREDERIK. Is that so? Not a bad idea to have a dealer in to look it over.

[PETER *stands listening, a faint smile on his face.*

MRS. BATHOLOMMEY. If I could have the old clock— cheap, Frederik, I'd take it off your hands.

FREDERIK. I'll find out how much it's worth. I shall have everything appraised.

[*Sets his watch by the clock.* MRS. BATHOLOMMEY *gives him a look and joins her husband at the door.*

COLONEL LAWTON. Good night.

[*Exit, closing the door.*

MRS. BATHOLOMMEY. [*As* REV. MR. BATHOLOMMEY *goes*

out—calling after him.] Henry: Catherine wants you to come back for supper.

[MRS. BATHOLOMMEY *leaves the room too disgusted for words.* FREDERIK *goes into the office.*

PETER. [*Now alone.*] We live and learn . . . and oh! What I have learned since I came back. . . . [*He goes to his own particular peg in the vestibule and hangs up his hat. He glances at the wedding presents. Presently he sees the flowers which* CATHERINE *has placed on the desk. With a smile, he touches the flowers.* MARTA *enters with another lamp, which she places on a table. As* PETER'S *eyes rest on* MARTA, *he nods and smiles in recognition, waiting for a response.*] Well, Marta? . . . Don't you know your old master? . . . No? . . . No? . . . [*She winds the clock and leaves the room.*] I seem to be a stranger in my own house . . yet the watch dog knew me and wagged his tail as I came in. [*He stands trying to comprehend it all.*] Well! Well!

FREDERIK. [*Looking at his watch, re-enters from the office and goes to the 'phone, which presently rings.* FREDERIK *instantly lifts the receiver as though not wishing to attract attention. In a low voice.*] Yes. . . . I was waiting for you. How are you, Mr. Hicks? [*Listens.*] I'm not anxious to sell, no. I prefer to carry out my dear old uncle's wishes. [PETER *eyes him—a faint smile on his lips.*] If I got my price? Well . . . of course in that case . . . I might be tempted. To-morrow? No, I can't see you to-morrow. I'm going to be married to-morrow and leave at once for New York. Thank you. [*Listens.*] To-night? Very well, but I don't want it known. I'll sell, but it must be for more than the price my uncle refused. Make it ten thousand more and it's done. [*Listens.*] You'll come to-night? . . . Yes, yes. . . .

[*Listens at the 'phone.*] The dear old man told you his plans never failed, eh? God rest his soul! [*Laughing indulgently.*] Ha! Ha! Ha!

PETER. Ha! Ha! Ha!

FREDERIK. [*Echoing* HICKS' *words.*] What would he say if he knew? What could he say? Everything must change.

[*A far-away rumble of thunder is heard—the lightning flickers at the window and a flash is seen on the telephone which tinkles and responds as though from the electric shock. Exclaiming "Ugh."* FREDERIK *drops the receiver—which hangs down.*]

PETER. [*The storm passes as he speaks into the receiver without touching the telephone.*] Good evening, my friend. We shall soon meet—face to face. . . . You won't be able to carry this matter through. . . . [*Looking into space as though he could see the future.*] You're not well and you're going out to supper to-night . . . you will eat something that will cause you to pass over . . . . I shall see you to-morrow. . . . A happy crossing!

FREDERIK. [*Picks up the receiver.*] Hello? . . . You don't feel well, you say? [*Then after listening to* HICKS' *answer.*] I see. . . . Your lawyer can attend to everything to-night—without you. Very well. It's entirely a question of money, Mr. Hicks. Send your lawyer to the Grimm Manor Hotel. I'll arrange at once for a room. Good-bye. [*Hangs up the receiver.*] That's off my mind.

[*He lights a fresh cigarette—his face expressing the satisfaction he feels in the prospect of a perfectly idle future.* PETER *looks at him as though to say, "And that's the boy whom I loved and trusted!"*]

FREDERIK *gets his hat, throws his coat over his arm and hastens out.*

PETER. [*Turns and faces the door leading into the next room, as though he could feel the presence of someone waiting there.*] Yes. . . . I am still in the house. Come in . . . come in. . . . [*He repeats the signal of the first act.*] Ou—oo. [*The door opens slowly—and* CATHERINE *enters as though at* PETER's *call. She looks about her, not understanding. He holds out his arms to her.* CATHerine *walks slowly towards him. He takes her in his arms, but she does not respond. She does not know that she is being held.*] There! There! . . . Don't worry. . . . It's all right. . . . We'll arrange things very differently. I've come back to change all my plans. [*She moves away a step—just out of his embrace. He tries to call her back.*] Katie! . . . Can't I make my presence known to *you?* Katie! Can't my love for you outlive *me?* Isn't it here in the home? . . . Don't cry.

> [*She moves about the room in thought. As* PETER *watches her—she pauses near the desk.*]

CATHERINE. [*Suddenly.*] Crying doesn't help matters.

PETER. She hears me. She doesn't know it, but she hears me. She's cheering up. [*She inhales the flowers—a half smile on her lips.*] That's right: you haven't smiled before since I died. [*Suddenly giving way to the realization of her loss,* CATHERINE *sighs. Correcting himself.*] I—I mean—since I learned that there was a happier place than the world I left. . . . I'm a trifle confused. I've not had time to adjust myself to these new conditions. [CATHERINE *smiles sadly—goes up to the window, and leaning against the pane looks out into the night.* PETER *continues comfortingly.*] The dead have never really died, you know. We couldn't die if we tried. We're all about you. . . . Look at the gardens: they've died, haven't they? But there they are all the better for it. Death is the greatest thing in the world. It's really a—ha!—delightful experience. What is it, after all? A nap from which we waken rested, refreshed . . . a sleep from which we spring up like children tumbling out of bed—ready to frolic through another world. I was an old man a few days ago, now I'm a boy. I feel much younger than you—much younger. [*A conflict is going on in* CATHERINE's *mind. She walks to the chair by the fireplace and sits—her back to the audience. He approaches her and lays a tender hand on her shoulder.*] I know what you're thinking . . . Katie! I want you to break that very foolish promise I asked you to make. You're almost tempted to. Break it! Break it at once; then—[*Glancing smilingly towards the door—as though he wished to leave—like a child longing to go out to play.*] then I could—take the journey back in peace. . . . I can't go until you do—and I . . . I long to go. . . . Isn't my message any clearer to you? [*Reading her mind.*] You have a feeling . . . an impression of what I'm saying; but the words . . . the words are not clear. . . . Mm . . . let me see. . . . If you can't understand me—there's the Doctor: he'll know how to get the message—he'll find the way. . . . Then I can hurry back . . . home . . .

CATHERINE. [*Helplessly—changing her position like a tired child.*] Oh, I'm so alone.

PETER. [*Cheerily.*] Not alone at all—not at all. I shall drop in very often . . . and then, there's your mother. [*Suddenly remembering.*] O yes, I had almost forgotten: I have a message for you, Katie. . . . [*He seats himself in a chair which is almost in front of her.*] I've met your mother. [*She sits in a deep thought.* PETER *continues with the air of a returned traveller relating his experiences.*] She heard that I had crossed over and there she was—waiting for me. You're thinking of it, aren't you? Wondering if we met. . . . Yes, that was the first interesting experience. She knew me at once. " You were Peter Grimm," she said, " before you knew better "— that's what *they* call leaving *this* world—" to *know better.*" You call it dying. [*Confidentially.*] She's been here often it seems, watching over you. I told her how much I loved you and said you had a happy home. I spoke of your future—of my plans for you and Frederik. " Peter Grimm," she said: " you've overlooked the most important thing in the world—love. You haven't given her *her right* to the choice of her lover—*her right!* " Then it came over me that I'd made a terrible mistake . . . and at that minute, you called to me. [*Impressively.*] In the darkness surrounding all I had left behind, there came a light . . . a glimmer where you stood . . . a clear call in the night. . . . . It seemed as though I had not been away one second . . . but in that second, you had suffered. . . . Now I am back to show you the way . . . I am here to put my hand on your dear head and give you your mother's blessing; to say she will be with you in spirit until she holds you in her arms—you and your loved husband—[CATHERINE *turns in her chair and looks towards the door of the room in which* JAMES *is working.* PETER *catches the thought.*]—yes, James, it's you. . . . And the message ended in this kiss. [*Prints a kiss on her cheek.*] Can't you *think* I'm with you, dear child? Can't you *think* I'm trying to help you? Can't you even hope? O, come, at least hope! Anybody can hope.

> [CATHERINE *rises with an entire change of manner—takes a bright red blossom from the vase on* PETER's *desk—then deliberately walks to the door of the room in*

which JAMES *is working*. PETER *follows her action hopefully. She does not tap on the door, however, but turns and sits at the piano—in thought. She puts* PETER'S *flowers against her face. Then laying the flowers on the piano, sings softly three or four bars of the song she sang in the first act—and stops abruptly.*

CATHERINE. [*To herself.*] That I should sit here singing—at a time like this!

PETER. Sing! Sing! Why not? Lift up your voice like a bird! Your old uncle doesn't sleep out there in the dust. That's only the dream. He's here—here—alive. All his age gone and youth glowing in his heart. If I could only tell you what lies before you—before us all! If people even *suspected* what the next life really is, they wouldn't waste time here—I can tell you *that*. They'd do dreadful things to get away from this existence—make for the nearest pond or—[*Pausing abruptly.*] Ah, here comes some-one who'll know all about it! [*The Doctor comes from* WILLIAM'S *room.* PETER *greets him in a cordial but casual way as though he had parted from him only an hour before.*] Well, Andrew; I apologize. [*Bowing obsequiously.*] You are right. I apologize.

CATHERINE. How is he, Doctor?

DR. MACPHERSON. William is better. Dropped off to sleep again. Can't quite understand him.

PETER. I apologize. I said that if I could come back, I would; and here I am—apologizing. Andrew! Andrew! [*Trying to attract* DR. MACPHERSON'S *attention.*] I have a message, but I can't get it across. This is your chance. I want *you* to take it. I don't wish Catherine to marry Frederik.

DR. MACPHERSON. He's somewhat feverish yet.

PETER. Can't *you* understand one word?

DR. MACPHERSON. It's a puzzling case. . . .

PETER. What? Mine?

DR. MACPHERSON. [*Getting a pad from his pocket—writing out a prescription with his fountain pen.*] I'll leave this prescription at the druggist's—

PETER. I'm quite shut out. . . . They've closed the door on me and turned the key.

DR. MACPHERSON. [*Suddenly noticing that* CATHERINE *seems more cheerful.*] What's happened? I left you in tears and here you are—all smiles.

CATHERINE. Yes, I—I am happier—for some reason. . . . For the last few minutes I—I've had such a strange feeling.

DR. MACPHERSON. That's odd: so have I! Been as restless as a hungry mouse. Something seemed to draw me down here—can't explain it.

PETER. I'm beginning to be felt in this house.

DR. MACPHERSON. Catherine: I have the firm conviction that in a very short time, I shall hear from Peter.

[*Sitting at the table.*

PETER. I hope so. It's high time now.

DR. MACPHERSON. What I want is some positive proof; some absolute test; some—er—

[*Thinks.* CATHERINE *has seated herself at the table. Unconsciously they both occupy the same seats as in the first act.*

PETER. The trouble is with other people, not with us. You want us to give all sorts of proofs; and here we are just back for a little while—very poorly put together—quite confused.

DR. MACPHERSON. Poor old Peter—bless his heart! [*His elbow on the table as though he had been thinking over the matter.* CATHERINE *sits quietly listening.*] If he kept that compact with me, and came back,—do you know what I'd ask him first? If our work goes on.

PETER. Well, now, that's a regular sticker. It has bothered me considerably since I crossed over.

CATHERINE. What do you mean, Doctor?

DR. MACPHERSON. The question *every man wants the answer to:* what's to become of me—*me—my work?* Am I going to be a bone-setter in the next life and he a tulip man. . . . I wonder. . . .

PETER. Andrew: I've asked everybody—Tom, Dick and Harry. One spirit told me that sometimes our work does go on; but he was an awful liar—you know we don't drop our earth habits at once. He said that a genius is simply a fellow who has learned his business in some other world and knows his business. Now then: [*Confidentially preparing to open an argument—sitting in his old seat at the table, as in the first act.*] it stands to reason, Andrew, doesn't it? What chance has the beginner compared with a fellow who knew his business before he was born?

DR. MACPHERSON. [*Unconsciously grasping the thought.*] I believe it is possible to have more than one chance at our work.

PETER. There . . . you caught that. . . . Why can't you take my message to Catherine?

DR. MACPHERSON. [*Rising to get his shawl—gruffly.*] Thought over what I told you concerning this marriage? Not too late to back out.

PETER. He's beginning to take the message.

CATHERINE. Everything's arranged: I shall be married as Uncle Peter wished. I shan't change my mind.

DR. MACPHERSON. Hm! [*Picks up his shawl.*

PETER. [*Trying to detain the Doctor—tugging at his shawl without seeming to pull it.*] Don't give up! Don't give up! A girl can always change her mind—while there's life. Don't give up! [*The Doctor turns, facing* PETER, *looking directly at him as he puts his hand in his coat pocket.*] You heard that, eh? . . . Didn't you? Yes? Did it cross over? . . . What? . . . It did? . . . You're looking me in the face, Andrew: can you see me? [*The Doctor takes a pencil out of his pocket, writes a prescription, throws his shawl over his shoulders—turning his back towards* PETER *and facing* CATHERINE.] Tc! Tc! Tc!

DR. MACPHERSON. Good night.

CATHERINE. Good night.

[CATHERINE *goes quietly to the fireplace, kneeling down, mends the fire, and remains there sitting on an ottoman.*

PETER. [*Calling after the Doctor.*] If I could only make some sign—to start you thinking; but I can't depend upon *you*, I see that. . . . [*Then changing—as though he had an idea.*] Ah yes! There *is* another way. Now to work. [*With renewed activity, he taps in the direction of the office door, although he himself stands three feet away from it. The door opens promptly and* JAMES *appears on the threshold—pen in hand—as though something had made him rise suddenly from his desk.* CATHERINE, *still seated, does not see* JAMES *who stands looking at her—remembering that she is to be married on the following day. Tempting* JAMES.] Yes, she *is* pretty, James . . . young and lovely. . . . Look! . . . There are kisses tangled in her hair where it curls . . . hundreds of them. . . . Are you going to let her go? Her lips are red with the red of youth. Every smile is an invocation to life. Who could resist her smiles? Can you, James? No: you will not let her go. And her hands, James. . . . Look! Hands made to clasp and cling to yours. Imagine her little feet trudging happily about *your* home. . . . Look at her shoulders . . . shaped for a resting place for a little head. . . . You were right, James: we should ask nothing of our girls but to marry the men they love and be happy wives and happy mothers of happy children. You feel what I am saying. . . . You couldn't live without her, could you? No? Very well, then—[*Changing abruptly.*] Now: it's your turn.

[JAMES *pauses a moment. There is silence. Then he comes forward a step and* CATHERINE, *hearing him, turns and rises.*

JAMES. [*Coldly—respectfully.*] Miss Grimm. . . .

CATHERINE. James. . . .

JAMES. I felt that you were here and wished to speak to me. . . . I—I don't know why. . . .

PETER. Good for James.

CATHERINE. [*Shaking hands with him.*] I'm very glad to see you again, James. [*When* PETER *sees that he has brought the two young people together, he stands in the background. The lovers are in the shadow, but* PETER'S *figure is marked and clear.*] Why did you go away?

JAMES. O—er— .

CATHERINE. And without saying a word?

JAMES. Your uncle sent me away. I told him the truth again.

CATHERINE. O. . . .

JAMES. I am going in a few hours.

CATHERINE. Where are you going? What do you intend to do?

JAMES. [*Half heartedly.*] Father and I are going to try our luck together. We're going to start with a small fruit farm. It will give me a chance to experiment. . . .

CATHERINE. It will seem very strange when I come back home . . . uncle gone . . . and you, James.

[*Her voice trembling.*

JAMES. I hope you'll be happy, Catherine.

CATHERINE. James: uncle died smiling at me—thinking of me . . . and just before he went, he gave me his mother's wedding ring and asked me to marry Frederik. I shall never forget how happy he was when I promised. That was all he wanted. His last smile was for me . . . and there he sat—still smiling after he was gone . . . the smile of a man leaving the world perfectly satisfied—at peace. It's like a hand on my heart—hurting it—when I question anything he wanted. I couldn't meet him in the hereafter if I didn't do everything he wished. I couldn't say my prayers at night; I couldn't speak his name in them. . . . He trusted me; depended upon me; did everything for me; so I must do this for him. . . . I wanted you to know this, James, because . . .

JAMES. Why haven't you told Frederik the truth?

CATHERINE. I have.

JAMES. That you don't love him? [CATHERINE *doesn't answer, but* JAMES *knows.*] . . . And he's willing to take you like that?—a little girl like you—in *that* way? . . . God! He's rotten all the way through. He's even worse than I thought. Katie: I didn't mean to say a word of this to-day—not a word; but a moment since—something made me change my mind—I don't know what! . . . [PETER *smiles.*] I felt that I *must* talk to you. You looked so young, so helpless, such a child. You've never had to think for yourself—you don't know what you're doing. You *couldn't* live under it, Catherine. You're making the greatest mistake possible, if you marry without love. Why should you carry out your uncle's plans? You're going to be wretched for life to please a dead man who doesn't know it; or, if he does know it, regrets it bitterly.

PETER. I agree with you now, James.

CATHERINE. You mustn't say that, James.

JAMES. But I will say it—I will speak my mind. I don't care how fond you were of your uncle or how much he did for you,—it wasn't right to ask this of you. It wasn't fair. The whole thing is the mistake of a *very* obstinate old man.

CATHERINE. James!

JAMES. I loved him, too; but he *was* an obstinate old man. Sometimes I think it was the Dutch blood in his veins.

PETER. A very frank, outspoken, fellow. I like to hear him talk—now.

JAMES. Do you know why I was sent away? Why I quarrelled with your uncle? I said that I loved you . . . he asked me . . . I didn't tell him because I had any hopes—I hadn't . . . I haven't now. . . . [*Struck.*] But in spite of what I'm saying . . . I don't know what makes me think that I . . . . I could take you in my arms and you would let me . . . but I do think it.

CATHERINE. [*Retreats, backing towards* PETER.] No! . . . Don't touch me, James—you mustn't! Don't . . . Don't!

> [PETER *pushes her into* JAMES's *arms, without touching her. She exclaims* "Oh, James!" *and fairly runs towards* JAMES *as though violently propelled. In reality, she thinks that she is yielding to an impulse. As she reaches him, she exclaims* "No!" *and turns back, but* JAMES, *with outstretched arms, catches her.*

JAMES. You love me. [*Draws her to him.*]

CATHERINE. Don't make me say that, James.

JAMES. I *will* make you say it! You *do* love me.

CATHERINE. No matter if I do, that won't alter matters.

JAMES. What? What?

CATHERINE. No, no, don't say any more. . . . I won't hear it. [*She stands free of* JAMES—*then turns and walks to the stairs.*] Good-bye, Jim.

JAMES. Do you mean it? Are you really going to sacrifice yourself because of—Am I really losing you? . . . Catherine! Catherine!

CATHERINE. [*In tears—beseechingly.*] Please don't. . . . Please don't. . . .

> [FREDERIK *enters. Until the entrance of* FREDERIK, PETER *has had hope in his face, but now he begins to feel apprehensive.*

FREDERIK. [*Throwing his hat and coat in a chair.*] I have some work to do—more of my uncle's unopened mail; then I'll join you, Hartman. We must—er—make haste.

> [JAMES *looks at* CATHERINE, *then at* FREDERIK. CATHERINE *gives him an imploring look—urging him not to speak.* FREDERIK *has gone to* PETER's *desk.*

JAMES. I'll come back later. [*Goes towards the hall.*

FREDERIK. Catherine: have you asked James to be present at the ceremony to-morrow?

CATHERINE. No.

FREDERIK. James, will you—

JAMES. I shall be leaving early in the morning.

FREDERIK. Too bad!

> [*Exit* JAMES. FREDERIK *lights the desk candles, takes the mail out of the drawer—opens two letters—tears them up after barely glancing at them—then sees* CATHERINE *still standing at the foot of the stairs—her back to him. He lays the cigar on the desk, crosses and taking her in his arms, kisses her.*

CATHERINE. [*With a revulsion of feeling.*] No! No! No! [*She covers her face with her hands—trying to control herself.*] Please! . . . Not now. . . .

FREDERIK. Why not *now?* [*Suspiciously.*] Has Hartman been talking to you? What has he been saying to you? [CATHERINE *starts slowly up the stairs.*] Wait a moment, please. . . . [*As she retreats a step up the stairs he follows her.*] Do you really imagine you—you care for that fellow?

CATHERINE. Don't—please.

FREDERIK. I'm sorry to insist. Of course, I knew there was a sort of school-girl attachment on your part; . . . that you'd known each other since childhood. I don't take it at all seriously. In three months, you'll forget him. I must insist, however, that you do *not* speak to him again to-night. After to-morrow—after we are married—I'm quite sure that you will not forget you are my wife, Catherine,—my wife.

CATHERINE. I shan't forget.

[*She escapes into her room.* FREDERIK *goes to his desk.*]

PETER. [*Confronting* FREDERIK.] Now, sir, I have something to say to you, Frederik Grimm, my beloved nephew! I had to die to find you out; but I know you! [FREDERIK *is reading a letter.*] You sit there opening a dead man's mail—with the heart of a stone—thinking: "He's gone! He's gone!—so I'll break every promise!" But there is something you have forgotten—something that always finds us out: the law of reward and punishment. Even now it is overtaking you. Your hour has struck. [FREDERIK *takes up another letter and begins to read it; then, as though disturbed by a passing thought, he puts it down. As though perplexed by the condition of his own mind, he ponders, his eyes resting unconsciously on* PETER.] Your hour has struck.

Frederik. [*To himself.*] What in the world is the matter with me to-night?

Peter. Read!

Frederik. [*Has opened a long narrow blue envelope containing a letter on blue paper and a small photograph. He stares at the letter, aghast.*] My God! Here's luck. . . . Here's luck! From that girl Annamarie to my uncle. Oh, if he had read it!

Peter. [*Standing in front of* Frederik—*looks into space—as though reading the letter in the air.*] "Dear Mr. Grimm: I have not written because I can't do anything to help William and I am ashamed."

Frederik. Wh! [*As though he had read the first part to himself, now reads aloud.*] "Don't be too hard upon me. . . . I have gone hungry trying to save a few pennies for him, but I never could; and now I see that I cannot hope to have him back. William is far better off with you. I—" [*Hesitates.*

Peter. [*Going back of the desk, standing behind* Frederik's *chair.*] Go on. . . .

Frederik. "I wish that I might see him once again. Perhaps I could come and go in the night."

Peter. That's a terrible thing for a mother to write.

Frederik. [*Who has been looking down at the letter—suddenly feeling* Peter's *presence.*] Who's that? Who's in this room? [*Looks over his shoulder—then glances about.*] I could have sworn somebody was looking over my shoulder . . . or had come in at the door . . . or . . . [*But seeing no one—he continues.*] "I met someone from home . . . if there is any truth in the rumor of Catherine's marriage—it mustn't be, Mr. Grimm—it mustn't be . . . not to Frederik. For Frederik is my little boy's—" [Frederik *gives a furtive glance upstairs at the door of the child's room. Picks up the small picture which was in*

the envelope.] Her picture. . . . [*Turns it over—looks at back—reads.*] "For my boy, from Annamarie."
[FREDERIK, *conscience stricken for the time being, bows his head.*

PETER. For the first time since I entered this house, you are yourself, Frederik Grimm. Once more a spark of manhood is alight in your soul. Courage! It's not too late to repent. Turn back, lad! Follow your impulse. Take the little boy in your arms. Go down on your knees and ask his mother's pardon. Turn over a fresh page, that I may leave this house in peace. . . .

FREDERIK. [*Looks about uneasily, then glances towards the door leading into the hall.*] Who is at the door? Curious. . . . I thought I heard someone at . . .

PETER. I am at the door—I, Peter Grimm! Annamarie is at the door,—the little girl who is ashamed to come home; the old mother in the kitchen breaking her heart for some word. William is at the door—your own flesh and blood—nameless; Katie, sobbing her heart out—you can hear her; all—we are all at the door—every soul in this house. We are all at the door of your conscience, Frederik. . . . Don't keep us waiting, my boy. It's very hard to kill the love I had for you. I long to love you again—to take you back to my heart—lies and all. [FREDERIK *rises—in deep thought.*] Yes! Call her! Tell her the truth. Give her back her promise. . . . Give her back her home. . . . Close the door on a peaceful, happy, silent room and go. Think—think of that moment when you gave her back her freedom! Think of her joy, her gratitude, her affection. It's worth living for, lad. Speak! Make haste and call her, Fritz. [FREDERIK *takes several steps—then turns back to the desk. He tears the letter in two, muttering to himself:* "Damn the woman," *and sinks into his chair.*] Frederik Grimm: stand up before me! [FREDERIK *starts to rise,* but *changes his mind.*] Stand up! [FREDERIK *rises—not knowing why he has risen. Pointing an accusing finger at* FREDERIK.] Liar to the dead! Cheat, thief, hypocrite! You shan't have my little girl. You only want her for a week, a day, an hour. I refuse. I have come back to take her from you and you cannot put me to rest. . . . I have come back. . . . You cannot drive me from your thoughts—I am there. . . . [*Tapping his forehead, without touching it.*] I am looking over your shoulder. . . . In at the window . . . under the door. . . . You are breathing me in the air. . . . I am looking at your heart. [*He brings his clenched fist down on the desk in answer to* FREDERIK's *gesture; but despite the seeming violence of the blow, he makes no sound.*] Hear me! You shall hear me! Hear me! [*Calling loudly.*] Hear me! Hear me! Hear me! Will nobody hear me! Is there no one in this house to hear me? No one? Has my journey been in vain? [*For the first time fully realizing the situation.*] Oh, must we stand or fall by the mistakes we made here and the deeds we did? Is there no second chance in this world?

FREDERIK. [*With a sneer on his lips as though trying to banish his thoughts.*] Psh!

> [MARTA *enters with a tray containing a pot of coffee and a plate of small cakes.* PETER, *who has watched her with appealing eyes, like a dog craving attention, glances from her to the desk and from the desk back to* MARTA—*trying to tempt her to look at the torn letter.* FREDERIK, *deep in thought, does not notice her.* PETER *points to the desk as though to say "Look!" After a pause she picks up the picture and the letter—holding them in*

one hand to clear a spot for the tray which she is about to set on the desk.

PETER. [*Speaking in a hushed voice.*] Marta: see what you have in your hand . . . that letter . . . there . . . read it. . . . Run to Catherine with it. Read it from the house-tops. . . . The letter. . . . Look! There you have the story of Annamarie. . . . It is the one way to know the truth in this house—the only way. . . . There in your hand—the letter. . . . He will never speak. . . . The letter for Catherine.

[MARTA *sets down the picture and the letter; but something prompts her to look at them; however, before she can carry out her impulse,* FREDERIK *starts up.*

FREDERIK. My God! How you startled me! [MARTA *sets down the tray.*] Oh! To be off and out of this old rat-trap. [*He wipes his forehead with his black bordered handkerchief.*] I mean—our loss comes home to us so keenly here where we are accustomed to see him.

MARTA. A cup of coffee, sir?

FREDERIK. No, no, no.

MARTA. [*Pathetically.*] I thought you wished to keep to your uncle's customs. . . . He always took it at this time.

FREDERIK. [*Recovering.*] Yes, yes, of course.

MARTA. . . . No word? . . .

FREDERIK. [*Hesitates.*] What do you mean?

MARTA. No letter?

FREDERIK. Letter? . . . [*Covering the letter with his hand.*] From whom? . . .

MARTA. From. . . . At a time like this, I thought. . . . I left . . . that Annamarie . . . that there should be some message. . . . Every day I expect to hear. . . .

FREDERIK. No.
  [PETER *gestures to* MARTA—*pointing to the picture and letter, now covered by* FREDERIK's *hand.*]
MARTA. [*Hesitating.*] Are you certain?
FREDERIK. Quite certain. [*She curtsies and leaves the room.* FREDERIK, *as though relieved to see her go, jumps to his feet and tearing the letter in smaller pieces, lights them in the candle, dropping the burning pieces on a tray. As the flames die out,* FREDERIK *brushes the blackened paper into the waste basket.*] There's an end to *that!* [PETER *crouches near the basket hovering over it, his hands clasped helplessly. After a pause, he raises his hand, until it points to a bedroom above. An echo of the circus music is faintly heard; not with the blaring of brasses, but with the sounds of elfin horns, conveying the impression of a phantom circus band. The door of* WILLIAM's *room opens and he comes out as though to listen to the music. He wears a sleeping suit and is bare-footed. He has come down stairs before* FREDERIK *sees him.* FREDERIK *quickly puts aside the photograph, laying it on the desk, covering it with his hand. Gruffly.*] Why aren't you in bed? If you're ill, that's the proper place for you.
WILLIAM. I came down to hear the circus music.
FREDERIK. Circus music?
WILLIAM. It woke me up.
FREDERIK. The circus left town days ago. You must have been dreaming.
WILLIAM. The band's playing now. Don't you hear it, sir? The procession's passing. [*He runs to the window and opens it. The music stops. A breeze sweeps through the room—bellies out the curtains and causes the lustres to jingle on the mantel. Surprised.*] No. It's almost dark. There's no procession . . . no shining horses. . . .

[*Turns sadly away from the window.*] I wonder what made me think the—I must have been dreaming. [*Rubbing his eyes.*]

FREDERIK. [*Goes to the window, closes it. The child looks at him and in retreating from him, unconsciously backs towards* PETER.] Are you feeling better?

WILLIAM. Yes, sir, I feel better—and hungry.

FREDERIK. Go back to bed.

WILLIAM. Yes, sir. [FREDERIK *sits.*

PETER. Where's your mother, William?

WILLIAM. Do you know where Annamarie is?

PETER. Ah!

FREDERIK. Why do you ask me? What should I know of her?

WILLIAM. Grandmother doesn't know; Miss Catherine doesn't know; nobody knows.

FREDERIK. I don't know, either.

> [*Tears up the picture—turning so that* WILLIAM *does not see what he is doing.* PETER, *who has been smiling at* WILLIAM, *motions him to come closer.* WILLIAM, *feeling* PETER'S *presence, looks around the room.*

WILLIAM. Mr. Frederik: where's *old* Mr. Grimm?

FREDERIK. Dead.

WILLIAM. Are you sure he's dead? 'Cause—[*Puzzled—unable to explain himself, he hesitates.*]

FREDERIK. [*Annoyed.*] You'd better go to bed.

WILLIAM. [*Pointing to a glass of water on a tray.*] Can I have a drink of water, please?

FREDERIK. Go to bed, sir, or you'll be punished. Water's not good for little boys with fever.

WILLIAM. [*Going towards the stairs.*] Wish I could find a cold brook and lie in it.

[*Goes slowly up the stairs.* FREDERIK *would destroy the pieces of the picture; but* PETER *faces him as though forbidding him to touch it, and for the first time,* FREDERIK *imagines he sees the apparition of his uncle.*]

FREDERIK. [*In a very low voice—almost inaudibly.*] My God! I thought I saw. . . .

[*Receding a step and yet another step as the vision of* PETER *is still before him, he passes out of the room, wipes the beads of sweat from his forehead.* WILLIAM, *hearing the door close, comes down stairs and running to the table at back, drinks a glass of water.*]

WILLIAM. Um! That's good!

PETER. William!

WILLIAM. [*Doesn't see* PETER *yet, but he feels his presence.*] Wish it *had* been the circus music.

PETER. You shall hear it all again. [*Gestures towards the plate of cakes on the tray.*] Come, William, here's something very nice.

WILLIAM. [*Seeing the cakes.*] Um! Cakes!

[*He steals to the tray, looking over his shoulder in fear of being caught.*]

PETER. Don't be frightened. I'm here to protect you. Help yourself to the cakes. William: do you think you could deliver a message for me . . . a very important message. . . .

[*The circus music is heard.* WILLIAM *sits at the table near the tray, and* PETER *seats himself opposite as though he were the host doing the honors.* WILLIAM, *being unconsciously coaxed by* PETER, *is pre-*

vailed upon to choose the biggest cake.
He takes a bite, looking towards PETER.

WILLIAM. [*To himself.*] Ha! . . . Think I am dreaming. [*Rubbing his little stomach ecstatically.*] Hope I won't wake up and find there wasn't any cake.

PETER. Don't worry: you won't. [WILLIAM *has taken another piece of cake which he nibbles at—now holding a piece in each hand.*] Pretty substantial dream, eh? There's a fine, fat raisin. [WILLIAM *eats the raisin, then looks into the sugar bowl.*] Don't hesitate, William. Sugar won't hurt you now. Nothing can hurt you any more. Fall to, William—help yourself. [WILLIAM *looks over his shoulder, fearing the return of* FREDERIK.] O, he won't come back in a hurry. Ha! Frederik *thought* he saw me, William; well, he didn't. He had a bad conscience—hallucination. [WILLIAM *nibbles a lump of sugar.*] Now, William: I have a message for you. Won't you try and take it for me, eh? [*But* WILLIAM *eats another lump of sugar.*] I see. . . . I can't expect to get any assistance from a boy while his little stomach's calling. [WILLIAM *empties the cream jug and helps himself to cakes. Presently the music dies out.*] Now I'm going to tell you something. [*Impressively.*] You're a very lucky boy, William; I congratulate you. Do you know why—of all this household—you are the only one to help me? . . . This is the secret: in a little time— it won't be long—you're going—[*As though he were imparting the most delightful information.*]—to know better! Think of *that!* Isn't the news splendid? [*But* WILLIAM *eats on.*] Think of what most of us have to endure before *we* know better! Why, William: you're going into the circus without paying for a ticket. You're laying down the burden before you climb the hill. And in your case, William, you are fortunate indeed; for there are some little soldiers in this world already handicapped when they begin the battle of life. . . . . Their parents haven't fitted them for the struggle. . . . Like little moon moths,—they look in at the windows; they beat at the panes; they see the lights of happy firesides—the lights of home, but they never get in. . . . You are one of these wanderers, William. . . . And so, it is well for you that before your playing time is over—before your man's work begins,—you're going to know the great secret. Happy boy! No coarsening of your child's heart, until you stand before the world like Frederik; no sweat and toil such as dear old James is facing; no dimming of the eye and trembling of the hand such as the poor old Doctor shall know in time to come; no hot tears to blister your eyes . . . tears such as Katie is shedding now; but in all your youth, your faith—your innocence,—you'll fall asleep and oh! the awakening, William! . . . "It is well with the *child*." [WILLIAM *lays down the cake and clapping his hands, thinks.* PETER *answers his thoughts.*] What? No—don't think of it! Nonsense! You don't want to grow up to be a man. Grow up to fail? Or, still worse—to succeed—to be famous? To wear a heavy laurel wreath? A wreath to be held up by tired hands that ache for one hour's freedom. No, no: you're to escape all that, William: joy is on the way to meet you with sweets in its outstretched hands and laughter on its lips. [WILLIAM *takes the last swallow of a piece of cake, exclaims "Hm!" in a satisfied way, brushes the crumbs off his lap, and sits back in his chair.*] Have you had enough? Good! William: I want you to try to understand that you're to help me, will you? Will you tell Miss Catherine that—

WILLIAM. [*Without looking up, his hands folded in his lap.*] Take me back with you, Mr. Grimm?

PETER. Can you see me, William?

WILLIAM. No sir; but I know.

PETER. Come here. [WILLIAM *doesn't move.*] Here
. . . here . . . [WILLIAM *advances to the center of
the room and pauses hesitatingly.*] Take my hand . . .
[WILLIAM *approaches in the direction of the voice.* PETER
takes WILLIAM's *outstretched hand.*] Have you got it?

WILLIAM. No, sir . . .

PETER. [*Putting his hand on* WILLIAM's *head.*] Now?
. . . Do you feel it?

WILLIAM. I feel something: yes, sir. [*Puts his hand on*
PETER's *hand which is still on his head.*] But where's
your hand? There's nothing there.

PETER. But you hear me?

WILLIAM. I can't really hear you. . . . It's a dream.
[*Coaxingly.*] O, Mr. Grimm: take me back with you.

PETER. You're not quite ready to go with me yet,
William—not until we can see each other face to face.

WILLIAM. Why did you come back, Mr. Grimm? Wasn't
it nice where you were?

PETER. It was indeed. It was like—[*Whimsically.*]
—new toys.

WILLIAM. [*To whom the idea appeals.*] As nice as
that!

PETER. Nicer. But I had to come back with this message. I want you to help me to deliver it.

[*Indicating the picture.*

WILLIAM. Where's the bosom of Abraham, Mr.
Grimm?

PETER. Eh?

WILLIAM. The minister says you're asleep there.

PETER. Stuff and nonsense! I haven't been near the
bosom of Abraham.

WILLIAM. Too bad you died before you went to the
circus, Mr. Grimm. But it must be great to be in a place
where you can look down and see the circus for nothing.

Do you remember the clown that sang: "Uncle Rat has gone to town?"

PETER. Yes, indeed; but let us talk of something more important. Come here, William: [*He starts towards the desk*] would you like to see someone whom all little boys love—love more than anybody else in the whole world?

[PETER *is standing at the desk with his finger on the torn pieces of the picture.*]

WILLIAM. Yes, the clown in the circus. . . . No. . . . it isn't a clown . . . it's our mother. . . . Yes, I want to see my mother, Annamarie. [*Unconsciously* WILLIAM *comes to the desk and sees the torn picture—picks up a piece and looks at it. Very simply.*] Why . . . there she is! . . . That's her face.

PETER. Ah! You recognize her. Mother's face is there, William, but it's in little bits. We must put her together, William. We must show her to everybody in the house, so that everybody will say: "How in the world did she ever get here? To whom does this picture belong?" We must set them to thinking.

WILLIAM. Yes. Let us show her to everybody. [*He sits and joins the pieces under the guidance of* PETER.] Annamarie . . . Annamarie . . .

PETER. You remember many things, William . . . . things that happened when you lived with Annamarie, don't you?

WILLIAM. I was very little. . . .

PETER. Still, you remember. . . .

WILLIAM. [*Evasively.*] I was afraid. . . .

PETER. You loved her.

WILLIAM. [*To the picture.*] O, yes . . . yes, I loved you.

PETER. Now, through that miracle of love, you can remember many things tucked away in your childish brain,

—things laid away in your mind like toys upon a shelf. Come: pick them up and dust them off and bring them out again. It will come back. When you lived with Annamarie . . . there was you . . . and Annamarie . . . and—

WILLIAM. —and the other one?

PETER. Ah! We're getting nearer! Who *was* the other one?

WILLIAM. [*Gives a quick glance towards the door—then as though speaking to the picture.*] I must put you together before *he* comes back. [*He fits the other pieces together*—PETER *trying to guide him. Presently* WILLIAM *hums as a child will when at play, singing the tune of* "*Uncle Rat.*"] "Uncle Rat has gone to town."

PETER. WILLIAM. [*Singing together.*] "Ha! Hm!"
  [*At this instant* PETER *is indicating another piece of the picture.*]

WILLIAM. Her other foot. [*Then sings.*]
  "Uncle Rat has gone to town,
    To buy his niece a wedding gown."
[*Adjusting a piece of the picture.*] Her hand.

PETER. WILLIAM. [*Together.*] "Ha! Hm!"

WILLIAM. Her other hand. [*Sings.*]
    "What shall the wedding breakfast be?
      Hard boiled eggs and—"
[*Speaking.*] Where's—
      [*Pauses—looking for a piece of the picture.*]

PETER. [*Finishing the verse.*] "A cup of tea."
      [*With a gesture as though knocking on the door of the adjoining room to attract* MRS. BATHOLOMMEY'S *attention.*]

WILLIAM. [*Speaks.*] There's her hat.

PETER. WILLIAM. [*Together.*] "Ha! Hm!"

WILLIAM. [*Stops singing and claps his hands with*

boyish delight—staring at the picture.] Annamarie! Annamarie! You're not in bits any more—you're all put together.

> [*By this time* PETER *is going up the stairs and as he stands in front of* CATHERINE'S *door, it opens.* PETER *passes in and* CATHERINE *comes out.*

CATHERINE. [*Astonished.*] Why, William! What are you doing down here?

WILLIAM. Miss Catherine! Come down! Come down! I have something to show you.

CATHERINE. [*Not coming down.*] No, dear—come upstairs: there's a good boy. You mustn't play down there. Come to bed.

> [*Passes into* WILLIAM'S *room.*

MRS. BATHOLOMMEY. [*Who has entered and seeing* WILLIAM.] William!

WILLIAM. Look—look! [*Pointing to the picture.*] See what old Mr. Grimm brought back with him.

MRS. BATHOLOMMEY. [*Alarmed.*] What are you talking about, William? *Old* Mr. Grimm is dead.

WILLIAM. No, he isn't . . . he's come back. . . . He has been in this room.

MRS. BATHOLOMMEY. Absurd!

WILLIAM. I was talking to him.

MRS. BATHOLOMMEY. You're feverish again. I must get the Doctor. [*Comes down to* WILLIAM.] And I thought you were feeling better! [*Seeing* CATHERINE, *who appears on the balcony as though wondering why* WILLIAM *doesn't come to bed.*] The child's mind is wandering. He imagines all sorts of things. I'll call the Doctor—

PETER. [*Who has re-entered.*] You needn't—he's coming now. Come in, Andrew. I'm giving you one more chance.

[*The Doctor enters, wearing his skull cap and carrying his pipe in his hand. It is evident that he has come over in a hurry.*]

MRS. BATHOLOMMEY. [*Surprised.*] I was just going for you. How fortunate that you came.

DR. MACPHERSON. I thought I'd have another peep at William.

[*By this time* CATHERINE *has seated herself on a chair and takes* WILLIAM *on her lap. He puts his arms around her neck.*]

MRS. BATHOLOMMEY. He's quite delirious.

DR. MACPHERSON. Doesn't look it. [*Putting his hand on* WILLIAM'S *cheek and forehead.*] Very slight fever. What makes you think he was delirious?

. .   [*Counting* WILLIAM'S *pulse.*]

MRS. BATHOLOMMEY. [*Interrupting.*] He said that old Mr. Grimm was in this room—that he was talking to him.

DR. MACPHERSON. [*Interested.*] Yes? Really? Well, possibly he is. Nothing remarkable in *that,* is there?

PETER. Well, at last!

MRS. BATHOLOMMEY. What? O, of course, you believe in—

DR. MACPHERSON. —In fact, I had a compact with him to return if—

MRS. BATHOLOMMEY. A compact? Of all the preposterous—

DR. MACPHERSON. Not at all. Dozens of cases on record—as I can show you—where these compacts have actually been kept. [*Suddenly struck—looking at* WILLIAM.] I wonder if that boy's a sensitive. [*Hand on his chin.*] I wonder. . . .

CATHERINE. [*Echoing the Doctor's words.*] A sensitive?

Mrs. Batholommey. What's that?

Dr. MacPherson. It's difficult to explain. I mean a human organism so constituted that it can be *informed* or *controlled* by those who—er—have—[*With a gesture.*] crossed over.

Mrs. Batholommey. I think I'll put the boy to bed, Doctor.

Dr. MacPherson. Just a moment, Mistress Batholommey. I'm here to find out what ails William. William: what makes you think that Mr. Grimm is in this room?

Mrs. Batholommey. I wouldn't have the child encouraged in such ideas, Catherine. I—

Dr. MacPherson. Ssh! Please, please. [*Taking the boy on his knee.*] What makes you think Peter Grimm is in this room?

William. [*Hesitating.*] . . . The things he said to me.

Mrs. Batholommey. Said to you?

Catherine. [*Wonderingly.*] William . . . are you sure he . . .

Dr. MacPherson. Said to *you,* eh? [William *nods assent.*] Old Mr. Grimm? [William *nods assent.*] Sure of that, William?

William. O, yes, sir.

Dr. MacPherson. Think before you speak, my boy: what did Mr. Grimm say to you?

William. Lots of things. . . .

Mrs. Batholommey. Really!

Dr. MacPherson. [*Raises his hand for silence.*] How did he look, William?

William. I didn't see him.

Mrs. Batholommey. Ha!

Dr. MacPherson. You must have seen something.

William. I thought once I saw his hat on the peg

where it used to hang. [*Looks at the peg.*] No, it's gone.

MRS. BATHOLOMMEY. [*Remonstrating.*] Doctor!

DR. MACPHERSON. [*Thinking.*] I wonder if he really did—

CATHERINE. Do you think he could have been Uncle Peter?

PETER. [*Pointing to the desk.*] William!

WILLIAM. Look! . . . [*Points to the picture.*] That's what I wanted to show you when you were upstairs.

CATHERINE. [*Seeing the picture.*] It's his mother—Annamarie.

MRS. BATHOLOMMEY. The Lord save us—his mother! I didn't know you'd heard from Annamarie.

CATHERINE. We haven't.

MRS. BATHOLOMMEY. Then how'd that picture get into the house?

PETER. Ah! I knew *she'd begin!* Now that she's wound up, we shall get at the truth.

MRS. BATHOLOMMEY. It's a new picture. She's much changed. How ever did it find its way here?

CATHERINE. I never saw it before. It's very strange. . . . We've all been waiting for news of her. Even her mother doesn't know where she is, or—could Marta have received this since I—

MRS. BATHOLOMMEY. I'll ask her.

[*Exit into dining room.*

CATHERINE. If not, who had the picture? . . . And why weren't we all told? . . . Who tore it up? Did you, William? [WILLIAM *shakes his head, meaning " No."*] Who has been at the desk? No one save Frederik . . . Frederik . . . and surely he—

[*She pauses—perplexed.*

MRS. BATHOLOMMEY. [*Re-entering.*] No: Marta hasn't heard a word; and only a few minutes ago, she asked

Act II] THE RETURN OF PETER GRIMM 191

Frederik if some message hadn't come, but he said, "No, nothing." I didn't tell her of the picture.

CATHERINE. [*Looking at the picture.*] I wonder if there was any message with it.

MRS. BATHOLOMMEY. I remember the day that picture came . . . the day your uncle died. . . . It was a long blue envelope—the size of the picture. . . . I took it from the postman myself because everyone was distracted and rushing about. It dropped to the floor and as I picked it up I thought I knew the writing; but I couldn't remember whose it was. . . . It was directed to your uncle. . . . [*Looking from the desk to the waste basket.*] There's the envelope,—[*Holding up a scrap of blue envelope.*] and paper . . . someone has burned it.

CATHERINE. Annamarie wrote to my uncle. . . .

DR. MACPHERSON. [*Not understanding.*] But what could Peter have to say to *me* concerning Annamarie? [*Making a resolution—rising.*] We're going to find out. You may draw the curtains, Catherine, if you please. [CATHERINE *draws the curtains. The Doctor turns the lights down and closes the door. A pause.*] Peter Grimm. . . .

PETER. Yes, Andrew? . . .

DR. MACPHERSON. [*Not hearing.*] If you have come back . . . if you are in the room . . . and the boy speaks truly—give me some sign . . . some indication . . .

PETER. I can't give you a sign, Andrew. . . . I have spoken to the boy . . . the boy . . .

DR. MACPHERSON. If you cannot make your presence known to me—I know there are great difficulties—will you try and send your message by William? I presume you have one—

PETER. Yes, that's right.

Dr. MacPherson. —or else you wouldn't have come back?

Peter. That's just the point I wanted to make, Andrew. You understand perfectly.

Dr. MacPherson. [*As before.*] I am waiting. . . . We are all waiting. [*Noticing that a door is a trifle ajar.*] The door's open again.

[Mrs. Batholommey, *without making a sound, closes it and sits as before.*

Peter. Sh! Listen!

[*A pause.*

William. [*In a peculiar manner—as though in a half dream—but not shutting his eyes. As though controlled by* Peter.] There was Annamarie and me and the other.

Dr. MacPherson. [*Very low, as though afraid to interrupt* William's *train of thought.*] What other?

William. The man . . . that came.

Dr. MacPherson. What man?

William. The man that made Annamarie cry.

Catherine. Who was he?

William. I don't know . . .

Peter. Yes, you do. Don't tell lies, William.

Dr. MacPherson. What man made Annamarie cry?

William. I can't remember. . . .

Peter. Yes, you can. . . . You're afraid. . . .

Catherine. [*In a low voice.*] So you do remember the time when you lived with Annamarie . . . you always told me that you didn't . . . [*To* Dr. MacPherson.] I must know more of this—[*Pauses abruptly.*] Think, William: who came to the house?

Peter. That's what *I* asked you, William.

William. That's what *he* asked. . . .

Dr. MacPherson. Who?

William. Mr. Grimm.

Act II] THE RETURN OF PETER GRIMM 193

Dr. MacPherson. When, William?

William. Just now . . .

Catherine. Mrs. Batholommey. [*Together.*] Just now!

Dr. MacPherson. Hm . . . you both ask the same question, eh? The man that came to see—

Mrs. Batholommey. [*Perplexed.*] It can't be possible that the child knows what he's talking about.

Dr. MacPherson. [*Ignoring her.*] What did you tell Mr. Grimm when he asked you?

Peter. You'd better make haste, William. Frederik is coming back.

William. [*Looking uneasily over his shoulder.*] I'm afraid. . . .

Catherine. Why does he always look towards that door? You're not afraid now, William?

William. [*Looking towards the door.*] N-no—but . . . Please don't let Mr. Frederik come back. 'Cause then I'll be afraid again.

Dr. MacPherson. Ah!

Peter. William? William?

William. [*Rising quickly.*] Yes, Mr. Grimm?

Peter. You must say that I am very unhappy.

William. He says he is very unhappy.

Dr. MacPherson. Why is he unhappy? . . . Ask him.

William. Why are you unhappy, Mr. Grimm?

Peter. I am thinking of Catherine's future. . . .

William. [*Not understanding the last word—puzzled.*] Eh?

Peter. To-morrow. . . .

William. [*After a slight pause.*] To-morrow. . . .

Peter. Catherine's—

William. [*Looks at Catherine—hesitating.*] Your—

[*Stops.* CATHERINE *gives the Doctor a quick glance—she seems to divine the message.*

DR. MACPHERSON. [*Prompting.*] Her—

CATHERINE. What, William? What of to-morrow?

PETER. She must not marry Frederik.

WILLIAM. I mustn't say *that.*

DR. MACPHERSON. What?

WILLIAM. What he wanted me to say.

[*Points towards* PETER. *All instinctively look towards the spot to which* WILLIAM *points, but they see no one.*

PETER. [*Speaking slowly to the boy.*] Catherine—must—not—marry Frederik Grimm.

DR. MACPHERSON. Speak, William. No one will hurt you.

WILLIAM. O, yes, *he* will. . . . [*Looking timidly towards the door.*] I don't want to tell his name—'cause . . . 'cause . . .

DR. MACPHERSON. Why don't you tell the name, William?

PETER. Make haste, William, make haste.

WILLIAM. [*Trembling.*] I'm afraid . . . I'm afraid . . . he will make Annamarie cry . . . he makes me cry . . .

CATHERINE. [*With suppressed excitement—half to herself.*] Why are you afraid of him? Was Frederik the man that came to see Annamarie?

MRS. BATHOLOMMEY. Catherine!

CATHERINE. [*On her knees before* WILLIAM.] Was he? Was it Frederik Grimm? Tell me, William.

MRS. BATHOLOMMEY. Surely you don't believe . . .

CATHERINE. [*In a low voice.* I've thought of a great many things to-day . . . little things . . . little things I'd never noticed before. . . . I'm putting them together just as he put that picture together. . . . I must know the truth.

PETER. William, make haste. . . . Frederik is listening at the door.

WILLIAM. [*Frightened.*] I won't say any more. He's there . . . at the door. . . .

[*He looks over his shoulder and* CATHERINE *goes towards the door.*]

DR. MACPHERSON. William, tell me.

PETER. William!

[CATHERINE *opens the door suddenly.* FREDERIK *is standing, listening. He is taken unawares and for a few seconds he does not move—then he recovers.*]

WILLIAM. Please don't let him scold me. I'm afraid of him. [*Going towards the stairs—looking at* FREDERIK.] I was afraid of him when I lived with Annamarie and he came to see us and made her cry.

DR. MACPHERSON. Are you sure you remember that? Weren't you too small?

WILLIAM. No: I *do* remember. . . . I always did remember, only for a little while I—I forgot. . . . I must go to bed. He told me to. [*Goes upstairs.*

PETER. [*Calling after* WILLIAM.] You're a good boy, William. [WILLIAM *goes to his room.*]

CATHERINE. [*After a slight pause—simply.*] Frederik: you've heard from Annamarie. . . . [*Gestures towards the desk.* FREDERIK *sees the photograph and is silent.*] You've had a letter from her. You tried to destroy it. Why did you tell Marta that you'd had no message—no news? You went to see her, too. Why did you tell me that you'd never seen her since she went away? Why did you lie to me? Why do you hate that child?

FREDERIK. Are you going to believe what that boy—

CATHERINE. I'm going to find out. I'm going to find out where she is, before I marry you. That child may be right or wrong, but I'm going to know what his mother was to you. I want the truth.

DR. MACPHERSON. [*Who has been in thought—now looking up.*] We've heard the truth. We had that message from Peter Grimm himself.

CATHERINE. Yes: it *is* true. I believe Uncle Peter Grimm was in this room to-night.

FREDERIK. [*Not surprised—glancing towards the spot where* PETER *stood when he thought he saw him.*] O! You too? Did you see him, too?

MRS. BATHOLOMMEY. [*Incredulously.*] Impossible!

CATHERINE. I don't care what anyone else may think —people have the right to think for themselves; but I believe he has been here—he *is* here. Uncle Peter: if you can hear me now, give me back my promise—or—or I'll take it back!

PETER. [*Gently—smilingly—relieved.*] I did give it back to you, my dear; but what a time I had getting it across!

Curtain.

ACT III

[*SCENE: The third act takes place at twenty minutes to twelve on the same night.*

The fire is out. The table on which PETER *took his coffee in the first act, is now being used by the Doctor for* WILLIAM'S *medicines, two bottles, two glasses, two teaspoons, a clinical thermometer, etc.* WILLIAM, *who has been questioned by the Doctor, is now asleep upstairs.* PETER'S *hat hangs on the peg in the shadow.*

Act III] THE RETURN OF PETER GRIMM

Although the hour is late, no one has thought of going to bed. FREDERIK *is waiting at the hotel for the lawyer whom* HICKS *was to send to arrange for the sale of* PETER GRIMM'S *nurseries, but he has not arrived.*

It is now a fine clear night. The clouds are almost silvery and a hint of the moon is showing.

AT RISE. The Doctor, full of his theories, is seated before the fire, writing the account of PETER GRIMM'S *return, for the American Branch of the "London Society of Psychical Research."*

DR. MACPHERSON. [*Reading what he has written.*] " To be forwarded to the London Society of Psychical Research: Dr. Hyslop: Dear Sir: This evening at the residence of Peter—" [*Pauses and inserts " the late " and continues to read after inserting the words*] " —the late Peter Grimm—the well known horticulturist of Grimm Manor, New York, certain phenomena were observed which would clearly indicate the return of Peter Grimm ten days after his decease. While he was invisible to all, three people were present besides myself; one of these a child of eight, who received the message. There was no spelling out of signals nor automatic writing, but word of mouth." [*A rap sounds.*] Who will that be at this hour? . . . [*Looks at the clock.*] Nearly midnight. [*Opening the door.*] Yes?

A VOICE. [*Outside.*] Telegram for Frederik Grimm.

DR. MACPHERSON. Not in. I'll sign. [*He signs, and receives the telegram, sets it against a candle stick on the desk and resumes his seat. Reads.*] " I made a compact with Peter Grimm while he was in the flesh, that whichever went first was to return and give the other some sign; and I propose to give positive proof—" [*He hesitates—thinks— then repeats*] " positive proof that he kept this compact and that I assisted in the carrying out of his instructions."

Mrs. Batholommey. [*Enters—evidently highly wrought up by the events of the evening.*] Who was that? Who knocked?

Dr. MacPherson. Telegram.

Mrs. Batholommey. I thought perhaps Frederik had come back. Don't you consider William much better?

Dr. MacPherson. Mm. . . .

Mrs. Batholommey. Dear, dear! The scene that took place to-night has completely upset me. [*The Doctor takes up his pen and reads to himself.*] Well, Doctor: [*She pushes forward a chair and sits at the other side of the table—facing him*] the breaking off of the engagement is rather sudden, isn't it? We've been talking it over in the front parlor, Mr. Batholommey and I. James has finished his work and has just joined us. I suggest sending out a card—a neat card—saying that owing to the bereavement in the family, the wedding has been indefinitely postponed. Of course, it isn't exactly true.

Dr. MacPherson. Won't take place at all.

[*Goes on reading.*]

Mrs. Batholommey. Evidently not; if the whole matter looks very strange to me—how will it look to other people; especially since we haven't any, any rational explanation —as yet. We must get out of it in some fashion.

Dr. MacPherson. Whose business is it?

Mrs. Batholommey. Nobody's, of course. But Catherine's position is certainly unusual; and the strangest part of it all is—she doesn't seem to feel her situation. She's sitting alone in the library, seemingly placid and happy. What I really wish to consult you about, is this: should the card we're going to send out have a narrow black border? [*The Doctor is now writing.*] Doctor: you don't appear to be interested. You might at least answer my question.

Dr. MacPherson. What chance have I had to answer? You've done all the talking.

Mrs. Batholommey. [*Rising—annoyed.*] O, of course, all these little matters sound trivial to you; but men like you couldn't look after the workings of the *next* world if others didn't attend to *this*. Someone has to do it.

Dr. MacPherson. I fully appreciate the fact, Mistress Batholommey, that other people are making it possible for me to be myself. I'll admit that; and now if I might have a few moments in peace to attend to something really important— [*The* Rev. Mr. Batholommey *has entered with his hat in his hand.*

Rev. Batholommey. Doctor: I've been thinking things over. I ran in for a moment to suggest that we suspend judgement until we investigate William's story. I can scarcely believe that—

Dr. MacPherson. Ump! [*Rises and goes to the telephone on the desk.*] Four—red.

Rev. Batholommey. I regret that Frederik left the house without offering some explanation.

Dr. MacPherson. [*At the 'phone.*] Marget: I'm at Peter's. I mean—I'm at the Grimms'. Send me my bag. I'll stay the night with William. Bye.

[*Seats himself at the table.*

Rev. Batholommey. Tell Frederik that if he cares to consult me, I shall be at home in my study. Good night, Doctor. Good night, Rose.

Dr. MacPherson. Hold on, Mr. Batholommey! [*The* Rev. Mr. Batholommey *turns.*] I'm writing an account of all that happened here to-night—

Rev. Batholommey. [*Dubiously.*] Indeed!

Dr. MacPherson. I shall verify every word of the evidence by William's mother for whom I am searching. [*The* Rev. Mr. Batholommey *smiles faintly behind his hand.*] Then I shall send in my report, and not until then. What I wish to ask is this: would you have any objection to the name of Mrs. Batholommey being used as a witness?

REV. BATHOLOMMEY. [*Looks perplexed.*] Well,—er —a—

MRS. BATHOLOMMEY. O, no, you don't! You may flout our beliefs; but wouldn't you like to bolster up your report with "the wife of a clergyman who was present!" It sounds so respectable and sane, doesn't it? No, sir! You cannot prop up your wild eyed—

REV. BATHOLOMMEY. Rose, my dear!

MRS. BATHOLOMMEY. [*Sweeping on*] theories against the good black of a minister's coat. I think myself that you have *probably* stumbled on the truth about William's mother.

REV. BATHOLOMMEY. *Can* it be true? Oh dreadful! Dreadful!

MRS. BATHOLOMMEY. But that child knew it all along. He's eight years old and he was with her until five—and five's the age of memory. Every incident of his mother's life has lingered in his little mind. Supposing you do find her and learn that it's all true: what do you prove? Simply that *William remembered,* and that's all there is to it.

REV. BATHOLOMMEY. Let us hope that there's not a word of truth in it. Don't you think, Doctor,—mind I'm not opposing your ideas as a clergyman,—I'm just echoing what *everybody else* thinks,—don't you believe these spiritualistic ideas leading *away* from the Heaven *we* were taught to believe in, tend towards irresponsibility—er—eccentricity—and—oftener—insanity? Is it healthy—that's the idea—is it healthy?

DR. MACPHERSON. Well, Batholommey, religion has frequently led to the stake, and I never heard of the Spanish Inquisition being called *healthy* for anybody taking part in it. Still, religion flourishes. But your old fashioned unscientific gilt ginger-bread Heaven blew up ten years ago—went out. My Heaven's just coming in. It's new. Dr. Funk and a lot of the clergymen are in already. You'd better get used to it, Batholommey, and get in line and into the procession.

Rev. Batholommey. You'll have to convince me first, Doctor—and that no man can do. I made up my mind at twenty-one and my heaven is just where it was then.

Dr. MacPherson. So I see. It hasn't improved a particle.

Rev. Batholommey. [*Tolerantly.*] Well, well. Good night.

Mrs. Batholommey. [*Follows him in the hall.*] Good night, Henry, I'll be home to-morrow. You'll be glad to see me, dear, won't you?

Rev. Batholommey. My church mouse!

[*He pats her cheek, kisses her good night and goes.*

Mrs. Batholommey. [*Who has gone to the door of her room—giving the Doctor a parting shot.*] Write as much as you like, Doctor; words are but air. We didn't see Peter Grimm, and you know and I know and everybody knows that *seeing* is believing.

Dr. MacPherson. [*Looking up.*] Damn everybody! It's everybody's ignorance that has set the world back a thousand years. Where was I before you—O, yes. [*Reads as* Mrs. Batholommey *leaves the room.*] "I assisted in the carrying out of his instructions."

[Frederik Grimm *enters.*

Frederik. Anybody in this house come to their senses yet?

Dr. MacPherson. I think so, my boy. I think several in this house have come to their senses. Catherine has, for one. I'm very glad to see you back, Frederik. I have a few questions to put to you.

FREDERIK. Why don't you have more light? It's half dark in this room. [*He picks up the lamp from the Doctor's table and holds it so that he can look searchingly in the direction of the desk to see if* PETER's *apparition is still there. His eye is suddenly riveted on the telegram resting against the candlestick on the desk.*] Is that telegram for me?

DR. MACPHERSON. Yes.

FREDERIK. O. . . . It may explain perhaps why I've been kept waiting at the hotel. . . . [*Tries to go to the desk but cannot muster up enough courage.*] I had an appointment to meet a man who wanted to buy the gardens. I may as well tell you, I'm thinking of selling out root and branch.

DR. MACPHERSON. [*Amazed.*] Selling out? Peter Grimm's gardens? So this is the end of Peter's great work?

FREDERIK. You'll think it strange, Doctor; but I—I simply can't make up my mind to go near that old desk of my uncle's. . . . I have a perfect terror of the thing! Would you mind handing me that telegram? [*The Doctor looks at him with scarcely veiled contempt, and hands him the telegram. After a glance at the contents,* FREDERIK *gives vent to a long drawn breath.*] Billy Hicks—the man I was to sell to—is dead. . . . [*Tosses the telegram across the table towards the Doctor, who does not take it. It lies on the table.*] I knew it this afternoon! I knew he would die . . . but I wouldn't let myself believe it. Someone told it to me . . . whispered it to me. . . . Doctor: as sure as you live—somebody else is doing my thinking for me . . . in this house.

DR. MACPHERSON. [*Studying* FREDERIK.] What makes you say that?

FREDERIK. To-night—in this room, I thought I saw my uncle . . . [*Pointing towards the desk*] there.

DR. MACPHERSON. Eh? . . .

FREDERIK. And just before I saw him—I—I had the . . . the strangest impulse to go to the foot of the stairs and call Kitty,—give her the house—and run—run—get out of it.

DR. MACPHERSON. O, a good impulse, I see! Very unusual, I should say.

FREDERIK. I thought he gave me a terrible look—a terrible look.

DR. MACPHERSON. Your uncle?

FREDERIK. Yes. My God! I won't forget that look! And as I started out of the room—he blotted out . . . I mean—I *thought* I saw him blot out; . . . then I left the photograph on the desk and—

DR. MACPHERSON. That's how William came by it. [*Jots down a couple of notes.*] Did you ever have this impulse before—to give up Catherine—to let her have the cottage?

FREDERIK. Not much I hadn't. Certainly not. I told you someone else was thinking for *me*. I don't want to give her up. It's folly! I've always been fond of her. But if she has turned against me, I'm not going to sit here and cry about it. I shall be up and off. [*Rising.*] But I'll tell you one thing: from this time, I propose to think for myself. I've taken a room at the hotel and a few things for the night. I've done with this house. I'd like to sell it along with the gardens and let a stranger raze it to the ground; but—[*Thinks as he looks towards the desk*] when I walk out of here to-night—it's hers—she can have it. . . . I **wouldn't** sleep here. . . . I give her the home because . . .

DR. MACPHERSON. Because you don't believe anything

but you want to be on the safe side in case he—[*Gesturing to desk.*] was there.

FREDERIK. [*Puzzled—awed—his voice almost dropping to a whisper.*] How do you account for it, Doctor?

DR. MACPHERSON. It might have been an hallucination or perhaps you did see him though it could have been inflammation of conscience. Frederik: when did you last see Annamarie?

FREDERIK. [*Angrily.*] Haven't I told you already that I refuse to answer any questions as to my—

DR. MACPHERSON. I think it only fair to tell you that it won't make a particle of difference whether you answer me or not. I have someone on the track now—working from an old address; I've called in the detectives and I'il find her, you may be sure of that. As long as I'm going to know it, I may as well hear your side of it, too. When did you last see Annamarie?

FREDERIK. [*Sits—answers dully, mechanically, after a pause.*] About three years ago.

DR. MACPHERSON. Never since?

FREDERIK. No.

DR. MACPHERSON. What occurred the last time you saw her?

FREDERIK. [*Quietly, as before.*] What *always* occurs when a young man realizes that he has his life before him, must be respected—looked up to,—settle down, think of his future and forget a silly girl?

DR. MACPHERSON. A scene took place, eh? Was William present?

FREDERIK. Yes. She held him in her arms.

DR. MACPHERSON. And then?

FREDERIK. I left the house.

DR. MACPHERSON. Then it's all true. [FREDERIK *is silent.*] What are you going to do for William?

FREDERIK. Nothing. I'm a rich man now—and if I recognize him—he'll be at me till the day he dies. His mother's gone to the dogs and under her influence, the boy—

DR. MACPHERSON. Be silent, you damned young scoundrel. Oh, what an act of charity if the good Lord took William, and I say it with all my heart. Out of all you have—not a crumb for—

FREDERIK. I want you to know I've sweat for that money and I'm going to keep it!

DR. MACPHERSON. You've sweat for—

FREDERIK. [*Showing feeling.*] —Yes! How do you think I got the money? I went to jail for it—jail, jail. Every day I've been in this house has been spent in prison. I've been doing time. Do you think it didn't get on my nerves? I've gone to bed at nine o'clock and thought of what I was missing in New York. I've got up at cockcrow to be in time for grace at the breakfast table. I took charge of a class in Sabbath school, and I handed out the infernal cornucopias at the Church Christmas tree, while he played Santa Claus. What more can a fellow do to earn his money? Don't you call that sweating? Yes sir: I've danced like a damned hand organ monkey for the pennies he left me and I had to grin and touch my hat and make believe I liked it. Now I'm going to spend every cent for my own personal pleasure.

DR. MACPHERSON. Will rich men never learn wisdom!

FREDERIK. [*Rising.*] No, they won't! But in every fourth generation there comes along a *wise* fellow—a spender who knows how to distribute the money others have hoarded: I'm the spender.

DR. MACPHERSON. Shame on you and your like! Your breed should be exterminated.

FREDERIK. [*Taking a little packet of letters from the desk.*] O, no: we're quite as necessary as you are. And now—I will answer no more questions. I'm done. Good night, Doctor.

Dr. MacPherson. Good night and good-bye. [*With a look of disgust, has gone to the table, held a medicine bottle to the light to look at the label, and poured a spoonful into a wine glass filled with water. As* Frederik *leaves the house, the Doctor taps on a door and calls.*] Catherine! [Catherine *enters and shows by the glance she directs at the front door that she knows* Frederik *has been in the room and has just left the house.*] Burn up your wedding dress. We've made no mistake. I can tell you *that!*

> [*Goes up the stairs to* William's *room, taking the lamp with him.* James *has entered and taking* Catherine's *hand, holds it for a moment.*

James. Good night, Catherine.

> [*She turns and lays her hand on his shoulder.*

Catherine. I wonder, James, if *he* can see us now.

James. That's the big mystery! . . . Who can tell? But any man who works with flowers and things that grow—knows there is no such thing as death—there's nothing but life—life and always life. I'll be back in the morning. . . . Won't you . . . see me to the door?

Catherine. Yes . . . yes. . . . [*They go out together,* Catherine *carrying a candle into the dark vestibule. The moment they disappear, a lamp standing on the piano goes out as though the draught from the door or an unseen hand had extinguished it. It is now quite dark outside, and the moon is hidden for a moment. At the same time, a light, seemingly coming from nowhere, reveals* Peter Grimm *standing in the room at the door—as though he had been there when the young people passed out. He is smiling and happy. The moon is not seen, but the light of it* (*as though it had come out from behind a cloud*) *now reveals*

Act III] THE RETURN OF PETER GRIMM 207

the old windmill. From outside the door the voices of
JAMES and CATHERINE are heard as they both say:] Good
night.

JAMES. Catherine. . . . I won't go without it. . . .

PETER. [Knowing that JAMES is demanding a kiss.]
Aha! [Rubs his hands with satisfaction—then listens—
and after a second pause exclaims, with an upraised finger,
as though he were hearing the kiss.] Ah! Now I can
go . . .

[He walks to the peg on which his hat hangs
and takes it down. His work is done.
CATHERINE re-enters, darting into the
hall in girlish confusion.

JAMES. [His happy voice, outside.] Good night!

CATHERINE. [Calling to him through the crack in the
door.] Good night! [She closes the door, turns the key
and draws the heavy bolt—then leans against the door,
candlestick in hand—the wind has blown out the candle.]
Oh, I'm so happy! I'm *so* happy!

PETER. Then good night to *you*, my darling: love cannot say good-bye. [She goes to PETER's chair and sitting
thinks it over—her hands clasped in her lap—her face
radiant with happiness.] Here in your childhood's home I
leave you. Here in the years to come, the way lies clear
before you. [His arms upraised.] "Lust in Rust"—
Pleasure and peace go with you. [CATHERINE looks towards
the door—remembering JAMES' kiss—half smiling. Humorously.] Y-es; I saw you. I heard . . . I know. . . .
Here on some sunny blossoming day when, as a wife, you
look out upon my garden—every flower and tree and shrub
shall bloom enchanted to your eyes. . . . All that happens—happens again. And if at first, a little knock of
poverty taps at the door and James finds the road hard and
steep—what is money?—a thing,—a good thing to have,—

but still a thing . . . and happiness will come without
it. And when, as a mother, you shall see my plantings with
new eyes, my Catherine,—when you explain each leaf and
bud to your little people—you will remember the time when
we walked together through the leafy lanes and I taught
you—even as you teach them—you little thing! . . .
So, I shall linger in your heart. And some day should your
children wander far away and my gardens blossom for a
stranger who may take my name off the gates,—what *is*
my name? Already it grows faint to my ears. [*Lightly.*]
Yes, yes, yes: let others take my work. . . . Why should
we care? All that happens, happens again. [*She rests her
elbow on the chair, half hides her face in her hand.*] And
never forget this: I shall be waiting for you—I shall know
all your life. I shall adore your children and be their
grandfather just as though I were here; I shall find it hard
not to laugh at them when they are bad and I shall worship
them when they are good—and I don't want them too good.
. . . Frederik was good. . . . I shall be everywhere
about you . . . in the stockings at Christmas, in a big,
busy, teeming world of shadows just outside your threshold or whispering in the still noises of the night. . . .
And oh! as the years pass, [*Standing over her chair*] you
cannot imagine what pride I shall take in your comfortable
middle life—the very *best* age, I think—when you two shall
look out on your possessions arm in arm—and take your
well earned comfort and ease. How I shall love to see you
look fondly at each other as you say: "Be happy, Jim—
you've worked hard for this." or James say: "Take your
comfort, little mother, let them all wait upon *you—you*
waited upon *them*. Lean back in your carriage—you've
earned it!" And towards the end—[*Sitting on a chair by
her side and looking into her face*] after all the luxuries
and vanities and possessions cease to be so important—

people return to very simple things, dear. The evening of life comes bearing its own lamp. Then perhaps as a little old grandmother, a little old child whose bed time is drawing near, I shall see you happy to sit out in the sunlight of another day; asking nothing more of life than the few hours to be spent with those you love . . . telling your grandchildren at your knees, how much brighter the flowers blossomed when *you* were young. Ha! Ha! Ha! All that happens, happens again. . . . And when one day, glorified, radiant, young once more, the mother and I shall take you in our arms, Oh! what a re-union! [*Inspired.*] The flight of love—to love. . . . And now . . . [*He bends over her and caresses her hand.*] Good night.

CATHERINE. [*Rises and going to the desk, buries her face in the bunch of flowers placed there in memory of* PETER.] Dear Uncle Peter. . . .

[MARTA *enters—pausing to hear if all is quiet in* WILLIAM'S *room.* CATHERINE, *lifting her face, sees* MARTA *and rapturously hugs her, to* MARTA'S *amazement— then goes up the stairs.*]

PETER. [*Whose eyes never leave* CATHERINE.] "Lust in Rust!" Pleasure and Peace! Amen! [CATHERINE *passes into her room, the music dying away as her door closes.* MARTA, *still wondering, goes to the clock and winds it.*] Poor Marta! Every time she thinks of me, she winds my clock. We're not quite forgotten.

DR. MACPHERSON. [*Reappears, carrying* WILLIAM, *now wrapped up in an old fashioned Dutch patchwork quilt. The Doctor has a lamp in his free hand.*] So you want to go downstairs, eh? Very good! How do you feel, laddie?

WILLIAM. New all over.

DR. MACPHERSON. [*Placing the lamp on the little table*

right, and laying WILLIAM *on the couch.*] Now I'll get you the glass of cold water.

    [*Goes into the dining room, leaving the door open.*
 PETER. [*Calling after the Doctor.*] Good night, Andrew. I'm afraid the world will have to wait a little longer for the *big* guesser. Drop in often. I shall be glad to see you here.

 WILLIAM. [*Quickly rising on the couch, looks towards the peg on which* PETER'*s hat hung. Calling.*] Mr. Grimm! Where are you? I knew that you were down here. [*Seeing* PETER.] Oh, I see you!

    [*Raising himself to his knees on the sofa.*
 PETER. Yes?

    [*There is an impressive pause and silence as*
     they face each other.

 WILLIAM. O, you've got your hat . . . it's off the peg. . . . You're going. Need you go right away—Mr. Grimm? Can't you wait a little while?

 PETER. I'll wait for you, William.

 WILLIAM. May I go with you? Thank you. I couldn't find the way without you.

 PETER. Yes, you could. It's the surest way in the world. But I'll wait: don't worry.

 WILLIAM. I shan't. [*Coaxingly.*] Don't be in a hurry. . . . I want—[*Lies down happily.*] to take a nap first. . . . I'm sleepy. [*He pulls the covering up and sleeps.*]

 PETER. I wish you the pleasantest dream a little boy can have in *this* world.

    [*Instantly, as though the room were peopled*
     with the faint images of WILLIAM'*s dream,*
     the phantom circus music is heard with
     its elfin horns; and through the music,
     voices call " Hai! Hai!" The sound of
     the cracking of a whip is heard and the

> *blare of a clown's ten cent tin horn. The phantom voice of the Clown (very faint) calls.*

CLOWN'S VOICE. Billy Miller's big show and monster circus is in town this afternoon! Don't forget the date! Only one ring—no confusion. Circus day comes but once a year, little sir. Come early and see the wild animals and hear the lion roar-r-r! Mind: I shall expect *you!* Wonderful troupe of trained mice in the side show.

> *During the above the deeper voice of a hawker—muffled and far off—cries.*

HAWKER'S VOICE. Peanuts, pop corn, lemonade—ice cold lemo—lemo—lemonade! Circus day comes but once a year.

> *Breaking in through the music, and the voices of the clown and hawker, the gruff voice of a " barker " is heard calling.*

BARKER'S VOICE. Walk in and see the midgets and the giant! Only ten cents—one dime!

> *As these voices die away, the* CLOWN, *whose voice indicates that he is now perched on the head of the couch, sings.*

CLOWN'S VOICE.
  " Uncle Rat has gone to town,
    Ha! Hm!
  Uncle Rat has gone to town,
    To buy his niece—"

> *His voice ends abruptly—the music stops. Everything is over. There is silence. Then three clear knocks sound on the door.*

PETER. Come in. . . . [*The door opens. No one is there—but a faint path of phosphorous light is seen.*] O, friends! Troops of you! [*As though he recognizes the unseen guests.*] I've been gone so long that you came for me, eh? I'm quite ready to go back. I'm just waiting for

a happy little fellow who's going back with us. . . .
We'll follow. Do you all go ahead—lead the way.

[*He looks at* WILLIAM, *holds out his arms and* WILLIAM *jumps up and runs into them.*]

Well, William! You *know better* now. Come! [*Picking up* WILLIAM.] Happy, eh?

WILLIAM. [*Nods, his face beaming.*] Oh, yes!

PETER. Let's be off, then.

[*As they turn towards the door.*

DR. MACPHERSON. [*Re-entering, goes to the couch with the water and suddenly setting down the glass, exclaims in a hushed voice.*] My God! He's dead!

[*He half raises up the boy that appears to be* WILLIAM. *The light from the lamp on the table falls on the dead face of the child. Then the Doctor gently lays the boy down again on the couch and sits pondering over the mystery of death.*

PETER. [*To the Doctor.*] O, no! There never was so fair a prospect for *life!*

WILLIAM. [*In* PETER's *arms.*] I *am* happy!

[*Outside a hazy moonlight shimmers. A few stars twinkle in the far-away sky; and the low moon is seen back of the old windmill.*

PETER. [*To* WILLIAM.] If the rest of them only knew what they're missing, eh?

WILLIAM. [*Begins to sing, joyously.*] "Uncle Rat has gone to town."

[PETER *dances up a few steps towards the door, singing with* WILLIAM.

PETER. WILLIAM. [*Together.*]
"Ha! Hm!
Uncle Rat has gone to town,

To buy his niece a wedding gown.
Ha! Hm!"

PETER. [*Gives one last fond look towards* CATHERINE'S *room To* WILLIAM.] We're off!

[*Putting the boy over his shoulder, they sing together, as they go up, the phantom circus music accompanying them.*

PETER. WILLIAM. [*Together.*]
"What shall the wedding breakfast be.
Ha! Hm!"

PETER. [*Alone.*]
"What shall the wedding breakfast be?
Hard boiled eggs and a cup of tea."

PETER. WILLIAM. [*Together.*]
"Ha! Hm!"

[PETER GRIMM *has danced off with the child through the faint path of light. As he goes, the wind or an unseen hand closes the door after them. There is a moment's pause until their voices are no longer heard—then the curtain slowly descends. The air of the song is taken up by an unseen orchestra and continues as the audience passes out.*

Curtain.

ROMANCE

By

EDWARD SHELDON

" *My thoughts at the end of the long, long day*
Fly over the hills and far away—"

EDWARD BREWSTER SHELDON was born in Chicago, February 4, 1886. Harvard was his college, from which he was graduated in 1907 and where he received his master's degree in 1908. His plays are *Salvation Nell* (1908), *The Boss* (1911), *Princess Zim Zim* (1911), *Egypt* (1912), *The High Road* (1912), *Romance* (1913), *Song of Songs* (1914) and *The Garden of Paradise* (1915).

Romance was first produced at Maxine Elliott's Theatre, New York, Monday, February 10, 1913, with Miss Doris Keane in the leading rôle as Mme. Margherita Cavallini. It was later produced in London, where its " run " of over one thousand nights was one of the longest on record. In the spring of 1920, it was produced as a motion picture with Miss Keane in the leading rôle.

[Copyright, 1912, 1913, 1914, by Edward Sheldon; Copyright in the Dominion of Canada; Copyright in Great Britain]

CHARACTERS

IN THE PROLOGUE AND EPILOGUE:
BISHOP ARMSTRONG
HARRY } his grandchildren
SUZETTE }

IN THE STORY:

THOMAS ARMSTRONG,
   Rector of St. Giles
CORNELIUS VAN TUYL,
   of Van Tuyl & Co.,
   Bankers
SUSAN VAN TUYL,
   his niece
MISS ARMSTRONG,
   the Rector's aunt.
MRS. RUTHERFORD
MRS. FROTHINGHAM
MISS FROTHINGHAM
MRS. GRAY

MISS SNYDER
MR. FRED LIVINGSTONE
MR. HARRY PUTNAM
SIGNORA VANNUCCI
BAPTISTE
LOUIS
FRANÇOIS
EUGENE
ADOLPH
SERVANT AT MR. VAN TUYL'S
BUTLER AT THE RECTORY
MME. MARGHERITA CAVALLINI

THE PROLOGUE: The Bishop's library in his house on Washington Square. New Year's Eve. About ten o'clock.

THE STORY: Act I. Over forty years ago. At Cornelius Van Tuyl's house,—58 Fifth Avenue. A November evening.

   Act II. The study in the Rectory of St. Giles', East 8th Street. The afternoon of New Year's Eve.

   Act III. Late that night. Mme. Cavallini's apartments in the Brevoort House. After her farewell appearance as "Mignon."

THE EPILOGUE: The Bishop's library again. Midnight.

PLACE: New York.   TIME: Now and the 1860's.

ROMANCE

THE PROLOGUE

[*SCENE: The Bishop's library in Washington Square. At right are two windows, with heavy curtains drawn. At left is a large fireplace, with a white marble mantel. At back is the door leading to the rest of the house. There are high bookcases, running up to the ceiling, set in both walls wherever there is any space. In a corner at back stands a Victrola, of sober mahogany. Before the fireplace, half facing the audience, is the Bishop's big armchair. At right, is a big mahogany table-desk, arranged in an orderly way with electric lamp, telephone, desk-furniture, books, memoranda, files, etc. The chair is behind it, between the windows. The whole room is one of quiet dignity,—slightly old-fashioned in effect, and very comfortable.*

It is night. The lamp on the desk is turned on and there is a cheerful wood fire burning. In his armchair before the fire sits Bishop Armstrong. He is a charming, drily humorous old man of about seventy. Suzette, —a decided young woman of seventeen,—is sitting at the desk, reading aloud from the evening paper.]

SUZETTE. [*Skimming over the headlines.*] "Regulation of Skyscrapers—Drastic Measures—" [*She yawns.*] "Borough President Gives to Board of Estimates the Report on Improvement." [*Looking up.*] Sounds dull, doesn't it?

THE BISHOP. No—but if you think so, try the next.

SUZETTE. [*Reading.*] "President in the West—Yesterday's Speech at Cheyenne"—Is that the way you pronounce it?—"Crops, Race Suicide, and Tariff Reform." [*As the noise of horns drifts in from the street.*] Oh, I do wish those boys would stop!

THE BISHOP. [*Philosophically.*] It's New Year's Eve.

SUZETTE. I know, but they needn't make such a fuss about it. [*Returning to her paper.*] The President talked two and a half columns and he looks dreadfully dull. Do you want me to read him? Now, grandpa, speak the truth! Wouldn't you much rather have me start the Victrola?

THE BISHOP. Well, my dear, perhaps I would. Where's Harry? He said he wanted to speak to me after dinner about something important.

SUZETTE. [*Busy with the Victrola.*] Oh, he just went out. He'll be back soon. [*The song begins.*] There, grandpa! Isn't that a splendid record?

THE BISHOP. [*Singing.*] Ta-ta-ta-ta! Yes—a very fine voice. Who is it?

SUZETTE. Tetrazzini.

THE BISHOP. Ah, you should have heard Patti sing this at the Academy in '72—!

SUZETTE. Now, grandpa, I can't help being young, and anyway I'm sure that Garden and Fremstad and Farrar are every bit as good as your Grisis and Pattis and Cavallinis. And as for Caruso—!

THE BISHOP. [*Softly.*] *I* have heard Mario! [*Humming again.*] Ta-ta-ta-ta! Now for the cadenza—[*He listens.*] Fair—quite fair! [*With a sigh.*] After all, there's no one like Verdi!

SUZETTE. Grandpa.

THE BISHOP. Yes, dear?

SUZETTE. [*Beguilingly.*] Which do you think would be

more apt to melt you into a perfectly angelic, Bavarian-cream sort of mood—*O Parigi* from *Traviata* or the *Sextette* from *Lucia?*

THE BISHOP. I'm melted already. I'm just running over the side of the dish.

SUZETTE. Really? No, I think you need one more. I want you very, very soft. [*Picking out a fresh record.*] Oh, here's a brand-new Destinn! That'll do it!

THE BISHOP. What's the opera?

SUZETTE. [*Adjusting the record.*] Wait and see. [*The voice is heard.*] Do you remember it?

THE BISHOP. [*Looking away.*] Yes—yes, I remember —[*He rouses himself suddenly.*] Don't play that, Suzette. I know I'm foolish, but it makes me rather sad.

SUZETTE. [*Stopping the record.*] I thought you'd like it. It's from *Mignon.*

THE BISHOP. Yes, I know—but—[*In a different tone.*] Suppose we have a little Harry Lauder for a change?

SUZETTE. [*Adjusting the record.*] Grandpa, your taste in music is low. That's the only word. And I've tried so hard to uplift it. Just think of those wonderful Boston Symphony concerts I dragged you to last winter! And now I think you'd rather hear *I Love a Lassie* than Beethoven!

THE BISHOP. [*Tranquilly.*] I would indeed.

SUZETTE. And you a Bishop of the Episcopal Church! [*She starts the machine.*] There!

THE BISHOP. [*Leaning back in his chair and singing under his breath.*]

"*I love a lassie,
A bonny Highland lassie—
She's the—*"

SUZETTE. [*Coming and perching on the arm of his chair.*] Oh, grandpa, you *are* such a dear old—baby!

THE BISHOP. Yes, ma'am?

SUZETTE. And I know I bully you an awful lot. Don't I?
THE BISHOP. Well, I'm used to it!
SUZETTE. How horrid of you! Why, I don't bully you at all! Of course there *are* times when you *do* need disciplining—
THE BISHOP. [*Smiling.*] So your grandmother used to tell me.
SUZETTE. And you haven't anyone to do it except me.
THE BISHOP. I know.
SUZETTE. [*Softening.*] But I don't want you to think I'm a tyrant—especially to-night!
THE BISHOP. To what am I indebted for this holiday?
SUZETTE. Well, I've got something to tell you.
THE BISHOP. Yes?
SUZETTE. And I don't know whether or not you'll like it.
THE BISHOP. I like everything. It's my greatest fault!
SUZETTE. [*Suddenly smiling.*] Oh! oh! What about Wagner?
THE BISHOP. [*Firmly.*] Except Wagner. Yes, that's true—I can't stand Wagner!
SUZETTE. Well, I doubt if you can stand this, either.
THE BISHOP. Suppose you give me a try!
SUZETTE. All right. [*She stops the record.*] It's Harry.
THE BISHOP. I thought so.
SUZETTE. He's gone and done it.
THE BISHOP. What?
SUZETTE. [*All in a rush.*] I mean he hasn't *really* gone and done it, because he naturally can't do anything without *her* and *she* says she won't do a thing until she's met you and you've said it's all right, so that's why Harry wanted to speak to you to-night and you mustn't breathe one word about my telling you—you see, he's planning to do it all himself, but when he said he thought the shock would kill you and he'd be held up for " episcocide "—yes,

that's what he called it!—I thought I'd better break it to you gently. [*Slight pause.*] Don't you think I've been wise, grandpa, to break it to you gently?

THE BISHOP. You haven't broken it at all, my dear. I don't know what you're talking about.

SUZETTE. Why, grandpa, I've just *told* you! Harry's engaged to a girl named Lucile Anderson!

THE BISHOP. Oh! I must be getting deaf. Dear me! And who is Lucile Anderson?

SUZETTE. Well, that's just it. Lucile's an—an artist.

THE BISHOP. You mean she paints?

SUZETTE. No, she doesn't exactly *paint*. You know, there're all kinds of artists, grandpa, and Lucile—well, Lucile's art is—er—a very beautiful art, it's the art of—er—

THE BISHOP. Well?

SUZETTE. The art of—er—impersonation on the stage. [*Slight pause.*]

THE BISHOP. In short, the young lady is an actress.

SUZETTE. Yes. [*Nervously.*] Well, it doesn't make any difference. Lots of nice girls are nowadays.

THE BISHOP. [*To himself.*] An actress—!

SUZETTE. [*Bursting out.*] But she's a perfect dear and her father was a well-known lawyer in Toronto, Canada, but he died and left her without a cent and her influence over Harry is very, *very* good and I'm sure you'll *love* her when you get to know her—I do, anyway, and I've only seen her four times— [*Coaxingly.*] Grandpa, say it's all right, please! Remember—it's our own Harry!

THE BISHOP. [*Drily.*] That's just what I am remembering, dear. He always did have very little sense!

SUZETTE. [*Reproachfully.*] Why, grandpa, he played quarter on the 'varsity! And you said yourself that took a lot of brains!

THE BISHOP. [*Smiling.*] Did I? Well, this proves I was mistaken.

SUZETTE. Oh, dear! I— [*Suddenly.*] Wait! I heard the front-door! That's Harry—! [*She slips off the arm of his chair.*] Now remember! Don't you get me into trouble!

THE BISHOP. I won't!

SUZETTE. Promise?

THE BISHOP. Cross my heart and hope to die! [*Enter Harry. He is an attractive young man of about twenty-two or three—restless, young and impetuous. He wears a dinner-coat.*] Well! We'd almost given you up!

HARRY. [*Ill at ease.*] I had to make a call. Didn't Suzie tell you?

THE BISHOP. [*Tranquilly.*] Oh, yes, she said something or other. Well, what about our little chat?

HARRY. [*Nervously.*] Your—your rheumatism isn't bothering you too much, is it, sir? To-morrow would—

THE BISHOP. Oh no! Suzie's played all my aches away with *Rigoletto* and *Trovatore*. I'm fit as a fiddle, my boy, so put another log on the fire and go ahead.

HARRY. All right, sir.

> [*He puts on the log, motioning the while for Suzette to leave.*]

SUZETTE. [*To the Bishop.*] I'll come in later and finish the *Post* to you before you go to bed. [*To Harry, in a lower voice.*] Don't worry! I've got him going!

HARRY. Thanks, old girl. [*She goes out.*]

HARRY. [*Turning resolutely to the Bishop.*] Grandfather, I have something I want to—

THE BISHOP. [*Gently.*] If you go to my desk, Harry, and open the second drawer from the top on the left-hand side, I think you'll see a box of cigars. [*As Harry obeys.*] Thank you. Can you find them? [*Harry returns with the box.*] Won't you have one? [*Harry shakes his head.*]

I know they're not as good as yours, but I can't afford the *very* best brands.

HARRY. I don't feel like smoking now. Grandfather, I've come to you in order to—

THE BISHOP. [*Gently interrupting.*] Er—just one moment. I haven't any match.

HARRY. Oh Lord! Excuse me! [*He lights the Bishop's cigar.*] There! Now I want to tell you what's on my mind, grandfather. It's been there for some time and I —I—

THE BISHOP. Yes?

HARRY. [*Embarrassed.*] I think I ought to—to get it off.

THE BISHOP. Well?

HARRY. You see—it's this way. [*Pause.*]

THE BISHOP. [*Mildly.*] What way?

HARRY. Hang it, I don't know how to put the thing, but —but—[*Looking up and seeing the Bishop smiling at him.*] Well, I'll be—! You're on! You've been on all the time!

THE BISHOP. Your intuition is overwhelming, Harry,— but it's correct. As you say,—I'm on. [*Pause.*]

HARRY. [*Wrathfully looking at door.*] I might have known no girl could keep a secret!

THE BISHOP. [*Hastily.*] It's my fault! I wrung it out of her! I kicked her shins! I squeezed her neck! I— twisted her arm!

HARRY. [*Disgusted.*] And now you're making fun of me! Well—! [*He straightens up defiantly.*]

THE BISHOP. [*Suddenly tender.*] I'm not making fun of you, Harry.

HARRY. [*Uncomfortably.*] I meant to tell you myself about Lucile. I didn't want anybody else butting in.

THE BISHOP. Of course—I know. You must love her a great deal!

HARRY. [*Still a little sulkily.*] Well, I do.

THE BISHOP. And she's very pretty, isn't she?

HARRY. [*Brightening.*] Did Suzie tell you?

THE BISHOP. No—I just guessed—that's all.

HARRY. [*Enthusiastically.*] And she's awfully clever, too —acts like a streak—and she has just bunches of character! Why, when it comes down to it, she's ten times too good for me! She's just too wonderful for anything!

THE BISHOP. [*With a little smile.*] Of course she is —of course—of course.

HARRY. I met her at the Randalls'—you know, that painter fellow—and now she's all alone in a rotten boarding-house on Tenth Street and she has no work and her family are all dead—and so I really think I ought to marry her right off. Now don't you agree with me? [*Pause.*] Well? Don't you?

THE BISHOP. [*Rousing himself with an effort.*] I don't know, Harry. You see, you're so young—you're just beginning life, and you may change, and grow, my dear boy, there may come a time when you'll need more than any little actress can ever give you—[*Harry makes a movement.*] Oh, it's all right now, you love her—I know that! But are you quite sure, Harry, that you'll always love her just the way you love her now and nothing hidden in the future—or in the past—can ever shake your faith and beat you down and break your heart?

HARRY. I don't know what you mean.

THE BISHOP. You must be very, very sure, my boy— or else you're not fair to yourself—and what's worse—I'm afraid you're not fair to *her*.

HARRY. [*Bursting out.*] Oh, what's the good of talking! I just knew it would be this way! There's absolutely no use trying to do things with my family—they're all alike —look at Uncle Thomas and Aunt Sarah and Cousin Ralph and the whole crowd of them—narrow, conventional, dry-as-dust! [*Turning away suddenly.*] If only dad and mummy were alive, *they'd* understand!

THE BISHOP. [*Hurt.*] Don't say things like that, Harry! You know I've done my best for Suzette and you.

HARRY. [*Penitent.*] I know you have. I didn't mean that, grandpa. But you see, it's a long time now since you've been young and I think it's sort of hard for you to remember back and realize what it's like and—*sympathize* with a fellow! [*Going on quickly.*] Oh, I know you're awfully wise and you can see clear through people and understand 'em *that* way, but this is different—I don't believe you ever felt the way I'm feeling now—and so—[*Gulping.*] Oh, well, there's no use going on. Thanks for trying, grandpa—I won't keep you up any longer. [*He is at the door ready to leave.*]

THE BISHOP. Where are you going?

HARRY. [*A trifle defiantly.*] I'm going to get married.

THE BISHOP. To-night?

HARRY. Yes, we got the license this afternoon. [*Slight pause.*]

THE BISHOP. Come in, Harry, and shut the door.

HARRY. [*Doing so.*] What do you want?

THE BISHOP. You said I couldn't remember back and realize how one felt when one was young—and life was just a glorious chaos of passion and beauty and despair. Well, I do remember. Because no matter how old one grows, Harry, there are always some things that keep a little youth still burning in one's heart.

HARRY. I didn't mean to hurt you, grandpa.

THE BISHOP. You didn't, my dear boy. But you've made me think of something that I'd supposed I'd forgotten—it's so long ago since it came up in my mind. It's something I never told to anyone before—I used to think I never would. Oh, well—times change, and I didn't realize then I was to have a grandson just like you. I wonder, Harry, if you'll have time to wait and hear about it?

HARRY. [*Distrustfully.*] If you think it's anything that's going to change my mind about Lucile, you might as well stop right here. [*As the Bishop rises with difficulty and goes slowly over to the desk.*] What is it, grandpa? Can't I get it?

THE BISHOP. [*Suddenly, with a sharp intake of breath.*] A-ah!

HARRY. [*Sympathetically.*] Your rheumatism, sir?

THE BISHOP. [*With a smile.*] Don't mention rheumatism now, my boy! [*He stands for a moment above the desk and shuts his eyes.*] I'm only twenty-eight years old!

[*Taking a bunch of keys from his pocket, he unlocks a lower drawer and, after some fumbling, comes up with a small mahogany box which he lays on the desk before him.*]

THE BISHOP. Do you know what's in this little box?

HARRY. No, sir. What?

THE BISHOP. [*With a radiant smile.*] Romance, my boy—the perfume of romance!

HARRY. How—how do you mean, sir?

THE BISHOP. Look!

[*He opens the box and takes out a little wisp of lace.*]

HARRY. [*Awed.*] What is it, grandpa? A handkerchief?

THE BISHOP. [*Nodding.*] A little handkerchief. [*He undoes it and discloses a few old flowers.*] White violets —[*He sniffs them, then smiles and shakes his head.*] They're dried and yellow now. Their sweetness is all gone.

I'm an old man, Harry, but somehow—why, it seems like yesterday—

HARRY. [*Wonderingly.*] What, sir?

THE BISHOP. [*Turning out the desk-lamp, and crossing to his chair again, holding the flowers and handkerchief very carefully in his hands.*] Ah, that's what I'm going to tell you now! Sit down, my boy—[*As Harry obeys.*] Are you comfortable there? That's right!—Well, it was over forty years ago—forty years—dear me, how the time flies!—and I was the young Rector of St. Giles, you know. That was before I married your grandmother—God bless her!—although I'd known her nearly all my life. Well, Harry, one night—in November, it was—I went to an evening party at old Cornelius Van Tuyl's house and there in that kaleidoscope of jewels and flowers and crinolines the great adventure of my life began—

> [*And, as he speaks, from far away comes the sound of a quaint old polka, and Harry and the Bishop and the whole room melt into the dark. The music swells and the lights, blooming again from crystal chandeliers, reveal the living vision of the past.*]

ACT I

[*SCENE: Evening reception at* MR. CORNELIUS VAN TUYL'S *house, about 1867. It is a small upstairs drawing-room. In the center is the stairway leading to the rooms below. At left is the door to the library. In foreground, at right, there is a couch, turned slightly to face the audience. At its head stands a small, marble-topped table. At left of foreground is a tête-à-tête chair. A seat runs along the balustrade which encircles the staircase well. Lamps in the foreground shed a mellow light which contrasts with the brilliance reflected from the rooms below.*

The lights go up upon an animated scene. The little room is filled with people. At back, leaning on the balustrade which surrounds the well, stand two men-about-town, looking out over the rooms below. Near them are a young man and a girl, talking, laughing, and flirting. Another young man and a girl—she on his arm—cross the stage, chatting gaily. They turn, descend the staircase, and disappear. Mrs. Rutherford,—*a rather pretty, affected woman,—is sitting on the couch at right. Beside her is* Miss Susan Van Tuyl, *a sensible, attractive young woman of about twenty-five, dressed simply and charmingly in white. They are listening to* Mr. Harry Putnam, *an elderly beau of the period, who stands twirling his moustaches, his feet crossed, ogling and talking to them.* Mrs. Frothingham,—*a buxom, florid dowager, very richly and fussily dressed,—sits on the tête-à-tête at left with her daughter, a pretty young girl of eighteen.*

The Young Man. [*To the young girl on his arm, as they cross the stage.*] A very brilliant party, don't you think?

The Girl. Oh, quite the most elegant affair of the winter! [*They turn to the stairs.*]

The Young Man. [*To another young man just coming up.*] Oh, Frank, is the dancing saloon crowded?

The Second Young Man. Not just now. They're beginning to serve supper.

The First Young Man. [*To the girl.*] Splendid!
[*They go downstairs.*

THE SECOND YOUNG MAN. [*To* MRS. FROTHINGHAM, *with a bow.*] Mrs. Frothingham, may I have the honor of this polka?

MRS. FROTHINGHAM. You droll wretch, don't you know my dancing days are over?

THE YOUNG MAN. [*To the girl.*] Miss Frothingham, then, may be persuaded to atone for—

MISS FROTHINGHAM. [*Rising.*] Of course I may! I love to polk! [*They turn towards the stairs.*

MRS. FROTHINGHAM. [*Rising.*] My dearest Susan—Agatha—forgive me if I come and talk to you.

> [*She joins the group at couch—right. Meanwhile the two men-about-town are heard to speak from the balustrade, where they are looking at crowd below.*

THE FIRST MAN. Who's that woman with the diamonds —down there by the door? I thought at first it might be Cavallini.

THE SECOND MAN. [*Turning away.*] No, Cavallini's singing that new opera—what's its name?

FIRST MAN. *Mignon?*

THE SECOND MAN. *Mignon*—of course! She's still at the Academy—she won't be here till twelve.

THE FIRST MAN. Shall we have supper now or shall we wait?

THE SECOND MAN. Now, my dear chap, now! This is one of the few houses where Blue Seal Johannisberger flows like water.

THE FIRST. [*At the stairs.*] And the '48 claret! I'd forgotten that—

> [*They disappear below, talking. A burst of laughter from the girl who is flirting with the young man at the back of the scene.*

THE GIRL. You mustn't talk to me that way any more! Now give me your arm and take me downstairs to mamma—

HER PARTNER. Do you know you have exactly the same effect on me as a glass of champagne!

THE GIRL. [*At the top of the stairs.*] Of course, I don't know anything about that!

HER PARTNER. No, of course not. It doesn't last long —still—while it lasts—

[*They descend, talking and laughing.*

MRS. FROTHINGHAM. [*Sitting on the couch, at right.*] You can say what you please, Miss Van Tuyl, the Rector's nose is *not* Grecian!

SUSAN. [*Very politely.*] Dear Mrs. Frothingham, are noses your only standard?

MRS. RUTHERFORD. [*Shaking her head.*] Ah, well— his grandfather on his mother's side came of very doubtful stock! An Irish peasant, I believe—he landed sometime about 1805.

SUSAN. Surely, Mrs. Rutherford, your memory doesn't take you quite as far back as all that?

PUTNAM. And to think we are condemned to listen to his sermons! Why, last Sunday I woke up just in time to catch the young puppy making scurrilous allusions to *me*—!

MRS. FROTHINGHAM. To you, Mr. Putnam? Dear me, I regret exceedingly that my neuralgia kept me from attending church! What did he—?

SUSAN. He said he didn't doubt that several of our elderly beaux would soon be making Heaven fashionable and organizing society among the more exclusive angels!

[TOM *is seen leisurely coming upstairs. He is about twenty-eight, healthy, positive, and determined. He is dressed very simply and a little shabbily. He has a very hearty, genial quality, but no humor.*]

Mrs. Frothingham. Abominable!

Mrs. Rutherford. Blasphemous, I call it!

Putnam. Hardly the remark of a gentleman!

Mrs. Frothingham. But he's not a gentleman!

Putnam. He dresses like a pen-wiper!

Mrs. Rutherford. He spends all his spare time with working men!

Putnam. [*To* Susan.] My dear young lady, why your excellent uncle ever gave him the church is more than I shall ever understand!

Susan. Because uncle knows he's the coming man—that's why! Look what he's done here in just these two years! Hasn't he built up the congregation from nothing at all to the third biggest in New York? Hasn't he started the athletic club for the young men and the cooking classes for the girls? Hasn't he founded our parish school for poor children, and got people to donate a playground, and a circulating library, and a big hall for free lectures and musical entertainments? Isn't he just as much at home and just as much loved down in a Bowery saloon as he is here in a Fifth Avenue drawing-room? Isn't he—

Putnam. My dear Miss Van Tuyl!

Mrs. Frothingham. He's impossible!

Mrs. Rutherford. Outrageous!

Putnam. A blot on the parish!

Mrs. Frothingham. A disgrace to the church—

Putnam. [*Suddenly seeing* Tom.] Er—what wonderful weather we're having!

Mrs. Rutherford. [*To* Mrs. Frothingham.] Rather cold for November, don't you think?

Mrs. Frothingham. [*Trembling.*] Yes—yes—very warm indeed—

Susan. [*Bewildered.*] But—[*She turns and sees* Tom.] Oh, I see! [*Smiling.*] We're talking about you, Tom.

Tom. [*Briefly.*] I heard. Thank you, Susan.

Mrs. Rutherford. [*Rising.*] We were all saying the most *flattering* things—

Mrs. Frothinham. [*Rising.*] Dear Dr. Armstrong, I—I wonder your ears weren't *burning*—

Putnam. [*Laughing nervously.*] By Jove, yes—so do I!

Tom. Don't let me drive you away.

Mrs. Frothingham. Er—I must look after Mabel. I mustn't let the dear child dance too much!

Putnam. And I was on the point of offering Mrs. Rutherford some supper.

Mrs. Rutherford. How very kind! [*To Susan.*] *Au revoir,* my dear—good-night, Dr. Armstrong.

Mrs. Frothingham. Good-night—good-night.

Putnam. [*Bowing.*] Your servant.

[*The three go downstairs.*

Susan. [*After them.*] Don't go before Madame Cavallini comes—she's promised to sing for us and you know what *that* means! Au revoir—au revoir! [*Turning to Tom.*] Cats! Two tabbies and one old tom! Did you hear what they were saying?

Tom. Just a little. [*Loftily.*] What does it matter? *They're* not the people I care about—they're not the people that really *count!*

Susan. I know. But I just can't bear their criticizing you! [*Looking at him.*] Oh, Tom! You've got on your oldest clothes! Why couldn't you have stopped to dress?

Tom. Well, I was going to, honestly I was. But this is my night at the athletic club and about ten o'clock, just as I'd taken on the heavyweight of the ward, little Jimmy Baxter came running in and said young Sullivan was drunk and killing his wife so would I please step over? [*Noticing her glance.*] What are you looking at?

Susan. Your hair!

Tom. [*Feeling it.*] Is it sticking up behind?

Susan. Just one lock—on the left. [*Coming up to him.*] Bend over! [*He does so and she smooths it down, as he goes on talking.*

Tom. [*Going on all the time.*] And I found Sullivan in a fighting mood and rather difficult to manage and in the middle of it all, if Mrs. Sullivan didn't go and have another baby!

Susan. [*Trying to take out a spot from his lapel with her handkerchief.*] How terrible!

Tom. That's what I told her. I said it was bad enough to have married Sullivan, but to bring a child of his into the world was almost worse than *murder!*

Susan. [*Always busying herself with him.*] But, Tom —she was longing for another baby!

Tom. I can't help that. However, now it's come, will you go round to-morrow and make a note of how she's doing?

Susan. [*Turning him round and looking at him critically.*] Of course. Does she need any baby clothes?

Tom. She had a few. Mrs. Baxter's given her the rest.

Susan. Very well—I'll take charge. [*The orchestra is heard below.*]

A Man's Voice. [*Coming upstairs.*] I say!

Susan. [*Looking over the balustrade.*] Oh, it's Mr. Livingstone!

[*Enter* Fred Livingstone, *a dandified young man of about thirty.*

Fred. [*Who is carrying a plate in each hand.*] There, Miss Van Tuyl! You owe that dab of mayonnaise to no less a person than the Golden Nightingale! [*To* Tom.] Hello, Tom—how goes it?

Susan. Why, Mr. Livingstone?

FRED. It's a fact. I never would have got it if it hadn't been for her. Why, all the literary and artistic talent in New York was fighting like a band of demons round the supper-table, when, thank the Lord! the band struck up and someone said that Cavallini had arrived!

SUSAN. [*Smiling.*] I see!

FRED. Two seconds—and there wasn't a soul in the dining room but me! Why, even the caterer's men were standing up on chairs to catch a glimpse of the divinity!

SUSAN. I really *must* go down and greet her.

TOM. If you see your uncle, Susan, tell him where I am.

SUSAN. Very well. [*To* FRED.] Mr. Livingstone?

FRED. Er—will you excuse me, Miss Van Tuyl? I want to have a word or two with Tom here.

SUSAN. Of course. *Au revoir.*

[*She goes downstairs.*]

FRED. [*Quivering.*] Well! This is the last time I bring my wife to *this* house!

TOM. [*Amazed.*] What—?

FRED. Of all the disgraceful insults that I've ever seen—! Why, the man must be out of his head!

TOM. Who?

FRED. Van Tuyl.

TOM. What on earth's he done?

FRED. [*Staring at him.*] Done—? Good Lord, man, don't you realize who's downstairs? Don't you know who's making a tour of the rooms on his arm, as the guest of honor? Don't you know whom he's introducing to every respectable woman that's been fool enough to come here to-night—

TOM. [*Interrupting.*] No, I don't—who?

FRED. [*Impressively.*] The Cavallini!

TOM. [*Puzzled.*] Oh, you mean that foreign opera singer? Well, what of it?

FRED. [*Exploding.*] What of it? By Jove, that's a cool one! I always knew you were advanced, Tom, but I'll swear I never thought you'd go as far as this!

TOM. What on earth—

FRED. [*Interrupting.*] It's bad enough to come and find the house all full of dirty painter chaps and female novelists! It's vile enough to see your wife rub elbows with those garlic-eating, gutter-born Italian Opera scoundrels—well, I won't talk about the others, they're old and fat and ugly, and I don't know anything against 'em—but Cavallini—

TOM. Well?

FRED. I know Van Tuyl's our biggest banker and a leading citizen and a pillar of the church—that's all right, but when it comes to asking all New York to parties given for his mistress—

TOM. What—?

FRED. It's true. She *is* his mistress!

TOM. [*Controlling himself with difficulty.*] Well?

FRED. I wouldn't have mentioned it if he hadn't brought her here to-night! I believe in letting a man's private affairs strictly alone, but gad! I expect him in return to show a little decency!

TOM. [*Ominously.*] I see.

FRED. And look here, Tom, so long as you're his rector and all that, I think you ought to speak to him about it—haul him over the coals and haul him jolly hard!

TOM. [*Holding himself in.*] And this is all you wanted to say to me?

FRED. Of course.

TOM. And you've quite finished?

FRED. I suppose so.

TOM. [*Coming close to him.*] Then *I* have one or two things to say to *you*. And I'll just begin by telling you what you are—and that's a miserable, sneaking, gossiping old woman—

FRED. [*Taken aback.*] Wait—hold on!

TOM. [*Continuing.*] A pitiful, cackling, empty-headed fool who hears a dirty story and can't wait until he's passed it on! Why, you apology for the male sex, do you know what you're doing? You're a guest in a gentleman's house—you've eaten his food and shaken him by the hand and now you're turning round and circulating filthy vicious lies behind his back—

FRED. [*Interrupting.*] They're not lies! He's lived with her for years—she has a villa on the Riviera that Van Tuyl gave her—it's called Millefleurs—Jack Morris saw them there together—

TOM. [*Thundering.*] Be still!

FRED. [*Angrily, as he gets behind the sofa and talks over it.*] I won't be still! Why, all the fellows know what Rita Cavallini is—except yourself and you're a clergyman. Ask Guvvy Fisk—he knew the French musician chap that found her singing under hotel windows years ago in Venice. And Guvvy knows just when she kicked him out and went off with that Russian grand-duke and lived with him in Petersburg, until the Prince de Joinville set her up in Paris! Why, she's notorious all over Europe—she's ruined whole families—run through fortune after fortune—it was outside *her* door that that young English poet shot himself—the Emperor borrowed money from the Rothschilds just to buy her diamonds—the King of Naples gave her—

TOM. [*Breaking in.*] Stop it, Livingstone!

FRED. [*Going right on.*] And as for Van Tuyl, well, everybody knows what *he's* been like—

TOM. Look out!

FRED. Why, Louis the Fourteenth couldn't beat him when it comes to—

Tom. [*Interrupting and making for him.*] You little cur you—

> [*Just here* Van Tuyl *comes up from downstairs. He is a man of about fifty, deep-voiced and strong—a powerful personality. His manner is gentle and full of a wise, quiet humor. He is dressed soberly, but beautifully and with great care.*]

Van Tuyl. [*Smiling.*] Well, my young friends! What's the matter?

Fred. [*Politely.*] Oh, nothing! Tom and I were arguing—that's all. [*He looks at his watch.*] Good gracious—twelve o'clock! You haven't seen my wife, sir?

Van Tuyl. But you're not going? Why, Mme. Cavallini's going to sing!

Fred. Er—I'm afraid we must. [*Offering his hand.*]

Van Tuyl. [*Taking it.*] Oh, why?

Fred. [*Simply.*] I'd rather my wife heard Mme. Cavallini across the footlights—a touch of prejudice, I suppose—don't let it bother you—good-night!

> [*He bows, smiles, and goes downstairs.*]

Tom. [*Simply and a little shyly.*] I'd have come downstairs to find you, sir, but I'm not dressed—as you see—and I thought you mightn't like it.

Van Tuyl. [*Heartily.*] Nonsense, my boy! Why, you've no time to prink up for our foolish parties. I think you're very good to come at all. I don't remember if you're interested in terra-cottas, Tom, but if you are—[*He is at the mantel, lifting one of the vases lovingly.*] Here's something that came in last week. It's a lekythos of the time of Pericles. Look at the exquisite grace and freshness of those figures! By Jove, they breathe a fragrance of eternal youth—and the hand that made them has been dust two thousand years!

Tom. [*Hastily.*] Er—very prety—very pretty indeed.

Van Tuyl. [*Looking at the vase.*] Two thousand years—I wonder where *we* were then—eh, Tom? [*He puts back the vase with a sigh.*] But I think you care more for pictures than for terra-cottas, don't you? Come and look at the new Millet. It's in my room where I can see it every morning, just as soon as I wake up. By Jove, he's a wonderful fellow, that Millet—and some day he's bound to be recognized, even if—

Tom. [*Firmly.*] Thanks, sir, but if you don't mind I'd rather stay here. I want to—to talk to you.

Van Tuyl. [*Genially.*] Of course—just as you say.

Tom. [*Awkwardly.*] I don't quite know how to begin, sir, as it's a rather important—and at the same time a rather—a rather *delicate* matter, but—but—[*Suddenly.*] I'm not by any chance keeping you from your guests?

Van Tuyl. [*Always smiling.*] Not at all.

Tom. [*Again awkward.*] But—it's—er—something that I really feel I ought to—er—I mean to say I—er—consider it in the light of—an obligation—to—er—to—

Van Tuyl. [*Interrupting.*] Tom.

Tom. Yes, sir?

Van Tuyl. [*Putting his hand on* Tom's *arm.*] It's about Susan, isn't it?

Tom. Yes, but—

Van Tuyl. Then it's all right. My boy, I'm as glad as I can be!

Tom. [*Puzzled.*] But *what's* all right? I'm afraid, sir, I don't follow you.

Van Tuyl. Why, aren't you asking me if—[*He looks at him sharply.*]

Tom. I'm sorry, sir, but it's advice I wish to offer you.

Van Tuyl. Advice—?

Tom. Yes, I regret it, but it's my duty.

VAN TUYL. In that case, pray go on. [*He sits.*] Won't you sit down? [*He lights a cigar.*]

TOM. No, thanks. [*Ingenuously.*] Mr. Van Tuyl, I suppose some people would say that after all you'd done for St. Giles and me, it wasn't in my place to suggest anything—

VAN TUYL. Nonsense, Tom. Do you know you're getting to look more like your dear mother every day?

TOM. No, am I? [*Resuming.*] But after all, I am your Rector and I feel I've got to—to—

VAN TUYL. Quite right, my boy, I respect your feelings. Well?

TOM. [*Struggling.*] Have you ever thought—I mean —wouldn't it be better if—that is to say—do you think you're wise, Mr. Van Tuyl, in opening your doors to these foreign opera singers? [*Going on quickly.*] Oh, I know how broad-minded you are and how interested in art and music and all that sort of thing, and it's splendid! It's so splendid, sir, that I couldn't bear to think anyone was imposing on your liberality.

VAN TUYL. [*Calmly.*] Whom do you mean?

TOM. This Madame Cavallini—isn't it? I know she's very distinguished, and I quite understand your public spirit in recognizing her genius by making her the center of one of your elegant entertainments. But after all, sir, are you quite sure she's the sort of lady—the kind of person—er —the type—[*With a gesture.*]—I say the type—

VAN TUYL. [*Mildly.*] It isn't Sunday, Tom.

TOM. [*Paternally.*] You know, sir, you're so generous and high-minded that anybody could take you in—oh, yes they could! [*With a shake of the head.*] And, personally speaking, I have always found that foreigners—particularly those belonging to the Latin races—have a distinct leaning towards immorality.

VAN TUYL. How old are you, Tom?

TOM. [*Lamely.*] Er—twenty-eight.

VAN TUYL. [*With a wistful smile.*] I wish *I* were twenty-eight. Life's a simple thing when you're twenty-eight.

TOM. [*Loftily.*] If one has standards—yes.

VAN TUYL. Standards?

TOM. Of right and wrong, I mean.

VAN TUYL. Oh, yes—I had those standards once.

TOM. [*Shocked.*] *Once,* sir?

VAN TUYL. [*Confidentially.*] And then one day I got 'em all mixed up—and the right seemed wrong and the wrong seemed right and I just didn't know where I was at.

TOM. Oh, come, sir!

VAN TUYL. That was a long time ago, my boy, but—[*With a chuckle.*] Well, I'm dashed if I ever got 'em straight again!

TOM. [*Distressed.*] Oh, sir, don't talk that way!

VAN TUYL. [*Soberly.*] I've learnt a few things, though—stray spars I've clung to in all this storm and ocean—just a few stray spars, but somehow they've managed to hold me up. One's how to value people that are good—that's why you're Rector of St. Giles, Tom—and another's how to pity people that are—

TOM. Bad.

VAN TUYL. No, not bad, my boy—there are no people that are bad. But there're some poor devils who find it harder to be good than you—that's all.

TOM. [*Hesitatingly.*] And Madame Cavallini?

VAN TUYL. If Madame Cavallini weren't fit to meet my friends, you never would have seen her here to-night. [*Slight pause.*]

TOM. [*Impulsively.*] Oh, what a fool I've been! I

might have known there wasn't a word of truth in what that puppy said.

VAN TUYL. What puppy?

TOM. A young he-gossip, sir, who reeled off lies about this woman. And I was ass enough to believe him, and come to you and talk like a—like a—like a confounded prig! I wonder you don't throw me out of the house!

VAN TUYL. [*With a twinkle.*] You're my Rector, Tom.

TOM. Do you think you can forgive me, sir?

[*Just here the band downstairs begins a beguiling Strauss waltz.*

VAN TUYL. [*Rising.*] There's nothing to forgive, my boy. And now go down and ask Susan for some supper.

TOM. But I'm not dressed—

VAN TUYL. Oh, nonsense! But if you'd rather go into the library, I'll tell her to bring it to you there.

[*Meanwhile, there is heard down the staircase the sound of men's voices, high and eager, and over and above them, a woman's laughter. This comes nearer and nearer.*

TOM. But I'm not—

VAN TUYL. [*Clapping him on the shoulder.*] Don't tell me you're not hungry! You're twenty-eight years old, and when a young man's twenty-eight—hello! who's this?

[*He turns and glances at back, as the sound of the voices and laughter grows nearer.*

A WOMAN'S VOICE. [*Just off, rising above the others.*] Go 'vay—go 'vay—you mus' not come vit' me—no—no—you are naughty—you are de mos' 'orrible naughty men I ever see— [*She sweeps up with the group of young dandies who have accompanied her and stands for a moment at the top of the stairway, laughing and talking, always facing in the direction whence she came, away from* Tom *and* Van Tuyl. *She is a bewitching, brilliant little foreign creature—beautiful in a dark, Italian way. She is marvellously dressed in voluminous gauze and her dress is trimmed with tiny roses. Her black hair hangs in curls on either side of her face and three long soft curls hang down her low-cut back. On her head is a wreath of little roses. She wears long diamond earrings, a rivière of diamonds is about her neck, diamonds gleam on her corsage, her wrists and hands. She carries a fan and bouquet in a silver filigree holder. She speaks in a soft Italian voice, with quick bird-like gestures. She seems herself a good deal like an exquisite, gleaming, little hummingbird.*

One of the Young Men. But it's my waltz!

Another. Don't listen to him, madame, you know you promised me to—

A Third. [*Interrupting.*] Nonsense, Willie—*my* name's on her card!

The First. It's no such thing!

The Second. I appeal to her!

The Third. Madame—

Rita. [*Interrupting.*] Oh—! Vhy you make such a beeg, beeg noise?

The First Young Man. [*Frankly.*] You're driving us crazy—can't you understand?

Rita. [*Mock serious.*] Vhat? *Me*—? Poor, leetle me? You beeg bad boy, you make of me—'ow you say?—vone seelly joke!

THE CHORUS. "We don't!" "It's true!" "Of course it is!"

RITA. [*Laughing.*] Go make de love to dose bee-eautiful Amer'can ladies vit' de long nose an' de neck full of leetle bones—!

ONE OF THE YOUNG MEN. But I want to make love to *you!*

ANOTHER. And so do I!

A THIRD. I do, too!

THE OTHERS. And I—and I!

RITA. Ouf! You cannot *all* make de love to me—so look! I tell you—[*They all gather nearer.*]

ONE OF THEM. What?

ANOTHER. Tell us!

RITA. [*Triumphantly.*] You shall not *any* of you make de love to me!

CHORUS. [*Disappointed.*] "Oh, madame!" "Please!" "You must!" etc.

RITA. No—no! I stay 'ere vit' Meestaire Van Tuyl—

CHORUS. "Oh, don't!" "What a shame!" "Please come downstairs!" etc.

RITA. But leesten now! Vhich vone of you, 'e catch dis peenk camellia—look!—'e drive me 'ome!

[*She holds up the flower.*

THE MEN. [*Surging forward to snatch it.*] "Give me it!" "Oh, madame!" "Get out the way!" "It's mine!"

RITA. [*Laughing and tossing it over the balustrade.*] It is all gone—so run—run qvick—qvick! Oh, 'e has fallen himself down—dat leetle meestaire! *Povrino!* [*Excitedly, looking over balustrade.*] Oh—! Oh—! You will be 'urted—[*Pointing.*] *O Dio! Guardi—guardi!* [*Clapping her hands and leaning over the balustrade.*] All right—all right—you meestaire vit' de beeg moustache—*Bene!* —*capito!* You take me 'ome! [*She kisses her hand and turns away, still laughing.*] Dey are so frightfully funny, dose— [*She suddenly sees* Tom, *who has been standing quite still, staring at her all the time. She stops. The words die away from her lips. She looks at him. An instant's pause.*

Tom. [*Indistinctly, as he tears his gaze away from her.*] I—I beg your pardon.

[*He passes her quickly, his head bent, and goes out. She turns and follows him with her eyes.*

Rita. [*Very simply, still looking after him.*] Please who is dat young man?

Van Tuyl. Tom Armstrong. He's a clergyman.

Rita. [*Vaguely.*] Cler-gee-man?

Van Tuyl. *Abbé*—priest, you know.

Rita. [*Almost to herself.*] Ah—! Den it vas *dat*—

Van Tuyl. What?

Rita. [*Turning away.*] I dunno. Jus' somet'ing in 'is eyes—

Van Tuyl. I don't suppose he'd ever seen anything like you in all his life.

Rita. No? My Lord, 'ow ver' sad! [*Glancing again downstairs—this time with a certain impishness.*] An' he vas 'an'some, too!

[Van Tuyl *chuckles. She hears him, turns, catches his eye and they laugh together.*

Van Tuyl. [*Coming up, still laughing, and taking her in his arms.*] You little monkey you!

Rita. [*Softly, her eyes closed, a smile of triumph on her lips.*] De beeg Amer'can, 'e like 'is leetle frien' to-night—yes?

Van Tuyl. [*Smiling.*] I don't think he could help it if he tried.

RITA. Den if 'e like 'er—[*She pauses.*]
VAN TUYL. Well?
RITA. [*Softly.*] Please vhy don' 'e keess 'er?
VAN TUYL. [*Laughing and kissing her.*] There!
RITA. [*Drawing herself away suddenly.*] My Lord, I 'ave forget somet'ing!
VAN TUYL. [*Following her.*] Come here!
RITA. I 'ave forget dat I am oh! mos' frightfully angry!
VAN TUYL. Not with me?
RITA. *Si—si!*
VAN TUYL. But why? What have I done?
RITA. [*Briefly.*] You know.
VAN TUYL. My dear, I don't!
RITA. [*Sitting right.*] Ssh! You mus' not say t'ings like dat—dey are not true! You 'ave treat me ver' bad to-night—yes, you 'ave treat me qvite, qvite—on-spikable!
VAN TUYL. Why, I've invited you to my house! I've introduced you to my friends—the most distinguished people in New York! I've entertained you before all the world—and isn't that exactly what you wanted?
RITA. You ask me to your *soirée*—dat is true—but you ask me as *artiste* not as *femme du monde.*
VAN TUYL. That isn't so!
RITA. [*Like a flash.*] Ah no? Den please vhy you ask de oder singers too?
VAN TUYL. Now, Rita, listen—
RITA. I vill not leesten! You t'ink I am a leetle—vhat you say?—*donnacia—une p'tite grisette—*
VAN TUYL. My dear, you know I don't think anything of the sort—
RITA. An' it is not to-night alone—oh, no! It is two—t'ree mont's—all de time since first I come to your mos' ver' diza-agree-a-ble country! [*With a smile.*] A-ah! It vas

not like dis at Millefleurs! I vas not dere a singer from de opera! At Millefleurs I vas a qveen!

VAN TUYL. Millefleurs—! Our Palace of a Thousand Flowers.

RITA. [*Caressingly.*] Do you remember de night I sing to you de Schubert serenade—vhen you valk up an' down below de vindow—yes? All de roses in de vorld, dey blossom in de moonlight. Dere vas no vind. De sea vas qvite, qvite steel—an' you valk up an' down—up an' down—an' alvays I sing to you—an' sing—an' sing—an' de vind an' de sea an' de beeg gol' moon—dey all of dem leesten to me!

VAN TUYL. [*Rousing himself.*] That was Millefleurs. The roses there had brought me back my youth. [*With a sigh.*] I came home, and I lost it, dear. I'll never find it again.

RITA. Ah, no—it vaits for you among de flowers!

VAN TUYL. I'm afraid—not any more.

RITA. Vhat you mean, please?

VAN TUYL. I'm fifty-one years old. [*She instinctively draws away from him a little.*] That frightens you?

RITA. Ah, no, but—

VAN TUYL. [*Gently.*] Don't deny it, dear—I know how—you must feel. [*Pause.*] Rita.

RITA. Vell?

VAN TUYL. Rita, suppose we finish our—our friendship —end it here to-night.

RITA. To-night—?

VAN TUYL. Give me your hand. There! Now we can talk!—I'm fond of you, dear—I always shall be that— but already I'm beginning to disappoint you. And I'm afraid I'll do it more and more as time goes on. [*Slight pause.*] Look at my hair! There wasn't any grey in it last year—at Millefleurs! But now—and next year there'll be more! And I've begun to be a little deaf and fall asleep in chairs and dream about to-morrow's dinner. My rheumatism, too, came back last week—[*She winces and draws away her hand.*] Don't blame me, dear—I can't help getting old.

RITA. [*Nervously.*] Don'—don' talk dat vay!

VAN TUYL. [*Quickly.*] God knows I'm not complaining! I've lived my life—and it's been very sweet. I've done some work, and done it pretty well, and then I've found time to enjoy a great many of the beautiful things that fill this beautiful world. [*Politely.*] Among them, my dear, I count your voice—and you! [*Resuming.*] And yet the fact remains I've *lived* my life, I'm in the twilight years —oh! they're golden yet, but that won't last, and they'll grow deep and dim until the last tinge of the sunset's gone and the stars are out and night comes—and it's time to sleep. [*With a change of tone.*] But you—Good Lord, *your* life has just begun! Why, the dew's still on the grass—it's sparkling brighter than your brightest diamonds! [*He touches the ornaments.*] The birds are singing madrigals, the meadow's burst into a sea of flowers— you wear the morning like a wreath upon your hair—don't lose all that, my dear,—don't waste your springtime on a stupid fellow, fifty-one years old! [*Pause.*]

RITA. [*Coldly.*] All right.

[*She turns away, whistling.*

VAN TUYL. [*Watching.*] What's the matter?

RITA. [*Casually.*] Oh, nodings.

VAN TUYL. Yes, there is.

RITA. Vone more—'ow you say?—frien-ship feenished—! [*In a hard voice.*] Vone more—! [*With a careless gesture.*] Oh, che m'importa—ce ne sono altri!

[*She yawns ostentatiously and sniffs her bouquet.*

VAN TUYL. [*Looking at her keenly.*] Rita?

RITA. Vell—Meestaire Van Tuyl?

Van Tuyl. [*Simply.*] Haven't you ever loved someone?

Rita. 'Ow you talk? 'Ave I not love *you* two—t'ree year?

Van Tuyl. [*Always very gently.*] I don't mean that. Isn't there someone whose memory is dear and—and sort of holy—like an altar-candle, burning in your heart?

Rita. [*In a hard voice.*] No.

Van Tuyl. Think back—way back. Didn't someone ever make you feel so tender that you didn't know whether to laugh or cry at the thought of him? Wasn't there ever someone you wanted to help so much that it—it hurt you, like living pain? Wasn't there someone that your heart and soul just rushed out to meet—and all the time you stood before him and looked down and—and couldn't say one single little word? Wasn't there someone who—

Rita. [*Rising suddenly.*] *Basta! Basta—!* Stop it—don'—don'—[*A little pause. She recovers herself.*] 'Ave *you* felt—like dat?

Van Tuyl. [*Nodding.*] Yes.

Rita. Who vas she?

Van Tuyl. [*Simply.*] Just a girl. Not wonderful or beautiful or gifted—and yet—well, somehow she meant the world to me.

Rita. Vhat 'appen?

Van Tuyl. She died before I ever told her that I loved her. [*Pause.*]

Rita. [*Not looking at him.*] It vas a good t'ing—dat she die so soon.

Van Tuyl. What?

Rita. Sometime I vish dat *I* 'ad died before I ever 'ear dose vords—"I love you."

Van Tuyl. What do you mean?

Rita. [*Ironically.*] I never tol' you of my first so-bee-eautiful romance? No—? Vell, I do not often t'ink of it—it make me feel—[*With a curious little shiver.*]—not nize. [*Pause.*] It vas in Venice. I vas jus' seexteen years ol'. I play de guitar wid de *serenata*—you know, de leetle company of peoples dat go about an' sing under de vindows of de great 'otels—[*With a sigh.*] *Ah Madonna! come sembra lontano!*

VAN TUYL. Well?

RITA. [*Not looking at him.*] A young man come join our serenata—Beppo, 'is name vas—Beppo Aquilone. 'E vas 'an'some an' 'ad nize voice—oh, ver' light, you know, but steel—*simpatica.* Ve stan' together vhen ve sing an' 'ave—I dunno—vone, two duet. An' so it go for two—t'ree veek an' e' say noding much, but every time 'e smile an' look at me my 'eart is full vit' great beeg vishes an' I feel like everyt'ing in all de vorld is new an' born again. An' so vone evening 'e come vit' me to my leetle room—an' den 'e tell me dat 'e love me—an' all night long 'e 'old me close an' kees me—an' I feel 'is 'ot breat' like a fire upon my face—an' de beating of 'is 'eart, it come like strong blows 'ere against my own. An' den 'e sleep. But I—I do not sleep. I lie still an' qviet an' in my mind I have vone t'ought—" Is dis vhat people mean vhen dey say—Love?" An' so de 'ours go by' an' de night is feenish, an' a—a—'ow you say?—a long, t'in piece of sunlight, it creep in my leetle vindow an' it shine on Beppo vhere 'e lie beside me. An' oh! 'e look so young!—an' den de sunlight—'ow you say?—it tease him, so 'e 'alf vake up, an' e' vink 'is eyes an' say, " *Ah, Rita, ti amo!*" An' den 'e sigh an' put 'is 'ead 'ere—on my shoulder—like a leetle baby dat is tired, an' go to sleep again. [*With passionate tenderness.*] An' oh! I put my arm about 'im an' I smile an' t'ink " For Love I vaited all night long, an' vit' de day—*it come!*"

VAN TUYL. And so it does, my dear.

Rita. [*In a different voice.*] You t'ink so? Vait—! [*She has turned away.*] In tvelve 'our—*tvelve* 'our—'e sell me to an English traveller for feefty *lire*. At first, I t'ink I die—I soffer so! An' den at las' I on'erstan'—an' laugh—an' know dat I 'ave been vone great beeg fool—

Van Tuyl. [*Protesting.*] My dear, I—

Rita. [*Shaking her clenched hands.*] A fool to t'ink dere vas some greater, better love—a love dat come at morning an' shine like sunshine—[*With a wide gesture.*]—yes, all t'rough de day!

Van Tuyl. There is.

Rita. [*Fiercely.*] Dat is vone lie! You 'ear—? vone lie! [*Voluptuously.*] Love—it is made of keeses in de dark, of 'ot breat' on de face an' 'eart beats jus' like terrible strong blows! It is a struggle—ver' cruel an' sveet—all full of madness an' of vhispered vords an' leetle laughs dat turn into a sigh! Love is de 'unger for anoder's flesh—a deep down t'irst to dreenk anoder's blood— Love is a beast dat feed all t'rough de night an' vhen de morning come—*Love dies!* [*Slight pause.*]

Van Tuyl. My dear, I think you must have suffered a great deal.

Rita. Yes—because I 'ave believe vonce in a lie, but— [*Shaking her finger.*]—not any more! [*With a grimace.*] Oh, vhy ve talk about dose bad ol t'ings?—see 'ere—I blow dem far avay! Pst—! Pouf—! [*With an enchanting smile.*] Now look! Dey are all gone! [*As he does not answer, but looks at her.*] Vell? Vhat you t'ink about so 'ard—yes?

Van Tuyl. Why don't you marry someone, Rita?

Rita. Marry—*me*—?

Van Tuyl. Well, why not?

Rita. Vhere vould I fin' a man to make of me 'is wife?

Van Tuyl. [*Protesting.*] Nonsense, dear, why—

RITA. [*Interrupting.*] My frien', you 'ave forget a leetle— vhat I am. [*Brief pause.*]

VAN TUYL. I'm sorry, dear.

RITA. [*Quickly.*] Sorry—? Bah! Do you t'ink I care? I—who 'ave 'ad de great men of de vorld among my lovers? Ah, no, my frien', I 'ave not come to dat!

VAN TUYL. I understand.

RITA. [*Turning and looking at him.*] De great men of de vorld! An' *you* are vone of dem—oh, yes, I know it vhen I see you first at dat beeg supper Rossini give for me. An' I ask 'im—I say "Maestro, who is dat man who seet next de Russian princess?" An' 'e laugh an' say, "Vhat? Not already you make up your min'?" an' den I see you look at me—

VAN TUYL. Of course!

RITA. An' I smile—oh, mos' sveet!

VAN TUYL. [*Rising.*] You little rascal you!

RITA. An' so—ve 'ave begin. [*She considers him.*] Come 'ere! [*He comes close to her. She takes him by the lapel and looks up at him.*] You know vhat I t'ink—yes?

VAN TUYL. [*Smiling.*] I never know.

RITA. I t'ink—ve 'ave not come *qvite* to de en'.

VAN TUYL. My dear, you make me very happy.

RITA. So you vill drive vit' me to-morrow afternoon at four?

VAN TUYL. I'm honored.

RITA. I tell you somet'ing—

VAN TUYL. Well?

RITA. You are naughty—but I like you frightfully much!

VAN TUYL. [*Kissing her hand.*] Madame, I'm more than grateful. [*The orchestra begins a waltz downstairs.*] Good Heavens, I've forgotten I'm a host! What will those wretched people think! My arm—? [*He offers it to her.*]

RITA. [*Like an unwilling child.*] Vhen mus' I sing?

VAN TUYL. Let's see. I've asked Artot and Capoul for the duet from *Traviata*—and then I want the sextette from *Lucia*—and after that we'll all be ready for the Golden Nightingale!

RITA. [*Lying on the sofa.*] De Golden Nightingale vill rest alone 'ere till de time is come. An' oh! sen someone vit' 'er red vine an' 'er lemon-juice! She is so tired—she cannot sing vit'out!

VAN TUYL. That's all?

RITA. Dat's all.

VAN TUYL. You're beautiful to-night.

RITA. [*Lying back and looking up at him.*] Vhy not? My star is Venus—I vas born for love!

VAN TUYL. [*Tenderly.*] "O love forever in thy glory go!" [*The sound of the waltz is heard full of insistent rhythm. With a sigh, she flings her arms above her head, stretches her body, and closes her eyes. Then, with a burst of chatter and laughter, three young couples rush up the stairs.*]

THE FIRST YOUNG MAN. [*To his partner.*] Come on!

THE GIRL. Oh, what fun! We'll have it all to ourselves!

THE FIRST YOUNG MAN. Quick! Before the others see us—[*They begin to dance.*]

ANOTHER GIRL. I'm dying to learn the Boston Dip!

HER PARTNER. It's perfectly easy—[*Dancing.*] One—two—*down!* One—two—*down!*

VAN TUYL. [*Turning from the couch.*] Ssh! Madame Cavallini's trying to rest a little before she sings! [*He smiles at the young people and puts his finger to his lips.*]

ONE OF THE GIRLS. Oh, of course, sir.

ANOTHER GIRL. We never noticed.

[*VAN TUYL goes downstairs.*

THE THIRD GIRL. [*Whispering.*] She's asleep!
[*They all gaze towards the couch.*]
ONE OF THE YOUNG MEN. [*Rapturously.*] I say! Isn't she a vision!
HIS PARTNER. Ssh! You'll wake her up!
THE SECOND YOUNG MAN. Let's go down to the conservatory.
THE THIRD YOUNG MAN. Tip-toe, you girls!
[*They begin to descend again.*]
TOM. [*Entering from the library.*] Mr. Van Tuyl, I— [*He stops on seeing the departing young people.*] Oh, it's you, my young friends!
ONE OF THE GIRLS. [*Whispering to him over her shoulder as she disappears.*] Mr. Van Tuyl's just gone downstairs.
TOM. [*About to follow her.*] Thank you.
RITA. [*Suddenly opening her eyes and speaking, from her couch.*] You are going?
TOM. [*Turning.*] I beg your pardon?
RITA. [*Smiling.*] Don't go—please—
TOM. [*Stuttering.*] But I—I—I—
RITA. I vas jus' begun to be a *leetle*—'ow you say?—lonely? An' now a nize young man come—oh, my Lord, I am so glad! [*She smiles at him bewitchingly.*]
TOM. You're sure I'm not—intruding?
RITA. But no! Come in an'—'ow you say?—oh yes! make yourself qvite to 'ome!
TOM. Er—thank you.
[*He sits down on other side of room.*]
RITA. Vhy you sit vay, vay over dere?
TOM. Why—er—er—I don't know—I—
RITA. [*Sweetly.*] Are you afraid of me? [*As one would talk to a young and timid baby.*] I vill not 'urt you—no, I *like* de young men! Please come! Sit 'ere!
[*She indicates a chair at foot of couch.*]

Tom. You're—very kind.

[*He comes over and sits down.*]

Rita. [*Lying back with a sigh.*] A-ah! [*She smiles at him. A pause. Then, curiously.*] Vhat make your face so red?

Tom. [*In consternation.*] My face—

Rita. [*Dreamily.*] It is de reddes' t'ing I ever see in all my life!

Tom. [*Agonized.*] It's rather—warm in here.

Rita. You t'ink so? *I* am qvite, qvite col'.

Tom. That's—very odd. [*Pause.*] I'm afraid I—I haven't had the honor of being—presented—er—my name's Armstrong.

Rita. Ar-rm-str-rong! But dat is not all—eh? Now vait—no—yes—*ecco!* I 'have it—*Teem!*

Tom. [*Slightly nettled.*] No, not Tim. That's Irish. Tom.

Rita. Tome!

Tom. Not Tome. *Tom!*

Rita. Tom—! Dat right—? [*Repeating it to herself.*] Tom—Tom! [*Laughing.*] My Lord—vhat a funny name!

Tom. It's not a *real* name. It's just short for Thomas.

Rita. [*Illuminated.*] Ah—Tomasso! *Si si!* Now I on'erstan'! I vonce 'ave a frien' name' Tomasso—oh, yes, ver' long ago! 'E 'ave jus' vone leg. 'T vas—'ow you say? —rag-picker!

Tom. Was he?

Rita. [*Critically.*] You look mos' ver' much like 'im!

Tom. [*Pulling uncomfortably at his coat.*] Do I?

Rita. [*With a sudden happy thought.*] Mebbe *you* are fine, beeg Amer'can rag-picker—no?

Tom. [*Severely.*] Madam, I am the Rector of St. Giles' Church!

Act I] ROMANCE 255

RITA. R-r-rector?

TOM. Yes—I mean I—I own it—I'm its minister—its clergyman—

RITA. [*Quickly.*] Oh, *cler-gee-man!* I 'ave forget! 'Ow bee-eautiful! An' Saint Gile'—who vas 'e? Some leetle Amer'can saint—*hein?*

TOM. [*Sternly.*] St. Giles is one of the most important figures in the great history of the Church of England!

RITA. [*Softly.*] Is dat so? Anodder cler-gee-man—yes? [*He nods.*] 'Ow frightfully nize! Ve never 'ear of 'im in Italy.

TOM. [*Struck.*] In Italy—! Why, you don't live in Italy.

RITA. I 'ave a house in Florence an' a villa on de Lago di Como—yes.

TOM. [*With a relieved laugh.*] Oh, that's all right, then. Do you know what I thought for just a moment?

RITA. No. Vhat you t'ink?

TOM. I thought that you were one of these Italian opera singers!

RITA. [*Laughing.*] You funny man!

TOM. Forgive me—do!

RITA. It vill be 'ard!

TOM. You see, there're lots of them downstairs,—but then, I ought to have known, because Fred Livingstone said they were all old and fat and ugly.

RITA. [*Dampened.*] Oh—! Did 'e?

TOM. With one exception—Madame Cavarini—or lini —or whatever her name is. You know.

RITA. [*Smiling.*] Yes—I know. An' you—vhat *you* t'ink? You fin' 'er bee-eautiful?

TOM. I—? Oh, *I* haven't seen her. *I* don't go to the opera.

RITA. [*Confidentially.*] You 'ave not miss much vhen

you miss La Cavallini. She is of a fatness—[*With a gesture.*] Oh, like dat!

Tom. You're sure?

Rita. [*Nodding.*] She eat tvelve poun' of spaghetti every day!

Tom. No!

Rita. [*Enthusiastically.*] An' ugly—oh, Madonna!—'ow dat vomans is ugly! Jus' to look at 'er give vone de nose-bleed!

Tom. But everybody says—

Rita. [*Interrupting.*] Leesten! Vone eye is made of glass—an' 'er nose—my Lord, 'er nose!

Tom. What's the matter with her nose?

Rita. [*Covering her face with her hands.*] She 'as not got vone—!!

Tom. But surely you're mistaken—why—

Rita. [*Shuddering.*] Jus' *papier-maché*—stuck to 'er face! O Dio!

Tom. Well, I suppose her figure is what makes them say—

Rita. [*Interrupting.*] I tell you somet'ing *terrible!* She 'as a 'ump!

Tom. A what?

Rita. [*With horrid emphasis.*] A 'ump—a 'ump upon 'er back!

Tom. You mean a *hump?*

Rita. [*Nodding.*] 'Er dressmaker in Paris—she tell me dat. *Now* vhat you t'ink—eh?

Tom. [*Rising.*] Do you really want to know?

Rita. Yes—tell me, please!

Tom. [*Very sternly.*] I think, madam, you have been guilty of the grossest cruelty!

Rita. Vhat—?

Tom. [*Oracularly.*] Yes—*cruelty*, I repeat the word!

To hear a woman, on whom an all-wise Providence has showered its choicest gifts of health and wealth and beauty—I say to hear a woman like yourself deride, hold up to scorn and gloat over the physical failings of a less fortunate sister—for, madam, you *are* sisters in the sight of God!—I say this heartless act deserves a far more serious rebuke than any I'm at—at liberty to offer.

RITA. [*Suddenly covering her face with her pocket handkerchief and gasping.*] Ah—don'—don'—

TOM. What if this unhappy lady *does* suffer from—exaggerated fleshiness? Beneath that bulk may beat the tenderest of female hearts! What if her face *is* repulsive even to the degree that you mention? The purest thoughts may animate the brain behind! What if one eye is glass? The other, doubtless, is the window of a noble soul! And even though she bears a hump upon her back, she may, with Christian patience, change it to a—[*Suddenly inspired.*]—a cross!

RITA. [*Her voice still covered, shaking.*] Don'—don'—! Dio mio—! I cannot bear it—

TOM. [*Professionally.*] I am glad my few, poor simple words have touched you. Never forget them—let them be with you always—and, should the temptation come again, remember that a soft, sweet tongue is Woman's Brightest Ornament!

RITA. [*Unable to control herself.*] Tschk—! Tschk—! Tschk—! [*She presses the handkerchief over her mouth.*]

TOM. [*Suddenly, taking a step toward her.*] Madam—!

RITA. [*Dropping the handkerchief and screaming with laughter.*] I cannot 'elp it—oh—! oh—! oh—!

TOM. [*Grinding his teeth and striking one palm against the other as he turns away.*] Madam—! You—a-ah!

RITA. [*Exhausted, gasping.*] Oh—! oh—! [*Wiping her eyes.*] My Lord—!

[*A servant comes from downstairs carrying a tray with
glasses, a carafe, and a decanter of wine.*

THE SERVANT. The wine, madam.

RITA. P-put it 'ere—on dis leetle table.

[*She indicates the little table by the head of
the couch. The servant places the tray
upon it.*

THE SERVANT. Is that all you will require, madam?

RITA. Yes—dat is all.

[*The servant goes downstairs.*

TOM. [*Stiffly.*] Good-night.

RITA. You are not going?

TOM. After what has occurred, I see no reason for staying.

RITA. [*Carelessly.*] All right.

[*She half-rises and occupies herself with an
elaborate mixing of the wine and lemon-
juice and water.*

TOM. [*Lingering.*] Aren't you sorry for making fun of me?

RITA. [*Always intent on the drink.*] Oh, frightfully sorry!

TOM. [*Doubtfully.*] You don't look it.

RITA. [*As before.*] Is dat so? Good-bye.

[TOM *walks to stairs, pauses, hesitates—then
slowly comes back and sits down in his old
chair.*

TOM. Madam—

RITA. [*Turning to glance at him.*] Oh! I t'ought you go!

TOM. [*With dignity.*] So long as you're sincerely sorry—so long as you truly repent—[*He pauses expectantly, awaiting her corroboration. But she whistles gaily and pays* no attention to him. *He finishes somewhat lamely:*] I don't suppose there's any need of my going.

RITA. [*Lightly.*] No? My Lord, I am dead vit' joy!

TOM. [*Sternly.*] Madam—

RITA. [*Gaily, as she pours the drink from one glass to another.*] Look—! See 'ow bee-eautiful I do it—! [*Her voice softening.*] Somevone who vas vonce ver' fon' of me, 'e teach me dis! [*He stares, hypnotized. She finishes and fills both glasses.*] Dere! [*She holds one out to him.*] Dat is for you!

TOM. [*Rousing himself.*] Thanks. I—don't take stimulants.

RITA. [*Very softly.*] Not even vhen *I* give dem—? [*A pause. She holds out the glass and smiles. At last he takes it.*] Ah, dat is right! [*She lifts her own glass.*] Now vhat ve dreenk to—eh? [*Suddenly.*] Ecco! Dat nice ol' cler-gee-man—Saint Gile'! You don't like dat—no? [*She pauses and considers, gazing at him. At last, in a slow, mysterious whisper:*] Den 'ow you like it if *I* dreenk to vhat I see in *your* eyes—an' *you* dreenk to vat you see in mine—?

> [*A pause. She stares at him steadily with a mysterious smile. He cannot take his eyes away. Together they slowly lift their glasses to their lips and drink, their gaze never faltering. From downstairs can be heard very faintly the voices of the other singers, singing the sextette from " Lucia," with the orchestra accompaniment.*

TOM. [*Oddly.*] Who are you? Tell me—I—don't understand—

RITA. [*Slowly and mysteriously.*] I am a cup all full of sacred vine! I stan' upon an altar built of gol' an' pearls an' paid for vit' de blood an' tears of men! De steam of perfume dat fills all de air, it is de t'oughts of me in poets' 'earts—de vhite flowers lying at my feet, dey are de young boys' bee-eautiful deep dreams! My doors are open vide to all de vorld! I shine in dis great darkness like a living star, an' somevhere—sometime every man 'as 'eard my voice—" Come, all you t'irsty vones—come, dere is vine for all!" [*Pause.*]

TOM. What's your name?

RITA. Ah, vhy you ask?

TOM. [*Always looking at her.*] Because I want to see you again—and again—I want to ask you a million things I never dreamed about until to-night—[*His voice rising.*] I want to know you right down to the very bottom of your soul—I want to—

RITA. [*Interrupting.*] Ah, poor young man—all dat can never be.

TOM. It will—

RITA. No—no!

TOM. [*Rising.*] It *must*—it's *got* to be!

RITA. [*Gently.*] Ssh—! Don' make a noise! [*Impulsively.*] Come 'ere! [*He comes up to the side of couch.*] Kneel down—[*As he does so.*] Dere—like dat! Close—close so ve can talk. [*Picking up her bouquet.*] You see my violets 'ere—so sveet an' fresh an' bee-eautiful? You see dem? Vell, 'ow long you t'ink dey las'?

TOM. A long time, if you treat them well.

RITA. Now look—! [*She pulls the flowers in handfuls from the bouquet.*] I press dem on my face an' neck—I feel dere freshness on my eyes an' 'air—I dreenk dere sveetness like I dreenk new vine—

TOM. [*Warningly.*] You're crushing them!

RITA. Vhat does it matter? I have kees dem—an' dey vere born to die! [*Taking up two great handfuls and covering his face with them.*] Dere—! Take long bret's of dere fragrance! Let dem cool your lips an' fall like vhite snow on your face! Don't t'ink sad t'oughts of vhat mus' be—jus' laugh an' love dem—dat is all dey need! [*Giving him more.*] Take dese—an' dese—take more—oh, take dem all—! [*She throws a last handful into the air. The flowers fall all about them.*] Dere—! [*Showing the bouquet holder.*] It is empty. Not vone is left to take 'ome vhen I go. You on'erstan'?

Tom. I don't know—

Rita. [*Tenderly.*] Our meeting 'ere to-night—vhat is it but a bunch of violets? Of flowers dat ve smell an' love an' t'row into de air? Vhy should ve take dem 'ome vit' us an' vatch dem die? I t'ink it is oh! much more vise to leave dem 'ere—like leetle memories—all sveet an' vhite an' scattered on de groun'.

Tom. Couldn't I keep—just one or two?

Rita. [*Smiling.*] Dey vere not meant for keeping. Dere whole life vas to-night!

Tom. [*Simply.*] I know—but I'd like to try. [*A little pause. She looks at him and shakes her head.*]

Rita. Ah, you are so young! [*She picks up a few flowers from where they have fallen and puts them in his buttonhole as he kneels beside her.*] Dere! [*Then, with her fingers still at his buttonhole.*] I vish—[*She hesitates.*]

Tom. What do you wish?

Rita. [*Very simply, almost like a child.*] I vish I knew some flowers dat vould never die.

> [*There is an instant's pause, then, quite suddenly, he seizes her hands and kisses them again and again.*]

Rita. [*Trying to rise.*] No—stop—vhat you do—?
> [*She manages to tear herself away from him just as* Van Tuyl *appears on the stairs.*]

*He pauses at the top and looks at them.
A brief pause.*

RITA. [*With complete self-command.*] Ah, 'ow nize you are to come!

VAN TUYL. [*Politely.*] You're ready, madame?

RITA. Gvite, qvite ready. [*To* TOM.] T'ank you, m'sieur, for your kin' politeness. Good-bye.

[*She bows to him and picks up her scarf,
gloves, and fan, preparatory to departure.*

TOM. [*Hoarsely.*] But I want to see you again.

RITA. You are—sure?

TOM. [*Gulping.*] Yes—

RITA. Gvite sure?

TOM. [*As before.*] Yes—

RITA. [*Very "femme du monde".*] Den vould you come to my 'otel to-morrow afternoon at four? It is de Brevoort 'Ouse—[*Pointing.*] Jus' over dere, you know.

TOM. [*With difficulty.*] All right—

RITA. [*Smiling.*] An' I vill take you for a leetle drive upon your bee-eautiful Fift' Avenue!

VAN TUYL. [*Always very polite.*] And *our* engagement, madame—what becomes of that?

RITA. *Our* leetle engagement is—is—'ow you say?

VAN TUYL. Postponed?

RITA. [*Finishing.*] In-definite-lee.

[VAN TUYL *bows. She moves towards the stairs.*

TOM. [*Who has never taken his eyes from her now steps forward as he sees her leaving.*] Wait—! I'm awfully sorry, but I—you know you haven't told me what your name is—

RITA. Oh, of course—I 'ave forget—so stupid! Vill you tell 'im—Meestaire Van Tuyl?

[*She gives them each the most correct of
smiles and bows, unconsciously dropping*

her handkerchief as she does so, then goes
downstairs. As she goes, there is a mur-
mur swelling up into loud applause which
comes from below. She is smiling and
kissing her hand to this unseen crowd as
she disappears.

[*A pause.* VAN TUYL *lights a cigar.* TOM,
*staring after her, comes slowly to the
top of the stairs, sees the handkerchief
and picks it up. He is fingering it aim-
lessly when he sees the initials at one
corner. He looks at them more carefully
—and then turns dumbly to* VAN TUYL.
The orchestra begins below.

VAN TUYL. [*Gently.*] Do you mean to say you really didn't know who she was?

TOM. [*Shaking his head and speaking almost inarticulately.*] No—I hadn't the least idea—

A WOMAN'S VOICE. [*Singing below.*]
" *Non conosci il bel suol*
    Che di porpora ha il, ciel?
Il bel suol ù de' rai
    Son più tersi ı colori?
" *Ove l'aura è più dolce*
    Più lieve l'augel

. . . . . .

[TOM *walks slowly to the balustrade and
stands there, looking down at the singer
in the room below.* VAN TUYL *watches
him rather sadly as*

The Curtain Falls.

ACT II

[*SCENE: New Year's afternoon. The study of St. Giles Rectory, a charmingly old-fashioned, spacious New York house, looking out upon a quiet street. The study is a square room. At the left are two windows, with heavy, rather faded curtains. In them hang holly wreaths, tied with scarlet bows. At the back is the double-doorway leading into the hall. At one side of it hangs the bell-rope. Over it is a long oar, and, above this a mounted stag's head. At the right is the white marble mantel and fireplace, in which a fire is burning. On the mantel are several silver cups, medals in their open cases, little old-fashioned photographs of young men, a big old clock, and two handsome candelabra. Over the mantel is a large steel engraving of Del Sarto's St. John. Near the fireplace is a rack containing rods and guns. A pair of boxing-gloves hangs here, too. There are bookcases at the back, filled with sober, pious, dusty volumes. On top these bookcases are a few more engravings of old Masters—a Last Supper, etc. In one corner stands an old-fashioned cabinet, with glass-covered shelves and drawers below.*

In front of the window is a very large, heavy table-desk; on it are a lamp, a water-pitcher and glass, desk-fittings, several books, a daguerreotype in a velvet case, a large, well-used Bible, a smaller Testament, etc. A big leather chair faces this desk. There are one or two other chairs near it. Across the room and placed so that the keyboard is not seen is a small, but exquisite old-fashioned square piano. There are candles on each side of the keyboard and several rather worn volumes of bound music, neatly ranged. Near the fireplace is a hair-cloth settee. All the furniture is old-fashioned black walnut, upholstered in black. An old-fashioned red carpet covers the floor.

The sunlight of a cold winter's afternoon comes through the windows. Outdoors the glitter of snow is seen. As the act goes on the sunlight changes to the ruddy glow of a winter's sunset, and then the twilight fills the room with shadows.

As the curtain rises MISS ARMSTRONG, *wearing a little black silk apron, is discovered arranging some roses in a bowl on the desk. The clock on the mantel strikes four.*]

[*The door opens and* GILES, *the old butler, appears.*
GILES. Miss Van Tuyl.
[SUSAN *enters, dressed in bonnet and mantle.*
SUSAN. [*Coming in.*] Tom, I— *Seeing* MISS ARMSTRONG.] Oh, Happy New Year, Miss Armstrong!
MISS ARMSTRONG. Don't be premature, my dear—it's only New Year's Eve. [*Kissing her.*] What nice cold cheeks you have!
SUSAN. [*Laughing.*] I ought to—I've been walking. Tom asked me to come in at four, and hear about the final arrangements for to-night.
MISS ARMSTRONG. To-night—?
SUSAN—Yes. The midnight New Year's service for the lost and friendless.
MISS ARMSTRONG. Oh, *that!*
SUSAN. [*Enthusiastically.*] We're going to have a brass band and torches and sing hymns and parade the streets for half an hour beforehand—oh, it'll be wonderful! Is Tom upstairs?

Miss Armstrong. [*Nervously.*] No. He went out after luncheon—er—to pay a call.

Susan. [*Meaningly.*] At the Brevoort House?

Miss Armstrong. [*Flustered.*] Oh, I'm sure he'll be here if you wait a moment! He has a Deaconesses' Meeting at a quarter to five and I *know* he never would miss that!

Susan. Wouldn't he? Well, we'll see—[*Noticing the flowers.*] What lovely roses!

Miss Armstrong. They're mine—they came just a moment ago. Without any card, too!

Susan. [*Chaffing her.*] Aha! An anonymous admirer—!

Miss Armstrong. [*Embarrassed and pleased.*] My dear, how foolish! But you know it's the first time in years that anyone's sent me flowers, and—

[*There is the sound of sleighbells outside.*

Susan. [*At the window.*] Oh, look! It's uncle's sleigh! He's driving his new team!

Miss Armstrong. Is he getting out?

Susan. Yes. He's come to call for me on his way uptown. [*Glancing at clock.*] I wonder if Tom—

Miss Armstrong. My dear, there's no telling when he'll be back. And as there's something I want to discuss with your uncle, I think you may as well go home.

Susan. Miss Armstrong, promise me not to tell him I came—unless he speaks of it himself, I mean. I don't want to be a drag on him. Oh, Miss Armstrong, promise—*please!*

Miss Armstrong. Very well, my dear—if you insist. and—

[Giles *enters.*

Giles. [*Announcing.*] Mr. Van Tuyl.

[*He stands aside to let* Van Tuyl *pass.*

VAN TUYL. [*Who wears a long fur coat and driving gloves.*] How d'you do, Miss Armstrong. Real New Year's Eve weather—eh? [*Taking off his coat and giving it to* GILES.] Well, Susannah! I thought I'd find you and Tom waving your arms and singing hymns and generally getting up steam for to-night's procession!

SUSAN. [*Smiling.*] Tom's out. Can Ralph take me home? [*She puts on her wraps.*]

VAN TUYL. Yes—good idea. I don't like to keep the horses standing. [*To* MISS ARMSTRONG.] Have you seen my new team, Miss Armstrong? The prettiest sight in New York—[*At the window.*] Look at that off mare there! Isn't she a little witch? The highest stepper on the Avenue and a mouth like a French kid glove!

MISS ARMSTRONG. She looks very wild indeed! [*To* SUSAN.] Good-bye, my dear. Tell Ralph to be careful.

SUSAN. [*Kissing* MISS ARMSTRONG.] Don't forget your promise. [*In a lower voice.*] And, dear, don't worry. *I* don't worry—I know it's going to be all right. [*She goes out.*]

MISS ARMSTRONG. [*Turning from the door.*] Oh, Mr. Van Tuyl, I—I am in great—in very great distress!

VAN TUYL. Dear lady, what is it?

MISS ARMSTRONG. [*Crying quietly.*] I'm ashamed to act like this—but—it's been so hard carrying it on my mind—all alone—

VAN TUYL. [*Soothingly.*] There—! Count on me.

MISS ARMSTRONG. You're Tom's oldest friend—and his father's and mother's before him—and you're his leading parishioner, too—and the chairman of the vestry—

[*She sniffs.*

VAN TUYL. [*Comfortingly.*] I know—I know—

MISS ARMSTRONG. [*Breaking down.*] Oh, save him, Mr. Van Tuyl—save him from that d-d-dreadful woman!

[*She sobs.*

Van Tuyl. I've done my best. He came to see me Saturday about the new gymnasium and I talked to him as I would have to my own son.

Miss Armstrong. What did he say?

Van Tuyl. He was very sweet, but somehow he wasn't there—the real Tom, I mean—it was only the outside shell that I was speaking to.

Miss Armstrong. I know! I've seen it! He's with *her!*

Van Tuyl. [*Reassuringly.*] Oh, come, Miss Armstrong! You mustn't be alarmed! Remember that she sails to-morrow morning, and—[*Glancing out window.*] Hello—!

Miss Armstrong. [*Stopping.*] What's the matter?

Van Tuyl. Why, her carriage is just stopping at your door!

Miss Armstrong. [*In amazed horror.*] Not Madame Cavallini—?

Van Tuyl. I rather think she's out to pay some calls. [*As* Miss Armstrong *goes and pulls the bell-rope.*] What are you going to do?

Miss Armstrong. Tell Giles I'm out.

Van Tuyl. [*Frankly.*] Let her come in. Perhaps I could say a word or two—

Miss Armstrong. [*Earnestly.*] You'll make her promise not to write to him?

Van Tuyl. I'll do my best.

Miss Armstrong. [*Vehemently.*] There ought to be a law against such women! Why, I'd sooner have a hungry tigress walk into this room than—

Giles. [*At door.*] Madame Cavallini.

> [*He enters and stands aside to let her pass. She comes in quickly. She wears a wonderful black velvet dress, an ermine coat,*

and a little ermine hat. Around her neck is a long rope of pearls; at the end hangs a cross. In her arms, as if it were a baby, she carries a great ermine muff. From one end of this peeps a monkey's head, adorned with a scarlet satin turban, a long green cigarette and a diamond clasp.]

RITA. [*To* MISS ARMSTRONG, *shaking hands.*] My dear meess, 'ow you do? I come in for vone meenute jus' to say good-bye an'—

MISS ARMSTRONG. [*Seeing monkey and drawing back with a cry.*] Oh—! What's that—?

RITA. What—? [*Noting her look.*] An' I breeng my leetle bab-ee to show you. You like bab-ees—yes?

MISS ARMSTRONG. That's not—a baby?

RITA. [*Laughing.*] Oh, no—no—no! Vhat you t'ink? I call 'er bab-ee—because I am so—lonely—you too 'ave no bab-ee, so you on'erstan'—yes? [*Seeing* VAN TUYL.] Oh—! [*Advancing to him.*] 'Ow you do, Meestaire Van Tuyl?

[*She shakes hands with him.*

VAN TUYL. [*Shaking hands.*] How do you do? It seems a long time since we've met.

RITA. Dat night I sing at your so bee-eautiful *soirèe!* To me, also, it seem a long, long time.

VAN TUYL. And Adelina—[*To the monkey.*] *Comment ça va, mademoiselle—hein?* I hope you find the weather not too cold—?

MISS ARMSTRONG. Adelina—?

RITA. Yes—because she look so much like Patti in *La Traviata.* [*To* VAN TUYL.] I t'ink she 'ave forget you, sir.

VAN TUYL. You ladies can forget so quickly.

RITA. Yes? Sometime—I vish you men forget a leetle—

too! [*Taking the monkey out from muff.*] *Tesoruccio mio, sei quasi gelato—non importa qui fa caldo!*
> [*The tiny animal wears a fantastic costume of bright green satin. Her skirt is ornamented with large diamond buttons.*

Miss Armstrong. Why, it's all dressed up!

Rita. [*In surprise.*] But surely she is dress! Do you vant she go—'ow you say?—naked? Dat vould be—ah! shockeeng!

Miss Armstrong. Are those—real diamond buttons?

Rita—Yes. De prince de Chimay, 'e give 'er dose. So pretty—eh?

Miss Armstrong. [*Indignantly.*] I call it sinful waste—!

Rita. [*Wistfully.*] You don' like de monkee—no?

Miss Armstrong. Certainly not—horrid little animals!

Rita. [*Warningly.*] Tschk—! Tschk—! You 'urt 'er feeling! *Ecco*—see—! She begin to cry! [*Suddenly thrusting Adelina into Miss Armstrong's arms.*] Kiss 'er please—tell her you like 'er jus' vone leetle bit—

Miss Armstrong. [*Frantically.*] Stop it! How dare you—? Take it away—oh! oh! It's going to bite me—Mr. Van Tuyl—

Van Tuyl. [*Taking the monkey.*] Come here, Adelina—there—that's right!

Rita. [*To monkey.*] *Bellezza mia! tu un' faresti male a nessuno!* [*Taking monkey.*] I t'ink she is like me, Meestaire Van Tuyl. [*With a reproachful glance towards Miss Armstrong.*] She is not 'appy when de peoples do not love 'er! [*Slipping the monkey into muff again.*] *Ti amo bambinello mio—si—ti amo!*

Miss Armstrong. [*Watching her.*] Ugh!

Rita. [*Putting both muff and monkey in big chair by fire where neither can be seen.*] I put 'er 'ere an' she vill take vone leetle nap! [*Bending over chair.*] *Dormi, bambina cara di mammà—e stai là—buona, buona—finche mamma ti sveglia!* [*Rising and turning quickly to* Miss Armstrong.] *Santi!* I 'ave forget! I 'ave a somet'ing to tell you from Meestaire Tom!

Miss Armstrong. You've seen him?

Rita. [*Innocently.*] But yes—'e drive vit' me. I leave 'im at de—oh, vhat you say?—de parish 'ouse. 'E mus' spik to de con-firm-a-tion class—[*To* Van Tuyl.] What is dat? Con-firm—

Miss Armstrong. [*Interrupting.*] Isn't he coming home?

Rita. Yes—jus' a leetle vhile, 'e say. [*Holding out her hand to* Miss Armstrong.] So I come firs'—to make my respec' to you, dear meess, an' say good-bye.

Miss Armstrong. [*Stiffly, to* Van Tuyl, *paying no attention to the outstretched hand.*] When Madame Cavallini goes, I hope you'll step up to my sitting-room and have a cup of tea? [*He bows.*]

Rita. [*Seeing the roses on the desk.*] A-ah! De roses—dey arrive all right? You like dem—yes? I 'ave choose each vone myself—! [*She smiles winningly at* Miss Armstrong.]

Miss Armstrong. [*Amazed.*] *You* sent me those—?

Rita. [*Wistfully.*] Jus' a leetle surprise—to remember me two—t'ree days after I 'ave gone—so far!

Miss Armstrong. [*After a speechless moment.*] Thank you—you were very kind. [*She goes over and takes up the bowl of roses from the desk.*] Mr. Van Tuyl will put you in your carriage whenever you're ready. Good-bye, madame, I wish you a pleasant voyage! [*She goes out at back.*]

Rita. [*Turning in wonder to* Van Tuyl.] Vhat for she go avay so qveeck?

VAN TUYL. I asked her to. I said I wanted to talk to you alone.

RITA. [*Turning away.*] Yes? Could you not come to my 'otel?

VAN TUYL. I may be wrong, but I thought I wouldn't be received.

RITA. [*Not looking at him.*] Mebbe you are not so wrong.

VAN TUYL. Come here.

RITA. [*Coming up to him.*] Vhat you vant?
[*She looks at him and suddenly smiles.*

VAN TUYL. [*Smiling, too.*] You little monkey, you—[*Recovering himself.*] Now pretend for five minutes I'm your father confessor!

RITA. You vant to scold me—yes?

VAN TUYL. [*Taking her by the shoulders.*] Well, that depends—we'll see. Has Tom asked you to marry him?

RITA. [*After a little pause.*] No.

VAN TUYL. I'm glad. And if he did?

RITA. [*Not looking at him, speaking with a rather sulky defiance.*] I vould not marry 'im—an Amer'can cler-gee-man. 'E vould vant I stop singing an' be so frightful good an' live 'ere in dis 'orrible New York—mos' col' diza-agree-ble place I ever see—! Adelina, in two—t'ree mont's she die—yes! An' 'e vould not let me go to Paris vhen I need de new dress—an' I vould be all bore—an' seeck—[*With a sniff.*] Mebbe *I* die, too—an' den—everyvone is glad—! [*She dries her eyes resolutely with her handkerchief.*] Oh, no, my frien', I vould not marry 'im—no—no—dat vould be vone beeg meestake!

VAN TUYL. Then why do you lead the poor boy on?

RITA. Lead 'im—?

VAN TUYL. He's not like the young gentlemen you're

accustomed to have circling round you—remember that, my dear! He's not a Baron Vigier or a Captain Ponsonby or a—who was that little Pole who singed his wings so badly when you sang last spring in Brussels?

RITA. No, my frien'—no—

VAN TUYL. [*Interrupting.*] Well, isn't that pretty much the way you're treating him? Aren't you amusing yourself—just a little bit at his expense?

RITA. You do not on'erstan'—ah! it is so 'ard to say! Leesten—! [*She speaks very seriously.*] 'Ow long I know 'im? Two mont's? Ver' vell—[*Solemnly.*] In all dat time 'e 'as not spik to me a vord of love—no, not vone leetle vord!

VAN TUYL. [*Amazed.*] What—?

RITA. At first I try to *make* him—oh, you know—jus' for fun! An' den—some'ow—I am so sorry for 'im—an' I don't try any more!

[*She sits on a hassock at his feet, leaning against his knees. He puts his hand on her shoulder.*]

VAN TUYL. [*Tenderly.*] My poor little Rita. Don't you know there's nothing in all this, dear, for you?

RITA. [*With a sigh.*] Oh, yes! I 'ave so often say, "Seelly voman, do not see 'im vhen 'e come today. Jus' tell de gentleman down-stair you vant to sleep an' no-bod-ee shall vake you up!"

VAN TUYL. Well, why didn't you?

RITA. I say no-bod-ee—like dat! No-bod-ee in all de vorld—[*Shamefacedly.*]—excep' jus' Meestaire Tom! [*With a sigh.*] O Dio, come e dura la vita!

VAN TUYL. So that's the way it went!

RITA. An' 'e come so much—oh! all de time! An' I cannot practice an' 'e take me for de valk in de Gran' Central Park. Vone day 'e keep me so late, dere is no re-

'earsal—yes, an' I sing dat night—! Oh! It vas mos' terr'ble! [*Shyly.*] But also it vas—nize!

VAN TUYL. [*Softly.*] I know—I know—

RITA. An' den ve go 'ome to de 'otel an' I play for 'im—an' sing—sometime I tell de fortune vit' de card. An' 'e sit near an' spik of many t'ings!

VAN TUYL. What sort of things?

RITA. Oh, I dunno. Sometime vhat 'appen vhen 'e vas a leetle boy—an' vhat de bee-shop say about 'is vork—an' of de new geem-nas-i-um 'e 'ave build—an' so much of de poor peoples dat 'e vant to 'elp.

VAN TUYL. He talks of them to you?

RITA. [*Nodding.*] Oh, yes! An' I—I tell 'im vhat I t'ink! I vounce vas poor—*I* know—*I* on'erstan'. [*Glancing up at him.*] I t'ink you smile a leetle—yes?

VAN TUYL. No, I'm not smiling, dear. [*Pause.*]

RITA. [*With a sigh.*] Ah, my frien', I am vone great big fool—I—who 'ave believe I vas so vise!

[*She smiles and shakes her head.*

VAN TUYL. Never mind, my dear. It's over now. You're leaving us to-morrow.

RITA. [*Glancing up.*] You t'ink 'e vill forget me—yes?

VAN TUYL. I'm sure you hope he will.

RITA. [*Looking off.*] I t'ink I vill not forget 'im—or if I do it take a long, long time!

VAN TUYL. Ssh! Nonsense! [*Putting his hands over her eyes.*] Shut your eyes and think of all that's waiting for you over there! Rome. Just say it yourself. Rome. Do you remember those last evenings on the terrace of the Villa d'Este? And inside the Abbé Liszt just playing and playing his—what did he call 'em?—"Consolations?" Do you remember that old piece of balustrade, and the Campagna, all purple like the twilight-laden sea? And far away, like smoke against the sky, St. Peter's dome? And that's not all—there's Florence, and the olive-covered hills of Fiesole! You'll be there for the first breath of the spring! And Como with the snow still on the mountains! And Paris—why, you'll see the first acacias on the Boulevard St. Germain—you'll smell the lilacs when you're driving in the Bois—! And Gounod will be there, and your dear old friend Rossini—! Think of the dinners at the Maison Dorée, and the violets in the forest of Compiègne—! Think of the suppers Cora Pearl will give! Do you remember when the Brohan poured her champagne down the prince's back? And Marianne de Murska—good old Gigi, too—why, don't you know what fun you're going to have?

RITA. Oh, dere is only vone t'ing dat I know!

VAN TUYL. What's that?

RITA. [*Passionately.*] I love 'im—I love 'im—

VAN TUYL. [*Covering her mouth with his hand.*] Ssh—! Rita, you oughtn't to have come here today. It isn't right—it isn't fair to either of you.

RITA. But 'e ask me so many time!

VAN TUYL. If you don't look out, you're going to make him suffer a great deal.

RITA. [*Quickly.*] Ah—no—no!

VAN TUYL. [*Gently.*] It rests with you, my dear—his happiness or pain.

RITA. [*After a pause, rising.*] All right. I go now—befor 'e come.

VAN TUYL. You won't regret it, dear.

RITA. [*Unpinning a bunch of white violets from her wrap.*] So vhen 'e ask for me—jus' give 'im dese—an' say it is—*adieu*—

[*She kisses the violets and holds them out to him. Just here the door opens and* TOM *bursts in, full of splendid spirits, utterly boyish and happy. He wears his overcoat and gloves.*

Tom. [*Entering.*] Well, did you think I never was—[*Seeing* Van Tuyl.] Oh, is that you, sir? How do you do? [*Shaking hands.*] I'm glad Madame Cavallini hasn't been waiting here alone. Where's Aunt Emma?

Van Tuyl. Upstairs.

Tom. [*Pulling off his gloves.*] Whew—! It's cold outside! I'm nearly frozen and I ran home, too! Those little rascals were so stupid—I wanted to spank the lot! [*Rubbing his hands.*] Now I'll just put some more coal on the fire and then we'll sit down and—

Van Tuyl. I think, Tom, Mme. Cavallini was just going when you came in.

Tom. [*Stopping.*] Going—?

Rita. [*Recollecting herself.*] Yes, I mus' sleep a leetle before tonight—my las' performance—I so much vant to give my best— [*She has moved towards the door.*

Tom. [*Running up and taking her hand.*] Oh, come now, you're not going!

Rita. [*Faltering.*] Please, Meestaire Tom, de performance—

Tom. [*Drawing her over to fire.*] Oh, that's all right—it's *Mignon* and you know it backwards.

Rita. [*Helplessly to* Van Tuyl.] You see—

[Giles *enters at back.*

Giles [*At door.*] Miss Armstrong's compliments, Mr. Van Tuyl, and tea is served in the sitting-room upstairs.

Tom. [*Quickly.*] Don't say we're here. We'll come up later. [Van Tuyl *looks at* Rita.

Rita. [*Pleadingly.*] In jus' vone leetle vhile!

[*With a shrug,* Van Tuyl *turns and goes out.* Giles *closes the door after him.*

Tom. [*With a sigh of pleasure as the door closes.*]

There! Now isn't this fine? I tell you, it's like a dream come true!

RITA. Vhat dream, please?

TOM. You—here in *my* big armchair—in front of *my* fire—in *my* study!

RITA. [*Wistfully.*] A dream—ah, dat is vhat I am! A leetle dream dat lose 'er vay an' rest vone meenute in your sleeping 'eart.

TOM. One minute? Always!

RITA. [*Smiling.*] Ah no, my frien'. To-morrow you vake up, an' pouf! dat leetle dream—she is all gone!

TOM. No—don't—

RITA. [*Softly.*] You 'ave been 'appy den, dese las' veeks—yes?

TOM. [*Lifting his eyes to hers.*] You know.

Rita. [*Very softly.*] I 'ave been 'appy too.

TOM. [*Impulsively.*] Don't go to-morrow!

RITA. Vhat you say?

TOM. Stay on till spring!

RITA. But 'ave I not tell you I mus' sing in Rome nex' mont'—? An' I go to Venice for de new opera Verdi 'ave compose—

TOM. Don't go—oh, please don't go!

RITA. An' den I mus' see Mapleson in London, an' de Russian concert tour begin in June—

TOM. I don't care—I just *can't* say good-bye!

RITA. [*Illumined.*] Den come vit' me!

TOM. [*Surprised.*] What?

RITA. Go qveeck an' buy de teecket—

TOM. Ticket—?

RITA. [*Enthusiastically.*] Yes—before dey are all gone!—an' to-morrow ve put de clo'es in de box an' de box on de carriage an' drive to de *quai* an' oh! ve stan' on de boat—you an' me an' Adelina—an' ve vave de 'an'-

kerchief an' t'row de kiss an' laugh!—oh! my Lord, 'ow ve laugh at all de stupid peoples ve leave behin'! Vhat you t'ink of dat? *Hein?*

Tom. I think it's wonderful. But I've got a meeting of the Board of Charities to-morrow at eleven, and Patrick Crowley's funeral at twelve, and after dinner I offer my annual report to the Vestry Committee, and in the evening my Knights of the Round Table boys—

Rita. [*Interrupting.*] I 'ave forget you are a clerg-ee-man.

Tom. And *I* forgot you were a Golden Nightingale. [*Pause.*]

Rita. [*Nodding to herself.*] I t'ink it is a ver' good t'ing I go avay to-morrow.

Tom. [*Much downcast.*] But you're coming back next year?

Rita. [*With a gesture.*] Ah, vhy talk about nex' year—it is so far avay!

Tom. In my profession, one has to think a great deal about things that are far away.

Rita. Den you are ver' foolish—[*As he starts to protest.*]—yes, you are! Leesten! I am ol' an' I know de vorld—so vhat I tell you now you mus' remember alvays.

Tom. Well?

Rita. [*Wistfully.*] Yesterday—it is a dream ve 'ave forget. To-morrow—jus' de 'ope of some great 'appiness—some joy dat never come! Before, behin'—all clouds an' stars an' shadow—nodings, nodings dat is real—only de leetle meenute dat we call to-day!

Tom. [*Bitterly.*] To-day's so short!

Rita. [*With a smile.*] Ah, you are young, my frien'! De time vill come vhen you are glad to 'ave dat leetle meenute—so glad you vould not t'ink to ask for more! [*Changing her tone.*] *Dio mio!* De 'ours, dey fly so fas'!

[*Pointing to a chair.*] Go sit down—fold your 'ands! Now ve vill see 'ow much Eetalian I 'ave teach you.

Tom. [*Disappointed.*] Oh, bother Italian! Don't let's waste time when—

Rita. [*Interrupting.*] De lesson 'ave begin. [*Primly.*] Buon giorno, signor.

Tom. [*Sulkily.*] Buon giorno, signora.

Rita. Sta ella bene oggi?

Tom. [*With some difficulty.*] Molto grazie io sono benissimo.

Rita. [*Smiling.*] Sono quelli i suoi istrumenti da pesca? [*Pointing to case—right.*]

Tom. [*Not understanding.*] Istrumenti da pesca?

Rita. [*Imitating the act of fishing.*] 'Ow you say—for de feeshes?

Tom. [*Understanding.*] Oh, *fishing* rods!

Rita. Si—si! Le piace pescare?

Tom. [*Shaking his head.*] Er—I'm afraid I don't get it.

Rita. You lika to 'unt de feeshes?

Tom. [*Enthusiastically.*] Do I? Well, I should say! There's a stream up in the Adirondack Mountains—you'd just love those mountains!—where I landed ninety-four trout in one day! Ninety-four—what do you think of that?

Rita. Poor leetle feeshes!

Tom. [*Tolerantly.*] Oh, *they* don't mind. They *like* to be caught.

Rita. [*Pointing to the stag's head over the door.*] E quel' cervo lo ha ammazzato lei anche quello?

Tom. Did I shoot him, you mean?

Rita. Si—si.

Tom. [*Enthusiastically.*] Well, you'd better believe I did! I got him all myself and—

Rita. [*Interrupting.*] Oh, là—là! Badi! Italiano—Italiano!

Tom. [*Pointing to himself proudly.*] Io—tutti io—guide three miles away! *Moltissimo grande*—Biggest *bucko* that season—tried to gore me with those antlers, but I plugged him just in time—*molto sporto*, I tell *you!*

Rita. [*Clasping her hands.*] *Santa Madonna!* You mus' be careful please—mebbe some day you get 'urted!

Tom. [*With a slight swagger.*] Oh, no, I won't!

Rita. [*Looking over the door.*] An' de beeg oar—vhy you keep 'im dere?

Tom. [*Proudly.*] I pulled that oar in the best race Yale ever won! I was number six—we beat Harvard by quarter of a boat-length. That was '59—my senior year. [*Anxiously.*] They didn't have anything about it in the European papers, did they? No—? [*Looking at the oar.*] Well, it was a great race just the same!

Rita. [*Softly.*] I am so glad you vin!

Tom. [*Pleased.*] We wouldn't have done it if it hadn't been for Dicky Parker. [*Going to the mantel and taking up a small photograph.*] He was our stroke—had the finest pair of legs in college, and as for his back—[*Reverently.*]—well, I just wish you could see the muscles in his back! [*Giving her the picture.*] Here he is—he looks sort of foolish in that picture, though.

Rita. [*Looking at it.*] He look ver' nize.

Tom. [*Giving her another picture.*] And here's Dave Sterling. He played first base on the college team. Dave went to China last year as a missionary—[*Giving her another.*] And here's Frank Willis—he was killed at Gettysburg, you know—[*Suddenly seizing another in a frame at the end of the mantel.*] Oh, and here's Wallie Fletcher—he's the fellow I told you about, that used to spend his summers with me up at Peekskill before father sold the place.

RITA. [*Taking the picture.*] De leetle boy dat sveem across de rivair?

TOM. That's the one! Didn't we have good times though? We always went barefoot—used to pick up things with our toes. I could beat Wallie running and jumping, but of course he had me when it came to swimming—and then he could whistle through his teeth! Dear me, when I think of the hours I spent in the back pasture all by myself, just trying to whistle through my teeth!

RITA. [*Sympathetically.*] A-ah!

TOM. But I made up for it when I learnt to turn a back somersault. Wallie used to rub himself every night with boiled angle-worms—he'd heard all acrobats did that —[*Suddenly.*] But there! I'm always talking about myself! Suppose you talk about *yourself* for a change?

RITA. Me—?

TOM. Yes, tell me about some of the larks *you* used to have. The good times—you know what I mean!

RITA. [*A little timidly.*] De good time—? I am afraid I did not 'ave dat ver' much—[*Suddenly.*] But vait! Yes, I remember vonce! My *baba*—

TOM. [*Interrupting.*] What?

RITA. Dat mean my fader—'e is dead—[*She closes her eyes, says something under her breath in Latin, crosses herself and then resumes brightly.*]—ve live in vone leetle room ver' ver' 'igh up—Calle San Polo on de Zattere. Vone morning de *baba*, 'e feel seeck—ve 'ad not anyt'ings to eat —so I mus' leave 'im qveek an' go an' sing to get de money. An' I sing an' sing, but no vone vill give nodings, an' de bad boys dey laugh, an' t'row de dirt at me, an' vone of dem, 'e break my guitar! An' de night come, an' I am so tired I don't know vhere I go or vhat I do—an' den I fin' myself before de 'Otel Danieli. An' I try to sing—but no vone leesten, an' de tears dey come so fas' I cannot see—an' jus' den I 'ear a voice say "Don' cry please!" I don' on'erstan' de Engleesh den, but I look up an' a leetle girl, all dress in vhite, she lean ovair de balcony an' smile at me an' drop an envelope an' in de envelope vas—vhat you t'ink?—a bee-eautiful bright piece of gol'! An' de tears, dey 'ave an en', an' I smile up at de leetle girl, an' keess my 'an' an' run avay an' oh! dat night I cook a—'ow you say?—a great beeg deesh of nize, fat, dee-licious fried eel! Dat suppair, it come back to me in dreams an' I seet again on de broken stool an' eat an' eat, an' de *baba*, 'e make de joke an' oh! my Lord, I am so *glad!* An' den I vake up—an' feel de pearls aroun' my neck—an' I cry —because it vas so long ago! [*Slight pause.*]

TOM. [*Whispering.*] You poor little thing—

RITA. [*Coming back to herself.*] So you see I 'ave de good time, too!

TOM. [*Whispering.*] You poor little thing—
[*He rises and comes to her.*

RITA. Vhat you say?

TOM. [*Passionately.*] Madam Cavallini—Margherita—I—

RITA. [*Shrinking from him in sudden nervousness.*] No—no—

[*Just here a hand-organ strikes up outside the window, playing the old waltz—"Il Bacio."*

TOM. [*Startled and furious.*] Drat that hurdy-gurdy!

RITA. [*Slyly.*] I t'ink it come jus' in time!

[TOM *goes over to the window where he looks out. Meanwhile* RITA *is dancing lightly and gaily about the room, whistling and snapping her fingers in time with the waltz.*

Tom. [*Opening the window and calling outside.*] Hi! [*Pause. The waltz continues.*] Hi—you there! Stop that racket! Stop it this minute! [*The waltz breaks off in the middle of a phrase.*] We don't allow any Italian mountebanks in the neighborhood of this church and if you don't—[*Suddenly spluttering with rage.*] Take that monkey off my gate!

Rita. Monkee—? [*She runs up to the window, and calls gaily outside.*] Buon giorno, amico! [Tom *stands petrified, staring at her.*] Che tesoro di una scimmietta avete! Come si chiama? [*The man calls back something in Italian.*] Hein? Tommaso—? [*To* Tom.] You an' de monkee 'ave de same name! [*Calling outside.*] Quanti anni ha? [*The man answers. She turns to* Tom.] 'E is two year ol'. [*Calling.*] Ha delle pulci? The man answers.] Davvero? [*To* Tom.] ' 'E use to 'ave de flea, but now 'e eat dem all.

Tom. [*Much annoyed.*] Really, I—

Rita. [*Suddenly struck with an idea and calling outside with mysterious importance.*] Aspettate un momento—voglio farvi veder qualche cosa! [*She runs across the room, picks up her own monkey and returns to the window.*] I make acqvainted Tommaso vit' Adelina!

Tom. [*Trying to stop her.*] Please, madame—remember my parishioners—

Rita. [*Holding up Adelina at the window and calling outside.*] Ecco—! Tommaso, questa è Adelina—siete compatrioti! [*To Adelina.*] Sii carina e saluta Tommaso—colla tua manina—[*Waving a hand for her.*] Brava—cosi! [*To the organ-grinder.*] E voi, amico, come vi chiamate? [*The man answers. She turns again to* Tom.] De gentleman's name is Meestaire Francesco Guerra. [*Calling outside.*] Da che provincia venite? [*To* Tom.] 'E come from Napoli. [*Calling.*] Da quanto tempo siete *in questo paese?* [*To* TOM, *as the man answers.*] 'E been 'ere vone year an' 'e vant like 'ell to go back! [*Calling.*] *Quanti bambini avete?*

TOM. [*Firmly.*] Madame, you'll catch your death of cold!

RIA. [*Turning to* TOM.] 'E 'ave five children an' anodder vone come nex' mont'!

TOM. [*Angrily.*] Tell him to go away, do you hear? Tell him to go away immediately!

RITA. [*To* TOM.] All right—give me de money—

TOM. [*Protesting.*] You're not going to—[*Meekly taking out his purse.*] Will ten cents do?

RITA. Qveeck—qveeck before 'e go avay! [*She snatches the purse out of his hand and throws it out the window, calling as she does so:*] Ecco—guardate bene dove cade—comperate qualche cosa pei bambini! Buona fine e buon principio, amico! [*Waving her handkerchief.*] *Arrivederci!*

[*She smiles and kisses her hand at the departing organ-grinder.*

TOM. [*Coldly.*] You talk to that man as if you'd known him all your life!

RITA. [*Turning away from the window with a little sigh and shrug.*] Ah, ve bot' make de music. [*Suddenly seeing the daguerreotype on the desk.*] Who is dat young lady?

TOM. That's my mother. [*Slight pause.*]

RITA. You let me look at 'er—yes?

TOM. Of course.

[*She takes up the picture very tenderly and studies it.*

RITA. [*Softly.*] Oh, she is bee-eautiful!

TOM. [*Coming up and looking at it over her shoulder.*] That was taken before she was married. My father always had it on his dressing-table.

RITA. [*Always gazing at the picture.*] I t'ink you look like 'er.

TOM. [*Looking at it, too.*] She died when I was fifteen. It was my first winter at boarding school. She'd come up to see me only two weeks before and brought me this—[*Picking up a small, worn book from desk.*]—my little Testament. I'd expected a fruit-cake—you can imagine how I felt! But now—[*He brushes it lovingly.*]—there's nothing else I value quite so much!

RITA. [*Whispering.*] She look like she 'old somet'ing in 'er 'eart—somet'ing dat make 'er 'appy—an' dat no vone know—[*Slight pause.*] Per-aps—per'aps it is de t'ought dat vone day she 'ave a son—like you—

    [TOM *has crossed the room and is unlocking a drawer in the corner-cabinet.*

RITA. [*Under her breath, to the picture.*] Forgive—
    [*She kisses it, then puts it back carefully on desk.*

TOM. [*Returning with a little box.*] There's something here I've been meaning to show you—[*He is opening the box and fumbling about in it.*] I keep it in this box with mother's little souvenirs—[*He has taken out a tiny, shabby, little shoe and put it on the desk to get it out of the way.*] Where on earth—[*Suddenly.*] Oh, yes!
    [*He takes out a small package done up carefully in tissue paper.*

RITA. [*Picking up the shoe as she interrupts.*] An' dis—?

TOM. [*Glancing at it.*] That? Oh, I believe that's my first shoe. [*His tone softening as he looks at it.*] Funny little thing—look! It's all worn out at the toes!

RITA. [*Half-laughing, half-crying.*] Oh!—oh, I t'ink it is so sveet!   [*She clasps it to her heart.*

TOM. [*Taking a little envelope from the box and giving it to her.*] Here's something else, too!

Rita. [*Tremulously, as she takes.*] Vhat—? oh, vhat you—[*Reading slowly from the envelope.*] " Curl saved from my son Thom-as Arm-strong's first 'air-cut—June seex —eighteen 'undred an' forty-vone—"

Tom. [*Smiling.*] Let's see—I must have been three years old!

Rita. [*Who has taken out the curl.*] Oh, look! De leetle curl—it is so soft—an' yellow—jus' like gol'—

Tom. I was blonde when I was young—you'd never think it now, would you?

Rita. [*Half-laughing, half-crying.*] An' she 'ave keep it in dis envelope an' write upon it—" Curl from my son Thom-as "—[*She cannot go on.*]

Tom. [*Half apologetic.*] She did that because she was very sentimental.

Rita. [*Bursting out.*] She did it because she love you such a much!

Tom. Here's what I really wanted to show you, though. [*He is unwrapping the little package he has been holding in his hand.* Rita *kisses the curl and puts it back in its envelope with great care.*] Now! Look at those!

Rita. [*Looking.*] A necklace—earrings —

Tom. They were father's wedding present! [*He holds up the necklace—it is made of seed pearls and has a locket.*] There! Isn't that pretty?

Rita. [*Admiringly.*] Oh, mos' ver' pretty!

Tom. There's one of my baby pictures in the locket. [*Trying to open locket.*] I wonder how—oh, yes, I remember—you press the back and then it opens! There—! [*He gives her the locket. She takes it eagerly, looks at it, glances at him, then breaks out into irrepressible laughter.*] What's the matter?

Rita. [*Trying to control herself.*] You are so—so *fat!*

Tom. [*Frowning.*] Fat—?

RITA. You 'ave such beeg cheek—jus' like dis—
[*She puffs up her own cheeks, loses her breath and starts laughing again.*]

TOM. [*Severely.*] I believe I was considered a *very* beautiful baby!

RITA. You are de mos' funny baby I ever see in all my life!

TOM. [*Coldly.*] Oh, very well. I'm sorry I showed it to you! I might have known that—

RITA. [*Interrupting.*] Ah, don't be angry.

TOM. [*Not turning.*] I'm *not* angry!

RITA. So? Den von' you turn your 'ead—please? [*Slight pause.*] I go avay to-morrow! [*Slight pause.*] Mebbe I never come back! [*Long pause. Then dreamily.*] I t'ink you are de mos' bee-eautiful baby in de whole world.

TOM. [*Loftily.*] No, you don't either.

RITA. [*Eagerly.*] *So—si!* It is true! *Softly to the picture.*] So good-bye, leetle fat boy—good-bye—good-bye! [*She kisses it twice.*]

TOM. [*Turning and seeing her.*] Thank you.

RITA. [*Shaking the locket.*] Dat vas for *'im*, my frien'—not you! [*She holds out the necklace for him to take.*]

TOM. [*Embarrassed.*] Er—don't you want to keep him then?

RITA. Keep 'im?

TOM. Yes, and the necklace, too. I wish—I mean I hope you will.

RITA. But no—I cannot—

TOM. Please—just as a favor to me!

RITA. It is your moder's—

TOM. [*Eagerly.*] I know—that's why!

RITA. But she vould not like it—

TOM. [*A little pompously.*] Of course I realize how you feel about accepting presents of jewelry from men, but I think in this case—it's—er—*quite* all right! [*Her hand has gone instinctively to her string of pearls.*] What are you doing?

RITA. [*Unclasping her own pearls.*] I make for it de place! [*She drops her string of pearls on the desk.*

TOM. [*Heartily.*] Aha! I knew you would! [*Giving her the rest of the package.*] Here! take the earrings, too!

RITA. [*With tender enthusiasm.*] Dio mio! dey are so bee-eautiful!

TOM. Can you see to put them on?

[*By this time the room is filled with twilight shadows. The firelight is warm and mellow.*

RITA. [*Standing on a footstool before the mantel and looking into the glass.*] Oh, yes I can see!

[*She takes off her own earrings, lays them on the mantelpiece and begins putting on his earrings and necklace. He watches her.*

TOM. You know how it clasps?

RITA. [*Busy with the necklace.*] Yes, it is all right— [*Finishing it, and turning gaily to him.*] Ecco! Are dey not be-coming? [*He does not answer.*] Vhy you look at me like dat? Vhat you t'ink of—*hein?*

TOM. [*Simply.*] I was just thinking how mother would have loved you.

RITA. Yes?

TOM. She loved everything that was beautiful and sweet and good. And then your music would have interested her so much! *She* was musical, too, you know.

RITA. Is dat so?

TOM. [*Continuing.*] Yes, that's why I kept her piano when the Worth Street house was sold. I put it over **there**

—so when I'm writing sermons and get all mixed-up, I can just look at it and imagine I'm eight years old again and hear her dear voice singing *Annie Laurie.*

RITA. [*Softly.*] "An-nee Laur-ee?"

TOM. That was her favorite song. [*Hesitating.*] I wish—I wish you'd sing it once before you go.

RITA. I tell you vhat—*I* play an' *you* vill sing!

TOM. [*Embarrassed.*] But I can't—I haven't any voice—

RITA. Come—vhere is it—in dis book?

[*She takes up one of the bound volumes of music lying on the piano.*

TOM. No—the big one underneath—page 27—but really —it's foolish—the idea of my trying to—

RITA. [*Finding it.*] Ah! Now light de candle, please.

[*She puts the volume on the rack.*

TOM. [*Lighting a long paper " spill " from fire and from it lighting the candles on either side of the keyboard.*] It goes up to E—that's pretty high, you know. Of course I wouldn't mind if you weren't a professional. I always help Mr. Gates with the choir, but they're not very critical. [*Taking up his position by her side.*] Give me the note when you come to it.

RITA. [*Playing the little prelude.*] Is dat too fas'?

TOM. A little bit—that's better! [*She strikes his note and pauses, glancing up at him. He hesitates.*] Just wait till I clear my throat—[*He coughs.*] It's so long since I've sung! Now I'm ready—go ahead!

[*He sings, she " conducting " him with her head and one hand whenever possible.*

" Maxwelton braes are bonnie
  Where early fa's the dew,
  And it's there that Annie Laurie
  Gie'd me her promise true."

[*Hastily clearing his throat and speaking.*] This is where it goes up! [*Resuming the song.*]

"*Gie'd me her promise true,*
Which ne'er forgot will be
And for bonnie Annie Laurie
I'd lay me down and dee!"

RITA. [*Playing.*] Bravo! Bravo! You sing ver' nize!

TOM. [*Flattered.*] I'll do better with the next verse—see if I don't! [*Singing.*]

"*Her brow is like the snowdrift,*
Her throat is like the swan,
Her—"

[*Just here Giles open the door at back.*

GILES. I beg pardon, sir. The Deaconesses.

TOM. Get rid of 'em!

GILES. What, sir?

TOM. [*Impatiently.*] I said get rid of 'em!

[GILES *bows and goes out closing the door.*
TOM *resumes the song.*
"*Her face it is the fairest*
That e'er the sun shone on.
That e'er the sun shone on,
And dark blue is her e'e
And for bonnie Annie Laurie
I'll lay me down and dee!"

RITA. [*Softly, not looking up at him.*] It is a song of love.

TOM. Yes. But I never knew it until now. Do you know why?

RITA. No. Tell me.

TOM. Because I never knew what love was—until now.

RITA. [*Sadly.*] An' vhat is love—to you?

[*She plays a little, idly, as she watches him.*

TOM. [*Leaning on the piano.*] It's finding the woman

you want to live with all your life. The woman who'll show you the right way and follow it with you, side by side, shoulder to shoulder, making all the good things seem a little better, and all the hard things—well, not quite so hard. It's knowing she'll be with you at your journey's end, when you're old, and she's old, and you can smile and look into each other's eyes and say " We've done our work together, dear—and I think we've done it well."

RITA. [*After a little pause, her eyes full of tears.*] Oh, my frien', dat love, it is for some, yes—but it is not for me.

TOM. I don't understand—

RITA. [*Wistfully and tenderly.*] For me, love is jus' a leetle light in all dis darkness, a leetle varmt' in all dis col', a leetle flame dat burn—not long, an' den go out. A star dat come an' is so bee-eautiful it bring beeg tears, an' vhen ve dry dee eyes an' look again—de star is gone. I t'ink it is to be a leetle 'appier togedder den ve are apart—vone meenute to lie still in de beloved's arms—vone leetle meenute to forget, my frien'—an' dat is all.

TOM. [*Brokenly.*] My dear—
    [*He comes swiftly to her and puts his hands on her shoulders.*

RITA. [*Rising.*] No—no—

TOM. [*Whispering.*] My dear—my dear—
    [*He draws her to him and holds her tightly in his arms.*

RITA. Oh, vhat you do?

TOM. [*Pressing her to him.*] I love you!

RITA. Don'—

TOM. [*Interrupting.*] And you love me. Now say it—

RITA. [*Piteously.*] No—

TOM. [*Through his teeth.*] You *must*.

RITA. [*Throwing her arms about his neck with deep abandon.*] All right—*I love you*—! Now ve are alone—

you 'ear—an' dere is nodings in de vorld but you an' me! Dis is our time—our leetle meenute dat vill never come again—so shut your eyes—an' 'old me close—an' *love*—

Tom. But, dear, I—

Rita. [*Putting her mouth to his.*] Ssh!

>[*A long kiss. They stand motionless, locked in each other's arms. And just here from the parish house next door comes the sound of an organ and men's voices singing " Ein Feste Burg "—all very faint and far away.*]

Rita. [*At last.*] Vhat is dat?

Tom. It's just the choir—they're practising for to-night—I love you.

Rita. [*Closing her eyes.*] A-ah!

Tom. When will you marry me?

>[*She slowly disengages herself from him and turns away.*

Rita. [*Almost to herself.*] I 'ave not t'ink de en' vould be so soon.

Tom. [*Eagerly.*] When—please tell me when?

Rita. Ask me anodder time—no, never ask me—it is jus' not possible—

Tom. But what's the matter? I don't understand!

Rita. [*Defending herself.*] Vhy you in such a 'urry? You mus' vait!

Tom. [*Coming nearer her.*] I'd wait forever—if there's any hope.

Rita. [*Retreating.*] Please don' come near—

Tom. There *is* hope—isn't there?

Rita. No—no—I 'ave make vone beeg meestake!

Tom. What—?

Rita. I 'ave le˙ you spik vords dat I mus' never 'ear—

Tom. My darling, I—

RITA. I t'ink I 'ave been mad for jus' vone leetle vhile, but now—I cannot marry you. Good-bye.

[*She goes towards door. He stops her.*]

TOM. Why not?

RITA. Oh, let me go!

TOM. Not till you've told me why.

RITA. Can you not on'erstan' vhat is so plain an' clear? Your frien's—dey know. De night I meet you you 'ave see de young men look at me—you 'ave see dere vives an' modders frown an' turn avay—

TOM. *Rita—!* [*He has guessed her meaning.*]

RITA. Dey know vhy I can never marry you—de whole vorld knows—[*Her voice softening.*] An' now I t'ink if you don' min'—I go avay.

[*There is a pause.* TOM *controls himself.*]

TOM. [*Very tenderly.*] No, my dear—not yet. [*He leads her to settee by fire.*] I think—I think you have something to tell me.

RITA. I cannot—no—please do not ask—

TOM. [*Always tender.*] I'm not going to ask—I'm just going to sit here and hold your hand and listen. [*He takes her hand.*] That's what I'm here for, you know—just to help people when they're in trouble and need a friend.

RITA. You are so good!

TOM. [*Quite pale.*] No, I'm not—but you'll find I'm very sympathetic. Why, I remember one day last week—Tuesday, it was, that a little tenement girl named McDougal, came in to see me. We sat here just as we're sitting now and after a while she told me all about it. She was going to be married the next day to a young carpenter over on 8th Street—but there was something she hadn't told him—poor child! She didn't dare. She'd been—treated badly by some brute of man when she was only sixteen years old. Of course he'd left her—and she'd tried to put together the pieces of her life and go on with her work—and then she met the carpenter and fell in love and was going to marry him—and at the last moment her conscience began bothering her—so she came to me.

RITA. An'—vhat you tell 'er?

TOM. Oh, I didn't say much! I just suggested things here and there, and in the end—God bless her! She made up her mind to do the right thing.

RITA. De right—?

TOM. She went home and told him all about it.

RITA. An' den—?

TOM. [*Cheerfully.*] He was a decent sort of fellow and he loved her, so of course he understood—and—well, I married them Wednesday morning and now they're two of the happiest people in New York!

RITA. An' vould *you* feel dat vay, too?

TOM. Me?

RITA. If somevone dat you love—[*Quickly.*] no, don't look at me!—[*Resuming.*] If somevone dat you love come an' say "I am not good—I mus' tell you now because ve love each oder! You are de first man I 'ave ever love—you are de first man I 'ave ever tol'!"

TOM. Well?

RITA. Could you forgive 'er—Meestaire Tom?

TOM. Forgive her—? [*Brokenly, as he catches her in his arms.*] You poor little child!

RITA. [*Wailing.*] No—no—you do not on'erstan'—it is *I* who am not good—

TOM. [*Soothing her.*] There, darling, there! Don't cry. It's all right. You've been fair and brave and honest. You've told me and I forgive you from the bottom of my heart!

RITA. [*Still sobbing.*] Oh—! Oh! I do not see 'ow it is possible—no, I do not see—I don'—I don'—

Tom. Why not? It was a long time ago, wasn't it? When you were poor and struggling and lonely. You didn't know anything about the world—how could you? And you had to live—hunger and misery were right behind you, driving you on—

Rita. Yes—oh, yes—

Tom. But you mustn't think of it any more! You must just remember how afterwards you pulled yourself together and raised your head and said to yourself, "I may have sinned, but that's all over—and from now on I'm going to be a good woman! I'm going to turn the rest of my life into a splendid, beautiful thing! I won't stop until I can be proud of myself!" And oh, my dear—I'm so glad—I'm so glad that you can be—now!

Rita. An' is dat vhy you can forgive me?

Tom. Is what, dear?

Rita. Because it 'appen—so long ago?

Tom. [*With a touch of his profession.*] I naturally believe that all sins, finished and truly repented of, should be forgiven by every Christian man or woman. [*Pause.*]

Rita. [*Gently releasing herself.*] I see—I see!

[*She rises and walks away.*

Tom. [*With an effort to shake off all these ugly things.*] And now that everything's cleared up between us, do you know what we're going to do?

Rita. No. Tell me.

Tom. [*Smiling.*] Go right upstairs, of course, and announce our engagement to Aunt Emma and Mr. Van Tuyl. Come on!

Rita. [*Instinctively.*] No—no—not now—

Tom. What—?

Rita. Vait a leetle—vait until to-morrow—

Tom. But you're sailing to-morrow!

Rita. Yes— dat is vhy—

Tom. [*Smiling.*] Nonsense! If you don't look out, I'll begin to think you're ashamed of me! Come along!
[*He puts his arm about her waist.*

Rita. [*Holding back.*] No, I say—it is too soon—I am not ready—ve mus' vait—

Tom. Wait? What for?

Rita. Mebbe—mebbe dey do not like it vhen ve tell dem!

Tom. Now don't you bother about Aunt Emma! She—

Rita. [*Interrupting.*] Ah, no! I do not bodder about 'er! But—[*She stops.*]

Tom. It surely isn't Mr. Van Tuyl that's worrying you? Why, he's my oldest friend—and father's and mother's, too. He's just like one of the family! Of course we must tell him right off!

Rita. Vhy don' you let *me* tell 'im?

Tom. What?

Rita. To-night—vhen I can see 'im all alone! [*Eagerly.*] Oh, please—please let me tell 'im!

Tom. [*Puzzled.*] But why? What's the matter?

Rita. If ve tell 'im now, 'e vill be so angry!

Tom. Nonsense! And even if he is, we don't care!

Rita. 'E vill say t'ings about me—oh yes, 'e vill!

Tom. But he doesn't *know* anything about you. [*She doesn't answer. He repeats in a different tone.*] Rita, he doesn't *know* anything about you, does he?

Rita. No—I mean—not ver' much—

Tom. What—?

Rita. Jus' a leetle—I tell 'im a leetle vone night in Paris—

Tom. You don't mean—what you've told *me?*

Rita. Yes, an' so if ve go upstairs now an'—

Tom. [*Interrupting.*] But you said just a minute ago that I was the only man you'd ever told—because I was the only man you'd ever loved!

Rita. [*Frightened.*] I 'ave forget—oh, it vas two—t'ree years ago—

Tom. [*Thinking.*] But wait! He's talked to me very openly about you—why, only last Saturday when I went to see him about the new gymnasium—

Rita. Vhat—?

Tom. He used every possible argument—except that one. Why, he never said so much as a word against—

Rita. I know. I—I ask 'im not to.

Tom. [*More and more surprised.*] You—? But—but he wouldn't take your side where *I'm* involved—why, it's incredible!

Rita. Oh, yes, 'e vould—you do not know!

Tom. But why?

Rita. [*Fighting for time.*] Vhy—?

Tom. Yes—there must be a reason.

Rita. Can you not guess?

Tom. No.

Rita. It is because—oh, long ago, you on'erstan'—'e was foolish enough to like me—jus' a leetle—

Tom. *What*—?

Rita. [*Quickly.*] It was not my fault—I cannot 'elp it vhen peoples—

Tom. [*Interrupting.*] When was this?

Rita. Oh, two—t'ree year ago! I did my bes' to stop 'im—but it vas not easy, I tell you dat!

Tom. [*Interrupting.*] Did he want you to marry him?

Rita. [*Trying to speak lightly.*] No—no—it was nodings—nodings at all—'e jus' like to sen' flowers an' 'ear me sing an'—

Tom. [*Interrupting.*] How long did his—attentions last?

Rita. I—I dunno.

Tom. [*Going towards her.*] You don't mean he's in love with you *still?*

Rita. [*With abandon.*] Oh, don't talk about dat any more! Jus' take me in your arms an' kiss me till—

Tom. [*Interrupting.*] And you knew he felt that way—you knew it all this time?

Rita. Yes—I knew—

Tom. Then why didn't you tell me?

Rita. I did not t'ink you vould—like it.

Tom. Like it! Why, it was all right. He can't help loving you, I suppose. There isn't anything to conceal—[*Stopping suddenly.*] Rita, there isn't anything to *conceal?*

Rita. Vhat—?

Tom. Tell me there isn't—tell me—

Rita. [*Retreating.*] I don't know vhat you mean—

Tom. Quick—for the love of God!

Rita. Don't look at me—

Tom. Not Mr. Van Tuyl? *Not he—?*

Rita. [*Terrified.*] Please—oh, please—

Tom. [*With a sudden cry.*] Oh—!

Rita. [*Frantically.*] It is not true! I say it is not true!

Tom. What—?

Rita. Dere 'as been nodings—you make vone terr'ble meestake—

Tom. How do I know?

Rita. [*Striking her breast.*] *I* tell you—*I!*

Tom. But you kept back something before—

Rita. No—

Tom. How do I know you're not doing it again?

Rita. No—I am not! I tell you I am not!

Tom. [*Pulling himself together.*] Ssh—be quiet! They'll hear you upstairs. [*His voice shaking.*] Now we must be calm, both of us,—quite calm and sensible. We must settle this matter here, once and for all. If it's true, I—I beg you—for both our sakes—as you will answer on the Day of Judgment—I beg you to tell me now. [*Pause.*]

RITA. If I say " Yes, it is true! " vould you—vould you again forgive me?

TOM. [*With a cry.*] Ah—! then it *is*—it *is*—

RITA. [*Wildly.*] No—no—

TOM. Will you swear it?

RITA. Yes—I vill swear.

TOM. Put your hand here—on my mother's Testament.

RITA. [*Obeying him.*] So?

TOM. And look me in the eye and say after me—

RITA. Yes?

TOM. " I swear there has been nothing wrong between Mr. Van Tuyl and me."

RITA. [*Faintly.*] O Madonna!

TOM. [*Harshly.*] Swear it!

RITA. [*Opening her eyes.*] Vhat—?

TOM. You won't—?

RITA. " I svear—dere 'as been "—vhat you say?—" nodings wrong betveen—Meestaire Van Tuyl—an' me—"

[*She sways a little.*]

TOM. [*With a sob of relief, as he catches her in his arms.*] Oh, my darling—forgive me—I've been a brute to doubt you—I'm—[*Suddenly.*] What's the matter? Rita—Rita! [*Her head has fallen. She has fainted. He carries her over to the settee, lays her on it, runs to the desk, pours out a glass of water, returns with it, kneels by her side and tries to make her drink.*] My poor little girl—there—it's all right—I'm never going to bother you again—forgive me—oh, my darling, just forgive me this once—[*She is gradually reviving under his caresses and endearments.*] I was out of my head—I didn't know what I was saying—please—please—[*She sits up dizzily.*] What's the matter? Aren't you going to speak to me—? [*She rises unsteadily to her feet.*] Rita—! [*He takes her hand.*

RITA. Let me go!

TOM. But, darling, just listen to me for a moment—

RITA. [*Interrupting.*] I vant to go avay—you don' believe me—you don' love me—

TOM. Yes, I do! I love you more than anything in the world—I love you and I'm going to marry you—

RITA. No—no—I vill never marry you now—never—never any more—

TOM. Rita—!

RITA. [*With passion.*] Vhy you make me to svear dose t'ings? Vhy you make me—?

TOM. Forgive me, dear—please—

RITA. I vill never forgive you. Good-bye.

TOM. No, wait!

[*He stops her at door, taking both her hands.*

RITA. I say—good-bye! [*He stares into her face. Her eyes drop.*] Oh, let me go please! I mus' return to de 'otel—it is so late—you know I alvays sleep before I sing an'—[*Suddenly.*] Vhat for you look at me like dat?

TOM. [*Trying to control himself.*] I believed you when you swore just now—I want it understood that I believed you—

RITA. Vell?

TOM. So—if you don't mind—I think—I think—I'll ask Mr. Van Tuyl to come down here—

Rita. Vhat—?

TOM. And then we'll tell him—we're engaged.

RITA. [*In a sudden fright.*] Ah, no—no—don' do dat—please—I ask you—jus' for me—vait a leetle vhile—

TOM. [*With a sudden wildness, pulling the bell-rope violently.*] Not a minute! Not a second!

RITA. Please—

Tom. I won't!

Rita. No—no—

Tom. Oh, my God—[*Pause. A knock.*] Come in!

[*Enter* Giles.

Giles. You rang, sir?

Tom. Yes. Ask Mr. Van Tuyl to step down here, please. Tell him I'll keep him only a moment.

Giles. Very good, sir.

[*Exit* Giles.

Rita. [*As the door closes.*] Ver' vell. You vill tell him alone. I vill not stay.

Tom. [*Before door.*] You've got to.

Rita. Vhat—?

Tom. I won't let you out.

Rita. Remembair my performance—

Tom. [*Snapping his fingers.*] I don't give *that* for your performance!

Rita. 'E come—I 'ear 'im—[*In desperation.*] O, let me go—*let me go!*

Tom. [*As if struck.*] Rita—don't tell me you're afraid—

Rita. Go avay—let me see 'im first—for jus' vone leetle meenute—it vill be all right—

Tom. [*His suspicions returning.*] I won't—

Rita. [*Wildly.*] Ver' vell den. I don' care!

[*She sits down at the piano and bursts into a Chopin polonaise. The door opens and* Van Tuyl *appears.*

Van Tuyl. [*Genially as he enters.*] Ah—! Still here? We thought you'd—[*Noticing* Tom's *face.*] Why, what's the matter, Tom?

[Rita *stops playing and sits at the piano, looking at the two men.*

Tom. [*Trying to speak naturally.*] Nothing, sir. I—

asked you to come down because—I wanted you to be the first to know of my good luck.

VAN TUYL. Good luck?

TOM. Yes. Madame Cavallini has been good enough to —[*Briefly.*] We're engaged.

VAN TUYL. [*In an expressionless voice.*] Engaged—?

TOM. [*Harshly.*] Yes—engaged—engaged to be married—this lady and myself. [*Pause.*]

VAN TUYL. [*Calmly.*] My dear boy, I congratulate you.

TOM. [*Choking.*] What—?

VAN TUYL. I congratulate you. Madame Cavallini stands alone, as I have always said. And while I confess I am—a bit surprised, I am flattered—[*Turning to her with a bow.*] that she has chosen one of my friends and countrymen for this—great honor.

TOM. Then it's all right—You approve—you give us your consent?

VAN TUYL. [*Turning to him.*] Consent?

TOM. Yes—for the parish, I mean—represented by yourself as senior warden and chairman of the vestry.

VAN TUYL. Most certainly, my dear boy. You know you can always count on me to wish you every happiness.

TOM. [*Baffled.*] Why, you talk as if you *liked* it—

VAN TUYL. [*Not understanding.*] I don't quite—

TOM. [*Interrupting.*] All I can say is, you must have changed your mind since Saturday.

VAN TUYL. Since Saturday?

TOM. Why, don't you remember warning me with tears in your eyes to keep away from this—this lady?

VAN TUYL. [*Smiling.*] Ah, that was Saturday!

TOM. You said we were perfectly unfitted for life together—we were as far apart as the poles through birth and training and career—

Act II] ROMANCE 303

VAN TUYL. [*Deprecating.*] Oh, don't bring up any foolish statements I—

TOM. [*Interrupting.*] You even went so far as to—to mention certain—flaws in Madame Cavallini's character.

VAN TUYL. My dear Tom!

TOM. [*Going on.*] Her temper—selfishness—an absence of stability—

VAN TUYL. Really, my boy, you mustn't hold me to account for—

TOM. [*Interrupting.*] And now, sir, I—I want to ask you here, before us both, if you were absolutely frank on Saturday—

VAN TUYL. What's that?

TOM. [*His voice almost breaking.*] If there were any argument against my—my attachment which you did not see fit to offer at the time—

VAN TUYL. Why, Tom, I don't understand—

TOM. If there was, sir, tell it now—tell it for God's sake —or else forever after hold your peace! [*Pause.*]

VAN TUYL. I don't see why you're so excited, but if it gives you any satisfaction to know I said all I could on Saturday—

TOM. [*Quickly.*] You held nothing back?

VAN TUYL. Why, no, of course not! What's the matter, Tom? [TOM *turns away in silent agony.* RITA *makes a sudden movement.* VAN TUYL *suppresses her with a glance. A moment's pause.* TOM *faces them again, controlling himself with difficulty.*

TOM. Sit down, sir, please.

VAN TUYL. [*Doing so.*] Well?

TOM. [*With difficulty.*] I—I want to apologize beforehand for what I'm going to say. I know I'm acting outrageously—but—I can't help it! [VAN TUYL *makes a move-*

ment towards him.] No, wait! You're my best friend, Mr. Van Tuyl—[*To* RITA.] and you're the woman I want to make my wife. So I—I'm sure you'll both of you be sympathetic and make—allowances for me.

VAN TUYL. [*Heartily.*] Of course, my boy, of course!

TOM. [*Still with difficulty.*] Madame Cavallini has been very frank and open with me, sir. She's just told me—about certain portions of her career—and of course, knowing as I do, how hard it is for girls when they're poor and young—and alone—why, I should be only too glad to tell her it's all right and blot it from my memory forever—but—but—[*He pauses, unable to go on, then rises, gripping the edge of the desk with both hands and leaning over it, haggard and terrible.*] Before I can do that, there's one thing I've got to be sure of.

VAN TUYL. Yes, Tom?

TOM. It seems—you've been an—an admirer of hers for some time—[*As* VAN TUYL *glances at her involuntarily.*] *For God's sake, don't look at her now!* [*Controlling himself.*] And what I've got—to be sure of is that—there never has been anything—you know—between you two—

VAN TUYL. *What—?*

TOM. [*Going on very quickly.*] I've asked her and she's denied it—and I believe her—implicitly, of course—but if—if *you'll* be good enough to deny it, too—oh, merely as a matter of form!—why, I—I shall be much obliged. Well?

VAN TUYL. [*After a slight pause.*] There's one thing I'm not going to deny, and that is my very deep and very true affection for Madame Cavallini. [*Looking at her.*] It is a sentiment none the less deep and true because it has lived for years with no response from her, and I am proud of my hope and my belief that it will continue so long as I'm alive to cherish it. [*Turning to* TOM.] As for the rest of your question, Tom, when you're yourself again you'll agree with me that it deserves no answer. I don't know how such thoughts have wormed their way into your mind, but one thing I *do* know, and that is the time will come when you would give your right hand never to have let them pass your lips. Good-bye—[*To her.*] Good-bye, madame—I offer you the best of wishes—

[*He is turning towards the door when Tom stops him.*

TOM. [*Seeing his hand.*] No, wait—you shan't go until I've begged your pardon—I've been a fool, sir—a perfect fool, but if you can, I want you to forgive me!

VAN TUYL. Don't you think, my boy, you'd better ask Madame Cavallini's pardon first?

TOM. [*Turning to her.*] Rita, darling—I don't know just what to say—but I think if you forgive me again—I can promise I'll never—never—oh, you *do* forgive me, dear, don't you?

RITA. [*Suddenly pulling herself away.*] No—no—I cannot! It is too much—

TOM. What?

RITA. [*Straightening herself up and looking at him.*] I love you—I mus' spik de truth—

VAN TUYL. Be quiet!

RITA. [*To* TOM.] It is all lies vhat ve 'ave said—all lies—*lies!*

TOM. [*Crying aloud.*] No—no—

RITA. I vas 'is mistress till de night I meet you!

TOM. Not Mr. Van Tuyl—not—[*He chokes.*]

VAN TUYL. Tom, listen to me for one minute—

TOM. [*Turning to him.*] Liar—thief—

VAN TUYL. For God's sake, Tom, don't—

TOM. [*With a cry.*] A-ah!

[*He rushes at* VAN TUYL *to strike him down, but she stands before him.*

RITA. [*Gasping.*] 'E lied for me—I tell you 'e lied for

me— [*Pause.* Tom *stands fighting for his control. He regains it, exhausted, and turns to the desk.*

Tom. [*In a whisper.*] Please go—both of you.
  [*He stoops to pick up the little Testament which has dropped to the floor, brushes it involuntarily, and puts it on desk.*

Van Tuyl. Tom, I'd have given everything I have in the world to have spared you this. I want you to remember that—if you can. [*coming towards him.*] Tom, I—

Tom. Don't!

Van Tuyl. [*Half to himself.*] Very well. Good-bye.
  [*He goes out quickly.* Tom *sits down slowly in his desk-chair.*

Rita. [*After trying once or twice to find her voice.*] Meestaire—Meestaire Tom—
  [*He shudders at the sound. She goes to the mirror, takes off his mother's earrings and necklace, kisses locket, and lays them on mantelpiece. Then she puts on her coat, picks up her muff and monkey from chair where she left them earlier in the act.*

Rita. [*Softly to the monkey.*] Basta—basta—poverina mia! [*She stands looking at* Tom. *He makes no sign. Then at last, very simply.*] T'ank you for 'aving loved me.
  [*She drops her veil and goes out. As he hears the door close, he has a few seconds of gasping for breath. Then, burying his face in his arms, he breaks into silent convulsive sobs. From far away comes the sound of the little hand-organ. It is still playing the old waltz.*
  The Curtain Falls.

ACT III

[*SCENE:* Mme. Cavallini's *apartment at the Brevoort House, that night, after the performance. At the left are doors leading to the hall. At the right are two long windows, with a tall old-fashioned gilt mirror and low consol table between. At the back—towards right —is an arch leading to the bedroom, covered with drawn portieres. At left, a smaller door. Opposite the windows are the fireplace and mantel. A fire is burning. A grand piano is covered with a confusion of music, hats, clothes, etc. Towards the centre are a couch and a table. The couch is strewn with various clothes, wigs, costumes, etc. Between the two windows is a perch on which sit, side by side, two stately scarlet macaws. Near the fire is the monkey's cradle—a charming cloud of lace and pale blue satin. There are several open trunks lying about the room in various stages of completed packing. Clothes, of all descriptions, are strewn about in the greatest disorder everywhere. The whole effect of the room is luxurious, yet filled with confusion and a sense of Bohemian life.*

When the curtain goes up, it is night. The gas is lit. Before the fire squats Signora Vannucci—*a fat, untidy old Italian woman with a moustache and long earrings, dressed very gaily, her skirts pinned up, a pair of old soiled pink satin slippers on her feet. She is telling her fortune with a pack of greasy cards, stopping every now and then to turn and stir two saucepans which are cooking over the fire.*]

Signora Vannucci. [*To herself.*] O Dio mio! Non imparta—riproviamo—! [*She gives the saucepan a stir, shuffles, and deals.*] *Picche! Il nove di fiori! Cosa ci hanno queste bestie di carte!—Ah! Il fante di cuori! Forse vuol dire un' amante—chi sà? Il dieci di quadri—! A-ha-he! Posso ancora esser ricca*—[*She laughs to herself. There is a knock at the door.*] *Avanti!*

[ADOLPH *comes in. He is an old German waiter carrying a tray with plates, napkins, glasses, bowl of salad, etc.*] You gotta da garlic—yes?

ADOLPH. [*Putting down tray.*] Two liddle beeces.

SIGNORA VANNUCCI. Cut dem ver' small an' put dem in vhen you maka da salad.

ADOLPH. Madame, she vill be hungry when she back comes from de opera.

SIGNORA VANNUCCI. She eata nodings before she go—she dreenka a leetle vine an' coffee, dat is all. So I come back qveeck an' maka myself da macaroni wid da tomat' sauce—she alvays lika dat!

ADOLPH. Ach! no great artiste vill eat pefore she sing! Do I not know? Have I not de first tenor of de Royal Court Opera of de city of Steichenblätter been? Do I not remember how I feel vhen—

SIGNORA VANNUCCI. [*Gloomily interrupting him.*] You 'ave forgetta da cheese.

ADOLPH. [*Crushed.*] *Du lieber Gott!*

SIGNORA VANNUCCI. [*With a retrospective smile.*] Ah, vhen I was *prima donna* at Bologna an' maka my *début* as *Linda di Chamonix* in da great, da bee-autiful, da gala performance—an' 'is—'ow you say—'is *eccellenza* da duca di Modena, 'e stan' an' clappa de 'an's an' say so loud—"Bravo, Vannucci! Bravo! Bravissimo!"—

ADOLPH. [*Interrupting.*] Your sauce, it burn.

SIGNORA VANNUCCI. [*Rushing to fire.*] *Madonna santa proteggeteci!*

[*She stirs the sauce vigorously.*

ADOLPH. [*Sadly as he mixes salad.*] Ach—so! De good old days—dey are all gone!

SIGNORA VANNUCCI. [*Stirring.*] Da opera now—vhat is ett? Vone beeg noise!

ADOLPH. Dis *Faust an' Mignon*—

SIGNORA VANNUCCI. [*Covering her ears.*] *Impossibili!*

ADOLPH. *Schreklich*—!

SIGNORA VANNUCCI. *Orribili!*

ADOLPH. *Ungeheuer*—!

SIGNORA VANNUCCI. [*Kissing her hand.*] *Ma La Favorita!*

ADOLPH. *Der Freischutz!*

SIGNORA VANNUCCI. *Bellissima!*

ADOLPH. *Wünderschön!*

SIGNORA VANNUCCI. *Celestiale!*

ADOLPH. *Kolossal*—!

SIGNORA VANNUCCI. [*Sighing.*] But ah! who now gotta da voice to seeng dem!

ADOLPH. [*Scornfully.*] Mario—? Bah!

SIGNORA VANNUCCI. [*Loftily.*] Grisi—? Pouf!

ADOLPH. Giuglini—? *Ein schwein*—!

SIGNORA VANNUCCI. La Patti—? *Un pulce*—!

ADOLPH. La Cavallini—?

SIGNORA VANNUCCI. *Ah, si*—la Cavallini!

ADOLPH. [*Patronizingly.*] She 'ave a leedle somet'ing—

SIGNORA VANNUCCI. You bet my life she 'ave! Ah! sometime vhen I stan' in de veengs an' 'old 'er shawl an' leesten—I t'ink it is myself again come back from long ago!

ADOLPH. *Ach, Gott!* I, too, haf treams! An' vhen I my half dollar pay an' de stairs up climb an' de orchestra begin—I shut my eye an' yet vonce more again I am in Steichenblätter—

SIGNORA VANNUCCI. [*Catching his enthusiasm.*] *Si—si!* Da box vhere seeta da duca di Modena—

ADOLPH. I see again the tears upon de ladies' cheeks—

SIGNORA VANNUCCI. Da "Bravos!" of da bee-eautiful young men—

ADOLPH. The opera—it is *Norma*—I am *Pollio*—

SIGNORA VANNUCCI. [*Clasping her hands.*] Ah *Norma—!*

ADOLPH. [*With the bottle of oil in one hand.*] De great duet—act dree—it come at last!

[*He sings softly in German.*

SIGNORA VANNUCCI. [*Rising from fire with spoon still in hand.*] *Più forte! Cosi! Ora! Crescendo!*

[*They sing the duet together in the very old-fashioned operatic way, tremendously in earnest. At the closing high note they fling themselves violently in one another's arms. Just here a small bellboy in buttons, enters from right, whistling between his teeth. He carries a card-tray, and stops, amazed at the sight.*

THE BELLBOY. Where's the madam?

SIGNORA VANNUCCI. [*Kneeling by the fire and stirring.*] She 'ave not yet return.

THE BELLBOY. [*Confidentially.*] Say, wotter ye t'ink she do if I asked her t' put her name in me autograph album?

SIGNORA VANNUCCI. Your—vhat?

THE BELLBOY. [*Proudly.*] Me autograph album! [*Taking it from breast.*] I got Sam McGuire, the famous murderer, an' Edwin Booth, the celebrated actor, not t' mention the lady author o' "Uncle Tom's Cabin" an'—

SIGNORA VANNUCCI. [*Impatiently.*] Go vay! Go vay! Vhat for you come an' talk so much an'—

THE BELLBOY. Hold yer horses, old lady! 'Tain't no use gettin' mad! There's a gent downstairs a-callin' on the madam—see? [*He holds out the salver with card.*

SIGNORA VANNUCCI. [*Irritably.*] Giva me da card—qveeck, leetle animal! Qveeck, I say!

THE BELLBOY. Quit callin' me names, ye big Eyetalian rag-bag, or I'll—

ADOLPH. [*Interrupting.*] Ssh! Keep still! I vip you good! [*The bellboy hands her salver.*

SIGNORA VANNUCCI. [*Reading card.* A-ah! It is milor! 'E 'ave come back! *Santi benedetti!* [*To the bellboy.*] Go—breenga 'im in! [*To* ADOLPH.] An' leesten, my frien', a bottle of champagne!

ADOLPH. [*With tray, at door.*] Champagne?

SIGNORA VANNUCCI. [*Joyously.*] You bet my life! Da besta you got!

[ADOLPH *goes out. She rises, puts card on piano, and begins unpinning her skirts, etc. The bellboy profits by this to steal some grapes and a cake from the table. She turns and sees him.*

Ah, demonietto!

[*She rushes at him with hand upraised.*

THE BELLBOY. Rag-bag!

[*He escapes. She hastily attempts to tidy the room, closes a couple of trunks, etc. Then, singing an incredible cadenza, she puts on a scarf, sticks an ostrich feather in her hair and is admiring the result in the long mirror, when there is a knock at the door to the hall.*

SIGNORA VANNUCCI. [*With a long trill.*] Avanti!

[*The door opens and* VAN TUYL *appears.*

VAN TUYL. [*Entering.*] Well, signora! I haven't seen

you for some time, have I? You're younger and more beautiful than ever!

SIGNORA VANNUCCI. [*Shaking hands.*] Ah, milor—you maka da joke as alvays! But I don' care—I am so full of joy because you 'ave come!

VAN TUYL. Thanks very much. [*Looking about.*] How's the menagerie? [*To the parrots.*] Remember me, old lady—eh?

SIGNORA VANNUCCI. Dey are full of love for milor—*ecco!* See! Manrico, 'e visha to keess 'is 'and!

VAN TUYL. Bite it, you mean. [*Going to fire.*] Where's Adelina—? [*Seeing the cradle.*] Oh!

SIGNORA VANNUCCI. She 'ave jus' eata vone greata beeg suppair.

VAN TUYL. [*Looking into cradle.*] Six olives—strawberry jam—a few hothouse grapes—

SIGNORA VANNUCCI. [*Rapturously.*] An' da cupa of chocolate! Ah, milor—'e 'ave recolleck ev'ryt'ings!

VAN TUYL. [*Seeing the saucepans by the fire.*] What's that you're cooking—not your famous macaroni?

SIGNORA VANNUCCI. It is for madame. She eata nodings alla da day. An' she looka so vhite an' seeck—*ah, Madonna!* I gotta vone great beeg fear!

VAN TUYL. How did she get through the performance?

SIGNORA VANNUCCI. Milor vas not dere—?

VAN TUYL. No.

SIGNORA VANNUCCI. 'E 'ave not 'eard—?

VAN TUYL. No.

SIGNORA VANNUCCI. [*Volubly.*] Ah, she maka—vhat you say?—*un triomfo enorme!* It maka me t'ink of dat so splendid night I sing *Lucrezia Borgia* an' 'is Excellenza da duca di Modena, 'e—

VAN TUYL. [*Interrupting.*] Yes, I remember. [*Looking at his watch.*] Madame is late.

Signora Vannucci. She say *addio* to Signor Strakosch an' de oder artistes an' receive da present—
Van Tuyl. Really?
Signora Vannucci. [*Nodding.*] Da pin vid da big rubee, an' de bracelet vid many pearl, an' ah! Madonna!—da di'mon' crown from alla da signora of New York!

> [*During the following she works at the packing and finally finishes and shuts one more of the trunks.*

Van Tuyl. [*Not paying much attention.*] It's true—the city's gone quite mad.
Signora Vannucci. *Dio mio!* Vhen I recolleck dat tomorrow ve go so far avay from dis country an' milor an' all da mon'—it maka my 'eart feel jus' like 'e vill break!
Van Tuyl. [*Smiling.*] Poor little heart!
Signora Vannucci. An' vhen do ve see milor again?
Van Tuyl. Soon, I hope. But in the interval, signora, I want you to enjoy yourself, so—

> [*Putting his hand in his pocket and taking out his wallet.*

Sigora Vannucci. [*Sidling up to him.*] Oh, milor—!
Van Tuyl. [*Selecting a bill.*] So here's a little something just to remind you that—
Signora Vannucci. [*Interrupting.*] Oh, no, milor—you already giva me so much—no—no—it is imposs'—

> [*She holds out her hand greedily.*

Van Tuyl. [*Putting bill in hand.*] Nonsense! As friend to friend! There! You can change it when you get to Naples.
Signora Vannucci. [*Enthusiastically, as she puts bill in stocking.*] Ah, milor—'e is so good! Jus' like 'is Excellenza da duca di Modena—

VAN TUYL. [*Interrupting.*] I believe you. [*Suddenly.*] Wait! What's that?

> [*There is an instant's pause. From far away come the distant strains of "Yankee Doodle," played on a brass band. During the following scene the music grows nearer, and beneath it can be heard the vague, confused noise of many people shouting.*]

SIGNORA VANNUCCI. [*After listening a moment.*] Da music— [*She goes quickly to window, opens it, steps out on balcony and looks up street.*]

VAN TUYL. [*Following her.*] A brass band!

> [*He stands by window.*]

SIGNORA VANNUCCI. [*As the music grows louder.*] Santi buonissimi! Vhat is dat dey play?

VAN TUYL. [*Opening the window wide and joining her on the balcony*]. "Yankee Doodle!"

SIGNORA VANNUCCI. [*Suddenly.*] Ah! Dey come! Dey come!

VAN TUYL. [*As the sound increases.*] Where? [*He leans out, too*]. Fourteenth Street! That's *en route* from the Academy—

SIGNORA VANNUCCI. [*Who grows more and more excited as the scene proceeds.*] Ecco! See—!

VAN TUYL. Torches—! By Jove, it's a regular Republican rally!

SIGNORA VANNUCCI. More peoples—an' more—an' more an' more dey come!

VAN TUYL. Every fellow with his hat off—[*Shivering.*] and zero weather, too.

SIGNORA VANNUCCI. [*Pointing.*] See—de peoples in de vindows! Dat so fat man—vhat is dat 'e say?

VAN TUYL. [*Raising his voice above the uproar.*] I can't hear! [*The music stops.*

SIGNORA VANNUCCI. [*At a loud roar of "Bravo!" "Cavallini!" "Hurrah!" etc.*] Ah! She come—she come! [*She claps her hands and leans far out.*]

VAN TUYL. [*Leaning out, too.*] Where?

SIGNORA VANNUCCI. [*Pointing.*] Dere—do you not see da carriage?

VAN TUYL. But where's the coachman—where are the horses—? Good Lord! if those young fools aren't dragging it themselves!

SIGNORA VANNUCCI. Ah! vhen I was prima donna at Bologna an' singa *Lucrezia Borgia* for—

VAN TUYL. [*Interrupting and chuckling to himself.*] In evening dress—without any overcoats! By Jove, what a lark!

SIGNORA VANNUCCI. [*Suddenly.*] Ah! Eccola là! Bellaza mia! Come è bella! You see 'er—yes?

VAN TUYL. No—that tall young devil's in the way! [*Suddenly.*] Ah, *there* she is! [*To himself.*] By Jove! By—*Jove!* [*He stares spell-bound. The band, now much nearer, slowly begins "Way Down Upon the Swaunee Ribber." The torchlight illumines the two figures on the balcony. The procession now is almost underneath them. The music stops. There is a burst of cheering.* SIGNORA VANNUCCI *waves her handkerchief wildly.*

SIGNORA VANNUCCI. Evivva! Evivva! Brava Cavallini! Brava regina! Ecco mi alla finestra! Guarda alla tua povera vecchia Vannucci— [*In delight.*] Ah! Ecco! Cosi va bene! [*She laughs and waves. To* VAN TUYL.] She look up—she see us!

[*Van Tuyl takes off his hat and bows in a very stately way. Suddenly the glitter of a rocket is seen in the street outside.*

SIGNORA VANNUCCI. *Ehi! Ehi! Cosa fate?* [*Another rocket goes off and the red glow of Bengal light is seen from the street below, lasting for a moment and then dying away.*] *Ah! Maledetti!*
 [*She clutches* VAN TUYL *and crosses herself.*
VAN TUYL. [*Reassuringly.*] It's all right—those fellows in the corner are setting off some fireworks, that's all.
 [*There is a great cheer from the crowd.*
SIGNORA VANNUCCI. She come—she descend from da carriage—Look! look 'ow da young men kissa 'er 'and! [*There are more rockets and the band begins to play "Kennst Du Das Land." From below is heard a volley of shouts and cheers and laughter.*] Dere! Up-a da step! So—! At las' she is inside— [*Coming back quickly into the room.*] Qveeck! Shuta da vindow—dis room is all dam' col'*—*[*He steps inside and closes the window. The fireworks are still seen, but the music and crowd are heard more faintly.* SIGNORA VANNUCCI *bustles about, putting a new log on the fire, adjusting furniture, etc.*] So! Dere! Ecco! Dat is right! Vill milor 'elp me vid dis chair—? an' da table—more near da fire—Lika dat! [*Suddenly.*] Madonna mia! I 'ave forget—[*She quickly pulls back the portières over arch at back, revealing the bedroom. There is a canopied bed, turned down, with elaborate pillows, etc. A small lamp burns on its head, casting a warm glow. On the bed is a nightgown case, heavily embroidered. A luxurious negligée of fur and velvet lies across a near-by chair, with a pair of slippers beneath.* SIGNORA VANNUCCI *picks them up and comes back immediately into the sitting-room. She hangs the robe on a chair close to fire and puts the slippers where they, too, will warm*] Milor, 'e recolleck dis robe—?
VAN TUYL. [*Helping her arrange it.*] Millefleurs!

SIGNORA VANNUCCI. [*Laughing.*] Ah, vhat good time milor 'e giva us dere! I vish dat—
> [*There is a knock at the door and before anyone can answer it is opened, and* ADOLPH *appears hurriedly, carrying a champagne bucket.*]

ADOLPH. [*Excitedly.*] You haf hear—? You haf seen? Look dere! [*He points to fireworks outside.*] Mein Gott im Himmel! [*He puts down the campagne by the table. The bellboy bursts in excitedly.*]

THE BELLBOY. [*With a long whistle.*] Whew—! Holy cats! This town ain't seen the like since the Prince o' Wales was here! [*There is an especially brilliant effect of fireworks outside.*] Jee-rusalem—! [*He rushes to the window. The Head Waiter, two subordinates and two hall boys in uniform come in, one after the other, talking among themselves and laden with " floral offerings " of all kinds. There are wreaths, " set-pieces " in the form of harps, hearts, etc. One large bird with " Nightingale " worked in white roses upon red, etc. Some have the American and Italian colors attached, others have sentiments such as " Say Not Good-bye," " Our Mignon," " Addio," etc.*]

ONE WAITER. Ouvrez la porte!

ANOTHER WAITER. Oui—ne voyez-vous pas que je suis occupé—?

HEAD WAITER. Où faut-il poser ces engins-ci, madame?

SIGNORA VANNUCCI. Sur le piano—bien! c'est ça! Dis-donc—et ce que tu as sur la table— [*To* VAN TUYL.] Are dey not bee-eautiful? Santi benissimi! [*To the waiters*]. Va doucement, idiot—! Tu vas l'abîmer—! Penchez celle-la à côté de la chaise—

HEAD WAITER. Vite! Vite! Espèce d'un escargot—! Madame va venir—toute de suite! Ah, la voilà—! Comme elle est ravissante—!

M. Baptiste. [*Outside.*] *Ah, madame, nous sommes infiniment heureux de prendre part dans le triomphe d'une artiste si célèbre—*

> [*As he has spoken, he has entered and stands respectfully on one side of the door, bowing and rubbing his hands. He is the hotel proprietor and wears a frock-coat.*

Rita. [*Entering.*] *Merci, monsieur—merci mille fois—vous êtes trop aimable—* [*To* Signora Vannucci *in a whisper.*] *Per l'amor di Dio, mettili fuori! Non posso più—* [*She is in gorgeous evening dress, glittering with jewels. On her head is a crown of diamonds. Her cloak is purple. In one hand she carries a wreath of laurel, tied with a golden ribbon. With the other she holds a great armful of white roses. She is very pale and exquisitely gracious. The music comes to an end just after her entrance. There is a renewed burst of cheering outside.*] *Ils sont toujours là? Ecoutez—qu'est-ce qu'ils disent?*

M. Baptiste. *C'est très confus, madame—* [*To the bellboy.*] Eh, you! Dose peoples out dere, vhat is it dey say?

The Bellboy. [*Shrilly.*] They're yellin' fer a speech!

> [*There are indeed heard loud cries of "Speech!" "Just a little one!" "Come on!" etc.*

M. Baptiste. [*To* Rita.] *Si madame était assez aimable de leur addresser—*

Rita. [*Drawing back.*] *Ah, non—non—c'est impossible—*

M. Baptiste. *Trois paroles, vous savez—*

Rita. *Vraiment, monsieur—je suis si fatiguée—*

The Bellboy. [*Yelling inside.*] They won't go way!

M. Baptiste. *Je vous prie, madame—pour l'honneur de l'hôtel—*

RITA. [*In a flash of petulance.*] Non. Je réfuse—entendez vous? Je réfuse absolument! [*Turning away.*] Ah, par example—c'est trop fort!

SIGNORA VANNUCCI. [*Coaxingly.*] Ti prego, cara.

RITA. [*Stamping her foot.*] Dio bono! Per che cosa mi prendete? [*There is a renewed outburst from the crowd.*]

VAN TUYL. [*Speaking for the first time.*] Madame, your public's calling you.

RITA. Vhat—?

VAN TUYL. [*Simply.*] You must obey. [*Pause.*]

RITA. [*In a low tone.*] Open de vindow.

> [*The bellboy does so, the noise is heard very much more clearly. She lays down her wreath, then goes slowly to the window.*]

M. BAPTISTE. Ah, que madame est bonne—

> [RITA *steps out on balcony. There is a great cheer as she appears, the red Bengal light, blazing up again, falls fitfully upon her figure. There is the hiss and glare of many rockets set off simultaneously. The band plays a fanfare—the general effect is a blare of light, noise and splendor. She stands in the midst of it all,—bowing, smiling and holding up her hand for silence. In the room behind her everyone is applauding.* BAPTISTE *utters an occasional " Bravo! " and* SIGNORA VANNUCCI *ostentatiously wipes away her tears. Then quite suddenly there is a silence. A man's voice is heard yelling " If you don't feel like talkin'—sing! " There is a burst of laughter, cries of " Shut up! " " Give her a chance! " etc., and silence again falls. A little pause.*]

RITA. [*Simply and tenderly.*] Sveet ladies—gentlemen—dear peoples who 'ave been so good to me! I do not know your names an' faces—I cannot follow you into your 'omes, an' laugh an' veep vit' you in every joy an' sorrow. I can jus' sing a leetle, an' pray de saints dat somet'ing in my song vill spik to you an' say—[*Holding out her arms to them.*] "I love you! You are all I 'ave to love in dis beeg vorld!" [*There are cheers from below, cries of "That's the ticket!" "Hear that?" "Shut up!" "Let her go on!" etc.*] Mebbe you don' on'erstan' jus' vhat dat mean—you who 'ave 'usban's, vives an' leetle children, too! [*With a smile.*] Ah, vell! I vould not like it dat you should! I only tell you so you feel like doing for me vone las' great kin'ness— [*There are cries of "What is it?" "Tell us!" "Give us a chance!" etc., from below. She takes a step forward and speaks very earnestly.*] To-morrow I go far avay. Mebbe sometime I sing for you again— [*Cheers and cries of "Of course!" "That's right!" "Come back soon!" etc. She puts up her hand for silence.*]—an' mebbe not. Who knows? But if t'rough all your 'appy, 'appy lives you carry, vay down deep, vone leetle t'ought of me—vone golden memory of my song—wherever I am, dear frien's, oh! I vill know it an' be glad! [*Shouts of "We will!" "That's easy!" "Couldn't help it!" "Trust us!" etc. Her tone changes. She continues with tender playfulness.*] In my country ve 'ave a leetle—vhat you say?—t'ing ve tell each oder vhen ve say "Addio"—"*Che le rose fioriscano nei vostri cuori fin ch'io ritorno a coglierle!*" May de roses blossom in your 'eart until I come to gadder dem again!

[*There is a great shout from the adoring crowd. "Good-bye!" "Good luck!" "Come back soon!" "We'll wait for you!" etc., etc., are heard. The band begins to* play, very slowly, "Auld Lang Syne." The cheering continues. There is a final burst of fireworks. RITA tosses one of her white roses over the balcony, there is a renewed shout, she smiles and follows it with another and another, until they are gone. Then, still smiling and showing her empty hands, she blows a last kiss and steps inside, shutting the window behind her. There has been applause from the people in the room at the close of her little speech, and now there is a general movement forward to congratulate her.

M. BAPTISTE. [*Effusively.*] Ah, madame, mes compliments! C'était parfait!

RITA. Merci—merci—

SIGNORA VANNUCCI. [*Embracing her.*] Amore mio—! Come sei bella!

RITA. Ah, non era niente—

VAN TUYL. [*Formally.*] Madame, my congratulations!

RITA. T'ank you ver' much—I—

[*She staggers suddenly, leaning on a chair and putting her hand to her head. There is a moment's pause, then everyone speaks at once.*

SIGNORA VANNUCCI. [*Rushing to her.*] Tesoro mio—! Cos'e'—?

M. BAPTISTE. Mais elle est malade—

VAN TUYL. [*To* ADOLPH.] A glass of water—quick!

[*He brings it hurriedly.*

SIGNORA VANNUCCI. [*To* RITA.] Bevi.

RITA. [*Recovering and refusing the glass.*] No—sto benone— [*To* BAPTISTE.] J'ai la tête en feu—mille pardons—[*She smiles.*]

M. Baptiste. [*Sympathetically.*] *Ah oui, madame—je comprends—des fois, vous savez, ça arrive—*

Signora Vannucci. [*To* Van Tuyl.] She 'ave eat nodings for vone—two day! [*To* Baptiste.] *Monsieur, vous savez madame—elle est au bout de ses forces—alors, vous comprenez—*

M. Baptiste. *Mais certainement—*[*To the waiters, chasseurs, bellboys, etc.*] *Assez—assez, mes enfants! Dites bon soir à madame et sauvez-vous—!*

[*They all huddle towards the door.*

The Bellboy. [*To* Adolph *who is trying to pull him along.*] Leggo o' me! Don't ye see this is my only chance? [*He struggles.*]

Adolph. [*Under his breath.*] Ssh! Be still!

A Waiter. [*Officiously*]. *Tais-toi!*

The Head Waiter. [*Angrily.*] *Nom d'un pipe—! Enlevez cet enfant-là—!*

The Bellboy. [*Loudly, as they all try to pull him.*] I will not! [*Calling to* Rita.] Say!

Rita. You vant to spik to me—yes? Come, I vill leesten! [*The waiters release him.*

The Bellboy. [*Triumphantly to them.*] Ya—ya! Did ye ever get left?

[*He turns to* Rita *and suddenly becomes horribly embarrassed.*

Rita. [*Smiling.*] Vell?

The Bellboy. [*All in one breath, speaking very rapidly.*] Beggin' yer pardon an' thankin' ye for all favors past an' present would it cause ye too much inconvenience t' affix yer autograph to this little album thus joinin' the large company o' famous ladies an' gents what have spread sunshine in the life of a po'r bellboy!

Rita. [*Bewildered.*] Vhat—? [*To* Baptiste.] *Que dit-il, le p'tit?*

M. BAPTISTE. [*Smoothly.*] *Oh, c'est votre autographe, madame*—[*Under his breath as he glances ferociously at the boy.*] *Sacré p'tit cochon*—

RITA. *Mais certainement*— [*To the bellboy holding out her hand for book.*] 'Ere—vhere shall I—?

THE BELLBOY. [*Gratefully giving her the book and a pencil.*] Say, yer a real Jim Dandy! [*Pointing to the page.*] Right there—between P. T. Barnum an' General Grant! [*As she writes.*] I've been savin' that space for two years, but holy Moses! I guess I'll never get anybody t' beat *you!*

RITA. [*Returning him book.*] So—! Be good boy—vork 'ard—an' grow up fine, big Amer'can man! Vait! [*Picking up a wreath of roses and smilingly putting it round his neck.*] A souvenir!

THE BELLBOY. T'anks. But if yer givin' away souvenirs, there's one I'd like more'n this!

RITA. [*Innocently.*] An' vhat is dat?

THE BELLBOY. [*Taking his courage in both hands.*] Would ye—would ye give me a kiss?

[*A movement of horror on the part of the waiters, proprietors, etc.*

RITA. [*Smiling as she makes believe to box his ears, then bending over and kissing him.*] Barabbin—! [*Pushing him towards door.*] Now run—qveek—qveek—!

THE BELLBOY. [*As he dashes out.*] S'elp me Gawd, I'll never wash that side o' my face again!

RITA. [*To all the waiters, etc., as they go out.*] *Bon soir! Bon soir! Merci bien*—*bon soir, Adolph*—

THE WAITERS. *Bon soir, Madame*—*bon soir*—

[*They go out.*

M. BAPTISTE. [*Kissing her hand.*] *A demain, madame*—! *Et dormez bien!*

RITA. *Merci*—*merci, cher m'sieur*—

HEAD WAITER. [*Kissing her hand.*] *Ah, madame, vous savez nous serons désolés de vous perdre—!*

RITA. [*Murmuring politely.*] *Ah, m'sieur—c'est très aimable de votre part! Bon soir—bon soir!*

[*They go out.* RITA, SIGNORA VANNUCCI *and* VAN TUYL *are left alone.*

RITA. [*Turning away with a sigh of lassitude.*] Oh—! Oh—! Oh—! *Son cosi stanca—*

SIGNORA VANNUCCI. [*Sympathetically.*] *Poverina!*

RITA. [*To the parrots.*] *Bèh, Manrico, come stai stassera—eh? E tu, Leonora bella—*[*Giving them a lump of sugar from the table.*] *Ecco—! Per celebrare!*

[*She turns away, takes a cigarette from a box on a small table and lights it.* VAN TUYL, *leaning against the piano, smokes a cigarette quietly and watches her.* SIGNORA VANNUCCI *bustles about the fire, preparing the negligée, slippers, etc.*

SIGNORA VANNUCCI. [*Always speaking as one would to a spoilt, tired child.*] *Vieni, piccina! Levati il mantello! Guarda! Ecco la tua veste da camera tutta bella calda—*

RITA. [*Blowing out her match and turning vacantly.*] Eh—? [*Understanding.*] *Ah, già—il mio mantello—*

[*She drops her cloak carelessly on the floor as she comes over to the fire and stops by the monkey's cradle. She draws over it a small monogrammed blanket, which hangs over the foot, and carefully tucks it in.*

RITA. [*Smoking and gently rocking the cradle.*] *Va bene—dormi—dormi, belleza mia! Mamma è qui, vicino a te—dormi, anima mia—dormi—dormi—*

SIGNORA VANNUCCI. [*Coming to her with a large jewel-case.*] *La tua corona, cara—e i tuoi gioielli—*

RITA. [*Putting her hand to her brow.*] Oh, my 'ead—it is so tired—*Eccola*—!

  [*She slowly and listlessly takes off the crown, her necklace, bracelets, brooches, rings, etc., and gives them to the* VANNUCCI. *The latter puts them in the jewel-case.*

SIGNORA VANNUCCI. [*While this is going on.*] *E la collana—così si fà—ora gli anelli—ora dammi il tuo braccio che ti levo i braccialetti—*

RITA. [*Petulantly, as* SIGNORA VANNUCCI *pinches her in unclasping a bracelet.*] *Fà attenzione—che mi fai male!*

SIGNORA VANNUCCI. [*Quickly.*] *Oh, scusa—scusa, cara!*

  [*She shuts the case and puts it in the inside room.*

RITA. [*Sitting down on the floor before the fire where the cards are scattered and speaking in an odd voice.*] *Per l'ultima volta—chissà cosa diranno?*

  [*She recovers herself with an effort, gathers up the cards, shuffles, and begins to deal, her cigarette still in her mouth.*

SIGNORA VANNUCCI. [*Coming from the inner room.*] *Ah, lascia le carte stassera!*

RITA. [*Paying no attention to her.*] *La carta di mezzo a destra—così!* [*Counting.*] *Una—due—tre—dieci! Così!*

  [*She deals and moves about the cards in a mystic pattern.*

SIGNORA VANNUCCI. [*Kneeling by her and taking off her slippers, trying not to disturb her.*] *Eccoci!* [*Feeling her feet.*] *Madonna mia! Come son freddi—!*

RITA. [*Busy with the cards.*] *Il rè di cuori cambia posto col fante—*[*She kicks viciously at the* VANNUCCI. *Then resuming.*] *E il fante coll'asso—*

SIGNORA VANNUCCI. [*Gingerly trying to put a slipper on the other foot.*] *Adagio! Adagio!* [*As she succeeds.*]

Ecco. E già finita! [*Undoing* Rita's *dress.*] *Adesso leviamo questo—ci vuole un momento solo—*

Rita. [*Over her shoulder.*] *Via!* [*Resuming.*] *Metto l'ultimo quadro su il primo cuore—*

Signora Vannucci. [*As before.*] *Ti prego, cara—un-momentino—*

Rita. [*In sudden anger.*] *Lasciami stare—! O ti do una lavata di capo—*

Signora Vannucci. [*Appealing to* Van Tuyl.] Milor —'e see—she villa not let me—

[Rita *solemnly crosses herself thrice.*

Van Tuyl. [*Tossing away his cigarette and rising.*] Rita.

Rita. [*Looking up.*] Vhat—?

Van Tuyl. [*Quietly.*] Stand up. The signora wants to put on your dressing-gown.

Rita. [*Whimpering as she tosses her cigarette into the fire and rises.*] Oh, dear! Vhat for you make me—

Van Tuyl. [*Interrupting.*] Ssh—!

[*During the following, with the* Vannucci's *help she slips off her ball-gown and puts on the elaborate negligée.*

Rita. [*Simply, still looking at him.*] Vhy you come 'ere?

Van Tuyl. Don't you want to see me?

Rita. Oh, I dunno—I am so tired—

Van Tuyl. [*Taking one of her hands.*] Poor little thing!

Rita. Yes, dat is right—poor leetle—[*Suddenly and viciously to* Vannucci.] *Per carità! Credi che sia fatta di legno—?*

Signora Vannucci. [*Panic-stricken.*] *Scusi tanto, cara mia! Va bene,—cosi!*

[*She goes off into the inner room, carrying the dress.*

Rita. [*In a sulky voice to* Van Tuyl.] She mos' ver' nearly break my arm!

> [*She drops on the floor again and lies at full length, her chin in her hands, studying the cards.*

Van Tuyl. [*Smiling.*] And what do the cards say—eh, little Italian sorceress?

Rita. Dey say—dey say—[*She looks far away.*] You did not see 'im veep!

Van Tuyl. What?

Rita. [*As before.*] 'E veep jus' like a leetle boy—vhen first 'e meet de badness of de vorld—

Van Tuyl. [*Concerned.*] Ah, don't, my dear! Don't think of it any more!

Rita. [*Looking down again at the cards.*] T'ree club —dat mean a long, long journey—

Van Tuyl. [*Cheerfully.*] Well! You're certainly going away. What comes next?

Rita. Vour—five di'mon'—an' good vones, too. Dat mean success an' money—vhat you say?—great fame. Only to reach it I mus' go t'rough much.

Van Tuyl. You'll get there—never fear!

Rita. [*Closing her eyes.*] Ah, my frien', I t'ink I am too tired to try.

Van Tuyl. [*Sympathetically.*] I know it's hard, my dear, but—

Rita. [*Interrupting.*] 'E vould not spik to me vone leetle vord! I say "T'ank you for 'aving loved me!"—jus' like dat!—an' den I vait. But 'e say nodings—so I go avay.

Van Tuyl. [*Pained.*] Don't, dear, it's no use! [*Pointing to a card.*] What's that jack of hearts doing up here in the corner?

Rita. Mebbe 'e is a blond young man who give to me 'is

'eart—[*Breaking off.*] 'Ow long you t'ink, before 'e vill forget?

Van Tuyl. Ssh!

Rita. [*Returning to cards.*] Ah, che m'importa? [*Pointing to the jack.*] Dat blond young man—look! 'Ow 'e is far from me!

Van Tuyl. [*Looking at cards.*] From you—? Oh, of course! You're the red queen down in the middle of all those spades. They're nothing bad, I hope?

Rita. You are among dem.

Van Tuyl. I—?

Rita. Yes, an' de oders, too—see! You are all about me—dere is no vay out.

Van Tuyl. But, dear, I—

Rita. [*Beginning with a little smile.*] My—vhat you say? [*Tenderly.*]—my flames—my splendid vones of whom I vas so proud—look! 'ow you are black, an' strong —ah, santa Madonna! I 'ave give you ev'ryt'ings, an' now vhen love, 'e come an' smile an' 'old out 'is dear 'ands, I cannot give—no, cruel vones! You 'ave leave me nodings —you 'ave take it all—

[*She sweeps away the cards and buries her face in her hands.*]

Van Tuyl. [*Gently.*] No. Not all. No one could do that. [*Changing his tone.*] Come and play for me! Please, there's a dear!

Rita. [*Vacantly.*] Play—?

Van Tuyl. [*Standing above her.*] Yes. A little music will do you good.

Rita. Music—?

Van Tuyl. [*Simply.*] That's left, my dear. [*Pause.*]

Rita. [*Half to herself.*] Yes—dat is lef'. [*To him.*] Vell, vhat you vant I play?

[*She holds out her hands for him to help her up.*

VAN TUYL. [*Doing so.*] Try something of our old friend Abbé Liszt. You know, that thing I used to like so much—all stars and jasmine—voices in the night—

> [*She sits at the piano and plays.*

VAN TUYL. [*Delighted.*] That's it! [*He hums the air lightly.*] By Jove—! Isn't that beautiful? What's it called?

RITA. [*Playing.*] A dream of love—

VAN TUYL. Of course! So it is! [*She breaks off.*] What's the matter?

RITA. I 'ave vake up—dat is all. De dream is gone—

> [*She buries her face in her hands.* VAN TUYL *puts his hand gently on her shoulder. There is an instant's pause.* SIGNORA VANNUCCI *comes bustling in from the other room.*

SIGNORA VANNUCCI. [*entering.*] Adesso! Siamo bell'e pronti per—[*She sees* RITA's *position.* VAN TUYL *makes a gesture for her to be still. She stops in the middle of her phrase. Then, under her breath.*] Poverina!

> [*She catches* VAN TUYL's *eye, makes a gesture towards* RITA, *then to macaroni at fire, next to table—then pantomime of eating. He nods assent. With every evidence of satisfaction she goes over to fire and takes up the macaroni, pours the sauce over it, and stirs it.*

VAN TUYL. [*Turning to* RITA, *speaking kindly and cheerfully.*] Supper's ready!

RITA. [*Stifled.*] I am not 'ungry.

VAN TUYL. [*Pleading.*] Oh, please! Why, the signora has taken all the trouble to cook your favorite macaroni—

SIGNORA VANNUCCI. [*From fire.*] Al sugo—sono buonissimi!

RITA. No—no—no—

VAN TUYL. Think how disappointed she'll be—[*Raising her.*] There! Come along, little girl—[*Showing her the table.*] Doesn't that salad look good? We'll sit you down in this big armchair at the head of the table—[*Doing so as he speaks.*] and I'll be butler, with my napkin over my arm—so! [*Imitating a servant's manner.*] And will madame drink Chianti or a little champagne—? [*Looking at the label on the bottle.*] Roznay et Perrault, '52—not too dry, I venture to recommend it. Champagne—? Very good, madame—I'll open it at once! [*He begins to do so.*]

SIGNORA VANNUCCI. [*Serving her with spaghetti.*] Ecco! Che buon odore? [*Sprinkling it with cheese.*] Mettiamo abbastanza formaggio—

VAN TUYL. [*Pulling the cork and filling a glass.*] There! That's a happy sight for any prima donna! Just taste it now and tell me if it's all right. If not, I'll send down and —[*As she refuses the glass.*] Please, dear! You really need it!

SIGNORA VANNUCCI. [*As one speaks to a child.*] Macchè! Non mangi? [*Coaxingly.*] Ti prego—!

VAN TUYL. [*Offering her again the glass.*] Just as a favor—please. [*She shakes her head.*

SIGNORA VANNUCCI. [*Winding a great coil of spaghetti around the end of a fork and holding it in front of* RITA's *mouth.*] Questo pochino—presto! presto! Apri la bocca! [*As* RITA *draws her head away and the spaghetti falls to the plate.*] Santo Dio!

> [*A pause of discouragement. She and* VAN TUYL *look at each other and shrug their shoulders. Then a happy idea comes to the signora. Behind* RITA's *back, she gestures towards* VAN TUYL, *then to the spaghetti, pantomime of his sitting at*

table opposite RITA, *and eating and drinking. He smiles and nods.*

VAN TUYL. [*To* RITA.] You know the sight of that macaroni's making *me* hungry? I wonder if there'd be enough to give me just a—

SIGNORA VANNUCCI. [*Interrupting and running to serve him.*] But certainly! Now if milor 'e jus' sita downa— [*As* VAN TUYL *does so, opposite* RITA.] Ah, dat is all right! *You* lika da macaroni, I bet my life!

[*She serves him.*

VAN TUYL. Here! That's enough! Thanks. [*As he pours himself a glass of wine.*] And just a swallow of champagne—I declare, I feel quite famished! [*Pause. He does not touch anything.*] Well! Are you going to let me starve?

RITA. [*Rousing herself.*] Vhat you say?

VAN TUYL. You know I can't eat anything until my hostess does.

RITA. [*Aggrieved.*] It is a treeck you play!

VAN TUYL. [*Humbly.*] No, on my word, I'm hungry!

RITA. [*Smiling unwillingly.*] Den jus' because I am so frightfully polite!

[*She eats a piece of spaghetti.* SIGNORA VANNUCCI *and* VAN TUYL *exchange glances.*

SIGNORA VANNUCCI. [*Hanging over* RITA.] Buoni?

RITA. [*Patting her cheek.*] Squisiti—!

SIGNORA VANNUCCI. [*Kissing her.*] Tesorino mio!

VAN TUYL. I'm thirsty, too!

RITA. [*Smiling.*] Blagueur!

[*She drinks some champagne. He smiles and follows her example.*

VAN TUYL. [*Putting down his glass.*] A thousand thanks! And now, my dear, the signora's had a hard day's packing and to-morrow she'll be up at dawn. Why don't you send her to bed and give her a good night's rest?

Signora Vannucci. *Grazia, milor*—I am nota much tired—

Rita. *Ha ragione. A letto! E metti in gabbia i pappagalli!* [*She drinks again.*

Signora Vannucci. [*Meaningly.*] *Capisco! Tu e milor avrete da chiacchierare un po'!* [*To the parrot.*] *E voi, povere bestie! Dovete avere un bel sonno.* [*Unchaining them and taking one on each wrist.*] *Andiamo*—! [*To* Van Tuyl.] I 'ope milor 'e sleep ver' fine! Good night!

Van Tuyl. [*Politely rising.*] Oh, thanks. Good night, signora.

Signora Vannucci. [*At door—back.*] *E tu, anima mia —mangia più che puoi!*

Rita. *Buona notte*—[*Suddenly putting down her glass, rising and running to* Signora Vannucci.] *Carissima mia, ti ringrazio tanto—tanto! Ti amo sempre—non dimenticare! Ti amo—Ti amo—*

[*She throws her arms around her neck and kisses her warmly.*

Signora Vannucci [*Half smothered by the embrace.*] *Madonna santissima, cosa vuol dire tutto questo?* [*Snivelling a little.*] *Corpo di Bacco! Mi fai piangere! Buona notte*—[*Kissing her.*] *Buona notte, milor*—! [*Kissing her again.*] *Carissima*—! *Buona notte—buona notte—*

[*She goes out, sniffing and smiling and carrying the parrots.*

Van Tuyl. [*Who has served her with salad.*] Now sit down and finish your supper.

Rita. [*Shaking her head.*] No—it is enough—

Van Tuyl. [*Filling her glass and lifting his own.*] Well, then, let's drink a toast—eh? I have it! To the splendor of your days to come! [*He bows and drinks.*

Then, seeing she has not followed his example.] What's the matter? Don't they tempt you?

RITA. [*Holding her glass.*] I do not drink to vhat I know mus' be, but to a dream I vill not dream again— de picture of a small room, varm an' bright, vit' 'im so busy writing at 'is desk,—an' me, before de fire, jus' rocking, smiling, vit' a little baby nursing at my breas'.

VAN TUYL. [*Suddenly.*] My dear, I want you to listen to a plan. [*Sitting in the big chair and drawing her down until she nestles at his feet.*] There—! That's right—! [*Cheerfully resuming.*] Now how would you like it if I sailed on the *Alaska* in April and met you in Paris and took you straight back to Millefleurs—

RITA. But my Russian concert tour?

VAN TUYL. They can get Patti in your place.

RITA. [*Not pleased.*] Patti—?

VAN TUYL. Yes, she'd be glad enough to go.

RITA. [*Less and less enthusiastic.*] But my dear frien', it is not—vhat you say?—it is not fair?

VAN TUYL. To whom?

RITA. To dose poor Russians!

VAN TUYL. [*Smiling.*] You're jealous!

RITA. [*Outraged.*] Of Patti? *Me*—? [*Very scornfully.*] My Lord!

VAN TUYL. [*Caressing her hair.*] Then why bother? Think of Millefleurs and how we loved it on those nights in May! And it's there now—asleep and empty, like some spellbound garden, just waiting for the touch of spring, and us, to give it life again.

RITA. [*Her head against his knee.*] You tol' me vonce you are too ol' to love Millefleurs—

VAN TUYL. [*Smiling.*] My dear, your sorcery can make me young again.

RITA. No—no—dat is imposs'ble—you don' on'erstan'—

VAN TUYL. [*Holding her.*]   What is it?   Tell me!

RITA. [*Rising.*]   I cannot do t'ings like dat any more. [*A pause.*]

VAN TUYL. [*Humbly.*]   Forgive me. It was a mistake. I didn't mean to hurt you.

RITA. [*Choking.*]   'Urt me? You—? My dear, dear frien', I am not vort' such kin'ness—[*She takes his hand.*] But in dese las' few veeks, I learn somet'ing all new an' beeeautiful—de goodness of de vorld—! It come like some great light dat burn an' blind an' strike me to de groun'! It show me for de first time to myself! *Ah, santo Dio!* vhat it is I see! But now I cannot change, an' yet I cannot jus' forget, an' go on as before—you see, I am—oh, vhat you call it? all meex up! [*Pointing to her bed.*] I almos' vish dat I could lie down dere tonight—an' say good-bye.

VAN TUYL. And what about Tom?

RITA. [*Quickly.*]   Don' spik 'is name—

VAN TUYL. I must. If knowing him has done all that for you—and God help me, dear, but up to now I didn't realize that it had!—don't you think you owe him something in return?

RITA. Somet'ing?

VAN TUYL. Yes, and I'll tell you what it is. You've got to pull yourself together, to raise your head and say, "I've been foolish in my time—but that's all over. From now on I'm going to be strong. I'm going to turn the rest of my life into a splendid noble thing. I won't stop till I'm the sort of woman Tom would be proud of"—

RITA. [*Interrupting.*]   Please—please—

VAN TUYL. [*With sudden tenderness.*]   I know it's hard, my darling, but that's no reason why you should give up. Why, it's your prize, your chance—the power to turn this dreadful business into something radiant and true—the final gift Tom's put into your hands!

RITA. [*Clasping her hands.*] Ah, Dio mio—

VAN TUYL. [*Going on.*] Be brave! live gloriously! And if responsibility's the price of love, love's worth it. Isn't it, my dear? [*A pause.*]

RITA. You are right. But oh, my frien'—my frien'—vhat 'ave I done—*vhat 'ave I done dat all dis come to me*—?

[*She bursts into agonized tears and throws herself on the couch, sobbing bitterly.*

VAN TUYL. [*Putting his hand on her shaking shoulder.*] My dear, I'm proud of you.

[*There is a knock at the door to the hall. They both turn. A moment's silence. The knock is repeated.*

RITA. [*Whispering.*] Vhat shall I—?

VAN TUYL. Go and open it.

RITA. [*Going to door.*] Who is dere?

THE BELLBOY'S VOICE. [*Outside.*] It's me, ma'am. There's a gent downstairs t' see ye.

RITA. Vhat—? [*She opens the door a crack.*

THE BELLBOY. They told him it was awful late an' you was tired, but he wouldn't go an' made 'em send up this.

[*He sticks in his arm with a tray, on which is a note.* RITA *takes it, looks at it, then opens it quickly and takes out a card, which she reads.*]

VAN TUYL. [*Watching her face.*] It's Tom?

RITA. [*Nodding.*] Yes.

VAN TUYL. [*In a low voice.*] What does he want?

RITA. [*Reading.*] " I mus' see you. It is life or death." [*Looking up.*] Dat's all.

VAN TUYL. What are you going to do?

RITA. I will say " no." [*She turns towards the door.*

VAN TUYL. Wait!

RITA. [*Shuddering.*] After vhat 'as 'appen, I can never look into 'is eyes again.

VAN TUYL. Perhaps this is the last time you two will ever meet. Be merciful. Don't leave the poor boy with the memory of this afternoon. Give him the chance of seeing you as you are. Give him the joy of knowing what he's done for you.

RITA. [*Nervously.*] Please don' ask me—no—I do not dare—

VAN TUYL. Be a brave child! Let me send for him!

RITA. No—not to-night—

VAN TUYL. This very minute. [*Going to the door.*] Ask the gentleman to come upstairs.

THE BELLBOY. All right, sir.

[*He closes the door.* VAN TUYL *turns to find his coat, hat and stick.*

RITA. [*Terrified.*] You are not going!

VAN TUYL. He mustn't find me here.

RITA. [*Trembling and clinging to him.*] Ah, don' leave me—please—I am afraid—

VAN TUYL. Afraid—when you can help him? I thought you loved him, dear. [*She releases her hold on him. He offers her his hand.*] Good-bye.

RITA. [*Taking his hand.*] Good-bye.

VAN TUYL. [*Still holding hers.*] Do you forgive me, Rita?

RITA. For vhat?

VAN TUYL. [*Wistfully.*] For everything.

[*With a little gasp she lifts his hand and touches it to her lips.*

VAN TUYL. [*Deeply moved as he suddenly gathers her in his arms.*] My darling—! Beautiful—! Joy of men—!

RITA. [*Brokenly.*] Oh, my good frien'—
[*She buries her face on his shoulder.*]
VAN TUYL. [*With infinite tenderness.*] Little bird—! I shall hear your singing in my heart forever, and I thank you from the bottom of my soul!

> [*He bends over and softly kisses her hair. Then, quickly and sharply, turns and goes out the other door.* RITA *is left alone. She looks after him for a moment, then runs to the window and opens it. Outside the gleam and swirl of falling snow can be seen. She stands there, one hand to her throat, breathing deeply. A knock is heard at the door to the hall. She closes the window and turns. The knock is repeated, more loudly. She tries to speak, but cannot. The knock is heard a third time. She controls herself with a great effort.*]

RITA. Come!

> [*The door opens and* TOM *appears. He closes the door and stands with his back against it, looking at her. He is quite white, his hair dishevelled, his eyes wild. He is without overcoat or gloves—the snow is still on his shoulders, his hands are red with cold. His voice is strange. He moves and talks as though devoured by some inward flame. During the entire scene he rarely, if ever, takes his eyes away from her.*]

RITA. [*With difficulty.*] You—you vant to—see me?
TOM. Yes.

> [*They look at each other, breathing deeply.*

RITA. [*Unsteadily.*] Vell?

TOM. Just wait. I—I'm sort of cold.

RITA. [*Her manner changing at once.*] De fire—please—go qveeck an' varm yourself—[*Taking him by the arm and drawing him across.*] Santi benissimi! You are all vet! [*Glancing at his feet.*] An' your shoe—*per capita!* You 'ave valk 'ere in dis snow!

TOM. [*Oddly.*] Yes. I've been walking. All the time that you were singing there. I think I got as far as Trinity, but I don't—quite remember.

RITA. Vhat for you come out on a night so bad? An', if you mus', vit'out dat beeg t'ick coat?

TOM. [*Looking down at himself.*] My coat? I suppose I—I forgot to put it on.

RITA. Forget—! [*With an exclamation.*] Madonna!

TOM. [*Again staring at her.*] I was thinking about something else. About you. I was praying for you in the twilight—in the evening—in the black and dark night—

RITA. Oh, Meestair Tom!

TOM. [*Continuing.*] I walked and prayed. And in my prayers I felt a little hand here on my arm. Some lost one offering herself, I thought. But when I looked down at the red mouth under the veil and the tawdry bonnet, my head swam. *It was you!*

RITA. [*Amazed.*] Me—?

TOM. I heard you crying as I ran away. And I ran and ran—I don't know where—till I saw some lights and people. And then a little beggar, playing on the curb, held up her hand. And when I gave her a penny, she thanked me—*with your voice.*

RITA. No—no—you vere meestake—

TOM. Of course! And then I saw you walking by me in the streets and looking at me out of windows—hundreds of different women, but every one was you. I couldn't move—you were so thick and close. And it began snowing, and I thanked God, because that would blot you from my sight. But no! Each snowflake was a tiny face. Your face. Some crowned with diamonds, some with loosened hair, some old and terrible, some sad and young. Some with your sweet lips parted and your cheeks all wet with tears. And you came and came and kept on coming. Thousands and millions of you, driving and swirling in your devil's dance by the glare of the gas-light on the corner. And not one spoke. You all just looked at me as if you wanted something—imploring—longing with your beautiful dumb eyes. And suddenly I knew! You were begging me to bring your soul to God before it was too late! And I called to you—I cried out that I would! And then you smiled and vanished, and I came here though the storm.

RITA. [*Clasping her hands.*] You poor, poor boy—

TOM. It's different now. Of course you understand. [*With emphasis.*] As man and woman, we've done with one another. Everything like that is over and forgotten—seared away. But I am still a minister of God's word and you are still a human being in mortal peril!

RITA. [*Tenderly.*] Ah, don' talk dat vay! But come—seet 'ere! You are all shaking—see! you vill catch col'!
[*She tries to make him sit by fire.*

TOM. [*Paying no attention.*] Do you know you're standing on the brink of life or death? You must choose between them.

RITA. [*Trying to calm him.*] Yes, yes—anodder time.

TOM. No, not another time! Tonight! This very minute! Now!

RITA. [*In deep distress.*] Oh, vhy you come?

TOM. To save you, dear. Now listen! At midnight I must lead my clergy through the streets. You know, my plan to gather in the vagrants for my New Year Service. And tomorrow you go away. So this is my hour—my hour of hours! And I'll never leave you till you've given me your soul!

RITA. Ah, if you only knew 'ow—

TOM. [*Interrupting and holding up his hand.*] Listen! Don't you hear it—now—above us—in this very room?

RITA. 'Ear vhat—?

TOM. [*In a sort of rapture.*] The sound of many waters—

RITA. [*Puzzled.*] Eh?

TOM. The Voice—[*Very solemnly.*] The thunder of an angel's wings! [*A pause.*]

RITA. I 'ear de vind blow, an' my eart' beat. Dat is all.

TOM. It's here! I feel it! [*Ecstatically.*] Oh, dear God! Dear God! You're giving me the strength to conquer her!

RITA. [*Anxiously.*] Conquair—? [*Suddenly.*] You vant to 'urt me! Ah, don' 'urt me—please!

TOM. [*Turning to her and speaking with sudden tenderness.*] My dear, I wouldn't hurt you for the world. It's love I'm offering you—[*As she makes a quick movement.*] —no, wait, my poor child. Not the sick passion of those luxurious beasts. Not even the great pity I once knew. Not theirs, not mine, the love I bring to you tonight is God's alone!

RITA. God's love—?

TOM. Yes, darling, His. The mighty tenderness that moves the stars, and understands when little children pray. It's ours *forever!* [*In sudden anxiety.*] Do you realize the meaning of that word?

RITA. [*Sadly.*] Your keess 'ave teach me.

TOM. [*Always staring at her.*] Little lost soul, I am

ready to carry you home! Little tired heart, eager for joy! Follow me and find it in His arms!

RITA. Vhat you mean?

TOM. Though your sins be as scarlet, they shall be white as snow. For you come out of great tribulation and have washed your robes in the blood of the Lamb—

RITA. Vhat is it—vhat you say?

TOM. [*More and more moved.*] You shall no longer hunger and thirst. For He will lead you to the living waters and the Tree of Life, and God himself will wipe away your tears!

RITA. [*Looking at him.*] I don'—qvite on'erstan'—

TOM. I thought our meeting was the work of chance—the call of a man for his earthly mate. But in bitter shame have I learnt my error. God drew you to me, over land and sea, that I might be the engine of His Word. You are a bride—but ah! not mine—[*His voice dropping.*]—not mine!

RITA. A bride—*me?* No—no—dat is imposs'ble—

TOM. [*His eyes gleaming.*] Don't you hear the midnight cry—" Behold! the Bridegroom cometh! Go ye out to meet him!" Don't you see Him, coming from the wilderness like a pillar of smoke, perfumed with myrrh and frankincense? His eyes are as a flame of fire, on his head are many crowns. He wears a garment dipped in blood and on it a name is written—*Lord of Lords and King of Kings!* Hark! He is outside, knocking at your door! O Rose of Sharon—Lily of the Valley! Cease your slumber, for the hour has come!

RITA. [*Nervously.*] I do not like it vhen you talk dis vay—

TOM. [*Coming nearer as she shrinks away.*] How can you sleep when His voice is calling—" Rise up, my love, my fair one—and come away! For lo! the winter is past, the rain is over and gone! The flowers appear on the earth, the time for the singing of birds is come! Open to me, my sister, my love, my dove, my undefiled—for my head is filled with dew and my locks with the drops of the night—"

RITA. [*Desperately.*] *Santa Madonna—! Vhat is it you say—?*

TOM. Awake, O fairest among women! Awake, and open wide the door! Awake and sing and shout and cry aloud—" My beloved is mine and His desire is towards me!"

RITA. Your eyes—dey bite me—oh, dey burn me up—

TOM. [*Breathing fast and deep as he comes nearer.*] My dear, He's tired! Don't keep Him standing there!

RITA. Meestair Tom—*Meestair Tom!*

TOM. [*Hoarsely.*] Darling, open your heart! For God's sake, let Him in!

RITA. [*In a spasm of nervous horror as he finally seizes her.*] Don' touch me—don'—don'—let me go!

> [*She drops writhing at his feet. He holds fast to her hands and speaks quickly bending over her.*

TOM. [*Changing his tone.*] So that's it, is it? So you're proud! You think you can close your soul against the Lamb! Well, let me tell you now that unless you repent, the day will come when your pride lies broken, shattered by His wrath! You're young and beautiful, but that won't last! Your head is burdened with the weight of gold and splendors. But, unless you pray God to forgive you, the time is near when the stench of your dead vanities will fill the world—

RITA. [*Interrupting.*] Let me go—*let me go*—

> [*She tears herself free and runs over to the*

fire where she crouches trembling against the wall.

Tom. [*With horrible intensity.*] When the kings of the earth have sealed themselves in pleasure on your heart—when the merchants of the earth have grown fat through the abundance of your delicacies—when you have glorified yourself and lived deliriously, and all lands are drunk with the wine of your abominations—when you have said in your soul, I sit a queen, and am no widow, and shall see no sorrow—*then* will the Son of Man thrust in His sickle! *Then* will He gather your grapes and cast them down and tread them in the winepress of God's rage!

Rita. It is not true—

[*A coal breaks in the grate behind her and her figure is bathed in a ruddy, flickering glow.*

Tom. [*With a cry, covering his face as if to shut out some dreadful sight.*] Ah! No! Not that! Dear God, not that—*not that*—

Rita. [*Terrified.*] Vhat? Vhat you say—?

Tom. [*Pointing at her.*] Look—! The red light—hell is burning—

Rita. [*Beginning suddenly to cry like a frightened child.*] Oh—! Oh—! I am afraid!

Tom. [*Wildly.*] Afraid—? *Afraid*—? Miserable sinner, how can you live with that horror staring in your eyes? The vision of that dreadful day when the sun is smitten, and the moon is blood, and the great stars reel and fall down from the sky—

Rita. I don' believe—no—no, I don'—I don'—

Tom. When the graves are broken, and the sea gives up its dead—and great and small they stand before Him and He sits in judgment—

RITA. [*Trying to interrupt him.*] Meestair Tom—jus' vait vone meenute—

TOM. [*Going on.*] Don't you hear that great Voice like a light that blinds—" I made you keeper of my vineyards. But your own vineyards you have not kept. So you shall drink from the cup of the wine of the fierceness of My wrath and be cast into the bottomless pit and the lake of fire. And there, in the midst of your eternal torment you shall hear the alleluias in the rainbow round My throne!"

> [*He sinks into a chair, and buries his face in his hands. A pause. Rita, who has risen, now comes nearer him.*]

RITA. [*Simply.*] I am qvite sure dis is de las' time dat ve spik togedder—de las' time dat I look upon your face. An' so I vant to tell you jus' a leetle somet-ing—an' den—vell, mebbe I can say good-bye. [*She comes a little nearer and speaks at first with some difficulty.*] You are ver' kin' to t'ink of me so much, aftair all de trouble I 'ave bring. An' I t'ank you—I shall alvays be oblige'. But, dear, you can forget me now. It is all right. Your vork is done.

TOM. What's that?

RITA. Before I meet you I did not know much vhat a voman's life should be. But now I know. You show me. An' I cannot do dose ol' t'ings any more.

TOM. [*Looking up at her.*] You don't mean—?

RITA. [*Her eyes shining.*] I vant to make my life all good—like yours! Ah, yes, I know dat vill be 'ard, but I don' care! An' mebbe de kin' Madonna she vill 'elp me, vhen she sees me try!

> [*She clasps her hands, the dawn of hope in her face.*]

TOM. [*Staring at her.*] Your lips drop as the honey-comb. Your mouth is smoother than oil. But your feet go down to death, and your steps take hold on hell.

Rita. [*A little anxious.*] You don' t'ink God, 'E vill forgive me—no? [*Smiling.*] Ah, foolish vone—! 'E vill! Did 'E not make my face so men 'ave alvays love me? Did 'E not put my voice 'ere to delight de vorld? Did 'E not give to vone poor leetle girl, who ask 'Im nodings, so much to carry dat she lose 'er vay? 'E vill not be surprise she stumble sometime. 'E vill not scol' much vhen she make meestake. 'E vill jus' smile an' keep 'Is candle burning. An' in a leetle vhile she see it, an' come 'ome!

Tom. Promise me something—

Rita. Vhat?

Tom. Take my hands and look me in the eyes and promise me never to give yourself to any man again.

Rita. Ah! I knew it! You 'ave not believe me!

Tom. [*Wiping the sweat from his forehead.*] Of course I believe you but promise me. For God's sake, promise just the same!

Rita. [*Turning away in agony.*] Ah, vhy don' you trust me? Vhy you doubt me so?

Tom. [*Loudly.*] You won't—?

Rita. [*Turning.*] 'Ere—take my 'ands. [*He seizes them.*] 'Ow col' you are! I promise—vhat you vant I say?—never to give myself to any man again!

Tom. [*Devouring her with his eyes.*] You swear it?

Rita. Yes, I svear! Now are you satisfied?

Tom. [*Suddenly uttering a cry of pain and hideous unrest.*] Ah! [*He pushes her away from him.*]

Rita. Vhat is it now—?

Tom. I've just remembered that you swore before!

Rita. [*Shrinking as she understands.*] No—no!

Tom. You put your hand on my dear mother's Testament and you looked up, just as you're looking now—

Rita. [*Putting up her hands as if to ward off a blow.*] No—stop it!

Tom. And you lied, and lied! You *lied* to me—

Rita. No—don'—please—it is all diff'rent now—

Tom. Different? I don't see it. Why, it's just the same!

Rita. No—no! I tell you *I* am diff'rent! *I* 'ave change! I am going now to be good!

Tom. But can you?

Rita. Listen! I tell you 'ow I show! I vill stop singing, fin' out a convent vhere dey take me in an'—[*Suddenly.*] Ecco! I 'ave it! Dere are some nuns near Geneva who nurse de sick. I vill go straight from Napoli, learn 'ow to 'elp, an' vork until dis flesh fall from de bone!

Tom. You'll do that just to show me you're sincere?

Rita. [*Imploringly.*] I vill do all you vant! Yes, anyt'ing! Only believe me, jus' believe—or else I die!

Tom. [*Deeply moved.*] All right. I take you at your word.

Rita. [*Hardly daring to believe.*] You mean it—?

Tom. [*Huskily, his face working.*] Yes. God bless you, dear. Good-bye. [*He turns away.*] Before I go—there's something I forgot—[*Remembering.*] Oh, yes! Your cross—your pearls. You left them at the Rectory.
> [*He has unfolded his handkerchief and taken from it the jewels. As he lays them on the table he sees* Van Tuyl's *card, left there by* Signora Vannucci *at the beginning of the act. He stands rigid. A moment's pause.*

Rita. T'ank you. [*Her voice changes as she sees his face.*] Vhat is it?

Tom. [*Trying to point.*] That card—Van Tuyl—
> [*He chokes suddenly.*

Rita. [*Anxiously.*] Meestair Van Tuyl. Yes?

Tom. [*With difficulty.*] He's been here then?

Rita. [*Looking at him.*] Si—si—

Tom. [*Putting his hand to his throat.*] To-night?
Rita. Yes.
Tom. [*Hardly able to contain himself.*] When?
Rita. Jus' before you come.
Tom. [*Seizing the card and crumpling it in both hands.*] Oh! What a fool I've been! What a fool! What a fool! What a blind, miserable, wretched *fool!*
Rita. Vhat is it? Tell me! Vhat 'as 'appen?
Tom. Why didn't I feel it as soon as I saw you in that indecent dress, with your hair unbound, and the night-light burning? Why didn't I smell it in the sickening perfume that this whole place reeks of—
Rita. Vhat you mean? O dear Lord, vhat you mean?
Tom. Don't try to cheat me any more! I know what's happened in this room to-night! While I was tramping through the storm and snow, praying with my whole heart for your soul's redemption—[*Pointing to the bedroom.*]— you lay there laughing in your lover's arms.
Rita. [*Stung.*] No—no! Dat is not so, I say—not so—not so! 'E come in kin'ness, jus' because 'e feel ver' sorry for me, an' vhen 'e ask me to go back to 'im, I 'ave refuse!
Tom. What—?
Rita. I 'ave refuse! You 'ear me? I 'ave tol' 'im "*No!*" An' 'e is great beeg man, an' on'erstan'. An' den I t'ank 'im, an' ve say good-bye.
Tom. [*Fiercely.*] You lie! Why, look at those two chairs—so close together! They look like a refusal, don't they? And those glasses—champagne—
Rita. No—no! It is qvite diff'ren'! You are all mees-take—
Tom. [*More and more fiercely.*] A private orgy, planned and thought out days ahead! Your last caresses—
[*He has seized the table cloth with both hands.*

RITA. Oh, take care!

TOM. [*Between his teeth.*] A farewell debauch—
[*He pulls the cloth and drags everything to the floor with a crash.*

RITA. [*Closing her eyes.*] Oh—!

TOM. [*Turning on her.*] Now do you dare deny Van Tuyl's your lover?

RITA. [*Her eyes still closed.*] Yes! Yes! I do! I do! [*Beginning to sway a little as she speaks.*] I 'ave refuse 'im an' I tell you vhy! I t'ought it was because my 'eart 'ave change, because I vant so much to be good! But now I know dat I vas all meestake! I 'ave *not* change! My 'eart, it is *not* good! *I break vit 'im because I love an-odder—*

TOM. [*Ready to kill her.*] Who is he?

RITA. [*Half-fainting, as she opens her eyes and sways towards him, holding out her arms.*] You—

TOM. [*Turning sharply as if she had struck him with a whip.*] Don't!

RITA. [*Pulling herself together.*] Forgive me—

TOM. [*Twisting his hands as if in prayer.*] Oh, my God! Oh, my God!

RITA. [*Her back to him, holding the big chair for support.*] An' now—if you don' min'—I mus' ask you—to leave me—it is almos' midnight—you 'ave your service in de church—an' I myself mus'—try to sleep a leetle—[*Turning with an enormous effort and holding out her hand with a smile.*] So good-night! I 'ope you—[*Her words die away as she sees the expression on his face. Then in a sudden paroxysm of terror.*] Vhy you look at me like dat? [*A brief pause.*] Please go avay! [*He doesn't move.*] Go avay!

TOM. [*Starting, wiping his forehead nervously, and trying to speak in his natural voice.*] All right. I'm going.

Yes, I'm going. [*His tone deepening.*] But first there's something we must do—what is it? I forget—oh, yes, of course—of course! We must pray together—that's it! Pray for your soul and for your soul's salvation—

RITA. [*Nervously.*] No—go now! I am in God's 'ands. 'E vill take care of me. [*In quick fear, he comes towards her.*] Oh, vhat you vant?

TOM. [*Thickly.*] Come here—[*He seizes her by the arm.*] Kneel down! [*He sits on the couch and draws her down before him between his knees.*] There! That's right! Give me your hands!

> [*He fumbles, finds them, and holds them tight against his breast. A silence, they look into each other's eyes.*

RITA. [*Suddenly in wild terror as she looks up at him.*] Pray! Vhy don' you pray? Pray! [*Half-smothered.*] O Gésu— [*In a silent fury of passion he has leaned forward, drawn her up to him, and crushed her in a terrible embrace.*

TOM. [*Triumphantly.*] It's all over! I thought I came here to save you, but I didn't! It was just because I'm a man and you're a woman, and I love you, darling—I love you—I love you more than anything in the world—

> [*He is kissing her frantically.*

RITA. [*Half-fainting.*] Oh—!

TOM. [*Between his kisses.*] My dearest—my precious —I've never felt this way in all my life before—[*With a laugh.*] What a fool—what a fool I've been! But that's all right, it's not too late—we're here—together—and the night is ours—

RITA. [*Terrified.*] No—no!

TOM. It's ours—the whole, long splendid night—it's ours, I tell you—every marvellous minute—why, God Himself can't rob us of it now!

Rita. [*Struggling.*] Don'—please—! Oh, take avay your 'ands—

Tom. I won't—

Rita. It is because I love you—

Tom. [*Leaning forward to kiss her.*] Ah—! I knew—!

Rita. [*Pushing him away from her.*] An' so, because I love you, I mus' save you from yourself!

Tom. You can't—it's too late—

Rita. Now leesten—please! It is you who 'ave teach me vhat is love! I 'ave know nodings—*nodings*—till you show me—all!

Tom. Till *I*—?

[*He breaks into a peal of jangled laughter.*

Rita. To love a man is jus' vone big forgetting of vone's self—to feel so sorry for 'im dat it break your 'eart—to 'elp 'im vhen 'e need 'elp if it cost your life—

Tom. [*Laughing again.*] Oh, darling—you don't really think that's love—?

Rita. I know it—now! [*With a sudden sob.*] But, oh, I learn it in such pain an' sorrow! [*In passionate entreaty.*] Don't take it from me, now dat it is mine!

Tom. Oh, nonsense! That's not love—why, that's the sort of thing *I* used to talk! [*Intoxicated.*] But I know better now! It's you who've taught me! Love isn't thinking or forgetting about anything—love's just *feeling*—it's being awfully sick and faint—as if you hadn't had anything to eat for years and years—it's—

Rita. [*Interrupting.*] Don'—! Don'—! You mus' not talk dat vay—

Tom. [*Moistening his lips.*] I love you—

Rita. [*In despair.*] Oh, t'ink of dat beeg lake—de lake of fire—de smoke an' torment dat you tell me of!

Tom. [*Recklessly.*] I know I'm lost! I'm done for,

damned forever! But I'll have had this night, so I don't care!

RITA. But *I* care! *I care!*

TOM. [*Panting.*] I'm going to kiss you—

RITA. [*Wild with fright.*] Don' touch me—no—go back —please—keep avay—

TOM. I won't—

RITA. [*Shrinking against the sofa.*] For God's sake—

TOM. [*Seizing her in his arms.*] My darling—

RITA. [*Closing her eyes.*] I am all alone. I 'ave no strengt'. I cannot fight against you any more. But now, before it is too late, remembair—oh, remembair vhat I say! Dis is de vone big meenute in my life. De kin' of voman I vill alvays be, it is for you to say—'ere—as ve stan' in dis room—now! [*Like a child.*] Oh, Meestair Tom! Please —please let me be good! Don' treat me like de odders 'ave! Don' make me bad—again! You are a man God send to 'elp de vorld. All right—'elp *me!* I need you! Go avay! My 'eart, it vill go vit' you alvays, but I don' care—jus' so you let me keep my soul!

> [*She stands transfigured. As she speaks he slowly releases her and sinks to his knees. His face is buried in his hands. There is a pause.*
>
> *Then, in the distance, sounds the first note of the midnight bell. As it continues, a choir of men's voices—sturdy and sweet —strikes up far away. It gradually comes nearer. They are singing the old Lutheran hymn " Ein Feste Berg." As* TOM *hears them he rises unsteadily to his feet. He passes his hand over his forehead, as one awakening from a dream.*

Tom. [*In his natural voice, very formal and polite, but a little constrained.*] I beg your pardon—I must take my leave—[*As he looks about for his hat.*] My church—the choir—procession—join them as they reach the Avenue—my apologies—disturbing you at such an hour—

Rita. [*Her eyes closed, crossing herself and murmuring almost inaudibly.*] Ave Maria gratia plena—Sancta Maria Mater Dei—

Tom. [*At the door.*] I beg you to accept—very best wishes—coming year—my—my—good-night—good-bye—

Rita. [*As before.*]—ora pro nobis peccatoribus nunc et in hora mortis—

> [*He is gone. Only her praying figure remains. The hymn swells to triumph as the lights fade. The scene is in darkness. For a moment the noise of the chimes and bells continues. Then it gradually dies away. The singing voices are no longer heard. A little band is playing the hymn. It is almost grotesque—so very thin and cracked and out of tune. To this music and the fading sound of the bells, the lights gradually appear. They reveal the scene set for the Epilogue.*]

THE EPILOGUE

[*SCENE: The* Bishop's *library again. The* Bishop *is sitting in the red glow of the dying fire, finishing his story. His grandson is at his feet. Outside are heard the last echoes of the bells and whistles. The little street band is still playing " Ein Feste Berg "—a lamentable performance.*

THE BISHOP. . . . And that's how I remember her—standing there with her hair loosened and her eyes shut. She crossed herself. I think now she was praying. And the next thing I knew I was on the sidewalk and my choir—God bless 'em!—were swinging round the corner of Tenth Street, marching like soldiers to the same tune those wretched Germans are murdering outside there now—[*As they strike a particularly distressing dissonance.*] Ah—! Really, that's too much! Give them a quarter, Harry, and tell them to go away. [*As the young man rises and goes to the window.*] "Ein Feste Berg"—! How well we used to sing it at St. Giles'—! [*He smiles and shakes his head.*

HARRY. [*Throwing up the window and calling.*] Hi—you! That'll be enough for to-night! Catch!

[*He throws out a coin. The music stops. There is silence, save for a few far-off horns.*

THE BISHOP. [*Rousing himself as* HARRY *returns and putting the dead violets and the handkerchief in his pocket.*] So that's what I wanted to tell you, my boy! I came home that night a different—and I think a better man. It was the following June that your dear grandmother and I were married. Mr. Van Tuyl came all the way from Madrid just to be there and to give his niece away. They're fine people—the Van Tuyls. But your grandmother was the finest of them all. She understood the world and loved it, too. She made my life a happy one—a very happy one indeed!

HARRY. [*Boyishly.*] And—Madame Cavallini?

THE BISHOP. [*Still looking in the fire and smiling.*] She became even more famous before her retirement. But, of course, you know.

HARRY. Where is she now?

THE BISHOP. Now? I'm not sure, but I believe she's in Italy somewhere—living rather quietly. [*Wistfully.*] She and Patti are the only ones left. A wonderful career, my boy. A very great artist. I never saw her again.

HARRY. [*Patting his arm awkwardly.*] I think you're just a corker!

THE BISHOP. [*Smiling.*] Nonsense! But now I hope you understand I haven't *quite* forgotten what it feels like to be young. And although it's true I always read the *Evening Post,* I still can sympathize—and even presume to offer some occasional advice!

HARRY. I know, and I appreciate it.

THE BISHOP. [*Very solemnly.*] My dear, dear boy, unless your love is big enough to forget the whole world and yet remember Heaven, you have no right to make this girl your wife.

[*A pause.*

HARRY. [*Rising abruptly.*] Grandfather, I've been an ass!

[*He puts his hands in his pockets and walks away.*

THE BISHOP. [*Whimsically, as he wipes his glasses.*] I suppose you have, Harry—I suppose you have.

HARRY. [*Turning back again.*] I've been an ass to hesitate one single minute! However, it's all right now. Your story's settled it. Lucille and I are going to get married as soon as ever we can.

THE BISHOP. [*Thoroughly startled.*] God bless my soul! But *that* isn't why I told it to you! I wanted to get this nonsense out of your silly young head!

HARRY. [*Laughing affectionately as he stands behind the* BISHOP's *chair and pats his shoulders.*] Never mind! You did something quite different and it's too late now to change—[*Suddenly.*] By the way, have you any engagement for to-morrow afternoon?

THE BISHOP. [*Still flustered.*] I—I can't say that I recall any at this moment—

HARRY. Then do you mind if we make one now? I want you to marry Lucille and me. How about four-thirty to-morrow?

THE BISHOP. [*Gasping.*] Four-thirty—?

HARRY. [*At the door, shyly.*] I don't know how to say it, grandpa, but—but Lucille and I—well, we'll be grateful all our lives for what you've done for us to-night.

> [*He goes out quickly, his head bent.*

THE BISHOP. Well! Well! I declare!

> [*He takes out his spotless handkerchief and passes it nervously over his brow. The door opens and* SUZETTE *appears, smiling brightly.*

SUZETTE. [*Standing at the door.*] Happy New Year, grandpa!

THE BISHOP. Happy New Year, my dear!

SUZETTE. [*Coming to his chair.*] Well—?

THE BISHOP. Suzette, I want you to order some white flowers and some black wedding-cake—

SUZETTE. [*With a wriggle of delight.*] Oh—!

THE BISHOP. [*Finishing.*] For to-morrow afternoon—four-thirty, I believe.

SUZETTE. [*Flinging her arms around his neck.*] You duck!

THE BISHOP. [*With some asperity.*] Don't kiss me in the ear!

SUZETTE. [*Triumphantly.*] I just *knew* Harry could get around you!

THE BISHOP. [*Drily.*] Oh, did you? Well, then, now that you two have arranged everything to suit yourselves, would you please finish reading me my paper and then go to bed? [*He leans back comfortably and closes his eyes.*

SUZETTE. [*Going to the desk.*] Where is it? Oh, yes! Wait till I turn on the lamp—

[*She does so, sits down, sighs, and unfolds the " Post."*]

THE BISHOP. Is there any foreign news?

SUZETTE. [*Carelessly.*] Oh, just some uprising in Portugal—a new Chinese loan—[*Turning the page.*] Why, Cavallini's dead! I thought she died a long time ago, didn't you? [*She reads to herself. A slight pause.*

THE BISHOP. What does—it say?

SUZETTE. Oh, it's just a cable. [*Reading.*] "Milan—December 30. Mme. Margherita Cavallini died this morning at her villa on the Lake of Como."

THE BISHOP. Is that—all?

SUZETTE. That's all the dispatch. There's a whole column of biography stuck on underneath. Shall I read it? [*Suddenly.*] Oh, of course! I forgot! She and Patti were your two great operatic crushes, weren't they? Well, she was born at Venice in 1841. That makes her—[*Looking up thoughtfully.*] Let me see—

THE BISHOP. Don't tell me how old she was!

SUZETTE. [*Smiling.*] All right. [*Running her eyes down the column.*] Début at Milan in 1859—*Forze della Destine.* I never heard of it, did you? Sang prima donna rôles at the Italian Opera in Paris under the direction of Rossini—brilliant figure during the last years of the Empire—success in London—hm!—brought to this country first by Strakosch—appeared as *Mignon* at the Academy of Music—[*Looking up.*] Everyone went mad over her, didn't they? [*Resuming.*] Opera and concert tours over all the civilized globe—retired in 1889—numerous charities—founded and endowed a home in Paris for poor girls who come to study music—in 1883 created Marchese Torrebianchi by King Umberto First—never married—that's funny, isn't it? [*Turning the page.*] Well, no matter what you say I bet she wasn't a bit more wonderful than my divine Geraldine! [*Reading headlines.*] "Anglican Congress at Detroit—City Chosen for June Conference—Federation of Churches—Further Plans." [*Bored.*] Oh dear! There's the old Conference again! [*She yawns and looking up, notices that the* BISHOP'S *head has fallen.*] Sleepy, grandpa?

THE BISHOP. [*Rousing himself.*] I—? No, my dear, I was just thinking—that's all.

SUZETTE. [*With affectionate impudence.*] I don't believe it! [*Yawning.*] Well, I am, anyway. May I go to bed now? There's so much to do to-morrow—and I think I've finished everything in this.

[*She puts down the paper and rises.*]

THE BISHOP. Of course, my dear, of course.

SUZETTE. [*As she alights like a bird on the arm of his chair and kisses the top of his head.*] Oh, grandpa, you *are* such an old darling!

THE BISHOP. Thank you, my dear.

SUZETTE. [*At door.*] And *please* don't sit up too late, will you? And don't forget to turn off *all* the lights before you come upstairs!

THE BISHOP. [*Meekly.*] I'll do my best.

SUZETTE. Grandpa—! [*He turns in his chair. She smiles and blows him a kiss.*] I love you!

[*She runs out.*]

THE BISHOP. [*Calling after.*] The same to you, my dear. Good-night.

[*He sits alone for a moment in silence, then, rising slowly, he closes the door and listens. There is no sound. Almost stealthily he goes over to the case where the phonograph records are kept, puts on his glasses, and looks over those lying on the top. Finally he selects one with much care and gingerly puts it on the machine.*

He starts it going. Then, switching off the lights, he returns to his armchair by the fire. The red glow from the coals lights up his face. He carefully takes from his inside pocket the dead violets and the woman's handkerchief. Looking at them, he smiles a tender little ghost of a smile and slowly sits down. The rich voice thrills through the darkness.

" —*Kennst du es wohl?*
Dahin! Dahin!
Möcht' ich mit dir, O mein Geliebter, ziehn! "

The Curtain Softly Falls.

THE UNCHASTENED WOMAN

A Modern Comedy in Three Acts

By

LOUIS KAUFMAN ANSPACHER

Louis Kaufman Anspacher was born in Cincinnati, Ohio, March 1, 1878. He received his A.B. at the College of the City of New York in 1897, his A.M. at Columbia University in 1899 and his LL.B. at the same institution in 1902. He studied in the Post-graduate School of Philosophy at Columbia from 1902-5 and was secular lecturer at Temple Emanu-El, New York City, for the same period. Since 1906, he has lectured for the League for Political Education, New York City, for the University Extension Center, New York City, and since 1908 at the Brooklyn Institute of Arts and Sciences.

His plays are *Tristan and Isolde* (1904), *The Embarrassment of Riches* (1906), *Anne and the Arch-Duke John* (1907), *The Woman of Impulse* (1909), *The Glass House* (1912), *The Washerwoman Duchess* (1913), *Our Children* (1914), *The Unchastened Woman* (1915), *That Day* (1917), *The Rape of Belgium* (1918), *Madame Cecile* (1918), *The Dancer* (with Max Marcin, 1919), *Daddalums* (England, 1919).

The Unchastened Woman was first produced by Oliver Morosco at the 39th Street Theatre, New York City, October 9, 1915, with Mr. H. Reeves-Smith as Hubert Knollys and Miss Emily Stevens as Caroline Knollys.

[Copyright, 1916, by Louis Kaufman Anspacher]

PERSONS OF THE PLAY

(Arranged in the order of their first entrances.)

HUBERT KNOLLYS
MRS. MURTHA, a charwoman
MISS SUSAN AMBIE
CAROLINE KNOLLYS, wife of Hubert Knollys
LAWRENCE SANBURY
HILDEGARDE SANBURY, his wife
MISS EMILY MADDEN
MICHAEL KRELLIN

TIME: The Present
PLACE: New York City

THE UNCHASTENED WOMAN

ACT I

[*The play opens in a morning in October. It is about ten o'clock. The first act presents the drawing-room of the* KNOLLYS' *house, situated on a corner in the fashionable fifties, New York City. The room is spacious, but a little old-fashioned. Up stage, at the right, is a large arch opening on a hall, which leads out to the front door off stage at the right. In the center of the arch there are three steps leading to a platform, from which a flight of stairs rises, going left, and leading to the rooms above. The balustrade continues on a level with the stage, and indicates that the stairs lead also downward from the front hall to the basement.*

In the middle of the right wall is a large marble mantelpiece, with an open fireplace. Above the mantel hangs an old family portrait. On the wall below the mantel hangs an ornamental Venetian mirror. In the rear wall of the room, toward the left, is a mahogany door, leading to the basement. Between this door and the arch stands a large bookcase, filled with books in expensive bindings. The left wall of the room is pierced by two large windows, with practical shades and blinds.

A library table and three chairs occupy the center of the room, under a heavy chandelier. There is a large divan chair with cushions and a foot-stool placed down left of the room. Set on an angle in front of the fireplace is a Davenport. Below this, also on an angle is a settle. *Several of the chairs and the Davenport are covered with linen slips or sheets, which indicate that the house has not been occupied for some time. The size and visible appointments of the room must suggest the atmosphere of large, though rather formal, luxury.*

The curtain rises on an empty stage. Dim light sifts through the closed blinds. There is a pause, and then the front door of the house is heard to open and close. A moment later HUBERT KNOLLYS *enters from the hall, through the arch, putting his keys into his pocket. He is followed by* MRS. MURTHA. HUBERT KNOLLYS *is a tall and distinguished looking man of fifty-three. He is dressed in a morning suit and a Panama hat. He carries a whisky and a couple of soda bottles under his arm. He also has a newspaper.* MRS. MURTHA *is an elderly Irish woman.*]

HUBERT. Phew! It's close in here! [*Goes to a window which he opens and lets in the sunlight, then he turns and looks at* MRS. MURTHA.] Is your name Agnes Murtha?

MURTHA. No. That's me daughter. D'ye see, Agnes was comin', the Lord love her, but she had a fall yesterday—

HUBERT. Oh, too bad.

[*He begins removing the slips from the furniture.*

MURTHA. [*Undoing her bonnet and showing her white head.*] Yis—She's a foine eddication, so she has; but she bez a little weak in th' knee. So Oi came over mesilf, as soon as Oi heard from Mrs. Sanbury.

HUBERT. [*Seeing her white hair.*] Perhaps you're not strong enough—

MURTHA. Oi'm as shtrong as ivir Oi wuz.

[*She energetically takes a slip from a piece of furniture.*

HUBERT. The whole house must be got in shape.

MURTHA. Yis, m'am. [*Awed.*] An' do yez own th' whole house entoire? [*He nods quizzically.*] Ah, glory be to God fer that!

HUBERT. [*Going to open the second window.*] I'll tend to the windows on this floor. [*Looking out, then turning.*] Oh, catch that ice-man and get him to leave a piece of ice.

MURTHA. Now do you be shtandin' there, son, so he don't get away. Oi'll let him in.

[*She starts to go off through the arch.*]

HUBERT. [*Pointing to the door.*] No, this way through the basement.

MURTHA *scrambles off quickly.* HUBERT *pauses, looking out, sees the ice-man, whistles and gesticulates to him to wait and go down into the house. During this,* SUSAN AMBIE *enters from the hall through the arch.* SUSAN *is a woman of forty-five. She has the soul of a chaperon. She enters in nervous haste.*

HUBERT. Why, Miss Ambie! [*Shaking hands.*] Where's Caroline?

SUSAN. Get your hat and come right down to the dock with me.

HUBERT. I'm never missed unless there's been some trouble. What is it?

SUSAN. Your wife has been grossly insulted, as I was! It's unheard of!

HUBERT. [*Dawning.*] Ah! trouble with the customs. Is that it?

SUSAN. [*Indignantly.*] They have dared to suspect us, your wife and me!

HUBERT. You mean they've found you out. You too!

SUSAN. I'm not speaking for myself. When I saw they were going to be disagreeable, I declared everything.

But suddenly I realized that a vulgar inspector woman had been watching Caroline. I saw her take Carrie off! All your wife's trunks are held!

HUBERT. [*Grimly relieved.*] Good!

SUSAN. [*Recoiling with a stare.*] Carrie's told me many things; but I never believed that you could be so heartless!

HUBERT. I've been prepared for this for many years. If she will do things in her own high-handed way, she'll have to stand the consequences. That's why I never meet her.

SUSAN. Then you refuse to go?

HUBERT. I refuse to be made a cat's-paw. That is, when I can help it.

SUSAN. Oh!

HUBERT. What is there for me to do? You must have made false declarations.

SUSAN. We didn't know they'd be so strict with us. We're not tradespeople or importers, or—

HUBERT. No, you're worse. Two women without even the wretched excuse of poverty, attempting to defraud the government!

SUSAN. Mr. Knollys!

HUBERT. Ha! The cold sweat isn't worth the money.
[*Wipes his brow.*

SUSAN. I don't know what she'll do!

HUBERT. She'll come home chastened in spirit, I hope, after having profited by this experience.

SUSAN. I really believe you're glad she's in trouble!

HUBERT. Not that. But I shall be glad if this population of a hundred million citizens in their corporate capacity are able, for once in her life, to demonstrate to my good wife that she can't do everything she likes with everybody. I've tried, her friends have tried, society has tried, perhaps the *government* will succeed.

SUSAN. Well, if I can't make you see your duty—

HUBERT. [*Interrupting.*] The question of my duty to my wife is one that I do not care to discuss even with you.

SUSAN. It's none of my business, I suppose . . .

HUBERT. [*Bluntly.*] Quite so.

SUSAN. [*Fixes her hat.*] Then I'll go back alone. Carrie's my dearest friend—[*Then, in a bravado of accusing tearfulness.*] And I can't help it if I'm not strong enough to stand by quietly and see her die of mortification!

HUBERT. [*Sarcastically.*] You might advise her to appeal to them for clemency.

SUSAN. She can't find less of it there than here!

[*He turns and goes up.* SUSAN *is about to exit when* CAROLINE KNOLLYS *enters from the hall.* CAROLINE *is a woman of forty, very young looking, handsome, commanding and self-possessed. She is faultlessly gowned.*

SUSAN. [*With a cry.*] Oh, Carrie!

CAROLINE. [*Entering.*] Oh, there you are, Susan. How are you, Hubert? [*Shakes hands with him. Then to* SUSAN.] I didn't know what became of you.

SUSAN. I came right here.

CAROLINE. You should have told me. Ninette and I looked every place.

SUSAN. I didn't want those men to see us together.

CAROLINE. Nonsense!

SUSAN. And I thought—

CAROLINE. [*Interrupting.*] You didn't think. You went right off your head.

HUBERT. [*Expectantly.*] Well?

CAROLINE. [*To* HUBERT.] You seem to thrive in my absence. [*To* SUSAN.] Doesn't he?

HUBERT. I return the doubtful compliment. The same to you, and many of them.

CAROLINE. Thank you. [*To* SUSAN.] You got through quickly, didn't you?

SUSAN. When I saw they were going to be disagreeable, I declared everything.

CAROLINE. What!

SUSAN. What could I do?

CAROLINE. [*Shrugging her shoulders.*] I told you exactly what to do.

SUSAN. But when that woman searched me, I—

CAROLINE. You lost your nerve.

SUSAN. Oh, Carrie, I'm not thinking of myself. What did they do to you?

HUBERT. [*Expectantly.*] Yes, what did they do to you?

CAROLINE. To me? Why, what's the matter?

SUSAN. [*Relieved.*] Nothing, dear, if you're all right. How brave you are!

CAROLINE. Don't be absurd!

HUBERT. [*Breaking in.*] I should hardly call it bravery. This was bound to come some time. I've always said so. I've always feared it.

CAROLINE. [*Calmly.*] Feared what?

HUBERT. Miss Ambie's told me everything!

CAROLINE. [*With a sharp look at* SUSAN.] Oh, indeed! Then there's nothing for me to say. [*Rises to cross.*

HUBERT. [*Nettled.*] Caroline, I want to know exactly what has happened; so if there's anything that can be done now, I—

CAROLINE. [*Sarcastically.*] My dear Hubert, I'm really sorry to disappoint you; but there's nothing to be done.

HUBERT. And how about your difficulty with the trunks?

CAROLINE. [*Smiling.*] Sorry again. There's been no difficulty.

HUBERT. Then why did you send for me?
CAROLINE. I didn't send for you.
HUBERT. You didn't! [*He looks at* SUSAN *inquiringly.*
SUSAN. I know, but—
CAROLINE. Whenever we are away from you, Hubert, we grow so accustomed to depend on the chivalry and courtesy of men, that on our return, *Susan* forgets, and has to learn her lesson of self-dependence over again. You must forgive her. Really, Susan, you gave yourself too much concern.
SUSAN. My dear, I was so frightened. Didn't that woman search you?
CAROLINE. Me? Oh, no! I very soon put her in her place. And then, besides, I was careful to have nothing dutiable on my person.
HUBERT. Where *are* your trunks?
CAROLINE. I couldn't carry them with me, all nine of them. They'll be here shortly, I suppose.
[*She stands before the Venetian mirror, takes off her hat and fixes her hair.*
HUBERT. Caroline, there's been quite enough of this bantering. *Did* you make a declaration?
CAROLINE. Sufficient for all practical purposes.
HUBERT. And what does that mean?
CAROLINE. I've done exactly as I've always done. I refused to argue the matter. I settled. Of course, as the law puts a premium on *dis*honesty, I found it expedient to—
HUBERT. [*Interrupting.*] To what?
CAROLINE. [*Smiling.*] To pay the premium.
HUBERT. It isn't only a question of expediency. It's downright lying!
CAROLINE. [*Sarcastically.*] Behold the moralist!
HUBERT. [*Continuing.*] And it's a question of decent, honest citizenship!

CAROLINE. But I'm not a citizen; and I don't care to be. If *you* were honest, you'd confess you're only irritated, Hubert, because you can't say: "I told you so." So don't moralize; it doesn't suit you; and don't talk like a husband the first day I arrive. That doesn't suit me.

[HUBERT *is about to say something, but is interrupted by the entrance of* MRS. MURTHA *from the basement.* CAROLINE *looks at her with an amused smile.*

MURTHA. Mr. Knowllez, the motor-man from the taxicab is ashkin' if you'll be wantin' him to wait any longer.

SUSAN. Oh, that's my cab! He's been there all this time! [*She flounces to the hall.*

HUBERT. Wait, I'll—

SUSAN. [*With acerbity.*] No, thank you. [*Exits.*

MURTHA. An' th' oice man will be wantin' twinty cints fer th' oice. [*To* CAROLINE.] Shure, it's the grand box ye have.

HUBERT. [*Giving her money.*] Here. [MURTHA *goes to door.*] Oh, you can fetch up some glasses now, with ice in them; if you will.

MURTHA. Yis, sor. [*Exits hastily.*

CAROLINE. [*Amazed.*] Where did you get her?

HUBERT. At a place that calls itself the "Co-operative Servant Agency."

CAROLINE. That must be the new name for the "Zoo." Have you a match?

HUBERT. Yes.

CAROLINE. [*Opening her cigarette case.*] Will you smoke?

HUBERT. Thank you, I prefer my own.

CAROLINE. These are contraband.

HUBERT. The kind you like.

CAROLINE. Yes.
  [*He strikes a match for* CAROLINE. *She lights her cigarette.*
HUBERT. Well, didn't you have a good time abroad?
CAROLINE. Certainly.
  [*He sits at left of table, and lights his cigarette. She sits at right.*
HUBERT. But you changed your plans rather unexpectedly?
CAROLINE. I hope that hasn't inconvenienced you.
HUBERT. Not at all.
  [SUSAN *enters from the hall.*
SUSAN. I hate America!
HUBERT. Eh?
SUSAN. When you sail up the harbor and see the Statue of Liberty, you feel a tremendous emotion of patriotism; but when you see your first cab charge, you want to turn around and go right back to Europe. I told the man there was something the matter with his meter! It jumped ten cents while I was arguing with him!
CAROLINE. Did you pay?
SUSAN. I *had* to!
CAROLINE. Then don't complain. Pay or complain; but don't do both. It isn't economical.
  [MURTHA *enters, carrying three glasses awkwardly.*
MURTHA. Here ye are, Mr. Knowllez!
  [CAROLINE *opens the newspaper on the table and begins to read.*
HUBERT. Thank you, that will do.
MURTHA. [*Putting down the glasses.*] Shure, they'll do. [*She suddenly stares as she sees* CAROLINE *smoking.*] Ah, fer th' love o' God! [CAROLINE *looks up.* MURTHA *continues:*] Shure, Oi do be fergittin' mesilf when Oi be

passin' rhemarks wid your hushband. [*Catching* CAROLINE's *eye.*] Oh, Lord, yis, m'am.

[*She wilts away and exits to basement.*
[HUBERT *opens the whisky bottle.*

HUBERT. Miss Ambie, will you have a Scotch and soda?

SUSAN. No, thank you, it always makes me silly. I'll go directly to my room.

CAROLINE. [*Not looking up from the newspaper.*] Take the front room on the third floor.

SUSAN. Don't worry about me. I'll have Ninette arrange your things.

CAROLINE. [*Turning over the paper.*] Thank you, dear.

[SUSAN *exits up stairs.*

HUBERT. She's going to stay here?

CAROLINE. Yes.

HUBERT. Oh, then, in that case— [*He ostentatiously doubles his drink.*] How do you stand her?

CAROLINE. She pays her own way and is very useful.

HUBERT. [*Sarcastically.*] I daresay; but to me she's simply an interfering nuisance.

[*Pours soda into his whisky.*

CAROLINE. [*Still reading.*] No. She's a constitutional altruist. That is, she has the soul of a servant.

HUBERT. A scotch and soda?

CAROLINE. I never take it in the morning.

HUBERT. [*Drinking.*] I always forget.

CAROLINE. [*Looking up.*] The Homestead stock at sixty-four?

HUBERT. It closed at seventy yesterday.

CAROLINE. What made the slump?

HUBERT. A series of muck-raking articles about Factory Reform, and a lot of talk about Child Labor.

CAROLINE. I hope you're not embarrassed.

HUBERT. I've got to keep buying *in* to steady them.

CAROLINE. [*Putting down the paper.*] I'll lend you, Hubert; but I won't invest.

HUBERT. [*Ironically.*] Really, Caroline, your generosity overwhelms me.

CAROLINE. Not at all. I know you have collateral.

HUBERT. I still hope to worry along without placing myself under *financial* obligations to you.

CAROLINE. [*Placing both her elbows on table and looking at him narrowly.*] Hubert, I've often thought you resented my having independent means.

HUBERT. It's foolish of me; but I believe it might have made some difference in our lives, if you'd been—

CAROLINE. [*Interrupting.*] If I'd been dependent upon you for everything. If I had had no individuality of my own, or the means of keeping it intact. In other words, if I'd been poor. Is that what you mean?

HUBERT. No. But the superfluous wealth you've had has deprived us both of at least *one* of the real things. If we'd been poor toegther, there might have been something in our lives . . . something we've missed—something at any rate *I've* missed. Some mutality—some interest together. [*Rising.*] Here we are, two people who have lived for twenty odd years together, and who have never really had even a trouble in common!

CAROLINE. [*With a remote smile.*] What trouble would you like to have me share with you?   [*Pause.*

HUBERT. [*With a changed tone.*] Oh, none.

CAROLINE. [*Laughing.*] Hubert, don't be romantic toward your wife. That's waste. You're neither old enough nor young enough to play that sketch convincingly. You're neither dawn nor twilight; and Romance needs something undiscovered, something in possibility, something not yet precipitated into noonday commonplace reality. And you and I—we know too much about each other to really carry that off without laughing in our sleeves. You say it isn't money. Oh, then I fear something has gone wrong with some object of your affection.

HUBERT. Please!

CAROLINE. Then what is it?

HUBERT. I—I was about to speak of Elsie and Stephen.

CAROLINE. [*Carelessly.*] Oh, yes. How are the happy couple?

HUBERT. I'm afraid our daughter's not very happy. Stephen is a fool.

CAROLINE. I can't help that.

HUBERT. Have Elsie down here with us a little while—

CAROLINE. [*Interrupting.*] Impossible!

HUBERT. She might occupy her old rooms.

CAROLINE. I have other plans.

HUBERT. But a little motherly counsel from you might—

CAROLINE. [*Waving the discussion aside.*] Oh, Elsie and Stephen bore me to extinction,—both of them. I did my best for her—gave her a coming out, a season in Newport and—

HUBERT. [*Interrupting.*] Then married her off, made her a settlement and got rid of her. Gad! A girl of nineteen married!

CAROLINE. How old was I?

HUBERT. Well, our married life is nothing to boast of.

CAROLINE. Pardon, my dear Hubert, we've made a brilliant success of marriage. We ought to be grateful to the institution. It has given both of us the fullest liberty—a liberty that I've enjoyed; and you've—

HUBERT. [*Interrupting.*] Yes, you've always done exactly what you wanted.

CAROLINE. [*Meaningly.*] And you?

HUBERT. It makes no difference where we begin, we always wind up at the same place; don't we?

Act I]   THE UNCHASTENED WOMAN   373

CAROLINE. Because you have abused your liberty.

HUBERT. Yes, I admit, it's my fault—if you like, *all* my fault. It's useless to go back over the old ruptures and recriminations. The prime mistake in both our lives was that we ever married. Well, we did. After about two years of doves, we had several years of cat and dog—and—

CAROLINE. I beg your pardon, in which class of animals do you place me?

HUBERT. We won't quarrel about the phrase. You refused divorce or separation at a time in life when we might have got one without making ourselves ridiculous.

CAROLINE. Divorce is always ridiculous. I made up my mind you'd never get free for anything *I* should do.

HUBERT. Yes, you've always been very careful about that. It isn't morality; but you never cared to relinquish an advantage. You refused divorce for your own reasons; and I agreed with you for Elsie's sake. Then Elsie married—a great relief to you; and we both agreed that the altitude of ideal husband and wife was too high for *me* to breathe in. You never cared about me; yet you were always very anxious that nobody else should. In the real significance of marriage, you have broken all your vows but one. I have kept all my vows,—

CAROLINE. [*Sharply.*] Eh?

HUBERT. But one.

CAROLINE. Ah!

HUBERT. [*Continuing.*] That one violation of mine has given you the whip hand over me for these long years.

CAROLINE. Have you broken with that woman?

HUBERT. What woman?

CAROLINE. That Madden woman—Emily Madden.

HUBERT. You know nothing whatever about her.

CAROLINE. Pardon, I have taken the trouble to gather all the intimate details.

HUBERT. Indeed?

CAROLINE. And my friends have seen you every place with her. That's all I really care about.

HUBERT. And they will continue to see us; whenever Miss Madden does me the honor to accompany me.

CAROLINE. [*Resuming her newspaper.*] Oh, very well. I shall continue to condone everything; because I do not wish the elaborate structure I have built for many years to be destroyed. Our marriage stands as a temple to the Gods of Convention. The priests are hypocrites; but be careful not to make the *congregation* laugh. That's all I ask of you. Quite simple, isn't it?

HUBERT. Yes, simple as all heartless things are.

[*Pause. She reads.* HUBERT *walks up as* SUSAN AMBIE *enters from up stairs.*

SUSAN. Carrie, I tried to 'phone the Intelligence Offices; but your 'phone isn't connected.

[*She looks accusingly at* HUBERT.

HUBERT. [*Irritated.*] Excuse me. [*Goes to door, then turns.*] Oh, Miss Ambie, there's a prize of fifty dollars for the first *good* news that you announce. [*Exits.*

SUSAN. [*Sentimentally.*] I can see by your face, dear, you've had a scene.

CAROLINE. No. Just our annual understanding.

SUSAN. [*Curiously.*] You don't have to tell me, Carrie. [*Pause.*] Has he broken with that Madden woman?

CAROLINE. [*Smiling.*] I hope not.

SUSAN. It's wonderful that all this hasn't made you bitter.

CAROLINE. Bitter? [*Laughing.*] I am very grateful to Miss Madden.

SUSAN. [*Quickly.*] Oh, Carrie, you didn't tell *him* that, did you?

CAROLINE. [*Laughs.*] Oh, dear no! I never let him

forget that at any moment I could name Miss Madden as a co-respondent. She is a weapon in my hands.

SUSAN. [*Admiringly.*] What a wonderful person you are! Only—

CAROLINE. Only what?

SUSAN. Only be careful, dear. Don't give *him* a weapon against *you*.

CAROLINE. In what way?

SUSAN. Of course you'd never think about it; and it's quite as well you shouldn't, as long as I can do that for you. But be careful, dear, about Lawrence Sanbury.

CAROLINE. Don't be absurd. You were practically always with me.

SUSAN. [*With a nervous whimper.*] Oh, no, I failed you, Carrie; I should have dragged along no matter how ill I was.

CAROLINE. [*Bluntly.*] Get that idea out of your head.

SUSAN. But if he should ever learn about your last days alone with Lawrence in the mountains . . .

CAROLINE. He'll never learn it.

SUSAN. And there is a *Mrs.* Sanbury, too!

CAROLINE. [*Impatiently.*] Of course! Susan, I've known artists all my life, and I've never had to bother with their wives; at least . . .

[MURTHA *enters excitedly from the hall.*

CAROLINE. Would you mind knocking on the door before you enter a room?

MURTHA. [*Pointing innocently to the arch.*] But there isn't any door, me dear.

CAROLINE. What is it?

MURTHA. Me great friend and sishter, Mrs. Sanbury, is here wid her hushband! They be a wantin' to see you!

SUSAN. [*Frightened.*] She's here!

CAROLINE. Tell them I'm at home.

MURTHA. [*Going to the arch.*] Why wouldn't you be? Shure, Oi told thim that already.

SUSAN. [*Anxiously.*] Oh, Carrie! She's here!

CAROLINE. [*Secretly.*] Don't be an ass!

MURTHA. [*Calling out into the hall.*] Come, Lord bless yer lovin' hearts! It's roight in here, yer to come! [*Re-entering.*] Shure Oi'd trust her wid a million dollars. It was Mrs. Sanbury, it was, that sint me to you.

CAROLINE. Oh, I've *her* to thank for *you*, have I?

MURTHA. Yis, m'am. Shure ye have.

> [LAWRENCE *and* HILDEGARDE SANBURY *enter from the hall. He is a handsome vital looking man of twenty-five. He has a quick and ingenuous, volatile manner.* HILDEGARDE, *his wife, is a woman of thirty, of sympathetic and responsive nature, full of exuberant gratitude to* CAROLINE, *whom she has never met. In dress* HILDEGARDE *is the exact opposite of* CAROLINE. *She is scrupulously neat, but* CAROLINE *is a perfect conscience of every allure of fashion. They enter followed by* MURTHA, *who goes up rear.* LAWRENCE *nods to* SUSAN.

CAROLINE. [*To* HILDEGARDE.] I'm very glad you've come.

LAWRENCE. Hildegarde, this is Mrs. Knollys.

> [HUBERT *enters quietly from the door leading to the basement. He is unnoticed amid the greetings. He goes nonchalantly towards window at left.*

HILDEGARDE. When I heard Larrie was coming to you, I just couldn't stay at home.

LAWRENCE. She wouldn't. So we—

HILDEGARDE. [*Interrupting.*] Oh, Larrie, you must let *me* speak! You've had Mrs. Knollys all to yourself for six long weeks—[HUBERT *turns as* LAWRENCE *goes to* SUSAN.] You see I've heard so much about you. Larrie wrote me reams and reams of letters right from the beginning.

CAROLINE. [*Purringly.*] Yes.

HILDEGARDE. Oh, yes! I've followed you every step you've taken.

[SUSAN *looks anxious and laughs a little hysterically.*]

CAROLINE. [*Noticing* HUBERT'S *presence.*] Indeed!

HILDEGARDE. [*Seeing* CAROLINE'S *face change.*] I hope we haven't intruded!

CAROLINE. Not at all. Oh, Hubert, let me present you to Mr. and Mrs. Sanbury.

HUBERT. Ah! How do you do?

[*They exchange greetings.*]

CAROLINE. I've persuaded Mr. Sanbury to accept the commission to remodel the house.

HUBERT. [*Surprised.*] Oh, have you! [*Pause.*]

HILDEGARDE. [*Continuing to* CAROLINE.] Oh, it was wonderful for Larrie to be with you. You were eyes to him in Italy.

CAROLINE. Let me present you to Miss Ambie. [*Pointedly.*] She was with us too.

[HUBERT *notes this closely, though seeming not to listen.*]

HILDEGARDE. [*Surprised.*] Oh, *were* you? [*Goes immediately to* SUSAN.] Larrie wrote me you were taken ill in Switzerland, and that he and Mrs. Knollys went on alone.

SUSAN. [*Nervously.*] Oh, dear no, I mean . . . I . . . It was really nothing serious.

HILDEGARDE. I hope you've recovered.

Susan. Oh, perfectly, thank you. I didn't miss much of the trip . . . You see it was really only . . .

Caroline. [*Seeing* Hubert's *eye on them.*] Oh, Susan, it's nearly twelve. [*To the others.*] Excuse me. [*Again to* Susan.] You might hail a taxi and settle the matter of servants for me.

Susan. [*Anxiously.*] Yes, yes, but hadn't I better—?

Caroline. [*Decisively, going to the hall with* Susan.] The club for luncheon. One o'clock. [Susan *exits.*

Murtha. [*Coming up from rear.*] Ah, it do be good to see thim together again, eh?

Caroline. Did you want to ask me anything?

Murtha. If it's a chambermaid ye want, me daughter Agnes—

Caroline. Would you mind closing the door?

Murtha. Ah, not at all.

[*She crosses and closes the door, then returns.*

Caroline. [*Cuttingly.*] I mean *behind* you.

Murtha. [*Catching* Caroline's *eye and meaning.*] Oh, yis, m'am. [*She exits.*

Caroline. [*Motioning* Hildegarde *to a chair.*] Do I understand you run an Intelligence Office?

Hildegarde. I've organized a general employment bureau in connection with the tenements.

Lawrence. But, my dear, it's hardly fair to Mrs. Knollys to send this old—

Hildegarde. [*Interrupting.*] We sent her daughter Agnes. You understand, only the derelicts come to us; but you'll see, Mrs. Murtha will do her work well.

Caroline. Tell me, do you really *live* among these people?

Hildegarde. Yes, at the model tenement. Have you ever seen one?

Caroline. No!

HILDEGARDE. I'd be delighted to show you around.

CAROLINE. Yes. Miss Ambie and I will come sometime together.

HILDEGARDE. Do, and take luncheon with us at our co-operative dining-room.

LAWRENCE. [*To* CAROLINE.] I wouldn't expect too much. You see, it's a fad of hers—Democracy and the Underdog.

HILDEGARDE. Oh, no, that's my real work.

HUBERT. [*Coming into the conversation.*] What?

HILDEGARDE. We believe in giving the poor people better living conditions first; so that then they will be better able to fight for other things.

HUBERT. Yes, and make them discontented all along the line.

HILDEGARDE. [*Fervently.*] If only we could make them sufficiently discontented!

HUBERT. [*Taking up the newspaper.*] I should say you were succeeding very well. Have you seen this series of furious articles on Factory Reform?

HILDEGARDE. [*Looking at paper.*] Yes.

HUBERT. What do you think of them?

HILDEGARDE. I ought to approve of them.

HUBERT. Why?

HILDEGARDE. Because I wrote them.

HUBERT. [*Amazed.*] What! You?

HILDEGARDE. Yes. They're mine.

HUBERT. You label these articles reform, but they read pretty much like anarchy to me.

HILDEGARDE. Do you know about our present factory conditions?

HUBERT. [*Grimly.*] Somewhat, to my cost. You've made me one of your horrible examples.

HILDEGARDE. What!!

HUBERT. I own the majority stock in the Homestead Mills.

LAWRENCE. [*Nervously.*] Good Lord, Hildegarde! Your crowd haven't been attacking Mr. Knollys, have they?

HILDEGARDE. [*To* LAWRENCE.] No one was mentioned by name. [*To* HUBERT.] Your manager refused to show his stock sheet to our committee; so we simply wrote up the mill.

HUBERT. Our manager has to compete with others. We give these people work. We don't force our hands to come to us.

HILDEGARDE. That's it. The whole system is wrong. The state must remedy it. Individuals can't. You've got to resort to the means of your lowest and most unscrupulous competitor; or leave the field.

HUBERT. Do you mind answering a few questions?

HILDEGARDE. Not at all.

HUBERT. [*To* CAROLINE *and* LAWRENCE.] Excuse us. [*He and* HILDEGARDE *go toward the hall. He takes some clippings from his pocket.*] In the first place you stated . . . [*They exit and pass out of sight, going toward the right, in earnest conversation.* CAROLINE *is sitting in the large divan chair at the left.* LAWRENCE *comes toward her.*

LAWRENCE. [*Enthusiastically.*] Isn't she splendid!

CAROLINE. [*Softly ironical.*] You treat us all alike; don't you?

LAWRENCE. How?

CAROLINE. [*Quietly.*] She, too, is older than you. Isn't she?

LAWRENCE. Oh, a year or two. That doesn't matter.

CAROLINE. How chivalrous you are. But for your sake, she ought to be wiser.

LAWRENCE. What do you mean?

CAROLINE. Her radical theories about Democracy and —the great Unwashed. . . . Do you agree with them?

LAWRENCE. I'm an artist. I take no side whatever.

CAROLINE. But don't you see, you'll *have* to take a side?

LAWRENCE. Why?

CAROLINE. People of our class won't support you, if your wife attacks the very sources from which they pay you.

LAWRENCE. [*With sudden anxiety.*] Oh, perhaps Mr. Knollys will resent what Hildegarde has done, and won't care to give me the work. Is that what you mean?

CAROLINE. I mean your wife mustn't add to my difficulties.

LAWRENCE. [*Sincerely distressed.*] Oh, Lord! In wrong the first crack out of the box; and I wanted you so much to like each other!

CAROLINE. Tell me,—is she really as frank as she seems?

LAWRENCE. Why, yes. What makes you ask that?

CAROLINE. I was a little startled when I learned you'd written her so definitely about our tour in Italy.

LAWRENCE. [*Relieved.*] Oh, that's all right. Hildegarde thinks nothing about that.

CAROLINE. But she mustn't give everybody credit for so much sympathetic understanding.

[*With a glance toward the hall.*

LAWRENCE. You mean your husband!

CAROLINE. [*Quickly.*] Don't speak so loudly! [*With a change to a seductive, problematical manner.*] I haven't told you everything about my life. I thought you guessed.

LAWRENCE. Why, surely, he wouldn't dare to misjudge you, would he?

CAROLINE. We move in a society that does not trust itself, so it is always suspicious.

LAWRENCE. I hope you'll forgive me. I'm just a fool about these things.

CAROLINE. [*Seeing* HUBERT *and* HILDEGARDE *approaching.*] Pst! Say nothing more.

HUBERT. [*Re-entering from the hall.*] [*To* HILDEGARDE.] If I'm on top, I know I'll treat the laborer as well as I can afford. If he's on top, I can't expect so much in return. They get a living wage.

HILDEGARDE. You'd better take a trip down South and see how well they live.

HUBERT. Perhaps I shall. And then I'll want to see you again.

HILDEGARDE. Do! [*To the others.*] Until then we part, good, class-conscious, cordial enemies.

HUBERT. [*Pointing to the newspaper.*] Very well. And how about these articles?

HILDEGARDE. To-morrow we begin on your competitors.

HUBERT. Good! That's fair play.

CAROLINE. Hubert, would you mind showing Mr. Sanbury about the house?

HUBERT. Now?

CAROLINE. Yes. Mrs. Sanbury will remain with me.

[HILDEGARDE *nods.*

HUBERT. We'll go this way.

LAWRENCE. Excuse me.

[LAWRENCE *and* HUBERT *exit through hall and are seen mounting the stairs.*

CAROLINE. [*Points to a chair in the full light.*] You don't mind the light?

HILDEGARDE. Oh, not at all.

CAROLINE. [*Speaking as she pulls up the shade full upon* HILDEGARDE.] I'm sure we shall understand each other thoroughly; because we both want your husband to succeed.

HILDEGARDE. It's fine of you to be so interested. He's never had a chance to prove what he can do.

CAROLINE. [*Sitting with her back to the light.*] My interest will excuse many personal questions. [*Charmingly.*] He being so young, we can discuss him and his future from the same point of view.

HILDEGARDE. Yes, Larrie for all his twenty-five years is just a great big boy.

CAROLINE. How did you come to live there in the tenements?

HILDEGARDE. Surely Larrie has told you!

CAROLINE. But I never trust a husband to tell me all about his home. [*Insinuatingly.*] If the wife loves him very much, he never really knows his circumstances.

HILDEGARDE. We've had no secrets from each other. We struggled on together right from the beginning. I sometimes got disheartened, but Larrie never did.

CAROLINE. Ah! Did *he* decide to live there?

HILDEGARDE. No. I lived there first, and when we married, we decided to settle there together, so I might continue my work.

CAROLINE. But do you think the tenement is quite the —ah—the atmosphere for him to work in?

HILDEGARDE. He hasn't complained; and offices cost lots of money.

CAROLINE. Yes.

HILDEGARDE. Your commission will enable him to start in business for himself; and then we hope to afford a better place.

CAROLINE. Yes. But have you ever considered how your very work in the world might hinder him?

HILDEGARDE. [*Puzzled.*] In what way?

CAROLINE. Art has always been the luxury of a leisure class. It has always been supported by the patronage of wealth; and you can't expect that the people whom you attack, and *publicly* attack, are going to reply by using their influence to promote your husband.

HILDEGARDE. Then Lawrence must work his way without their influence.

CAROLINE. [*With narrowing eyes.*] In the school of adversity, eh?

HILDEGARDE. [*Proudly.*] That school has brought out the best in many artists!

CAROLINE. And has killed thousands of others that we never hear of. My dear, the school of adversity is a very good school; provided you don't matriculate too early and continue too long.

HILDEGARDE. I'd rather continue just as we are now to the end of our days, than have him sell his soul and abandon all he's stood for.

CAROLINE. *You* would; but how about *him?*

HILDEGARDE. He would too!

CAROLINE. Perhaps I know him better than you do.

HILDEGARDE. I don't think so.

CAROLINE. Then some day, you may have to reproach yourself for his failure.

HILDEGARDE. I?

CAROLINE. Yes.

HILDEGARDE. Why should he fail?

CAROLINE. Just because of his unusual qualities. The world at best is a cruel place. It gives its prizes to the ordinary. It martyrizes the exceptional person, because it doesn't understand him, and what it doesn't understand, it fears; and what it fears, it destroys, or worse than that, it allows to die unnoticed. The world will make your husband suffer, *just because he is exceptional.*

HILDEGARDE. I can't believe that!

CAROLINE. [*Sarcastically.*] One must indeed be an

optimist to be a fanatic. With your help I hoped to place him where I know he belongs. But I cannot; if you oppose it. [*Pause.*]

HILDEGARDE. I don't see how *I* stand in his way!

CAROLINE. You have already made a difficulty with my husband.

HILDEGARDE. How?

CAROLINE. My dear, you can hardly expect my husband to give your husband an expensive commission; when you spend your time writing articles that lower the value of the most important investment he holds.

HILDEGARDE. Then Lawrence will have to choose.

CAROLINE. Oh, no. You mustn't put that on him. You mustn't bind him by his love for you. For if he fails to choose properly, you will be forced to bear the burden of his bitterness. And there's nothing so bitter in the world as an artist's bitterness. [*Looking at her closely.*] It won't come now. I grant you a few years more of his hopeful illusions and youthful courage; but then your awakening will come . . . when you are gray—at heart, and he still in his prime; but with the sources of his faith run dry—eaten with disappointments, sick with postponements, his inspiration festered by discouragement; while he still knocks listlessly at the doors, which would be open to him now; but will be closed hereafter, when his opportunities have passed him by.

HILDEGARDE. That can't be true!

CAROLINE. [*Continuing ruthlessly.*] And in the cruel retrospect, then *his* awakening will come; and he will see that it has been [*Cynically*] what you call your "life-work" that has hindered him. And then, what will his love for you be worth to *you* or *him?*

HILDEGARDE. [*Obstinately.*] He has his work, I have mine. It's for him to choose.

CAROLINE. And is your muck-raking worth his career? Knowing that he loves you now, and will be influenced by you, have you a right to make him choose?

HILDEGARDE. No more than you!

CAROLINE. There is this difference:—*I* do it for his sake purely.

HILDEGARDE. So do I!

CAROLINE. I doubt it.

HILDEGARDE. [*Passionately.*] Don't you think it would be easier for me to see him settled? I've walked the floor at night! I've agonized over his career, while he's been sleeping like a child!

CAROLINE. [*Quickly.*] Ah, then there *have* been secrets!

HILDEGARDE. [*Continuing.*] Yes! I've made it a point of honor not to allow him to spend one cent on me! [*Suddenly.*] You're looking at this dress! I know it's shabby—You've noticed it—He hasn't . . .

CAROLINE. My dear, you mustn't feel sensitive about your clothes!

HILDEGARDE. [*Choking back her tears.*] It's the first time that I ever was!

CAROLINE. You must let me give you a gown or two.

HILDEGARDE. [*Recoiling.*] Oh, no! I couldn't accept them—I couldn't!

CAROLINE. But, my dear—

HILDEGARDE. [*Proudly.*] Excuse me, don't presume!

CAROLINE. I hoped you'd understand. Your husband's profession has a social side. There are people he must meet—people that will be of use to him. I want to arrange it. You won't object?

HILDEGARDE. Oh, no!

CAROLINE. It's always easy for a man—a dress suit and

there you are. But we women are at a disadvantage without the proper equipment, and . . .

HILDEGARDE. Please leave me out of all your calculations. I shan't complicate matters.

CAROLINE. My dear, I merely intended to save you from embarrassment.

HILDEGARDE. I am very grateful. But I repeat, it's impossible I should accept anything from you. We belong to two totally different orders.

CAROLINE. Then as you're unwilling to meet the social requirements, you will understand perfectly, if you're not included in . . .

HILDEGARDE. Certainly. I shall not expect to be invited.

CAROLINE. I must compliment you, Mrs. Sanbury. You're stronger than I thought you were.

[*Pause. The two women look at each other.* HILDEGARDE *is dazed.* CAROLINE *is smilingly confident.*

LAWRENCE. [*Coming down stairs.*] We'll have a jolly job introducing Queen Victoria to the Renaissance. You've plenty of room; that is, if you'll let me smash the conventional partitions.

CAROLINE. [*Meaningly.*] I always like to smash conventional partitions; provided the outside walls remain intact. Have you explained to Hubert?

LAWRENCE. He couldn't follow the sketch.

CAROLINE. [*With a veiled sneer.*] You'll have to build models before he can see.

LAWRENCE. [*After a slight hesitation.*] Will you really need models?

CAROLINE. I am afraid so. How long would it take you?

LAWRENCE. Well, you know, I've left my old firm; and I'll first have to look about for larger quarters.

HILDEGARDE. [*Involuntarily.*] Oh!

LAWRENCE. [*Confidently.*] I've been thinking of changing. It's only been a question of the proper place.

CAROLINE. [*Knowingly smiling at* HILDEGARDE.] Oh, of course. But I've an idea. In insisting upon models, I appreciate I am asking the unusual; but I want to expedite matters.

LAWRENCE. Yes . . . Yes . . .

CAROLINE. You've seen the fourth storey?

LAWRENCE. Yes.

CAROLINE. Couldn't you build your models there?

LAWRENCE. [*Eagerly.*] Splendidly! [*Relieved.*] That would solve everything; wouldn't it, Hildegarde? [*To* CAROLINE.] And I could consult with you at every step.

CAROLINE. Yes. [*To* HILDEGARDE.] And in that way, we needn't interfere with your plans at the tenement.

HILDEGARDE. Oh!

CAROLINE. Perhaps you'd better advise with your wife before you decide. I'll speak with Hubert. Excuse me.

[*She exits through the hall.*

LAWRENCE. [*Watches her out of the tail of his eye. As soon as she is off, his manner changes, and he comes to* HILDEGARDE *in hushed excitement. He takes her hands and speaks quickly.*] I'm glad, old girl, you didn't butt into any of my bluffs! I got a cold sweat when she spoke about models! [*Wiping his brow.*] Phew! That was a poser! But did you see me do it? [*Imitating his former manner.*] "Just looking for a proper place." [*With a flourish of his hand.*] Money no object. Did you see me? With not enough to the good to keep the sheriff off any place for a single month! [*Sitting.*] That fourth storey is too good to be true! [*Devoutly.*] God bless the ugliness of Queen Victoria! God bless the rich with big houses and small families! Don't wake me!

HILDEGARDE. Then you're going to accept her top floor?

LAWRENCE. [*Flabbergasted to an echo.*] Am I going to accept her . . . ? Watch me! I've never told you; but I haven't been able to work there in the tenements. This address alone will get me credit for materials. And right now, I'm in no position to deny her anything.

HILDEGARDE. Evidently.

LAWRENCE. [*Rubbing his chin.*] Gosh! The old man was pretty mum about the plan. [*Suddenly.*] He may be sore about those articles of yours! I hope they haven't queered it.

HILDEGARDE. Oh, I fancy she'll arrange it.

LAWRENCE. I hope she will. [*Suddenly.*] Golly, you don't seem to realize what this job means to me!

HILDEGARDE. Perhaps I do, even more than you.

LAWRENCE. [*Intensely.*] Money! That's what it means . . . Money! A thing we've never had, and a thing we've got to get!

HILDEGARDE. Is money everything?

LAWRENCE. Yes, now—everything. . . . Money! I want money—money to be free to do things—money to get things for you. Do you think I like to see you wearing rags like this?

[*Pointing to her dress.*

HILDEGARDE. [*With a quick pain.*] Oh, as for me—

LAWRENCE. I've had enough of the tenements! I've never told you—

HILDEGARDE. Larrie!!

LAWRENCE. [*Excitedly.*] That's all right, my dear. You're a fanatic about some things. I don't interfere with you, and you mustn't interfere with me! [*Change.*] Perhaps you'd better go. . . . I mean if you're not in sympathy with the scheme, for God's sake, don't hang on.

HILDEGARDE. [*Slowly.*] There's lots that I could say, Larrie. . . .

LAWRENCE. Yes, I know, but not here. Listen— Open your head! I've got to nail this job. I want to do it on my own hook. Then if I take it to a firm, I collar some of the swag and get some credit for my work. . . . I may never wing a chance to start like this again. [*She is about to say something but he continues.*] We're broke—and no instalment until the plans and models are accepted. Here I get a place rent free, materials on tick, with Lawrence Sanbury I-N-C upon the signs. . . . I'll incorporate my debts. Otherwise, back again into an old thirty a week job to sweat for the other fellow all my life. [*Quickly giving* HILDEGARDE *her coat.*] Hildegarde, here—take your rags and run.

HILDEGARDE. [*Quietly.*] Shall I wait luncheon?

LAWRENCE. Hang luncheon. I'm going to eat this job.

HILDEGARDE. But on your first day home, after . . .

LAWRENCE. There'll be lots of days like this coming. [*Holding her coat.*] Here—here she comes. Just say good-by.

[*Enter* CAROLINE *from the hall.*

CAROLINE. Well, I've spoken with my husband.

LAWRENCE. [*Restrained.*] Yes . . . ?

CAROLINE. He thinks it an admirable plan for you to work here.

LAWRENCE. [*Relieved.*] Ah, then that's settled!

CAROLINE. So we can begin immediately . . . that is . . . if—

[*Looks at* HILDEGARDE.

HILDEGARDE. I was just going. [CAROLINE *is silent.*] Good-by, Mrs. Knollys.

CAROLINE. [*With feigned surprise.*] Oh! [*Then in a commonplace tone.*] Good-by. I shan't forget your invitation to the tenements.

LAWRENCE. Excuse me, Hildegarde, I'll be home—ah—shortly.   [HILDEGARDE *goes quickly to the arch, and exits through the hall.*
[LAWRENCE *makes a move to follow her, then pauses perplexed.* CAROLINE *watches him narrowly.*

LAWRENCE. [*Scratching his head.*] By Jove! What makes a fellow a brute sometimes to the woman he cares for?

CAROLINE. [*Slowly.*] It's the artist in *you,* Lawrence, that is instinctively unscrupulous toward anything that hinders its development.

LAWRENCE. But Hildegarde wouldn't hinder me!

CAROLINE. Not intentionally, certainly not. She's an exceptional person. [*Sitting.*] I'm sorry she doesn't like me.

LAWRENCE. [*Fighting against his own conviction.*] What makes you think she doesn't like you?

CAROLINE. She has her—ah—principles. Unfortunately they oppose everything I stand for.

LAWRENCE. You don't know her, she . . .

CAROLINE. Perhaps not, and I'm so sorry! for I hoped we should agree about you.

LAWRENCE. But she must see how much you mean to me, and—

CAROLINE. Perhaps you've been too frank with her.

LAWRENCE. I never conceal anything from Hildegarde.

CAROLINE. [*Ironically.*] No. . . .

LAWRENCE. [*Continuing.*] And I'd hate any person that made me lie! [*Sitting disconsolately.*] What can I do?

CAROLINE. That you must decide yourself. You stand at a crossing, Lawrence. The one road means the old limitations and the commonplace: the other leads to freedom and opportunity. It's difficult to choose, because she loves you . . . dearly.

LAWRENCE. Of course she does!

CAROLINE. Therefore it's quite natural she should resent any one having the power to do for you what she would like to do; but can't. I'd feel that way myself, if . . .

LAWRENCE. If what?

CAROLINE. If I loved you the way she does. If I weren't ambitious for your *great* work!

LAWRENCE. But she wants me to do big work.

CAROLINE. [*Shaking her head.*] You feel things in you that she never dreamed of. That's why . . . [*With a change.*] But I oughtn't make you conscious.

LAWRENCE. What is it?

CAROLINE. [*With a show of reluctance.*] That's why you aren't at your best, when you're with her. Now there, I've said it.

LAWRENCE. But I haven't had the chance of really explaining to her all I want to do, and . . .

CAROLINE. [*Unscrupulously.*] An *artist* justifies himself by *doing:* not explaining! Consider everything that helps you to your end as good. That is the conscience of an artist. His work is always greater than his life.

LAWRENCE. By Jove, I always see clearer when I talk to you!

CAROLINE. [*Passionately.*] I am unscrupulous for the best in you!

LAWRENCE. [*Taking her hands.*] You're wonderful!

CAROLINE. I mustn't be mistaken in you!

LAWRENCE. [*Kissing her hands.*] You won't be.

CAROLINE. I have a problem too, because of you.

LAWRENCE. [*Dropping her hands.*] Yes, I know.

CAROLINE. And you must justify *me as well*. We made a compact. Have you forgotten it?

LAWRENCE. The afternoon we left Florence.

CAROLINE. And climbed the hills toward Fiesolé . . . alone.

LAWRENCE. [*Rapt.*] In the flaming orange scarfs of mist, with the whole world behind us in the valley.

CAROLINE. Where you said the world should always be for the artist with the vision and the will to create a new form of art. You were splendid then!

LAWRENCE. And afterward, the long ride on to Brescia and Como and—

CAROLINE. Psch! That lies behind us. [*Pause. With a change.*] I thought that memory belonged to us alone.

LAWRENCE. It does!

CAROLINE. [*Raising her finger.*] You shared it.

LAWRENCE. Forget that, please.

CAROLINE. I hope the others will.

MURTHA'S VOICE. [*Up stairs.*] Will I hang the things up here, sir?

HUBERT'S VOICE. [*Up stairs.*] Yes, just put them in the closet, please.

CAROLINE. [*Quickly to* LAWRENCE.] Sit down. [*He starts to sit in a chair near her. She points to one at right of stage.*] No; over there. [*He goes quickly to the other side. She continues.*] We'll lunch together. The Colony Club at one o'clock.

LAWRENCE. I thought that Hildegarde might—

CAROLINE. [*Interrupting peremptorily.*] I *must* see you.

LAWRENCE. But on my first day home—

CAROLINE. [*Impatiently.*] Between Susan's nervousness and your thoughtlessness, I . . .

LAWRENCE. Very well.

[*Enter* HUBERT *from the hall.*]

HUBERT. H'm! Still talking over plans?

LAWRENCE. [*Rising, embarrassed.*] Yes . . . yes . . . and I want to thank you, Mr. Knollys.

HUBERT. Me? For what?

LAWRENCE. The fourth storey. It'll be a great help to me. [HUBERT *looks perplexed.*

CAROLINE. You know, I have asked Mr. Sanbury to build his models there.

HUBERT. [*Grimly.*] Ah . . . have you! I didn't know.

LAWRENCE. [*Filling in the awkward pause.*] Then you can see exactly how the rooms will look.

HUBERT. Oh, as for me . . . [*Smiles.*] Quite so. Very kind of you—very. Where's your wife?

LAWRENCE. She's already gone.

HUBERT. [*Sarcastically.*] If you should *see* her again, you might tell her that I've decided to go South immediately.

LAWRENCE. [*Jerking at his watch.*] Yes—ah . . . She'll be delighted to hear that . . . and . . . ah . . . I was delighted to meet you, Mr. Knollys; and if you'll excuse me—I'll—I'll . . . be going now.

[*He stands awkwardly.* HUBERT *goes to the hall, then turns to* LAWRENCE.]

HUBERT. Good morning.

LAWRENCE. Oh, good-by, Mrs. Knollys. [*To* HUBERT.] Good-by, Mr. Knollys.

CAROLINE. Good-by.

[HUBERT *nods.* LAWRENCE *exits. Pause.*

HUBERT. [*Laughing softly.*] Caroline, I think your latest is a light-weight!

CAROLINE. [*Changing the subject.*] You're going South?

HUBERT. I hope you'll endure my absence. [*Pause.*]

What was your object in giving your young man the impression that you had to consult me in anything?

CAROLINE. I generally consult you.

HUBERT. Yes. After you've completed your arrangements. It's your house. I've nothing to say. But I see now why you needed Elsie's room.

[*A furious knock is heard in the hall. They both start as* MURTHA *enters.*]

MURTHA. [*Proudly.*] Ah, did ye hear me knock?

CAROLINE. What is is?

MURTHA. A young lady's in th' front hall. [*To* HUBERT.] She wants to see you, Mr. Knowllez.

HUBERT. To see me?

MURTHA. [*Hesitating.*] She says she's from th' Cushtoms office, so she says.

HUBERT. [*Grimly to* CAROLINE.] I fancy it's about your trunks.

CAROLINE. [*To* MURTHA.] Send her in here.

MURTHA. Shure Oi will—whoy wouldn't Oi?

[*Exits to hall.*]

HUBERT. Why should the young lady want to see me?

CAROLINE. Have you money with you?

HUBERT. [*Taking out his bill case.*] Yes.

CAROLINE. [*With a smile.*] I gave her my card.

HUBERT. But—

CAROLINE. [*Taking his bill case and going to window.*] Let me see. All she's come for is more money.

[HUBERT *during the above goes toward the hall.* CAROLINE's *back is to him.* EMILY MADDEN *enters nervously from the right. She is a young woman of about twenty-eight.* HUBERT *makes a quick recoil of amazement and a half-smothered exclama-*

tion: "Emily!" *She, seeing* CAROLINE, *gives him a quick gesture of silence.*

EMILY. [*In a breathless staccato and a forbidding manner.*] This is Mr. Knollys, I believe.

HUBERT. Yes.

CAROLINE. [*Turning and coming down.*] I hope you've had no difficulty.

EMILY. You evidently did not understand.

CAROLINE. Oh, I see. In that case, why, of course, I wish to pay you for any further—

EMILY. [*Violently.*] Please!

HUBERT. Caroline!

CAROLINE. Oh!

EMILY. Mrs. Knollys, all your trunks are held.

CAROLINE. [*Savagely.*] The insolence!

EMILY. It was the only way to save you from a charge of smuggling and . . .

CAROLINE. Indeed!

EMILY. I couldn't make you realize it. That's why I've come to see your husband.

CAROLINE. [*With a smile.*] Thank you very much.

HUBERT. Caroline, you'd better let me settle this.

CAROLINE. [*Crossing to the hall.*] By all means. You always settle things so adequately. [*To* EMILY.] Good morning. [*She starts to go up stairs, then turns and says significantly to* HUBERT:] Oh, your purse!

[*She throws it gracefully over the balustrade. He, standing below, catches it. She continues up stairs. He watches her out of sight, then turns and comes down to* EMILY.

HUBERT. [*Giving way to his astonishment.*] Emily! I'm all in the dark! How are you mixed up in this?

EMILY. [*Quickly.*] I left the newspaper and got a position in the Customs. This morning I saw her name on the list of passengers. She fell into the hands of one of the sourest old inspectors. He found some jewels in a sachet bag. Then he caught her in a lie. As usual, he asked her to reconsider her declaration. She refused . . .

HUBERT. [*Unconsciously.*] The damned fool!

EMILY. Then he insisted she be searched.

HUBERT. Naturally.

EMILY. As I was standing there, the officers deputed me to look her over.

HUBERT. [*Appalled.*] But she didn't know who you were, did she?

EMILY. Oh, no, but I took the chance to tell her of the penalty: ten thousand dollars' fine, or two years' imprisonment, or both.

HUBERT. I hope that sobered her!

EMILY. Judge for yourself. She said she had a list, and gave me this envelope. [*Giving him an envelope out of her bag.*] Open it.

HUBERT. [*Opening it.*] Two one hundred dollar bills.

EMILY. One for my partner. There were two of us.

HUBERT. [*Putting envelope on table.*] The same old game.

EMILY. I felt like throwing it into her face; but then I thought of you, and held my temper. The inspectors were waiting.

HUBERT. What did you do?

EMILY. I told your wife I'd tend to everything, and got her off. Then I reported for her that she had reconsidered, had nothing on her person, she was ill and didn't know what things were dutiable; and therefore wanted all her stuff to be appraised.

HUBERT. Good! And then?

EMILY. Then I tried to 'phone you everywhere, and

finally I had to take the chance of even meeting—her again, and come right here to tell you.

HUBERT. You little thoroughbred.

EMILY. Hubert, do nothing until you hear from them. Dispute nothing, but make her stick to the story that I framed up for her, and pay on their appraisal. I hope I've done right.

HUBERT. Right! I don't know how to thank you.

EMILY. Return this to your wife with my compliments.
[*Points to envelope.*

HUBERT. I guess you're all in, Emily.

EMILY. Oh, don't mind about me.

HUBERT. Filthy business, this. [*Suddenly anxious.*] There'll be no consequences for you?

EMILY. I guess not.

HUBERT. [*Walking about.*] I don't know how it is. She never learns. She does exactly what she pleases. Experience means nothing to her; because in some way she always manages to get protected, no matter what she does. She's skated over thin ice all her life—she *courts* the danger signals; and just when anybody else would fall through, an unknown somebody reaches her a hand out of the universe and lands her safe! Gad! and to think that it was you that helped her!

EMILY. I don't think that would appeal to her sense of humor.

HUBERT. Did she bring over much stuff?

EMILY. They said about six thousand, off hand.

HUBERT. Six thou . . . Phew! Well, that's *her* affair. But sit down a moment. [*He puts her on settle, then sits at right of the table.*] Tell me, how did *you* get into the Customs office?

EMILY. I got tired of the paper. My friend Hildegarde Sanbury suggested the Customs, and helped me get it.

HUBERT. Oh, Mrs. Sanbury's a friend of yours.
EMILY. Yes, why?
HUBERT. They were here this morning.
EMILY. Were they? Isn't Hildegarde fine?
HUBERT. Tell me about *him!*
EMILY. You mean Lawrence?
HUBERT. Yes.
EMILY. They say he's a genius, full of all wonderful things, and just waiting for his opportunity to express them.
HUBERT. Yes, just the type!
EMILY. What type?
HUBERT. Do you know where he and Caroline met?
EMILY. I've no idea; except that they spent some time together in Italy.
HUBERT. What was he doing there?
EMILY. Studying and making sketches. Hildegarde slaved and saved every cent she could to send him over.
HUBERT. So this is her latest!
EMILY. What do you mean?
HUBERT. I wonder if I can explain it. Caroline has a mania for depredating the next generation. She poses to herself as the heroine of a belated romance.
EMILY. But she knows Lawrence is married; doesn't she?
HUBERT. She prefers them married. Takes all the perfume and the blossoms, and lets the wife grub at the roots. She likes to be the destiny and let the wife assume the utility. Does he love his wife?
EMILY. Why, of course, devotedly. That's the finest thing about him.
HUBERT. Better yet. She enjoys making a test of her power.
EMILY. [*Impulsively.*] Hildegarde's the best in the world, Hubert, and . . .

HUBERT. Then I pity her.

EMILY. You don't mean your wife will hurt Hildegarde, do you?

HUBERT. [*Bitterly.*] She won't bleed; that is, outwardly. She'll just wake up and find her happiness evaporated.

EMILY. You mustn't allow it. She's just a child before a sophisticated person.

HUBERT. [*Desperately.*] What can I do? Caroline has done this all her life; and as she operates under the protection of my name, I've had apparently to stand by and sanction it.

EMILY. Can't you stop her?

HUBERT. [*Again walking about.*] How? You'd respect her if she showed one real emotion. She's physically chaste; but is absolutely unchastened in soul; and yet she feeds on the souls of others. That's how she keeps young. She's a mental *Bluebeard,* and I'm the hotel clerk for her castle . . . I know where all her miserable relics hang . . . What rooms and what days of their lives they've offered her!

EMILY. Why, this is horrible, Hubert!

HUBERT. [*Continuing.*] I'd give my eyes to stop her! If not for the sake of others, for my own sake! She's broken me! I tried to get free for years at the beginning. But she plays so absolutely safe . . . She protects herself so completely that she is unassailable.

EMILY. Can't *he* be warned?

HUBERT. Not if she gets him first. Her kind of poison strikes them blind. There's nothing to be done for him. Just *you* keep out of her way.

EMILY. Don't worry. I will. Well, I must get back to work. [*She starts to go again.*

HUBERT. My dear, why will you work? Why won't you let me take care of you?

EMILY. I wish to earn my own living, Hubert. You know that.

HUBERT. Yes. But I want to ask you . . . Why have you avoided me for this long time?

EMILY. Hubert, I didn't want to write it; but it's over between us.

HUBERT. [*After a pause.*] Yes, I've realized that.

EMILY. [*Very tenderly.*] Hubert, I've no reproach to make you; and I don't want you to reproach me, or to feel any bitterness. What we gave was a free gift from both —a free gift and no regrets. A break had to come some time, I suppose; and as soon as I met *him*, I—I realized that it had to come right away. [*Looking away from* HUBERT.] He asked no questions; but that's why you haven't seen or heard from me. Hubert I'm going to marry Michael Krellin.

HUBERT. [*After a pause.*] Good luck to you. [*He takes her hand in both of his.*] But I thought you didn't believe in marriage.

EMILY. Neither did he. But I'm afraid we both believe in marriage now. I can't tell you how it happened; but it's *different*, Hubert . . . That's all . . . I know you'll understand.

[HUBERT *nods and releases her hand. She goes toward the hall.*]

HUBERT. Emily . . . [*She stops and turns.*] We've been good chums for a long time; and, do you know, you've never allowed me to give you anything?

EMILY. That was our agreement, Hubert.

HUBERT. Yes; but I want you to promise me this. If you should ever get into a blind alley, and need anything, a friend or money, and need it without strings, I want you to think of me. I'd like to feel you'd do that much for the sake of Auld Lang Syne.

EMILY. [*Coming to him.*] All right. I promise. [*Extends her hand.*] Good-bye.

HUBERT. [*Quietly, as he takes her hand.*] Krellin's a very lucky fellow.

EMILY. That's like you, Hubert.

HUBERT. I'll call you a cab.

EMILY. Never mind. Don't come with me, please. I'll run right along. [*She turns and says very tenderly:*] Good-by.

HUBERT. Good-by.

> [*She exits through the hall. After she is off, HUBERT stands looking after her until the front door is heard to close. He drops his hands disconsolately and walks mechanically to the table at center. His eyes fall upon the envelope still lying there. He takes it up. His mood changes. He gets a sudden idea. He looks up, throws the envelope down on the table again with an angry gesture, and goes with vehement determination toward the stairs. He pauses at the bottom of the stairs, shakes his head perplexed, and then decides upon a different attack. He calls very pleasantly:*]

HUBERT. Ah, Caroline!

CAROLINE. [*Up stairs.*] Yes.

HUBERT. I'd like to see you for a moment.

CAROLINE. Are you alone?

HUBERT. [*Still pleasantly.*] Yes. Oh, yes.

CAROLINE. I'll be right down.

> [HUBERT *walks round the room gathering his confident anger with every step. He hears her coming, controls his humor, and*

stands with his hands behind him, full of exasperation, as she enters.

CAROLINE. Did you settle it?

HUBERT. [*Deliberately giving her a chair.*] One moment.

CAROLINE. Susan is waiting me for luncheon.

HUBERT. [*Decidedly.*] Very sorry.

CAROLINE. [*Inquiringly.*] Well?

HUBERT. *Very* sorry, but I'm afraid *I'll* need some of your time this afternoon.

CAROLINE. [*After sitting, looks up demurely.*] What for?

HUBERT. [*With great distinctness.*] The Customs office.

CAROLINE. Oh, no. You ventured to criticize me. You asked me to leave it to you. I do.

HUBERT. [*Losing control.*] About six thousand dollars' duty for you to pay!

CAROLINE. I? Perfectly ridiculous! I settled it. Of course, if you . . .

HUBERT. [*Angrily.*] You did, eh?

CAROLINE. [*Laughing.*] If you were fool enough to let that woman—

HUBERT. If "that woman" treated you as you deserve—

CAROLINE. I think I treated her very well.

HUBERT. It was only out of consideration for me that she—

CAROLINE. Oh, for *you!*

HUBERT. Yes, for me. If "that woman" didn't happen to be a friend of mine, you might be publicly disgraced by now as well as I!

CAROLINE. [*Laughing.*] A friend of yours! Why, really, Hubert, I must say you have strange friends— A woman that would use her friendship to extort money . . .

HUBERT. [*Enraged.*] Listen to me! Your trunks are

in the hands of the appraisers. You've been caught in a ridiculous lie; and she—

CAROLINE. [*Triumphantly.*] She can't say that, because *I bribed her!* Your friend!

HUBERT. [*Flinging the envelope on the table.*] There's your two hundred dollars, and you'll have to pay six *thousand* dollars on your trunks, and be grateful to *Miss Madden* for having saved you!

CAROLINE. To whom?

HUBERT. [*With great confidence.*] Miss Emily Madden, the woman you maligned.

CAROLINE. [*In a moment of rage.*] She looked me over! She dared!

HUBERT. [*Gloating.*] It was Miss Madden. [*He walks away from her, turns with supreme elation.*] Yes.

CAROLINE. [*In a peal of laughter.*] Then I understand perfectly why she came to you! But I'm not so easy. The matter of the trunks was settled. [*Walking to the hall.*] Of course, if you feel that you are subject to her extortions, or that perhaps you want to give her a token of your gratitude, that's *your affair*. [*Turning to him.*] It would really be indelicate of you to insist that *I* should pay your *mistress!*

HUBERT. [*Foiled and following her furiously.*] You . . . [*Chokes.*]

CAROLINE. [*Very pleasantly.*] Good morning. Susan is waiting. *She exits as the Curtain descends.*

ACT II

[*The stage presents the combined kitchen and living room of the* SANBURY *flat in the model tenements, New York City. The whole atmosphere betrays great neatness, but equal constriction and narrowness of quarters. At* the first glance, the room is apparently all doors. The walls are done in waterproof white. There is a window in the rear wall, a little to the left. This opens on a fire-escape, and gives a view of other tenements in the rear. There is a shade over the window, which is further hung with chintz curtains, that are visibly cheap, but in good taste as far as the design is concerned. In front of the window is an upholstered window-seat. To the left of the window is a small serving table, with cruets of vinegar and oil, and a salad-bowl upon it. Below this table hang sundry cooking utensils. Next to the table stands the gas-stove with a coffee-pot upon it. High on the wall above the gas-stove is a gas-meter of the kind commonly in use in the tenements. It is automatic, and releases a supply of gas only when a quarter is dropped into it. At the left of the stove and in the corner of the room is a combination sink and wash-tub of white porcelain ware. The dwellers in the tenements use the wash-tub as an ice-box. At the opening of the act, a four-fold screen hides both the sink and the stove from view. However, above the screen, a towel rack with clean dish towels is visible. In the upper left wall of the room is a door leading to LAWRENCE's bedroom. Below this, there is a combination wall book-case and mirror. The book shelf is jammed with well-used books. Directly underneath the book-case stands a flat table upon which are a typewriter and a telephone.

In the rear wall of the room, to the right of the window, is the door leading from the hall. To the right of this is the dumb-waiter shaft, with a sliding panel door. In the right wall of the room is the entrance to HILDEGARDE's bedroom. A little below this is the door leading to the bathroom.

There is an electric bell above the hall door, another electric bell above the dumb-waiter. Next to the dumb-waiter is a speaking tube, which rejoices in a very shrill whistle.

RUNNING around the whole room is a plate shelf with colored plates upon it. There are framed pictures of Tolstoy, Ruskin and Prince Kropotkin conspicuously hung upon the walls.

At the center of the room is a large mission table, set with a plate, knife, cup and saucer, napkin and a bowl of fruit. The morning newspaper lies opened. Between the dumb-waiter and the door to HILDEGARDE'S *room is a large mission cupboard. There are five chairs in the room. Three are around the table, and one is placed before the typewriting stand. There is a hat-rack upon the wall next to the hall door.*

It is about eleven-thirty in the morning, some weeks after the preceding act. The blind is up, and the room is very light.

Off rear a hand-organ is heard playing. HILDEGARDE *is discovered at the typewriter. She works on, disregarding the hum of incoherent tenement life about her. The organ stops. A street vendor is heard hoarsely crying his wares:*]

VENDOR'S VOICE. [*Off.*] Apples! Apples! Ten cents a qu-a-art!

WOMAN'S VOICE. [*Off.*] Hey-hey! Epples! Yas—you! Noomber seven! A helfft quart!

VENDOR'S VOICE. [*Off.*] All right, number seven!

WOMAN'S VOICE. [*Off.*] I schick de nikkel down.

[*The* VENDOR'S *voice ceases. Suddenly the sound of a window crashing is heard quite close.* HILDEGARDE *pauses attentively.*

LAWRENCE *bursts into the room from the left. He appears in a dressing gown, with a ball in his hand. He is shaved, but still has lather on his face.*

LAWRENCE. Look here!

HILDEGARDE. Was it your window?

LAWRENCE. Almost my *head*. Say, does anybody own those brats?

HILDEGARDE. [*Goes quickly to the window, throws it up and calls out:*] Vincent! Joey; Don't run away. I told you, you mustn't play ball in the court. I'll have to tell your mothers.

LAWRENCE. [*Giving her the ball, which she puts on a shelf.*] A lot of good that'll do.

HILDEGARDE. It's hard to be severe with them. [LAWRENCE *goes toward the bathroom.*] They oughtn't play in the street. Little Jamie Kirk was killed by a car last week.

LAWRENCE. There's plenty of them left. [*The dumbwaiter whistle gives a piercing scream.*] What's loose again? [*He opens the tube, listens and yells down.*] No! don't want any apples!

HILDEGARDE. [*Opening dumb-waiter.*] Wait, Lawrence. [*She calls down quietly.*] Mrs. Pannakin is number seven on the other side. [*Shuts dumb-waiter door.*] Will you have breakfast now?

LAWRENCE. What time is it?

HILDEGARDE. [*Taking screen away from stove.*] About half-past eleven.

[*She tries to light gas-stove.*]

LAWRENCE. We've got to hurry. [*Turning.*] What's the matter now?

HILDEGARDE. The meter. Have you a quarter?

LAWRENCE. [*Giving her a coin.*] No credit there, eh!

[*He goes into bathroom.*

[*She gets up on chair and puts coin in the meter, winds it and proceeds to heat the coffee.*

HILDEGARDE. [*Calling to him.*] It'll be ready in a moment. You finish dressing.

[LAWRENCE *enters from the bathroom with a towel, drying his face.*

LAWRENCE. What have you ordered for lunch?

HILDEGARDE. I told Mrs. Pannakin to take especial pains to-day.

LAWRENCE. [*Grimly disguste*d.] Mrs. Knollys will enjoy one of Mrs. Pannakin's co-operative dinners; where all the last week's vegetables co-operate to make this week's soups. I wonder why they want to come here anyway.

HILDEGARDE. [*Slowly.*] I can't imagine.

LAWRENCE. [*Reproachfully.*] *You* invited them. I tried to head it off.

HILDEGARDE. They are your friends; and you know I never miss a chance of interesting rich people in this philanthropy. Go, dear, and finish dressing.

[*He exits to his room.*
[*She takes a script from the typewriter, folds and signs it, then addresses it in an envelope, and stamps it. She hums while she works.* LAWRENCE *re-enters carrying his collar, tie, coat and vest. He wrestles with his collar and then throws the other things down.*

LAWRENCE. This life is killing me! I'm as nervous as a cat!

HILDEGARDE. Didn't you sleep well?

LAWRENCE. [*Pointing to the typewriter.*] Sleep! What

time was it when you began banging that instrument of torture?

HILDEGARDE. I had to get my copy ready for this evening's edition.

LAWRENCE. [*Continuing to dress.*] What is it?

HILDEGARDE. A report of last evening's Labor Meeting for Krellin's column.

LAWRENCE. You know, you'll have to stop this kind of thing. That's if you care anything for me.

[*She gets butter out of improvised ice-box in the wash-tubs.*

HILDEGARDE. [*Cheerfully.*] My little writing and my job here are at present our only means of support.

[*She puts butter on table.*

LAWRENCE. Oh, don't rub it in. [*With a change.*] I'm sorry enough to see you slave the way you do; but Krellin and your friends are attacking the very people from whom I'm going to get my living.

HILDEGARDE. [*Cheerfully.*] Yes, Mrs. Knollys took the trouble to inform me of that some weeks ago.

LAWRENCE. Well, they don't *like* to hear how their money is made.

HILDEGARDE. There's very little danger of their listening to me.

LAWRENCE. And how about Mr. Knollys?

HILDEGARDE. He and I understand each other completely.

LAWRENCE. Yes, no doubt. But this is how it's worked out for me. I've finished the preliminary plans, and should have got the first instalment to begin my work three days ago.

HILDEGARDE. Well?

LAWRENCE. [*Continuing.*] Your articles have driven him down South, to look over that factory of his.

HILDEGARDE. Oh, I'm glad of that.

LAWRENCE. I'm glad you're glad. But I get not a cent till he O.K.'s the plans.

HILDEGARDE. [*Cutting bread for him.*] When does he get back?

LAWRENCE. He was expected yesterday. [*Turning away.*] Oh, I don't want a lot of breakfast. I'm rickety! I'm all in! Just give me some coffee!

HILDEGARDE. [*Getting coffee from gas-stove.*] It's ready now. [*Pouring it.*] Where do you go to-night?

LAWRENCE. Mrs. Millette.

HILDEGARDE. Mrs. Who?

LAWRENCE. Millette,—what's the difference what her name is? Mrs. Knollys says she wants to build a house.

HILDEGARDE. Good.

LAWRENCE. I'm invited to dine with her and go to the play to-night to talk things over.

HILDEGARDE. Any prospects?

LAWRENCE. [*With a tone of justification.*] There's a social side to my job. You must see that. I've got to make that solid first.

HILDEGARDE. Yes. [*Pause.*]

LAWRENCE. Why? You're not offended that you're not asked, are you?

HILDEGARDE. Oh, dear no; I'm thinking only of what they'll think of you.

LAWRENCE. In what way?

HILDEGARDE. I don't want you to be known as the kind of man these woman can invite without his wife.

LAWRENCE. And I don't want to be known as the kind of man that always drags his wife about, either.

[*He opens the newspaper.*]

HILDEGARDE. It's an affront to you, not to me. [*The bell rings over the hall door. Opening the door.*] Oh, thank you. [*Takes letters from some one outside.*] Wait, will you drop this in the mail for me? [*She fetches her typewritten article and an orange. As she passes* LAWRENCE *she says:*] These are for you. [*She gives him some letters. Then she returns to the door and gives the letter and the orange to the little girl evidently standing outside.*] Here, Annie. Thank you. [*She closes the door.*

LAWRENCE. [*Reading a letter which he has opened during the above business.*] From my old firm. [*Proudly.*] They offer me a raise of ten a week if I'll come back.

HILDEGARDE. [*Looking through her mail.*] Bills, bills, bills. [*She sits at her typewriting table.*

LAWRENCE. They'll have to wait. I've got to. [*Showing his letter.*] How would you answer them?

HILDEGARDE. That you must decide yourself.

LAWRENCE. [*Pointing to the bills humorously.*] Say, ain't it the devil how the money goes?

HILDEGARDE. [*With a smile.*] I can manage the necessities; if you'll keep down the luxuries.

LAWRENCE. [*Looking at a bill.*] Seven dollars and fifty cents for flowers. [*Looks up at her.*

HILDEGARDE. To whom did you send them?

LAWRENCE. Mrs. Knollys, of course. She needs flowers. Always has them. [*With attempted justification.*] I eat two meals a day on her; I've got to keep my end up some way.

HILDEGARDE. Certainly, by all means.

LAWRENCE. [*With another letter.*] Tailor's bill. One hundred and twenty-five cold plunks. [*Boyishly.*] That's the swell dress suit, all right. [*Looks at her.*] Do you know, I'm sometimes tempted to drop in and see my old firm; not that I'm aching to go back to them, but—

HILDEGARDE. You might call on them, and tell them what you're doing.

LAWRENCE. What do you think?

HILDEGARDE. I'd play the game out for all its worth. It's no use weakening now.

LAWRENCE. [*Pointing to bills.*] What will we do with these?

HILDEGARDE. [*Encouragingly.*] We'll meet them with your first instalment.

> [*The bell over the dumb-waiter rings loudly.*

LAWRENCE. [*Going to dumb-waiter.*] I'll open.

> [*He opens door. The bell continues its ringing.*

VOICE. [*Below, yelling up.*] Sanbury?

LAWRENCE. [*Shouting down.*] Yes. [*Roaring.*] Take your finger off that bell! [*Bell stops.*

VOICE. [*Cheerily.*] Thought you might be a-hangin' out the wash!

LAWRENCE. No, I'm not hangin' out the wash! What do you want?

VOICE. Look out! It's coming up!!

> [LAWRENCE *just ducks back as the dumb-waiter shoots up.*

HILDEGARDE. It's the grape-fruit and salad from the grocer's. [LAWRENCE *takes it off.*] Put them in there.

> [*He puts them as she indicates inside the wash-tubs.*

LAWRENCE. What time is it now?

HILDEGARDE. After twelve. You'll have to hurry.

LAWRENCE. [*Suddenly.*] Say, can't we have the screens up? [*Putting them hastily back before the stove.*] And you know, there's nothing very handsome about this view.

> [*Jerks down the blind over window rear.*

HILDEGARDE. Larrie, please don't fuss.

> [*He has gone quickly for his coat hanging on a peg behind his door. He re-enters struggling into his coat.*

LAWRENCE. Say, my room looks like hell!

HILDEGARDE. Agnes will clear it up while I'm setting the table.

LAWRENCE. [*Nervously.*] Where is she? You know she never comes when you want her!

HILDEGARDE. [*Clearing table quietly.*] She'll *be* here.

LAWRENCE. [*Attempting to fix a picture straight on the wall.*] Have all your orders come?

HILDEGARDE. Yes. Please don't get nervous.

LAWRENCE. [*Turning nervously.*] Well, I'm only trying to help *you* out. I pass the grocer's.

HILDEGARDE. [*Pausing.*] You silly boy. I guess you can't help fussing.

LAWRENCE. I like things to be right. [*Suddenly.*] Are you going to wear that dress?

HILDEGARDE. What's the matter with my dress?

LAWRENCE. [*Dubiously.*] Oh, I suppose it's all right; only I thought your green—and honestly now, your feet aren't as big as that. It's those Consumer's League boots, just like your gloves! You'd wear anything with a Trade Union label on it, wouldn't you? No matter what it looked like!

HILDEGARDE. They won't see my feet.

LAWRENCE. .Won't they? [*Exploding.*] That skirt hikes!!

HILDEGARDE. [*With an obvious effort to be patient.*] I'll be all right; if you'll only get out before you make *me* nervous. [*A bell rings. He goes toward dumb-waiter again.*] [*Lifting the blind he has pulled down.*] No. That's the door. I guess it's Agnes.

LAWRENCE. I hope so. [*He opens the hall door and* MURTHA *bounds into the room.*] Oh, Lord!

MURTHA. [*Effusively.*] Th' top o' the marnin' to you, Mishter Sanbury! [*Seeing* HILDEGARDE.] Ah, Sishter! Shure, yer hushband do be lookin' loike a capitalisht to-day.
[*Shakes both her hands.*

LAWRENCE. Where's Agnes?

MURTHA. [*With feigned surprise.*] Ah, Agnes, is it? [*Cunningly.*] Shure, she's all roight. She do be havin' th' gran' good loock to-day!

LAWRENCE. Where is she?

MURTHA. She's got a job-to-day, yis, wid Mishter Curtis, her auld boss.

HILDEGARDE. Why didn't you tell me she couldn't come?

MURTHA. Oi wouldn't dishappoint ye. Oi know yer goin' to have a shindy; and is it any wonder that Oi'm here before th' wind.

HILDEGARDE. [*Practically.*] Then go right to Mr. Sanbury's room and clear it up.

MURTHA. Shure Oi will; whoy wouldn't Oi?

[*She exits left with aged agility.*]

LAWRENCE. Can't you get rid of her?

HILDEGARDE. I've got to have somebody.

LAWRENCE. Mrs. Knollys hates the sight of her. [*To the ceiling.*] Oh, we're going to have a lovely party!

HILDEGARDE. [*Nervously.*] Then call it off entirely.

LAWRENCE. I tried to. But she was determined to come here to-day.

HILDEGARDE. [*Abruptly.*] Then stop complaining! I wish you'd go! [*Seeing the futility of chiding him, she changes to a very reassuring manner.*] Now go, dear. You look very handsome.

[*She adjusts his necktie and goes with him toward hall door. He has his hands in his pockets.*]

LAWRENCE. Do I look like ready money?

HILDEGARDE. [*Laughing.*] Yes.

LAWRENCE. [*Shamefaced.*] Well, I haven't got any. Mine's in the gas meter.

HILDEGARDE. How much will you need?

LAWRENCE. I've got to get those dames here, haven't I? And I might be stuck for a taxicab. You know, such things have happened!

HILDEGARDE. [*Going to cupboard.*] Wait.

[*She brings out a china bank and shakes it.*]

LAWRENCE. What's that?

HILDEGARDE. My linen bank. [*Shaking it.*] There must be several dollars in it.

[*She breaks it with a knife; and a mass of small coins is exposed.*]

LAWRENCE. [*Sweeping up the coins.*] I feel like a man that's robbed a nursery.

[*As he puts them uncounted into his pocket, some of them roll on the floor.*]

HILDEGARDE. The grocer will be glad to give you bills.

LAWRENCE. It 'ud take me an hour to count up this chicken feed. [*Suddenly.*] There's some on the floor. [*As he starts to lean over, his soft hat falls from his head. He steps on it.*] Gad!! Sure thing! This is my lucky day! [*He punches his hat savagely.*]

HILDEGARDE. I'll pick it up. [*She does so.*] Larrie dear, will you let me say something? And you won't get angry?

LAWRENCE. [*Defensively.*] Well . . . ?

HILDEGARDE. [*Going to him.*] Dearest, first try to be calm—for your own sake, don't be irritated. It's unbecoming.

LAWRENCE. Oh, I'm all right; but all these little things . . .

HILDEGARDE. I know, dear, it *is* hard; but for the sake of my pride in you, be careful about showing any impatience to me, particularly in front of Mrs. Knollys. I don't care how angry you get when we're alone. I understand.

She doesn't. And judging from the last time she saw us together, she might think . . .

LAWRENCE. Please don't refer to that again. I thought you had forgotten it. [*Contritely.*] I lost my head.

HILDEGARDE. If you remember it, I shall forget it. [*She kisses him.*] Now, good-by, dear.

LAWRENCE. Good-by.

[*He exits through the hall door, as* MURTHA *re-enters from his room at the left.*

MURTHA. That's done.

HILDEGARDE. Then you can lay the table.

MURTHA. Shure Oi will, me dear.

[*She goes quickly to the cupboard for the necessary things.*

[*While* MURTHA *is busied at the table, center,* HILDEGARDE *gets the salad and grapefruit from wash-tubs. She cleans and prepares them during the following scene.*

HILDEGARDE. You know, Mrs. Murtha, it isn't quite honest for you to say that Agnes will go to places, and then you go to them yourself.

MURTHA. [*Busying herself at table.*] No, ma'm.

[*She crosses herself with a mechanically devout expression.*

HILDEGARDE. Then why do you do it?

MURTHA. Whoy wouldn't Oi? There's Aggie, th' Lord love her, can hardly keep herself, and Tim's no good at all, and Mary in th' hoshpital, and Joey wid th' haughty lady that he's married and th' twins!

HILDEGARDE. But aren't you getting a little too old for . . . ?

MURTHA. [*Interrupting savagely.*] There yer sayin' it! And d'ye see, if Oi wuz to tell thim: " It's me, ma'm, that's lookin' fer th' job," Oi'd nivir git it! And a little loi loike that doan't hurrt. [*Wheedling.*] Fer Oi'm as shtrong as ivir Oi wuz.

HILDEGARDE. [*With a sigh of futility.*] The knives on the *right* side.

MURTHA. [*Very gently.*] Yis, ma'm.

[*Pause.*

HILDEGARDE. Have you ever waited on a table?

MURTHA. Me! Naw, ma'm.

HILDEGARDE. [*Pausing.*] Then perhaps—

MURTHA. [*Confidently, while* HILDEGARDE *works at straightening out the table.*] Ah, ye jusht tell me what to do, and Oi kin do it. Shure, Oi'm not wan av thim thick Micks.

HILDEGARDE. Then first of all you must roll down your sleeves.

MURTHA. [*Obeying like a child.*] Yis, ma'm. Yer a laidy. Oi can't say naw liss than that.

HILDEGARDE. [*Smiling.*] What is a lady?

MURTHA. Ha! A laidy is wan av thim that has all th' beer an' skittles, an' doan't have to do no worrk. [*Laughing.*] Shure, Oi allus says moy auld man's th' loocky laidy av our house. Me an' his chilthren does th' worrk fer him; and' he schmokes in th' corner all day long.

HILDEGARDE. Well, I don't smoke in the corner all day long.

MURTHA. Ah, doan't ye be lishtenin' to me gush!

HILDEGARDE. You just bring the things from Mrs. Pannakin to me.

MURTHA. Yis, ma'm.

HILDEGARDE. And if there's anything you don't know how to do, you just ask me *quietly,* and I'll tell you.

MURTHA. Yis, ma'm. [*She pricks up her ears.*] What wuz that!!! [*She makes a dive for the window rear and looks out.*] That's Mickey Doolan! Shure it's Doolan!!

[*She flings open the window. As she does so, a violent quarrel in Irish between a man and woman is heard.* MURTHA *yells out:*] Mickey! Mickey!! You lave her be! [*Solemnly.*] Moy Gawd! He's hit her, th' poor woman, and she wid th' young un comin'! [*She jumps up on the sill.*] Mickey! Mickey!! You lave her be!! Fer th' love o' God and th' shame o' man, you let her be!! You dhrunken pesht!

> [DURING *the above speech,* HILDEGARDE *has tried vainly to hold* MURTHA *back and stop her yelling; but* MURTHA *has got speechless with rage. She tears loose from* HILDEGARDE, *goes through the window and is heard clattering down the fire-escape execrating* DOOLAN.

HILDEGARDE. [*Calling.*] Mrs. Murtha!! Wait—Mrs. Murtha!!!

> [MURTHA *has disappeared into the mêlée. The row is heard suddenly to increase with* MURTHA'S *advent. A woman's shrill scream is heard, and than a man's growl. The row increases.* HILDEGARDE, *seeing the futility of trying to control things at a distance, decides to follow. She also exits over the fire-escape, and descends.* MURTHA'S *high voice is heard above the noise, calling for "Tim." Then some other woman's voices are heard in high excitement calling. A hushed subsidence due to* HILDEGARDE'S *appearance follows. Finally an absolute pause of silence. Then a key is heard turning in the lock of door from the hall. The door opens. Whistling is heard on the steps. The whistling evi-*

Act II] THE UNCHASTENED WOMAN 419

dently is paced to keep time with some one climbing slowly up stairs. LAWRENCE *enters.*

BOYS' VOICES. [*Outside, heard as the door opens.*] Give us the ball! You got it!

LAWRENCE. Go on, boys, chase yourselves. [*To* CAROLINE.] Come in.

[CAROLINE *enters.*

BOYS' VOICES. [*Derisively.*] Git a hair-cut! Git a hair-cut! G'wan, you dude!

LAWRENCE. [*Closing the door.*] This is the living room. Plain living and high thinking.

CAROLINE. [*Laughing.*] I should admit it's rather high.

LAWRENCE. [*Calling.*] Hildegarde! We're here! [*To* CAROLINE.] Sit down, please.

CAROLINE. [*Not sitting.*] Are you sure that she expected me?

LAWRENCE. Certainly. She may be in my room.

[*Crosses left and opens his door.*

CAROLINE. [*Crossing.*] I want to see where you sleep.

LAWRENCE. Behold my couch of dreams.

CAROLINE. [*Murmuring.*] You poor boy!

LAWRENCE. [*Closing window rear.*] I don't care where I sleep, as long as I've a place to *work* in.

[*He starts to pull down the blind.*

CAROLINE. What's there?

LAWRENCE. [*Cheerfully.*] Excellent view of a fire-escape and Mrs. Pannakin's kitchen, where our nectar and ambrosia are prepared; which later you are to be privileged to taste.

CAROLINE. [*After looking.*] Ah!

LAWRENCE. [*He pulls down the blind. Then he goes toward* HILDEGARDE'S *room at right, calling.*] Hildegarde!

CAROLINE. [*Insinuatingly.*] Do you object to this little chat with me alone?

LAWRENCE. Of course not! But I wanted to leave you here with Hildegarde, while I looked for Miss Ambie. She may have trouble finding us.

CAROLINE. I hope so. [*He looks at her.*] I have trouble enough in losing her.

LAWRENCE. [*Laughing.*] Do you know, you sometimes perplex me terribly?

CAROLINE. [*Sitting.*] Do I? [*Smiles.*] Sit down and let me look at you. [*He sits and looks at her inquiringly.*] I want to see if I can fit you into this environment. How do you manage it?

LAWRENCE. Oh, Caroline, you're so used to luxury, you can't understand how a little plain living rather helps a fellow to dream true. That's why I didn't want you to come down. I was afraid it would discourage you.

CAROLINE. [*Slowly and with a caressing glance.*] It has made many things about you very clear to me.

LAWRENCE. There's nothing complex about me.

CAROLINE. Yes, if you can do what you have done down here, what will you do, when—? Oh, it's only because you are *you* that all this squalor hasn't killed your genius!

LAWRENCE. [*Humorously.*] Oh, come now, Caroline, it's hard for me not to agree with you when you speak of me as a genius and all that. I tell you frankly I adore it; but I'm really quite an ordinary sort of a chap. I've got enough ambition and enthusiasm to draw cheques on my future. I hope I've learned my job; so if the big things come along, I'll be able to measure up to my opportunities. And—when I'm with you, I feel my luck is with me.

CAROLINE. Then my faith in you does really help you, does it?

LAWRENCE. How can you ask that?

CAROLINE. Keep your confidence, Lawrence, but remember that patience is a virtue of the underlings. *I don't possess that virtue; and you cannot afford to.*

LAWRENCE. What's that to do with it?

CAROLINE. [*Vehemently.*] Oh, I can't bear to see you in circumstances like these! I can't lie to you! It's useless to disguise it. I hate to see you pulling down the blinds! I hate anything that ties you here! The world is full of people that can plod and wait for opportunities. *We've* got to *make* them and before it is too late! I knew that you had wings the first time that I saw you. I hate the idea of a half a loaf, when by the right of the power in you, you are entitled to the whole! I hate even the patchwork you're doing on my house! [*She rises.*

LAWRENCE. Don't say that! The work you've given me has enabled me to leave my firm with a free conscience.

CAROLINE. [*Smiling.*] What have *you* to do with conscience? People have conscience only when they *fail.*

LAWRENCE. [*Rising.*] By Jove, you have a liberating way of saying things!

CAROLINE. Have I helped to liberate you?

LAWRENCE. I've chucked a lot of litter since I've met you.

CAROLINE. That's right. I love to hear you say that. Oh, I want to see you free—free from all the petty scruples that would hinder you! That's my work now. For while you're building houses, *I* shall be building your career.

> [LAWRENCE *takes her enthusiastically and impulsively into his arms, and kisses her full on the mouth. He looks at her as if hypnotized. She is full of the disguised triumph in her seduction. They pause.* LAWRENCE *becomes thoughtful with a disturbing realization of what he has done.*

LAWRENCE. I beg your pardon.

CAROLINE. For what?

LAWRENCE. Forgive me. I had no right to—

CAROLINE. [*Interrupting.*] You have a right to everything if you only want it *enough!* [*Passionately.*] I want you—[*Quickly correcting herself.*] I *want* you to succeed; and we shall find a means. [*Suddenly.*] You must get that studio immediately.

LAWRENCE. [*Dazed.*] What—?

CAROLINE. [*In a low voice.*] You can't work any longer at my house. [*He looks up.*] Hubert arrives to-day.

LAWRENCE. [*Absently.*] Good!

CAROLINE. A little less enthusiasm, please.

LAWRENCE. I mean, then I can get his O.K. on the plans.

CAROLINE. You'll get your first instalment to-morrow. You've got to draw up plans of an Italian country house for Edwalyn Millette.

LAWRENCE. She has decided?

CAROLINE. She will. She has money; and I can tell her exactly what she thinks she wants. [*Humorously.*] There I can help *you* too. You'll need your studio. [*Dreamily.*] I know exactly how we'll furnish it. I know just where I shall sit and pour your tea. [*The bell rings over the door. They start.*] And we won't have bells like that!

LAWRENCE. That's Hildegarde. [*Turning.*] I'll tell her of the studio.

CAROLINE. [*Quickly.*] Not a word. Leave that to me. [*He hesitates.*] Oh, we drive to Edwalyn's Long Island place this afternoon. I want you to see the grounds before you dine with her to-night.

LAWRENCE. Oh, all right. [*He opens the door to the hall, and discovers* SUSAN AMBIE.] Come in, Miss Ambie.

SUSAN. [*Entering, her hat awry.*] Oh, there you are! [*Grieved.*] Well, Carrie, I *must say*—

CAROLINE. We decided you weren't coming.

SUSAN. [*Looking at her watch.*] I thought I was on time.

CAROLINE. Think again, my dear.

LAWRENCE. Did you have trouble finding us?

SUSAN. [*Straightening her hat and speaking to* LAWRENCE.] You oughtn't let those children play ball in the street. Their ball just missed me!

CAROLINE. Too bad! Too bad!

SUSAN. Carrie, I've something I must say to you . . .
[*Looks significantly at* LAWRENCE.

LAWRENCE. Excuse me. I'll hunt up Hildegarde. She may be in her office.

[*As soon as* LAWRENCE *exits* SUSAN *betrays a most uncontrolled and nervous anxiety. She is nervous almost to the point of incoherency.*

CAROLINE. Well, what is it?

SUSAN. Carrie, I'm sorry . . . but I haven't slept! I can't take any more responsibility. That's all.

CAROLINE. Then don't.

SUSAN. [*On the raw.*] They ask me if I'm *blind!!*

CAROLINE. Well, if you're not, what do you care?

SUSAN. [*Gushily.*] People are talking about you and Lawrence. Of course, *I* understand—but . . .

CAROLINE. [*Interrupting.*] If you give your time thinking about what other people say, you'll never have time for anything else.

SUSAN. [*Impatiently.*] But people know that Hubert's been away . . . and they see you and Lawrence together everywhere, and . . .

CAROLINE. There's comfort in that. Just think what they imagine when they *don't* see us.

SUSAN. My dear, you can't stop wicked tongues from wagging. . . . Of course, I tried to defend you all I could. . . . People are saying that you've lost your head over this young architect that you have *living* with you in your house. *Everybody's* talking—

CAROLINE. Everybody has nothing else to do.

SUSAN. Where is his wife? Perhaps *she's* heard things and *means* to be rude!

CAROLINE. Rude to *me*? She couldn't be.

SUSAN. You know, Lawrence tried to discourage our coming. What *can* you and she have in common?

CAROLINE. [*Meaningly.*] Nothing! Lawrence sees that already. When *she* realizes that we can have *nothing in common*—not ever her—well, the rest is easy.

SUSAN. [*Alarmed.*] Carrie! You're up to something mad! [CAROLINE *laughs.*] I haven't seen you look or act like this, not since . . . Italy! [*Suddenly with a cry.*] Yes, they're right! It's true!!

CAROLINE. [*Calmly.*] What?

SUSAN. You've lost your head about him.

CAROLINE. [*Recklessly.*] Oh, there's no law against a woman losing her *head*.

SUSAN. But his wife! What do you mean to do?

CAROLINE. I? Nothing.

SUSAN. Carrie, come back with me. We'll leave our cards; and we'll have done our duty.

CAROLINE. Go if you like.

SUSAN. [*With a nervous whimper.*] I won't desert you, Carrie!

CAROLINE. [*Rising.*] Oh, then shut up!

SUSAN. Don't be rash, dear, she may know more than you think.

CAROLINE. In big things I do nothing underhand.
[*There is heard a fearful shaking of the window.*
SUSAN. What's that!!
CAROLINE. I'll see.
[*She goes toward window rear, pulls up the blind. The person outside on the fire-escape flings up the window and scrambles into the room.*
SUSAN. [*Tearfully.*] [*During* CAROLINE'*s movement.*] I don't know what we're doing here anyway!
CAROLINE. [*Seeing* MURTHA.] The gorilla!
SUSAN. [*Frightened.*] Carrie, this is the way out!
[MURTHA *has scrambled into the room talking incoherently to herself. She looks rather damaged, and is carrying her apron and purse in her hand. Her hair is tousled and her eye is red.*
MURTHA. [*Recognizing* CAROLINE.] Ah, fer th' love o' God, Mrs. Knowllez, is it you! D'ye see me oye? [*Pointing to it.*] That's phwat ye git whin ye come interferin' between a hushband and a woife! Shure, it wuz *her* that guv me that. [*Laughing.*] Hah, there wuz wigs on th' green! I licked him wance before, and Mrs. Doolan she knows it, moind ye; and whin I wuz trou' wid him, a dog wouldn't ha' lapped his blood!
[CAROLINE *and* SUSAN *have tried in vain to retreat before* MURTHA'*s stream of hysterical verbiage.*
SUSAN. [*Completely appalled.*] Yes, that's all very interesting . . .! [*Retreats around table.*
MURTHA. Now doan't ye moind me. Shure O'im only talkin' to mesilf, and Oi couldn't foind a bigger fool to talk to. [*She opens a purse she still carries in her hand, sees her money.*] Ah, that's all roight.

[*She puts purse down on the table.* CAROLINE *and* SUSAN *are chasséing toward the door, which is suddenly opened and* HILDEGARDE *is heard talking to some one at the entrance.*]

HILDEGARDE. [*Calling in.*] Mrs. Murtha, go bathe that eye in cold water.

MURTHA. [*Subdued immediately.*] Yis, ma'm.

[*She goes to the sink and does so.*]

HILDEGARDE. [*Continuing to some one outside.*] No, Doolan; if you're sobered up at four o'clock, come to my office. The ejection officer will be there. [*She closes the door sharply as she enters, then suddenly sees* CAROLINE *and* SUSAN. *She continues with complete composure.*] Oh! [*Shakes hands with* CAROLINE.] I'm sorry I wasn't here to receive you. [*Shakes hands with* SUSAN.] I hope you'll forgive me. There's been an unfortunate difficulty with a couple of our tenants. Excuse me!

CAROLINE. Certainly.

[HILDEGARDE *exits into her room.*

[CAROLINE *and* SUSAN *look at each other while the noise of running water is heard at the sink, where* MURTHA *is bathing her eye.* SUSAN *is frightened.* CAROLINE *is enjoying her usual parasitic amusement.*]

SUSAN. What do you think, Carrie?

CAROLINE. The worse it is, the better I like it.

[HILDEGARDE *immediately re-enters with a small bottle and some lint, which she puts down on the table.*]

HILDEGARDE. [*To* CAROLINE *and* SUSAN.] Won't you lay off your wraps in Larrie's room? [*Pointing left.*] [SUSAN *passes and enters the room at left.*] [*Continues.*] I'm sure there's more excitement than real injury.

[CAROLINE *goes toward room.* HILDEGARDE *takes a bowl from plate rack and moves to* MURTHA.

CAROLINE. [*To* SUSAN *whose train is still visible showing the smallness of the room.*] Susan, go in.

SUSAN. [*Excitedly.*] I can't walk through the wall, my dear.

[*The train is however snatched in, and* CAROLINE *enters, closing the door behind her.*

MURTHA. Oh, me oye—me oye!

HILDEGARDE. [*To* MURTHA.] Now quick, let me look at that eye.

MURTHA. Shure Oi will, me dear!

HILDEGARDE. Bathe it with this stuff. Here, use this too. [*Going to table to get the lint pad, she sees* MURTHA's *purse.*] Oh, you've found your purse. Where was it?

MURTHA. [*Guiltily.*] I must ha' dhropped it runnin' down.

HILDEGARDE. You see you were wrong to accuse Mrs. Doolan. That only made more trouble.

MURTHA. [*Cannily.*] It wuz th' loocky thing thim Polacks didn't know 'twas loyin' jusht outside their window.

[LAWRENCE *enters from the hall door.*

LAWRENCE. [*To* HILDEGARDE.] Where *have* you been?

MURTHA. [*Groaning.*] Oh, Mother! Me oye . . . me oye. . . .

[*She sits wretchedly at the left.*

LAWRENCE. What's the matter!

MURTHA. [*In a loud regretful tone.*] If I had only hit him whin he thripped!!

HILDEGARDE. There's been trouble with the Doolans.

LAWRENCE. In here?

HILDEGARDE. No. And everything is all right now.

LAWRENCE. Yes, but where are the ladies?

HILDEGARDE. [*Trying to quiet him by her tone.*] In your room, laying off their wraps.

> [*During the above, MURTHA has been fighting over the battle in pantomime, while bathing her eye, and mumbling to herself.*

LAWRENCE. Did you get anybody else to help you?

HILDEGARDE. [*Barely holding her nerves.*] I've been quelling a riot!

LAWRENCE. [*Pointing to MURTHA.*] What are you going to do with her?

HILDEGARDE. Go to Mrs. Pannakin's, and see if *she* won't serve the dinner herself.

LAWRENCE. I was just there looking for *you!* I asked her then. . . .

HILDEGARDE. Well . . . ?

LAWRENCE. [*Throwing up his hands and speaking to the ceiling.*] She can't come! She isn't dressed! And dinner's ready!!

HILDEGARDE. [*To MURTHA.*] Go to Mrs. Pannakin's, smooth your hair, borrow an apron and bring in the dinner.

MURTHA. [*Rising.*] Oh, yis, ma'm. [*With a savage gesture.*] The durrty A.P.A.! [*She crosses to the hall door muttering.*] Oh, Lord, I'm as blind as Doolan's goat! I'll nivir see out o' that oye again. . . . To hit me whin Oi wasn't lookin'. . . . [*She exits.*

LAWRENCE. Good Lord!

> [*He swings around the room in an ecstasy of exasperation.*

HILDEGARDE. [*Going to him.*] Larrie, no matter what happens, don't be betrayed into any rudeness to me before Mrs. Knollys.

> [*The door left opens and SUSAN enters.*

HILDEGARDE. The excitement has subsided. Won't you

sit here? [*She fixes a chair at her right.*] [SUSAN *sits with her back to the door.* CAROLINE *enters.*] [*Continuing.*] And, Mrs. Knollys, won't you sit there? [*She motions* CAROLINE *to the chair at* LAWRENCE's *right. He helps her. She faces the door.* HILDEGARDE *faces the audience.* LAWRENCE *has his back to the audience. Note: the* LADIES *have just removed their wraps.* CAROLINE *has not taken off her gloves.*] Don't mind my jumping up. [*She gets bread and butter from the wash-tubs.*] How is Mr. Knollys?

CAROLINE. Well, thank you, the last I heard.

HILDEGARDE. [*Puts the bread on table and helps them to butter.*] [*To* CAROLINE.] Let me help you. We hear the Homestead Mills are going to begin work again. I'm glad. Sugar?

CAROLINE. [*Waving a "no."*] And the percentage on investments lowered again.

[*They all, except* CAROLINE, *eat grape-fruit.*]

SUSAN. [*Changing the conversation.*] Mrs. Sanbury, have you any nerves left?

HILDEGARDE. This is by no means a typical day.

CAROLINE. No?

HILDEGARDE. Many of the workmen living here are idle. Unfortunately, they drink.

CAROLINE. If that is how they spend their leisure, why agitate for shorter hours and bigger pay?

SUSAN. [*Vigorously.*] What good bread!

HILDEGARDE. Many laboring people drink because they have to work, and—

CAROLINE. [*Interrupting sarcastically.*] Precisely, and they don't like it. I agree with you so far.

HILDEGARDE. Perhaps. But oftener they get the habit of drink because they haven't decent food.

LAWRENCE. [*Rising.*] That being the case, ladies, I

propose we fortify ourselves against the possible vagaries of our co-operative cook.

[*He goes to tubs and takes out bottles.*]

SUSAN. [*Looking.*] Your what?

HILDEGARDE. [*To* SUSAN.] Perhaps Larrie has told you, this is a co-operative dining-room. Several of the people living here chip in to pay the rent.

LAWRENCE. [*To* CAROLINE.] A little Scotch?

[*She refuses it. He helps* SUSAN.]

CAROLINE. [*To* HILDEGARDE.] A sort of socialistic mess.

SUSAN. [*Incredulously.*] But you're not Socialists, are you? [*She drops her bread and knife.*]

HILDEGARDE. Not all of us.

SUSAN. [*Reassured and beginning to eat again.*] Oh, that's better.

HILDEGARDE. But then we've got an Anarchist or two among us.

SUSAN. [*Anxiously, pausing in a mouthful.*] Oh!

HILDEGARDE. [*Continuing.*] All interested in improving conditions.

SUSAN. [*Approving charitably.*] Ah.

[*She resumes eating.*]

LAWRENCE. [*Rising.*] Psh! [*Mysteriously.*] It's coming! [SUSAN *is apprehensive, as he goes to the hall door and opens it.*] I've got a long distance nose! The soup!! [*He returns to his chair as* MURTHA *enters carrying four soup-bowls on a very presentable tray. She never takes her eyes from* HILDEGARDE. MURTHA *is very neat and important.* HILDEGARDE *motions her to serve her first.* MURTHA *does so.*]

SUSAN. [*Seeing* MURTHA.] Oh, she's all right again. I'm glad.

HILDEGARDE. [*To* MURTHA.] Then serve Mrs. Knollys.

CAROLINE. [*Waving a gloved hand.*] I never eat soup.
       [MURTHA *goes to* SUSAN *and helps her, then* LAWRENCE. *She stands awkwardly for a moment, but very quietly.*]
HILDEGARDE. [*To* MURTHA.] You can come back in a moment and clear off the bowls.
MURTHA. Yis, ma'm.
HILDEGARDE. Leave the door ajar.
       [MURTHA *is about to exit, carrying the tray with* CAROLINE'S *bowl of soup on it, when she is passed in the door by* MICHAEL KRELLIN. KRELLIN *is a Russian by birth, but speaks English with a scrupulous, scholarly exactness, though with a slightly foreign accent. Physically, he is of medium height, lithe and slender in figure, rapid and exact in his movements. His dress is clean but careless. Everything about him betokens a fearless definiteness of mind. He has a shock of curly hair. His face is pale, his eyes are very keen; and when he looks at a person, he is likely to peer a little closer into their faces than the usual man. His speech is fluent and incisive. He is mentally a combination of the political dreamer and the practical meliorist, who has saved his optimism by fighting for the next reform at his hand. His manner is above all things humorous and easy, with a sort of detached impersonal impertinence. He has the assurance of the platform orator.*]
MURTHA. [*Meeting him at the door.*] Good marnin', Mishter Krellin.

KRELLIN. Good morning. Eh? Wait!
　　　　　　[*Stops* MURTHA *and peers into the tray.*
LAWRENCE. [*To* CAROLINE.] There's our Anarchist.
　　　　　　　　　　　　　　　　　[HILDEGARDE *rises.*
KRELLIN. [*Continuing to* MURTHA.] Here . . . Hello—Hello! I'll *take* that soup.
　　　　　　[*He has already deftly lifted it from the tray.*
MURTHA. Doan't let yer modesty wrong you.
　　　　　　　　　　　　　　　　　　　[*She exits.*
KRELLIN. [*Joyously.*] Hildegarde, Hildegarde! I've news for you! Good news!
　　　　　　[*He goes immediately to the cupboard, puts down his soup-bowl deftly, pulls out a drawer, finds his napkin with a cheap ring on it, picks out a knife, fork and spoon, puts the napkin in his mouth, takes the bowl, with knife, fork and spoon in one hand, then picks up a chair with his remaining hand and advances toward the table.*
HILDEGARDE. [*Hesitatingly.*] Yes, Michael . . .
KRELLIN. [*During the above business.*] Just wait. I'm as hungry as a wolf. All night at the office.
HILDEGARDE. You must be tired, Michael.
KRELLIN. [*His voice is merry, but his body is relaxed.*] Not very.　　[*He puts down his chair between* SUSAN'S *and* HILDEGARDE'S, *and places his eating paraphernalia on the table.* SUSAN *draws away, as he sits down.* CAROLINE *is imperturbed.* LAWRENCE *is annoyed.*
KRELLIN. [*Peering near-sightedly at* SUSAN.] Oh, you're having a party. I didn't see. [*Rising.*] Pardon, I am very near-sighted; and I have broken my glasses. [*About to withdraw.*] I'll step in later.

HILDEGARDE. Wait, Michael. [*To* CAROLINE *and* SUSAN.] Mr. Krellin is one of our friends.
KRELLIN. Yes, yes. I only wanted to ask; did you finish your article?
HILDEGARDE. Yes. It's gone. What's the news?
KRELLIN. You'll have to write a special. Despatches from the South tell of the final settlement by arbitration with the Homestead Mills. Another victory!
[*He shakes* HILDEGARDE's *hands enthusiastically.*
HILDEGARDE. Splendid, but—[*Turns toward* CAROLINE.]
KRELLIN. [*Continuing.*] A ten hour day, and a dollar ninety cents!
LAWRENCE. The Homestead Mills! those are . . .
[*Turning to* CAROLINE.
CAROLINE. Yes, I'm interested.
HILDEGARDE. My friend is one of the reporters on the "ECHO." He's just had news. May I present him?
CAROLINE. And which way has the strike been settled?
KRELLIN. [*Coming toward her.*] You will be glad to hear in favor of the shorter hour and the living wage. Another milestone passed!
HILDEGARDE. Mrs. Knollys, this is Mr. Krellin. A member of our co-operative club. We don't usually have the pleasure of seeing him till dinner time.
KRELLIN. [*Has leaned toward* CAROLINE.] Mrs. Knollys . . . Knollys? [*Peers at her, then at* HILDEGARDE, *then again at* CAROLINE.] I am delighted to find you here. [*Laughs softly.*] God is a great dramatist!
CAROLINE. Why?
KRELLIN. I've seen you before, Madame; and I've heard of your husband.
HILDEGARDE. [*Quickly.*] And this is Miss Ambie.
KRELLIN. [*Bowing.*] Ah, yes . . . Miss Ah . . .
[*He goes toward her.*

SUSAN. [*Frightened.*] How do you do! . . .
       [KRELLIN *sits between* HILDEGARDE *and* SUSAN. *Pause.*]

KRELLIN. [*Partially rising with his knife in hand and peering.*] Is that the butter? [*He takes some and puts it on bread. To* CAROLINE, *as he settles back in his chair.*] Mrs. Knollys, I put you on your guard. Before you know it, Hildegarde will persuade you to invest in tenements and make you a five per cent, philanthropist.

LAWRENCE. [*Decidedly.*] No, she won't! She—

KRELLIN. [*Interrupting.*] Wait! She will induce you to put up better dwellings for the poor; so they can live a little more decently on their miserable wages. You will feel charitable towards them, because they will give you a steady five per cent.; and the workingmen will be made more contented with conditions, that otherwise they might be encouraged to radically change.

SUSAN. [*Horrified.*] But don't you believe in charity?

KRELLIN. [*Throwing up his hands.*] Ah, I see! Another sentimentalist. I surrender!

SUSAN. I'm no such thing!

KRELLIN. [*Gracefully looking at* SUSAN *and* CAROLINE.] But neither of you is old enough to be the real conservative.

CAROLINE. [*Smiling.*] You're a radical?

KRELLIN. I am a social physician, whose prescriptions nobody respects, because I do not believe in wasting time disguising or trying to cure *symptoms*. *Poverty is the real disease.*

CAROLINE. Other people have a name for your kind of man.

KRELLIN. They call us lots of names. Which one?

CAROLINE. They call you "muck-rakers."

KRELLIN. [*Good humoredly.*] Oh, that never offends me. To make all beautiful things grow, there must be some one to stir up ... ah ... unappetizing things about the roots. We do that. [*Pointing to* CAROLINE.] Unfortunately, however, it is the "other" people that wear the flowers. So! [*He eats his soup.*

LAWRENCE. You mustn't take him seriously, Mrs. Knollys.

KRELLIN. Never listen to the artists. *They* must take nothing seriously; else they could find very little beauty in anything. They are spiritual toy-makers and seducers. They gather the flowers and forget the roots. At least don't take them seriously when they *speak*. Admire them when they *do;* because they are permitted to do, and don't know *how* to speak. Listen to *us* when *we* speak; because the government will allow us no other liberty.

[*Eats.*

LAWRENCE. Nonsense, Michael.

KRELLIN. [*Appealing to* CAROLINE.] You see, that is my great misfortune. My friends never know when I am in earnest. What else is there to eat?

[*At this moment* MURTHA *appears with a tray on which are chops and vegetables.*

HILDEGARDE. [*To* MURTHA.] Take these things off before you serve the chops.

[MURTHA, *without a word, puts the tray on the cup-board, and deftly removes the empty soup-bowls.*

KRELLIN. [*To* HILDEGARDE.] Emmy will be late.

[MURTHA *during the next speeches serves chops.*

CAROLINE. [*Resuming.*] Do you take yourself seriously, Mr. Krellin?

KRELLIN. [*With a quick glance.*] That means *you* don't. But I did once. That's why I left Russia.

HILDEGARDE. Mr. Krellin wrote a book for the Radical movement, and the government didn't like it.

CAROLINE. Wise government.
> [*Henceforward* LAWRENCE *and* CAROLINE *form a party against* HILDEGARDE *and* KRELLIN.

KRELLIN. Yes, my friends, the enemy, were making Russia too hot for me; and Siberia has always been too cold; and—

CAROLINE. [*Interrupting.*] So you decided to make trouble over here.
> [SUSAN *has got an eating devil and is despatching food.*

KRELLIN. Precisely.

CAROLINE. And in that work, do you take *other* people seriously?

KRELLIN. Sometimes. You see, I am neither an artist [*Bowing to* LAWRENCE] nor a sentimentalist [*Bowing to* SUSAN].

SUSAN. [*Putting down her knife and fork.*] Now he means me again, Carrie!

CAROLINE. [*To* KRELLIN.] Then you and I might understand each other.

KRELLIN. Ah,—you mustn't ask me to take *you* seriously, Mrs. Knollys; that would be too much to ask.

CAROLINE. Why?

KRELLIN. You see, I know you. You're a spoiled American woman; which means you take neither our government nor yourself seriously. I don't blame you; neither do I. In other words, *we* have a sense of humor. And then you are a *Saxon* woman; which means to a Russian, that you have elevated hypocrisy until it takes rank with a virtue. Otherwise you could never do as you do. [*He eats.*

LAWRENCE. [*Growing nervous.*] For heaven's sake, stop him!

HILDEGARDE. Please, Michael, eat.

LAWRENCE. [*To* CAROLINE.] He's our interminable talker.

HILDEGARDE. [*Laughing a little nervously and speaking to* CAROLINE.] People say anything they think here.

KRELLIN. [*In the midst of a mouthful.*] Yes, *when* they think! [*Then to* SUSAN.] *When* they think!

HILDEGARDE. But we try to argue about *principles,* not persons.

CAROLINE. But I'm not interested in principles.

KRELLIN. [*To* CAROLINE.] Right you are! Only involve people in *principles,* and you keep them harmless.

CAROLINE. [*To* KRELLIN.] But do go on. You said you saw me once before.

KRELLIN. Yes. I was detailed at the dock when you arrived.

CAROLINE. [*Not so pleasantly.*] Oh.

[SUSAN *puts down her knife and fork again.*

KRELLIN. [*Continuing.*] And a dear, a very dear friend persuaded me to lose fifteen dollars on your account.

CAROLINE. That was a very *dear* friend, indeed.

KRELLIN. Ah, yes, I had a beautiful article written, which for *her* sake, I was weak enough to drop . . . an article about the humor and hypocrisy of the American woman,—with special reference to yourself, Mrs. Knollys . . . [LAWRENCE *is fearful, pushes back his chair.* CAROLINE *has waved aside the chop and peas that* MURTHA *has offered her.*] [*To* MURTHA.] Bring that to me. I've had no breakfast. [*During the next speeches he has the business of taking* CAROLINE's *chop, etc.*] Shall I continue?

LAWRENCE. [*Decidedly.*] No!

CAROLINE. By all means.

KRELLIN. [*To the others.*] You see, she already treats me as an artist. I amuse her.

CAROLINE. Immensely.

KRELLIN. That's why I permit myself to speak. Well, to resume: strange to say, I wrote that the people whose fortunes have been made in industries protected by the government are always the very ones most eager to evade the customs imposed by that government to *protect* their industries.

SUSAN. [*Fearfully.*] Carrie!

KRELLIN. [*Impatiently.*] Miss Nambie—Miss Pambie —Miss . . .

SUSAN. *Ambie* is my name.

KRELLIN. Pardon, quite so. I do not include you; because on that day you personally *lost* your sense of humor. [*To* CAROLINE.] *Your* money is made in protected tin plate. Your husband's in protected woollen mills. [*Laughs.*] You see, you have a sense of humor and a genius for hypocrisy. [*Seriously.*] You don't *respect* a government that will let your factories work the *poor* the way they do. Neither do I. And so you refuse to pay the customs to support that government. No more do I!

LAWRENCE. Michael!

KRELLIN. [*Continuing unperturbed.*] I admire you! Your personal discernment and your sense of humor were almost worth six thousand dollars to you. I admire you personally—fifteen dollars worth; and that's a great deal for a man who is saving up in order to get married.

CAROLINE. [*Quietly leading him on.*] Oh, you still believe in marriage. That's interesting.

KRELLIN. You mean, as soon as we are *inconsistent* we are interesting. [*Wisely.*] *You* believe in conventions that you do not observe; *I* for a time observe conventions in which I do not believe.

SUSAN. [*Horrified.*] *Don't* you believe in marriage?

KRELLIN. [*Bowing to her.*] Oh, yes, as all the *un*married people do.

SUSAN. I'm sure I don't know what you mean, but it makes me very uncomfortable.

LAWRENCE. [*Laughing.*] Gag him!

HILDEGARDE. I'll mix the salad.

[*She gets the salad bowl.* MURTHA *helps her.*]

CAROLINE. Then you believe in *women* too?

KRELLIN. Boundlessly. And in every capacity of citizenship. [SUSAN *pushes back her chair with an exclamation of disgust.* KRELLIN *continues to* CAROLINE.] I believe especially in *one,* the one I'm going to marry. I believe in eugenics and endowed maternity—in everything that makes for a superior humanity. [*To* SUSAN.] I believe that by our foolish laws we can sometimes save people from doing what they'd like to *do*. [*To* CAROLINE.] I should like to save people from being what they *are*. I believe— Oh—I believe that I'm a stupid fool for telling you sincerely all that I do believe in—and—[*To* HILDEGARDE.] Don't put too much vinegar in the dressing.

SUSAN. [*Outraged.*] I've listened long enough!

CAROLINE. Why, Susan! What's broke loose in you?

SUSAN. I'm bound to protest!

KRELLIN. Ah, then there's hope for you.

SUSAN. [*Scathingly.*] Oh, I'm not clever! but I think your ideas are perfectly ridiculous and detestable—all of them!

KRELLIN. Thank you. I would have doubt of them if you thought otherwise.

SUSAN. [*Continuing.*] And as for women as citizens—women voting and doing the work of men . . . Well, it's bad enough now as it is, when they happen to hold office under the government . . .

KRELLIN. [*Amused.*] I remember. You had difficulty.

SUSAN. [*Unheeding his interruption.*] Yes, we had an experience at the customs!

CAROLINE. [*Warningly.*] Susan!

SUSAN. [*Impetuously.*] There was a hussy there when we arrived . . . Of all the insolence in office . . . Hah! If I had *my* way . . .

[*Stops breathlessly.*

KRELLIN. You *didn't* have your way. That was the trouble, wasn't it?

SUSAN. Well, I'd like to meet her some time face to face—That's all; when she didn't have her little badge upon her; and without the authority of the government behind her— I'd . . .

KRELLIN. Yes—yes. Excuse me.

[*The door to the hall has opened and* EMILY MADDEN *appears.* KRELLIN *has risen alertly.*

SUSAN. [*Bewildered.*] What's the matter?

[*She continues to talk to* CAROLINE.

KRELLIN. [*At the door with* EMILY.] Ah, Emmy, you're late.

[*He starts to bring her down. She resists a little, seeing strangers present.*

CAROLINE. [*Seeing* EMILY.] Susan, you're a fool!

SUSAN. [*Seated with her back to the door, doesn't see* EMILY. *She continues to* CAROLINE, *mournfully:*] I had no right to drink that whisky. It always makes me silly. [*She suddenly turns, following* CAROLINE'*s glance, and exclaims, terrified:*] There she is!! Don't *you* see her? [*Crumpled.*] Oh, Carrie, it's gone to my head!!

[*She makes a mad clutch at her head.*

CAROLINE. Keep quiet!

LAWRENCE. [*To* CAROLINE.] I'm so sorry. [*Then savagely to* HILDEGARDE.] Now, you see! . . .

[*He becomes incoherent and swings up rear, sees* MURTHA, *stops short and goes to window.*

Act II] THE UNCHASTENED WOMAN

KRELLIN. [*Bringing* EMILY *down.*] Emily, there is a lady here, who has just expressed a great desire to meet you.

EMILY. [*Advancing a step.*] Oh, then, I'd be deligh—
  [*She stops and recoils as she recognizes* CAROLINE.

SUSAN. [*Waving her hands.*] I've had quite enough! I've had quite enough!! [*She rises as if to go.*

KRELLIN. [*Gallantly.*] Mrs. Knollys, Miss Madden is the reason for my belief in marriage.

CAROLINE. [*Amused and pausing.*] Oh! That is remarkable.

  [*She suddenly realizes that a weapon has been placed in her hands; she immediately becomes calm.* EMILY *is in silent desperation.*

KRELLIN. [*Proudly.*] It was due to *her* persuasion that the article I wrote about you was never published in the papers.

CAROLINE. [*To* EMILY.] I am glad of this opportunity to thank Miss Madden for that, and [*Significantly*] for many other favors.

EMILY. [*Uncertainly.*] Oh, I am sure . . . I . . .

KRELLIN. [*To* EMILY.] I needed you, my dear, to save me from Miss Ambie and defend the government. Miss Ambie agrees with you about the government. [*To* SUSAN.] No?

SUSAN. [*Vehemently.*] I don't!

KRELLIN. [*To* EMILY.] She does not! Another convert! [*Gesture of amusement.*] While Mrs. Knollys and I maintain the government is ridiculous. [*To* CAROLINE.] No? [*Suddenly remembering.*] I'll get a chair.

  [*He looks for one, but there are no more.*

CAROLINE. [*To* KRELLIN.] Don't bother, please. Miss Madden can occupy my place.

EMILY. Oh, no!

HILDEGARDE. [*To* CAROLINE.] Please don't disturb yourself. [*To* LAWRENCE.] Larrie, get a chair from your room. [LAWRENCE *immediately exits left.*

CAROLINE. It won't be a new experience for Miss Madden. She has already *occupied my place* before this, many times; and for a long time, I have been accustomed to yield to her.

KRELLIN. [*Perplexed.*] Is that so! How?

EMILY. [*In terror.*] Oh, Michael, why did I come here!!

KRELLIN. What's the matter, Emmy?

CAROLINE. [*To* EMILY.] Have no fear, Miss Madden. Your intended husband believes in women " boundlessly," and " in every capacity." He has a sense of humor and admires hypocrites. He will be consistent to his views; but I am sure he will allow me to be equally consistent with mine.

KRELLIN. Carte blanche! [*Seeing* LAWRENCE *re-enter with the chair.*] Here we are. Now we can listen.

CAROLINE. I have no principles, but I have some prejudices. And either Miss Madden or I must leave the room.

SUSAN. Oh, Carrie!

KRELLIN. What do you mean! That isn't argument. That is evasion!

LAWRENCE. [*Quickly.*] Emily and Michael, you've said about enough! Now please go!

[*He bangs down the chair.*

HILDEGARDE. [*To* LAWRENCE.] By no means. Mrs. Knollys will be good enough to explain herself.

KRELLIN. What is your reason, Mrs. Knollys?

CAROLINE. [*Charmingly.*] Since you insist, it is simply because I refuse to sit at the same table with my husband's *mistress.*

KRELLIN. [*Dawning.*] Ha!!

HILDEGARDE. [*Simultaneously.*] Oh!

KRELLIN. [*Fiercely.*] That's a lie! A black, malicious lie!!

CAROLINE. Oh, no!

KRELLIN. [*Continuing.*] She doesn't even *know* your husband!

CAROLINE. [*Confidently taunting.*] Ask her!

KRELLIN. Madame, I am not here to insult her myself; but to defend her against *your attempt* to do so.

CAROLINE. Ask her, and you will learn it was for my *husband's* sake that your article was suppressed. But he, no doubt, has *paid* Miss Madden for any loss *you* may have suffered. Come, Susan. [*To* HILDEGARDE.]. I've had a most delightful luncheon. My wrap, Lawrence.

[*He exits left.*

KRELLIN. [*Quite aggressive.*] Mrs. Knollys, of course you cannot go until I have relieved your mind from any misapprehensions you may have concerning your husband.

CAROLINE. But unfortunately I seem to affect Miss Madden disagreeably.

[LAWRENCE *re-enters with wraps.*

MURTHA. [*Suddenly coming up from the rear.*] Fer th' love o' Gawd, th' poor gurrl's goin' t' faint!!

[*She takes* EMILY *in her arms.*

EMILY. [*Weakly.*] Take me home, Michael. . . . Oh . . . !

MURTHA. Now there, there, there, dearie, doan't ye moind. . . .

KRELLIN. [*To* MURTHA.] Yes, take Miss Madden home!!

EMILY. No! Not without you, Michael!!

SUSAN. [*Terrified.*] Carrie, Carrie! Come with me! Come home!! I'm sorry we ever came! These awful people!! [*Gets into her wrap.*

LAWRENCE. Come, Mrs. Knollys. [*Then to* KRELLIN *and* EMILY.] If *they* haven't sense enough to go!

KRELLIN. [*Fiercely to* CAROLINE.] You *cannot* go!

LAWRENCE. [*To* KRELLIN.] What do you mean?

KRELLIN. I have something to say to Mrs. Knollys!

SUSAN. [*As he comes forward.*] Carrie, if you don't come, I . . . [*Weeps in fright.*] God knows what they will do!

HILDEGARDE. [*Beseechingly.*] Michael, go with Emily!

KRELLIN. [*Shaking his mane.*] Mrs. Knollys has permitted herself to utter a filthy, vicious lie! And I—

HILDEGARDE. [*Going to him.*] But this is not the time to—

KRELLIN. [*In fury.*] A filthy LIE!!

LAWRENCE. [*To* KRELLIN.] See here, you can't use that kind of language to my friend!

KRELLIN. [*Savagely to* LAWRENCE.] Your *friend!* You little lap-dog! I want nothing from you! Just look to yourself!! [*He flings* LAWRENCE *aside.*

HILDEGARDE. [*Beseechingly.*] Michael, go with Emily! She *needs* you.

[*She turns him around, and he sees* EMILY *being helped to the door by* MURTHA.

EMILY. [*As she leaves with* MURTHA.] Michael. . . . Michael. . . .

KRELLIN. [*With suppressed vehemence.*] Mrs. Knollys, I shall give myself the pleasure of continuing this conversation in the presence of your husband.

[*He bows and exits, after* MURTHA *and* EMILY.

SUSAN. [*Incoherently.*] Carrie, here are your things! Here! Of all the frightful experiences! [*Spinning around.*] Where's my glove? You must get out of this!!

HILDEGARDE. Mrs. Knollys, *I* must have a word with you.

SUSAN. [*Dizzily.*] Now *she's* going to begin! Why did we ever . . . ?

LAWRENCE. [*Angrily.*] Hildegarde, don't you think you'd better drop it?

HILDEGARDE. [*Meaningly.*] It isn't only in reference to *Miss Madden* that I wish to speak.

SUSAN. [*Hysterically.*] I knew it, Carrie! [*To* HILDEGARDE.] But you're wrong! No matter what you think. . . . People have such vile minds! [*Specifically.*] I was with Mrs. Knollys all the time, except once when I took sick. . . . Your husband knows it—and so does Mr. Knollys. . . .

LAWRENCE. What are you talking about?

SUSAN. [*Continuing.*] And if her kindness is to be misinterpreted—then—

LAWRENCE. [*Angrily.*] Say, Miss Ambie, what's on your mind?

CAROLINE. [*To* LAWRENCE.] Psch!

SUSAN. [*Collapsing.*] Oh, everybody's crazy!

LAWRENCE. [*Disgusted.*] You're right there. [*He turns helplessly.*] Hildegarde, I hope that. . . . Oh, what's the use!

CAROLINE. [*Abruptly.*] Quite so, Lawrence; get Susan home.

[SUSAN *has got rapidly to the hall door.*

LAWRENCE. But, Hildegarde, I—

CAROLINE. Please go. I wish to talk with your wife. [LAWRENCE *takes his hat.*] Send the motor back for me immediately. [*He crosses to the door. There is a look full of crowded meaning between* HILDEGARDE *and* CAROLINE; *then* CAROLINE *continues to* LAWRENCE.] Oh, and remember, you have engagements for this afternoon. [LAWRENCE *exits with* SUSAN. HILDEGARDE *closes the door after him. There is a pause of sizing up between the two women.*] [*Amused.*] You're not going to lock me in; I hope.

HILDEGARDE. [*Gravely.*] No. But after you leave this room, I want you to pass out of our lives forever.

CAROLINE. *Your* life? That's very simple. You have something else to say to me?

HILDEGARDE. So many things,—I hardly know where to begin.

CAROLINE. Let me help you. We'll eliminate Miss Madden.

HILDEGARDE. We will *not* eliminate Miss Madden. We have a different sense of values, you and I; but we both are *married* women. Emily is different. She has nothing but her friends, Michael and me. And we together will force you to retract.

CAROLINE. Retract the truth! What else?

HILDEGARDE. And make a full apology to her.

CAROLINE. I have never apologized in my life.

HILDEGARDE. Then you have a new experience in store for you. [*Pause.*] What was your purpose in coming here to-day?

CAROLINE. [*With charming frankness.*] You know. My interest in your husband.

HILDEGARDE. And now, you think you can eliminate *me*.

CAROLINE. Why? Your husband has his own career; and you are sensible.

HILDEGARDE. It's a dangerous thing to interfere with other people's lives.

CAROLINE. Yes. We discussed that some time ago.

HILDEGARDE. You told me then that I might hinder him,—that my very work in the world might be an obstacle. Since then I've left him free. I haven't influenced him—

CAROLINE. Oh, don't make virtues of your inabilities.

HILDEGARDE. You mean?

CAROLINE. Don't boast of what you *couldn't* do. You know you couldn't keep him here. Don't say you didn't *want* to. That would be weak.

HILDEGARDE. I don't wish to speak of Lawrence. I wish to speak of you. I am told the world of art needs women of your kind. You have everything—wealth, influence, position. You hold patronage and opportunity in your hands.

CAROLINE. [*Interrupting.*] Why don't you add: " You hold my husband too "? In other words, that you regret your bargain; and you want me to send him back to you.

HILDEGARDE. [*Scornfully.*] Oh, no! But don't make the price for your patronage so high, that a man must sacrifice his self-respect to gain the prize you offer.

CAROLINE. [*Quietly, after a look.*] I never dreamed that you'd be jealous; are you?

HILDEGARDE. [*Fervently.*] Yes, I am jealous—jealous *for* him, but not *of* him!

CAROLINE. I've given him the opportunity. *He* has chosen.

HILDEGARDE. He hasn't!

CAROLINE. Then why are you so anxious?

HILDEGARDE. [*Continuing.*] To choose, one must be independent. He isn't. He thinks he dare not choose against you. He fears to jeopardize commissions. There's where you make unscrupulous use of your advantages!

CAROLNE. [*With a smile.*] My dear Mrs. Sanbury, I may be mistaken; but you seem bent on telling me your husband doesn't care for me. Is that what you mean?

HILDEGARDE. No. [*Suddenly.*] What are you trying to make me think?

CAROLINE. Think what you like. *I* make no disguises. But I marvel at you.

HILDEGARDE. At me!

CAROLINE. I thought you weren't a feminine woman. You're interested in so many things beside your husband. I've interested myself in him. If, in that interest, you think that *he* has gone beyond what you expected; why not speak to *him?*

HILDEGARDE. He's lost his senses! You've blinded him!

CAROLINE. I thought I had *opened* his eyes. You see, Love isn't blind. The trouble is, it sees too much! [*Obliterating her with a glance.*] It sometimes sees things that aren't there at all. It isn't *my* fault if *now* he sees things as they are. I open everybody's eyes. That's my profession. [*Significantly.*] I've opened *yours,* I hope. I've opened Mr. Krellin's. [*She laughs.*]

HILDEGARDE. Yes, and tried wantonly to destroy his faith in Emily, as now you're trying to destroy my faith in Lawrence.

CAROLINE. Ah, then you *are* afraid!

HILDEGARDE. [*Uncertainly.*] Afraid of what!

CAROLINE. You fear to lose your husband's love. Of course, you'll struggle.

HILDEGARDE. I never struggle for what is mine.

CAROLINE. Hum.

HILDEGARDE. [*Nervously.*] I'm not afraid of Lawrence. Your insinuations don't affect me—you . . .

CAROLINE. Indeed. Then why this argument?

HILDEGARDE. [*Amazed.*] You'd like to make me think my husband is your lover! [*She draws a sharp breath.*]

CAROLINE. And if that were the case— What then?
[*Pause.*]

HILDEGARDE. Oh, no! You wouldn't boast of it!

CAROLINE. [*Quietly.*] I never boast. Only the insecure do that.

HILDEGARDE. It's a lie! It's a lie!! It's a lie!!!

CAROLINE. Ask him.

HILDEGARDE. You mean you would have me ask my husband such a question?

CAROLINE. Why not?

HILDEGARDE. [*Suddenly calm, and seeing through* CAROLINE.] Because it isn't important enough, Mrs. Knollys.

CAROLINE. You mean, your husband's fidelity isn't important to you?

HILDEGARDE. Oh, yes, but there's far more at stake. For his sake, I've stepped aside. I've given you every chance with him; because you may have helped him. . . . I don't know. You've taken his time, his mind, his work, his energy. He has amused you, fed your vanity and gratified your sense of power over people. I've been patient. I've left him free to choose. For if a woman like you can take the rest of him from me; he isn't worth my energy to keep. I don't want even a part of him; if anything is withheld—

CAROLINE. [*With an amused sneer.*] And what have *I* to do with your ideal of marriage?

HILDEGARDE. I don't approve of the way that you make use of the protection of your husband's name!

CAROLINE. Then you'd better see my husband.

[*She goes toward the hall door.*

HILDEGARDE. Perhaps I shall.

CAROLINE. He'll be delighted to discuss Miss Madden. Mr. Krellin also wants to speak with him. He'll welcome you both; I'm sure. [*Turning casually.*] He's just back from the South. He'll be in splendid humor after all you've done for him in shutting up the mills. Good-by.

[*She exits in smiling good humor.*
[HILDEGARDE *stands by the table and slowly sinks into a chair. The hum of tenement life becomes audible. A baby is heard crying; and every detail that can be de-*

veloped, pointing to the barren squalor of her life is emphasized as in contrast with the elegance of MRS. KNOLLYS. HILDEGARDE *sits lost in thought, while the hub-bub swings around her. Suddenly the telephone begins to ring.* HILDEGARDE *doesn't notice it at first. The bell continues.* HILDEGARDE *seems to come to her senses with a start. She goes to the 'phone, takes receiver and listens mechanically.*]

HILDEGARDE. Yes. . . . This is Mrs. Sanbury. . . . Who is this? . . . Oh, Miss Ambie. . . . Yes. . . . Mrs. Knollys has just left. . . . [*Coldly.*] I quite understand. Yes. . . . Good-bye. . . . [*Suddenly.*] Wait! Hello! [*Quietly.*] Is Mr. Sanbury still there? [MURTHA *has entered softly from the hall, and goes to clear up the table.*] . . . Yes. . . . I should like to speak with him. [*Pause. She speaks very tenderly.*] Is this you, Larrie? . . . I'm sorry; but it couldn't be helped. . . . She's just left. . . . Yes. . . . Nothing has happened. . . . I'd just like to speak with you; as soon as you can get here. . . . Larrie! . . . What? . . . You can't? . . . [*Long breath.*] Then I'll wait for you. . . . This evening too . . . ? . . . Well, listen, Larrie, you *must* come. . . . No. . . . I can't speak of it over the 'phone. . . . I must see you; and as quickly as possible. . . . But this is important too! [*Pause.*] No! I can't wait! . . . Do you understand, Larrie, I *won't* wait!!!

[*She claps up the receiver and crosses to her room exclaiming hysterically:* "I won't wait!! I won't wait!!" MURTHA *goes on quietly clearing up the dishes at the* table. HILDEGARDE *is heard pulling out drawers violently and pushing them back again.* MURTHA *shakes her head sorrowfully. She has cannily sensed the situation.* HILDEGARDE *re-enters, carrying a small satchel, which she places on a chair next to the table. During the following scene she packs it with a dressing gown, tooth brush, hair brush and comb, slippers, night gown, etc. Several times during the scene she exits rapidly to her room for these toilet articles, and returns, without interrupting the dialogue.*

MURTHA. [*As* HILDEGARDE *enters carrying her satchel.*] Ye ain't goin' away; are ye?

HILDEGARDE. [*Jamming things into the grip.*] Yes . . . yes . . .

MURTHA. [*Suddenly.*] Ah, where's me head! I saw th' Doolans. They've got a date wid you, they say.

HILDEGARDE. [*Going to her room.*] I don't want to see them.

MURTHA. [*Calling after* HILDEGARDE.] Th' agent says he's goin' to throw him out.

HILDEGARDE. He deserves it.

MURTHA. Ah, but jisht a word from you. . . . Moy, th' poor woman an' th' fambly. . . .

HILDEGARDE. [*Entering and continuing her packing.*] I can't help them.

MURTHA. Doolan wanted to come here to apologoize; but Oi told him he'd bedther not. He'd be met on th' doorshtep wid a lump av his death!

HILDEGARDE. You can tell them the ejection office will tend to them.

[*She exits again and immediately re-appears.*

MURTHA. Shure, it's not *you* that's talkin', dearie; and Oi can't go down there! Th' avvicer would see me oye, and know th' Doolans done it. . . . Oh, where's that shtuff? They say it's goin' blue on me. . . . An' you wouldn't have thim turned out in th' shtreet. . . .

HILDEGARDE. [*Pointing to the shelf above the sink.*] It's over there. You'd better take it with you.

MURTHA. Thank ye. [*Tenderly coaxing.*] Go on now, you. Go on now, shishter. . . . Take him back and let him shtay.

HILDEGARDE. After what they've done to you; it seems queer that you . . .

MURTHA. Shure ye can't be angry wid th' min folks. . . . They're chilthren all av thim. [*Piling up dishes.*] Some gits crazy over the *booze,* and some gits crazy over *polyteecks* . . . and some gits crazy over *wimmin* . . . [*Picking up all the dishes*] and th' resht gits crazy over nothin' at all. [*Coaxingly.*] Go on now. . . . Give iviry body anither chanct. That's what I allus says. [*Singing out.*] Ha! Now there's moy Tim—Ha! Oi could ha' left him any toime this forty years fer what he done to me —and what he *didn't* do. . . . G'wan now, dearie, give th' man anither chanct. [HILDEGARDE *leaves the grip.*] Th' Lord love ye, that's roight . . . and it's th' gran' good heart ye have. [HILDEGARDE *goes toward door of her room.* MURTHA *continues with a wise and tender canniness.*] And . . . ah . . . ye'll not be needin' these things roight away. . . . [*She throws the grip into her room.*] You'd bedther shleep here fer to-night. . . . [HILDEGARDE *has exited sobbing brokenly.* MURTHA *returns to the work of clearing up the table. She shakes her head and exclaims:*] Shure, they're chilthren! Ivery blessed wan of thim—just chilthren.

[*The* CURTAIN *descends on the Second Act.*

ACT III

[*The scene is the same as Act II. It is about eight-thirty of the evening of the same day. The table has been cleared and everything is restored to order. The door of* HILDEGARDE'S *room is open. There are no lights on the stage, but the scene is dimly lit by the glow of lights from the flats in the rear.*

After the rise of the curtain, KRELLIN *enters from the hall door, and goes immediately to the telephone on the typewriting desk.*]

KRELLIN. [*With the 'phone.*] Hello—give me seven-one-one Plaza—yes, if you please. No, seven-*one*-one.
[*Enter* LAWRENCE *from the hall, flinging the door back.*
KRELLIN. Say, be quiet, will you?
LAWRENCE. [*Nervously.*] Oh, that you, Krellin? Where's Hildegarde?
[*He turns on a light over the table.*
KRELLIN. Psch! [*To 'phone.*] Hello, seven-one-one Plaza? Yes. Mr. Krellin of the "NEW YORK ECHO" would like to speak with Mr. Knollys.
LAWRENCE. [*Startled.*] See here, Krellin, you'd better drop it.
KRELLIN. [*To 'phone.*] Then I'll ring up again—yes, later. [*As soon as* LAWRENCE *has gathered that* HUBERT *is out, he makes a gesture of relief and flings into* HILDEGARDE'S *room. He finds her bag and immediately re-enters carrying it.* KRELLIN, *in the interim, has hung up the receiver.*

LAWRENCE. What does this mean? Where is she?
 [*He drops the bag and goes uncertainly toward his room at the left, and opens the door.*

KRELLIN. Have you been drinking?

LAWRENCE. [*Fiercely.*] That's my business!

KRELLIN. H'm! Have you any other?

LAWRENCE. [*Coming towards him.*] I want to know where my wife is; and I want to know why you're telephoning my friends!

KRELLIN. Because I won't let your friends treat my Emmy the way you let them treat your wife.

LAWRENCE. Don't you interfere between Hildegarde and me! Because, if you do, by God, I'll—

KRELLIN. I don't mix in with you. I have my own score to settle with Mr. Knollys and his wife.

LAWRENCE. [*Seriously.*] Krellin, I advise you to leave Mr. Knollys out of it.

KRELLIN. Ah, you are afraid, eh?

LAWRENCE. It isn't me—it's— [*He hesitates.*

KRELLIN. [*Violently.*] So! You too!! That woman has made you believe that Emmy—[*He goes toward* LAWRENCE *angrily, but stops and laughs.*] I don't wonder Mrs. Knollys thinks all women are like she is!

LAWRENCE. [*Violently.*] You—?

KRELLIN. [*Quietly.*] All the more am I determined now.

LAWRENCE. [*At his wits' end.*] There'll be an awful mix-up! I don't know what to do! [*Sits down blankly.*

KRELLIN. Don't think that I don't know why you're afraid of Mr. Knollys. It isn't business—it isn't Emmy—it's *you*. [*Scathingly.*] I am ashamed of you! You'd let this lie rest on my Emmy's shoulders, rather than have the truth revealed about yourself. Of course you don't want the truth to come out. But you see, *I'm* different. I don't fear the truth. And if your conduct with Mrs. Knollys cannot stand her husband's or your wife's investigation, I am sorry. That is all.

LAWRENCE. Get that idea out of your head! I don't fear the truth. It's Hildegarde I'm thinking of, and only Hildegarde.

KRELLIN. [*Scornfully.*] You've thought so much of her these last four months, since—

LAWRENCE. I have. We're down to rock-bottom, Krellin. We're full of debts—even my life-insurance is gone. I've given up my job. We've pawned everything that we could raise a cent on; and Hildegarde's stood by me. That's why you can't go on and spoil things now, by dragging Mr. Knollys in. [KRELLIN *laughs scornfully.*] I know it looks as if I had neglected Hildegarde; but *she* understands. I've had to hold on to this one chance, tooth and toe-nail. [*Desperately.*] I won't let anything interfere with it! Not you, nor Hildegarde—nor Emily—nor—

KRELLIN. [*Interrupting.*] *Is* that so! Well, no matter what it costs to you or anybody else, we make Mrs. Knollys *eat* those lying words she said about my Emmy. So.

[KRELLIN *exits through the hall door.*

[LAWRENCE *stands perplexed for a moment, then goes decidedly to the 'phone and rings up.*

LAWRENCE. Hello—give me one-four-three-three Plaza —yes—in a hurry, please. [*Pause.*] Central, they *must* answer. It's a private wire and they are expecting me to ring them up. [*Pause. Then with an exaggerated change to a very polite manner.*] Oh, hello—Is that you, Caroline? I've been very busy—yes—all afternoon. Yes, I'm so sorry, but I shan't be able to get back— Nothing's happened to my *voice;* but—ah—the fact is I've had an accident

... only my ankle— Oh, nothing serious—I'm sure, so don't be alarmed. . . . Yes, getting out of the cab. . . . I'm telephoning from a drug store. . . . Yes, it *is* painful; but I'm sure it's only wrenched. . . . Yes, I'll ring up my doctor as soon as I get home. . . . I shall be quite alone. . . . Please don't worry. . . . Oh, I can tend to everything. [*Pause.*] I've already telephoned to Mrs. Millette. . . . Mercy, no, I wouldn't have a nurse touch me. . . . Yes, I'll telephone in the morning . . . yes, then as soon as he has left, I'll ring you up and tell you what his diagnosis is. . . . Hildegarde? . . . No, I haven't seen her. . . . Oh, not because of anything that happened here. . . . She's— she left this afternoon to spend the week-end with some friends—yes—somewhere in the country—Westchester. . . . No, I shan't send for her. . . . Yes, if there's anything—but—Oh, thank you so much. . . . Good-by.
[*He rings off. During the last part of the above speech,* HILDEGARDE *has quietly entered from the hall door.*

LAWRENCE. [*Relieved and confused.*] Oh—Westchester!—I mean, I've just been telephoning.

HILDEGARDE. I didn't expect to see you this evening.
[*She goes to her typewriting desk for some letters, etc.*

LAWRENCE. Well, there was something in the sound of your voice over the 'phone that made me nervous; and I lied out of my engagements. As usual, said the first foolish thing that came into my mind. Now I'll have to stick to it, I suppose.

HILDEGARDE. Why do you always lie these days?

LAWRENCE. I never lie to *you*.

HILDEGARDE. Is *that* really the truth?

LAWRENCE. Why, yes!

HILDEGARDE. Why did you say I was in Westchester?

LAWRENCE. I didn't know where you'd gone to, and—

HILDEGARDE. Didn't you say I'd gone to Westchester because you were afraid that Mrs. Knollys would be jealous of your spending an evening alone with me?

LAWRENCE. What have you got in your head? [*She looks at him. He continues.*] I had to say something to get out of things. Then I come home and find your bag packed. Where *are* you going?

HILDEGARDE. I think it best I go away a little while.

LAWRENCE. Away? Where to?

HILDEGARDE. I haven't decided. I was going to leave a note for you; but Michael told me you were here; so I—

LAWRENCE. [*Bursting.*] Michael! Do you know what he's doing? And just now, of all times! When everything depends on Mr. Knollys?

HILDEGARDE. Yes, I advised him.

LAWRENCE. What! [*Pause.*] Hildegarde, suppose what Mrs. Knollys said about Emily is true?

HILDEGARDE. [*Turning sharply.*] Larrie!

LAWRENCE. Well, I said, *suppose* it's true.

HILDEGARDE. It's not. And even if it were, *she's* not the one to make the accusation.

LAWRENCE. Why not? [*Pause.*] What's in your mind? *Krellin's* been saying things!

HILDEGARDE. Oh, no.

LAWRENCE. I know it. Why, just a moment ago he said that I was afraid to meet Mr. Knollys.

HILDEGARDE. Afraid? Why?

LAWRENCE. He thinks that I—

[*He hesitates.*

HILDEGARDE. [*In a level tone.*] What—?

LAWRENCE. That I've forgotten you. [*Recklessly.*] Oh, I don't care what he thinks, except that I don't want *you* to get wrong-headed. I thought at least, *you'd* understand. There's not a thing I've done that anybody can't question.

HILDEGARDE. That's ambiguous, Larrie; but I shan't question you.

LAWRENCE. I mean that anybody can't investigate. I've never *really* lied to you; have I?

HILDEGARDE. No—not lied exactly—just disguised things to make it easier for me. . . . Oh, yes, Larrie, my clothes, my work, our home, our life together, *your* work and all the circumstances and people that have come between us.

LAWRENCE. Oh, those things! I don't mean them.

HILDEGARDE. What do you mean?

LAWRENCE. [*Blurting it out.*] I mean Car—Mrs. Knollys. That's what *you* mean; and that's what Krellin means.

HILDEGARDE. [*Tremulously.*] Yes. [*She turns away.*]

LAWRENCE. I want to explain everything, right from the beginning—everything. [*She moves away. He follows.*] I want you to know the whole truth, and nothing *but* the truth; and then you can judge for yourself. Oh, I'm not proud of what I've had to do; but there isn't a single thing that you can't know about—or that I'm really ashamed of—I swear! [*There is a knock at the hall door.* LAWRENCE, *after a gesture of impatience, continues:*] If that's Krellin, tell him I want to be alone with you. He can't telephone. He's got to leave Mr. Knollys out of this. I don't want Knollys to get wrong-headed too!

[*He has followed* HILDEGARDE *who has moved up to the door.*]

HILDEGARDE. [*At door, to* LAWRENCE.] Please!

[*She opens the door and discovers* HUBERT KNOLLYS *standing there.*]

HUBERT. [*To* HILDEGARDE.] I couldn't find the bell.

Lawrence. [*Retreating.*] Oh, Lord!

Hubert. Mrs. Sanbury, I'm very glad to see you.
                    [*Extends his hand. She takes it.*

Hildegarde. I've been hoping you'd come.
                              [Lawrence *is surprised.*

Hubert. Thank you.

Lawrence. Yes—we—

Hubert. [*Laconically to* Lawrence.] Oh—how are you?

Lawrence. [*Embarrassed.*] Oh, finely . . . been pretty busy since you left; but—

Hubert. [*Abruptly.*] Yes, so I hear. [*He turns to* Hildegarde *and points to a chair.*] May I?

Hildegarde. [*Nodding.*] Let me take your things.
                    [Lawrence *takes his hat and coat.*

Hubert. [*Sitting and speaking to* Hildegarde.] I've just got back from the South.

Lawrence. [*Effusively.*] Yes, we heard you were away.

Hubert. [*Turning quietly.*] I was rather of the opinion that you *knew* I was away.

Lawrence. Yes, to be sure—of course. Did you have a successful trip of it?

Hubert. [*Ironically.*] Have you had time to read the papers?

Lawrence. I was interested and all that; though I haven't followed the strike very closely. A little out of my line, you know. So if you're going to talk economics, hadn't I better—?   [*He starts toward his room.*

Hubert. [*Interrupting.*] There are some things I wish to discuss with your wife. I'd rather you'd be here. That is, if you don't mind.

Lawrence. [*Vaguely.*] By all means—not at all.
                    [Hildegarde *turns anxiously to* Hubert.

HUBERT. [*To* HILDEGARDE.] You know, it was due a little to your suggestion, I went South.

HILDEGARDE. And?

HUBERT. We've increased the operative's salaries and killed the child labor.

HILDEGARDE. We know about the splendid settlement you forced.

HUBERT. [*Grimly.*] I couldn't have done it by myself. You opened fire on my competitors. That made it easy. It looked like a general lock-out; so I called a committee of the managers, and we all agreed to meet the strikers' terms. Alone, I would have made a Quixotic failure. Well, we've yielded. You've kept *your* word; I've kept mine. Now we'll see what the workers will do with more money and shorter hours. Personally, I think they'll invest in more phonographs and liquor; and their children will continue to go barefoot.

HILDEGARDE. Perhaps. But the use of time and money must be learned.

HUBERT. They'll have their chance. Now, for the matter that brings me here immediately. [*He takes out a letter.*] I received this by messenger this afternoon—from Miss Madden.

HILDEGARDE. Yes.

HUBERT. Miss Madden urges me to see *you*.

HILDEGARDE. She told me.

HUBERT. So I am here to do anything I can in the way of reparation.

HILDEGARDE. There's only one possible reparation. Your wife must withdraw her statement absolutely. The circumstances are such that—

HUBERT. I know.

HILDEGARDE. What can have been her motive?

HUBERT. There is no question of Miss Madden's innocence. She suffers from two misfortunes. Firstly, she is a very dear friend of mine; and secondly, she was of service to my wife. Gratitude makes some natures resentful. I, however, feel a great obligation to Miss Madden for averting a scandal, that my wife's ignorance of the law nearly precipitated.

HILDEGARDE. Mr. Krellin helped her hush the matter up. But now, unless your wife withdraws her statements, he is determined to publish everything.

HUBERT. So his telegram informed me. But Mr. Krellin's threat could have very little weight either with Mrs. Knollys or with me.

HILDEGARDE. Why?

HUBERT. You must surely see that after doing all he could to keep the matter from the press, it would be ridiculous for Krellin now to make an exposure. His own conduct couldn't stand investigation. [*Pause.*] Will not my personal apology for Mrs. Knollys to Mr. Krellin and Miss Madden suffice?

HILDEGARDE. Considering the accusation and the way you are involved, I should say not.

HUBERT. Perhaps you're right. [*Rises.*] I suggested it merely to show you how really powerless we are. A money damage for defamation is out of the question—

HILDEGARDE. Quite.

HUBERT. Then what do you propose?

HILDEGARDE. [*Firmly.*] That right here, and before the very people in whose presence Mrs. Knollys *made* the accusation, she must *retract* and with full apologies. Nothing less.

HUBERT. [*Involuntarily.*] I'd love to see it!

LAWRENCE. Hildegarde!

HUBERT. [*To* HILDEGARDE.] Your husband's exclamation proves that he and I know my wife much better than you do, Mrs. Sanbury. *He* appreciates her force of will. [*To* LAWRENCE.] Don't you, sir?

[LAWRENCE *looks on guard and says nothing.*

HILDEGARDE. Is your wife absolutely indifferent to the social consequences of her own conduct?

HUBERT. [*Sitting.*] Ah! Why do you ask?

HILDEGARDE. Because immediately after having accused Emily, she did her best to make *me* believe my husband had become her lover.

HUBERT. [*Attempting to be surprised.*] What!!

LAWRENCE. [*Bounding out of his skin.*] Hildegarde!! [*To* HUBERT.] This is outrageous!

HILDEGARDE. Yes.

[LAWRENCE *is open mouthed.*

HUBERT. [*To* HILDEGARDE.] Are you sure you're not mistaken?

HILDEGARDE. Oh, no. On the contrary, she took the greatest pains to impress it on me with all the malicious insolence of triumph she could command.

HUBERT. But—why do you tell *me* this?

HILDEGARDE. To ask you to use it as you think best, to help me to force your wife to make just reparation to my friend.

LAWRENCE. [*Finding his voice.*] It's all a damnable lie! A whole-sale rotten—!

HUBERT. [*Interrupting.*] Pardon, I should reserve such language until you have a better right to use it.

LAWRENCE. Wh-what do you mean?

HUBERT. Remember, sir, the lady you are speaking of is still *my* wife.

LAWRENCE. [*Wildly.*] I can't help *that!* I have *my* wife to consider, Mr. Knollys, and—

HUBERT. [*Scornfully.*] Indeed!

LAWRENCE. [*Continuing.*] And with all deference to

your wife, I must repeat that if *your* wife said those things to *my* wife, your wife uttered a lie!!

HILDEGARDE. So I told her myself.

HUBERT. [*Promptly.*] You did that to shield your husband.

LAWRENCE. [*Vehemently.*] And I protest that if *your* wife—

HUBERT. [*Sternly to* LAWRENCE.] Keep quiet!

LAWRENCE. [*Spinning about.*] For God's sake, some one do me the favor to tell me that one of us is blind or deaf or—

HUBERT. [*Severely.*] Sit down!!

LAWRENCE. [*Landing into a chair and wailing.*] She's old enough to be my mother!

HUBERT. [*To* HILDEGARDE.] Did she say anything further? Come!

HILDEGARDE. She wantonly taunted me with my failure to hold my husband. When I told her I did not believe her, she even urged me to question him. I refused. Please to observe I have not questioned him.

LAWRENCE. [*Imploringly.*] Oh, why didn't you?

HUBERT. [*To* HILDEGARDE.] Why did you *not* question him?

HILDEGARDE. Because—simply because I did not believe your wife.

LAWRENCE. [*Fervently.*] Thank God!

HUBERT. But if you do not believe her statements, why repeat them to me?

HILDEGARDE. To serve my friend, I shall deliberately *choose to believe* your wife; and if you will help me—

HUBERT. [*Interjecting.*] Rely on that.

HILDEGARDE. Then I shall act as if everything she said were absolutely true.

LAWRENCE. Oh, Hildegarde! How *can* you!?

HILDEGARDE. [*To* HUBERT.] In that way we can turn her arrow against Emily into a boomerang to recoil upon herself.

HUBERT. Hum. Then you will name her as a co-respondent?

HILDEGARDE. [*Genuinely frightened.*] What! You mean divorce my—divorce Larrie?

HUBERT. Yes.

LAWRENCE. [*To* HILDEGARDE.] See here! *I'm* the one that your damned boomerang is hitting!

HUBERT. [*To* HILDEGARDE.] This is unavoidable.

LAWRENCE. See here!—

HILDEGARDE. [*Expostulatingly to* HUBERT.] But don't you see that I do *not* believe her. She did it to provoke a jealous quarrel; and if I judge her rightly, she will withdraw her insults rather than endure disgrace. It won't have to go that far! D-Don't you see that?

HUBERT. Thank you for your assurance, but I must differ with you.

LAWRENCE. [*To* HUBERT.] Why?—do you think that I—?

HUBERT. [*Calmly.*] I think there is an important person that you both have so far overlooked—myself. [*To* LAWRENCE.] You have chosen to protect my wife by calling her a liar. [*To* HILDEGARDE.] You protect your husband by calling her a liar, too. It seems *my* attitude has been neglected. [HILDEGARDE *is appalled.*

LAWRENCE. [*Bravely.*] Well—?

HUBERT. Yes. Here's where *you* come in.

LAWRENCE. [*Crumbling.*] What do you intend to do?

HUBERT. I choose to believe these statements for my *own* sake.

HILDEGARDE. You can't! You can't!!

LAWRENCE. [*To* HUBERT.] You don't mean to say!—

[*To* HILDEGARDE, *wildly.*] He believes it! He believes it!

HUBERT. [*Quietly.*] I always believe my wife when she affirms, *never* when she denies.

HILDEGARDE. [*Stupefied.*] But, Mr. Knollys, you don't *really* think that . . .

HUBERT. [*Interrupting.*] My dear lady, you are too gullible. [*To* LAWRENCE.] Now, I want the truth, and I expect it manfully.

[*He approaches* LAWRENCE, *who retreats.*]
LAWRENCE. This is perfectly ridiculous!

HUBERT. [*Taking out a note-book.*] Please have the courtesy to remember that it is *you* who has made us both ridiculous; and don't thrust it down our throats. [*Consulting his book.*] You spent at least a week with Caroline alone in Italy.

LAWRENCE. That isn't true! Susan Ambie . . .

HUBERT. [*Promptly.*] I have seen Miss Ambie. She did more than confess. She attempted to defend it.

LAWRENCE. Miss Ambie is a fool!

HUBERT. Quite so. [*Continuing.*] Do you admit being alone with Mrs. Knollys?

LAWRENCE. [*Pausing.*] Why—I—

HILDEGARDE. [*Gone white.*] Don't deny it, Larrie.

HUBERT. [*To* HILDEGARDE.] I heard you say some weeks ago you had letters to that effect.

LAWRENCE. [*Imploringly.*] Hildegarde!

HILDEGARDE. Yes. I have them.

HUBERT. Very good. I trust you to produce them at the proper time. [*To* LAWRENCE.] You crossed on the same steamer.

LAWRENCE. [*Grasping at a straw.*] Miss Ambie was with us!

HUBERT. Yes; and since your arrival on October 5th

you have devoted all your time, practically day and night, to each other.

LAWRENCE. [*Angrily.*] I won't stand here and have you say such things about your wife!

HUBERT. Am I to be the only one who does *not* say them?

LAWRENCE. She simply—

HUBERT. [*With feigned anger.*] Pray do not explain my wife to me. [*Continuing from his note-book.*] On October 7th you actually installed yourself under my roof —a most tasteless procedure, which I refused to countenance. I went South. You thought, no doubt, that openness would disarm suspicion. It doesn't work. As part of that same plan, my wife openly confesses her infatuation to your wife, boasts of her power, and then further openly denounces an innocent woman, in order to produce the impression that her own actions are not subject to criticism. Truly, this is the very blindness of infatuation. [*Laughs.*] I admire your brass—but really it won't do. The rest of us are not so blind. I compliment you on your conquest [*Ironically*]. But how long did you imagine I would allow this to continue?

LAWRENCE. Mr. Knollys, all that I can say is—

HUBERT. [*Scathingly.*] At least, sir, have the courage of your actions. [*Snapping his book closed, and looking at* HILDEGARDE, *who sees she has awakened a Frankenstein.*] I have a further list of rendezvous, which I shall not ask you to verify in the presence of your wife!

LAWRENCE. My wife knows everything that can be said about me!

HUBERT. I doubt it. In any case, your protection until now has been your wife's credulity. We shall see. When my lawyer—

LAWRENCE. [*Interrupting.*] All right. *Get* your

lawyer. Now I'll thank you, Mr. Knollys, to leave me alone with my wife, who's never doubted me, and has no reason to doubt me now. I *have* the courage of my actions! I'll bring the whole thing right into the open—and if *you* can stand it, *I* can.

> [*The two men look each other squarely in the eye. Suddenly the bell rings over the hall door.*]

HUBERT. [*Turning to* HILDEGARDE.] Is that your bell?
> [HILDEGARDE *goes directly to the hall door, opens it and discloses* MRS. KNOLLYS. *She is magnificently dressed in a long opera cloak over her evening gown. She has also a heavy veil about her head.* CAROLINE *enters swiftly, then stands appalled.*]

HUBERT. [*Recognizing her.*] Ah, Caroline! [*Surprise of all.* CAROLINE *undoes her veil and faces him.*] You come most apropos. [*Sarcastically.*] Did you call to see *Mrs.* Sanbury?

CAROLINE. [*After a pause.*] I . . . I have called for *you*. [*She comes into the room.*

HUBERT. Indeed! How is that?

CAROLINE. I am on my way to the opera. I assumed that Miss Madden had summoned you. I thought I'd pick you up.

HUBERT. How kind of you. But may I ask why you assumed that I'd be here in Mrs. Sanbury's apartment?

CAROLINE. Quite naturally. Mrs. Sanbury is the only other person interested with you, in deceiving Mr. Krellin and whitewashing Miss Madden.

HILDEGARDE. Mrs. Knollys, my husband telephoned you that I had gone to Westchester; so you couldn't have expected to see *me*. [LAWRENCE *is desperate.*

HUBERT. [*To* CAROLINE.] Oh, you expected to find

Mr. Sanbury alone. [*After a glance at* Lawrence, *he turns to* Hildegarde.] Well, then, Mrs. Sanbury, let us no longer intrude. Will you direct me to Miss Madden?

Hildegarde. [*Moves to the hall door, then turns.*] Mrs. Knollys, I think it only fair to tell you, that I have repeated to Mr. Knollys the whole substance of your conversation with me this afternoon.

> [Hubert *opens the door.* Hildegarde *exits; and he follows, closing the door behind him.* Lawrence *is standing stupefied down left.* Caroline *is at center. Pause.*

Caroline. [*In an unsteady voice.*] I think I'm going to faint.

Lawrence. [*Putting her into chair at the table, anxiously.*] Oh, don't! For Heaven's sake, don't do that. [*She sits.*] I'll get you a glass of water. [*He goes quickly to the tubs and pours one out of a bottle. Coming to her.*] Here, drink this. Is there anything else I can get you? [*She sips the water.*] Shan't I send for some one?

Caroline. [*Ironically.*] For whom?

> [*She drinks the water.*

Lawrence. You feel better now, don't you? Shall I get you some salts?

> [*He moves quickly toward* Hildegarde's *room.*

Caroline. No. I'll be all right. [*Suddenly.*] You walk very well.

Lawrence. [*Stopping.*] Why, yes, I— Shall I get you home?

Caroline. [*Caustically.*] No. I have no trouble with *my* ankle.

Lawrence. [*Suddenly remembering.*] Oh, forgive me, Caroline.

Caroline. [*In a rage.*] Don't call me Caroline! I

imagined you here alone, in pain, too ill to telephone—I thought you might be glad to see me. I lost my prudence. [LAWRENCE *turns away*.] How much of what you've said to me for all these months is true? What did you mean by taking me into your arms to-day and . . . Agh—!!
                                        [*She turns from him.*
  LAWRENCE. [*Simply*.] I've done a great wrong.
  CAROLINE. [*Sarcastically*.] And when did you discover that?
  LAWRENCE. After I kissed you to-day—the way I did.
  CAROLINE. That's why you left so suddenly.
  LAWRENCE. Yes.
  CAROLINE. And came right back to *her?*
  LAWRENCE. I tried to find her, but I couldn't. I was frantic. I looked every place. I really thought that she had left me. [*In a low voice*.] And I thought that I deserved it. Then I telephoned to you; and she came in.
  CAROLINE. The kiss that woke *your* prudence put *mine* to sleep. How strange! And you were thinking all the time of *her!*   [*She laughs hysterically.*
  LAWRENCE. Why, yes. Always! My work, my ambition,—even my gratitude to you has been for her sake.
  CAROLINE. Then I was merely the ladder on which you proposed to climb and pluck the golden fruit for *her!*
  LAWRENCE. I've been a miserable cad! I know what you must think of me!
  CAROLINE. And what do *they* think of you?
  LAWRENCE. Oh, how can I tell you? Your husband insists upon putting the worst interpretation upon everything!
  CAROLINE. You mean?
  LAWRENCE. I did all I could to make him see that he was wrong in doubting *you*. [*A withering look from* CAROLINE.] Oh, but what made you tell those outrageous falsehoods about us to Hildegarde!?

CAROLINE. [*Rising in a cold rage.*] The word falsehood can only be applied to *your* attitude to me. I took you for an artist, eager to rise above and to be free from the commonness and squalor of your surroundings, and I was willing to help you. But I find you only a little entrepreneur, afraid of your conscience, and satisfied with your mutton! Well, return to it! [*She moves away, then turns.*] I have one more direction to give you. Kindly refrain from any further defense of me. I wish to speak to my husband. Will you tell him I am waiting?

> [LAWRENCE *exits through the hall door.*
> [CAROLINE *pauses in intense thought, then gathers herself together, takes her vanity-box from her opera bag, opens the mirror and scrutinizes herself closely. She adjusts her hair, smooths her eyebrows and puts a little rouge on her lips. She regains her absolute composure by a supreme effort.* HUBERT *enters. He is very self-possessed.*

HUBERT. You wished to see me?

CAROLINE. [*Charmingly.*] I have been waiting.

HUBERT. For what?

CAROLINE. If you've quite finished your visit, I thought perhaps you would enjoy an hour at the opera.

> [*She gives him her cloak.*

HUBERT. [*Taking the cloak.*] No, thank you.

CAROLINE. You wish to go right home?

HUBERT. For the present I have decided to—ah—live at the club.

CAROLINE. Very well. Can I drop you there?

HUBERT. No. [*Putting her cloak on a chair.*] I shall need you here.

CAROLINE. Oh, then our meeting was most fortunate.

HUBERT. Yes. I was wondering how to get you here.

CAROLINE. As it is probably the last time I shall ever come, if there's anything that you would like me to do for you while I am—

HUBERT. [*Interrupting her, admiringly.*] Caroline, you're magnificent! We'd better get right to the point. [*Looking at his watch.*] I needn't detain you very long. I've told Miss Madden and the others to—ah—come downstairs in five minutes.

CAROLINE. [*Acting as if perplexed.*] I wonder what she can have to say to me; or [*Incredulously*] do *you* want me to meet her again?

HUBERT. I am afraid I shall be obliged to insist upon it. I have already satisfied Mr. Krellin.

CAROLINE. Dear, dear! That must have been fatiguing; but how very nice! I believe he wants to marry her.

HUBERT. Yes.

CAROLINE. A very amusing man. Too bad! But how am I concerned?

HUBERT. In the presence of all the people before whom you made your accusation against Miss Madden, I should like you to retract it and apologize.

CAROLINE. [*Very graciously.*] My dear Hubert, I consider that you've never had any fault to find with me in any of your former affectionate waywardnesses. Of course, I have regretted them, but my pride has never been involved till now. *This* adventure is different. You might at least have chosen a woman of your class. I closed my eyes even to *this*, until the unfortunate woman was forced upon me in a manner I felt obliged to resent. I'm very sorry. I know so little of how these people act. You might have put me on my guard. Now you wish me to apologize to her for having said the truth. [*She laughs.*] Really, Hubert, don't you think you ask too much?

HUBERT. I have assured them you would do so. That was the purpose of my visit.

CAROLINE. [*Still smiling.*] I'm very sorry to disappoint the audience and perplex the impresario. [*Distinctly.*] You may cut my salary if you like, but I give no performance this evening. [*Rises.*]

HUBERT. [*Gracefully.*] Having heard you once, the audience refuses a substitute.

CAROLINE. Then I suggest you reimburse them.

HUBERT. No, that won't do.

CAROLINE. Have you tried?

HUBERT. I explained that you came here with the best intentions, and that you would fulfil their expectations.

CAROLINE. [*Merrily.*] I couldn't keep my face straight in the tragic parts.

HUBERT. I must really insist that you be serious.

CAROLINE. It's no use my trying.

HUBERT. [*Looking at his watch.*] We're wasting time.

CAROLINE. Hubert, you're so good-humored, you almost make me feel that you're in earnest.

HUBERT. I am.

CAROLINE. And if I still refuse?

HUBERT. Then you force me to resort to measures that we both decided were ridiculous. I have waited for this moment for twenty-five long years. For all that time *you've* held the whip; *I've* had to canter to your wish. But now, my dear, if you do not retract your statement and protect Miss Madden absolutely, *I* shall sue for a divorce and name your—latest as a co-respondent.

CAROLINE. [*Calmly.*] You can't.

HUBERT. I have persuaded Mrs. Sanbury to allow me to assume the suit.

CAROLINE. [*Slowly.*] So, you stand with her.

HUBERT. Precisely.

CAROLINE. I compliment you on your associate.
HUBERT. You left me no choice.
CAROLINE. Well?
HUBERT. It's been your policy to overlook *my* trespasses; but note *I* have not condoned either in private or in public. That is why I do not wish to appear with you in our box to-night—that is why I left your house, as soon as ever I discovered the—intrigue; and I shall not return. Whatever was lacking in my evidence, Mrs. Sanbury and others have supplied.
CAROLINE. Go on.
HUBERT. I should like to settle matters amicably, but really, my dear, it's no longer in my power. If *I* do not sue for the divorce, Mrs. Sanbury *will;* and she will name *you* as a co-respondent. That might be more annoying.
CAROLINE. I have done nothing!
HUBERT. You have always told me that our society deals in appearances; and you have done sufficient here and abroad to create a prima facie case. The burden will rest upon you to prove that we are wrong.
CAROLINE. [*Snapping her fingers.*] That for your appearances!
HUBERT. They are far more damning than any you may know about me and Miss Madden. Come, you're too much a thoroughbred and too wise a woman not to know when you are beaten.
CAROLINE. [*Leaning forward.*] Let me understand you. If I give Miss Madden a certificate of virtue, you will withhold the suit. That is your price, is it?
HUBERT. As far as I'm concerned, yes. I can make no bargain for Mrs. Sanbury.
CAROLINE. Then what's the use of my withdrawing anything, if she—?

HUBERT. You will have me *with* you instead of *against* you.

CAROLINE. And what of that?

HUBERT. If I stand by and make no objection to Sanbury's attentions, who else *can?* They become immediately innocent, and her proceeding is discouraged; but if I join with her—which I mean to do unless you meet my terms, you become immediately defenseless and every suspicion is justified. [*A movement from* CAROLINE.] Without me, to whom can you appeal for help? To Society? It would rend you and rejoice in it, as you have rended others. You can ill afford to have your name publicly coupled with this young Sanbury's in any dirty proceeding.

CAROLINE. [*Sharply driving a bargain.*] In other words, if *I* protect Miss Madden from the truth, *you* will protect *me* from a lie.

HUBERT. Precisely; and we all enter into our usual, polite conspiracy of silence. I advise you to reflect.

CAROLINE. [*Rising.*] I shall. I'll think it over.

[*She sits in the chair down left.*]

HUBERT. [*With his watch.*] You've just two minutes to decide.

CAROLINE. [*Ominously.*] Hubert, I advise you not to humiliate me before these people.

HUBERT. It's either these few people here, or the grinning congregation you will be forced to face alone, in your temple of Convention. [*Pause.*] I know what this must mean to you. [CAROLINE *shudders.*] You've been hard hit to-day. [*He goes toward her.*] With all your bravado, I know you're covering a wound. I believe that you seriously cared about this young man. For the first time in your life you've cared about anything outside of yourself. That's why you forgot yourself and went so wrong. [*She looks up at him.*] Oh! There's hope in that. I didn't think that it was *in* you. You made yourself vulnerable for him, and the disillusionment has come, and hurt you far more than you will ever confess. [*He turns away.*] And then I'd like to spare you for another reason. After all, you are the mother of my child, and we've negotiated something of a life since we were young together. [*Pause.*]

CAROLINE. [*Rising.*] Send them in!

    [*He goes to the hall door, opens it and makes a gesture to them outside.*]

HUBERT. [*To* CAROLINE.] They're coming now.

CAROLINE. [*A malicious expression crosses her face. It passes. She turns and asks:*] Do you want to stay and see me take my medicine?

HUBERT. [*Bowing.*] I know that you will do it gracefully.

    [LAWRENCE *enters from the hall.* CAROLINE *turns immediately toward the audience.* LAWRENCE *is very uncomfortable as he passes* HUBERT. LAWRENCE *is followed by* KRELLIN *and* EMILY. KRELLIN *is uneasily defiant.* EMILY *looks down.* HILDEGARDE *is the last to enter. She looks uncertainly at* HUBERT. CAROLINE *is the only one who is completely self-possessed.* HILDEGARDE *closes the door. The others have gathered awkwardly around the table, center.* CAROLINE *stands in her position down left. There is an awkward pause.* HUBERT *turns to* CAROLINE, *who shrugs her shoulders gaily and turns away.*]

HUBERT. [*To all.*] Hum—As I explained to you, my wife so much regretted her unfortunate mistake that she was unwilling to allow the night to pass before she came down personally to rectify it. [*To* KRELLIN *and* EMILY.] You have assured me that her *personal* retraction will be satisfactory. My wife desires to make it.

[KRELLIN. [*Taking out a paper.*] Mr. Knollys, I have drawn up a paper for your wife to sign.

HUBERT. But—

CAROLINE. Hubert!

[*She passes him and goes to the table, center.*

KRELLIN. I think that she will find it accurate.

[KRELLIN *puts the paper on the table, center, and takes out his fountain pen, which he lays carefully next to it.* CAROLINE *sits at the table, takes the paper and reads aloud.*

CAROLINE. "November twenty-ninth, nineteen-fifteen. I, Mrs. Hubert Knollys, having permitted myself to make a certain disparaging, slanderous and criminal statement [HUBERT *would interfere. She continues*] on this date, concerning the chastity of Miss Emily Madden,—in the presence of Mr. Krellin, Mrs. Sanbury and Mr. Sanbury, do herewith wish to recant it absolutely, and to state over my signature that my statement was groundless. To wit: I said that Miss Madden was improperly intimate with my husband, Mr. Hubert Knollys. I now declare this statement to be absolutely false, mistaken and unwarranted. Signed "— [*She looks up questioningly.*] [KRELLIN *points to the bottom of the page.*] Here?

KRELLIN. Please.

CAROLINE. [*While writing.*] In addition, I wish to make my humble apology for any misinterpretation I may have made in regard to Miss Madden's . . . generous services to my husband and to me. At least I've learned that lies are futile, and that truth crushed to earth will rise again. [*She rises.* EMILY *sinks down into a chair* at the right. *The rest of them shift in an embarrassed way.* CAROLINE *folds the signed retraction, leans toward* KRELLIN *and asks gently:*

CAROLINE. Is there anything else? [*Pause.*
LAWRENCE. [*Coming forward.*] Mrs. Knollys . . . [CAROLINE *passes him, disdaining to reply. He then turns to* MR. KNOLLYS.] Considering the circumstances, I think it better that I resign the contract for remodeling your house.

HUBERT. Very well. Then—ah . . . Caroline, if you've quite finished . . . that is . . .

CAROLINE. [*Taking her cloak, which he holds for her.*] Yes. I told Morgan to wait. [*With a little shiver.*] I'm afraid it's raining. Hubert, will you please see if the motor is at the door?

[HUBERT *gives her a swift, suspicious look. She meets his returning glance with an assuring smile. Pause.*

HUBERT. Yes, certainly. [*He quickly takes his hat and coat from the hatrack at the door, then turns.*] Good night. Good night.

KRELLIN. [*Picking up the signed paper.*] Good night.
[HUBERT *exits.*

[CAROLINE *sweeps around as if to follow* HUBERT, *but pauses a second to look mockingly at* EMILY, *who is still seated at the right, with bowed head.* CAROLINE's *soft laugh is interrupted by* KRELLIN, *who speaks just as she has got to the door.*

KRELLIN. Mrs. Knollys . . . [*She turns in the door, with her hand on the knob.*] You have signed this paper. [*Triumphantly.*] But I wish you to know that, for me, this was not in the least necessary. I had no belief whatever in your assertions. It was only because they distressed Miss Madden that I exacted this satisfaction.

CAROLINE. [*Graciously.*] Quite so . . . *Quite* so. It's a pity that I cannot go further and silence all rumors about a little trip on the Chesapeake, Miss Madden made with Mr. Knollys on his yacht . . . [*Looking at* EMILY.] Or any malicious inuendoes about my husband's too frequent visits at odd hours to her apartment in East Thirtieth Street. [*A movement from* KRELLIN.] Don't be alarmed! When rumors of this kind come to you, I want you to feel sure that I am always at your service to help you to discredit them. [EMILY *has cowered under* CAROLINE'S *speech.* KRELLIN *starts for the door with an inarticulate cry of rage and surprise.*

CAROLINE. [*Very graciously.*] Good night.

[*She closes the door behind her.*

KRELLIN. Stop! Wait!!

[EMILY *has quickly risen, and intercepts him.*

EMILY. Michael! Please!

KRELLIN. But Emmy, this is worse!!

EMILY. You can do nothing more!

KRELLIN. This time I'll . . .!

EMILY. No, no! I'm done for! I've got to give you up! What she said is true!!

KRELLIN. What!?

HILDEGARDE. Oh!

EMILY. I couldn't have stood it any longer! I'm glad the truth is out!! . . . I'm glad . . .

[KRELLIN *makes over to her, takes her by the shoulders and peers into her face. She sinks under his gaze. He recoils with an almost savage exclamation.*

HILDEGARDE. Stop, Michael!

KRELLIN. [*Tearing up the retraction.*] Women! Women! [*Then, with a bitter cry.*] Faith is a virtue only when it is *blind;* and then it makes a fool of you . . . a fool!

EMILY. No, Michael, *I'm* the fool! I should have trusted you . . . I should have told you everything. *You* would have understood. But how can you forgive me for the *lie* I've *acted!* [*She goes toward him.*] But don't . . . don't lose your faith in other women, because *I've* been a fool . . . [*She turns sobbing toward the door.*] Yes, I'm the fool . . . I'm the fool . . . [*She exits.*]

HILDEGARDE. Michael, go with Emily.

KRELLIN. [*With infinite pity.*] So, my poor little Emmy. Oh, we primitive males! We create idols, and when the truth comes, what do we find? Only pitiful humanity! [*He goes to the door and turns with a wry smile.*] But you see, all of us together, fighting blindly, were not strong enough to fight against the *truth!* [*He suddenly breaks out into an hysterical laugh.*] God is a great humorist! . . . A great humorist!! [*He exits through hall door.*]

[*As soon as the door closes on* KRELLIN, HILDEGARDE *also breaks out into a bitter laugh of disillusionment.*

LAWRENCE. [*Frightened at her laughter.*] How can you laugh?

HILDEGARDE. Because I too have been a fool! And when one's faith is dead, one needs a sense of humor. [*Grimly.*] So, she spoke the truth, your friend Mrs. Knollys—the truth about *you* as well.

LAWRENCE. Hildegarde, if she told you that I had ever been unfaithful to you, she lied.

HILDEGARDE. Did she lie when she said your nature couldn't stand poverty—that you couldn't work in this environment,—that you had to court the rich to get your chance to rise,—that I, with my principles and my work stood in your way? Did she lie about your *character?* Oh, no, she showed me the truth.

LAWRENCE. Hildegarde, you frighten me! How can we live together if you believe such things?

HILDEGARDE. Do you think that I could speak like this, if I didn't realize that we *can't* live together?

LAWRENCE. [*Terrified.*] Hildegarde!

HILDEGARDE. I see it now. It's been a huge mistake, our marrying. I've got to leave you.

LAWRENCE. Why—why?

HILDEGARDE. You can't live *my* way any more. You've got another call. I won't live *your* way. I try not to judge; but I can't approve of what you do.

LAWRENCE. Then you really believe all that she said about me!

HILDEGARDE. How little you understand!

LAWRENCE. But she lied—she lied!!

HILDEGARDE. I know she's neither big enough nor small enough to really give herself; but there's much more at stake than physical fidelity. She's seduced you away from your *self*,—from every ideal I built my faith in,—from everything that consecrated us.

LAWRENCE. But you're my *wife;* aren't you?

HILDEGARDE. You're not the man I married; and this isn't the kind of life together that we contemplated.

LAWRENCE. [*Agonized.*] But you love me; don't you?

HILDEGARDE. How far off that sounds!

LAWRENCE. [*Imploringly.*] What are you *saying!?*

HILDEGARDE. Larrie, you've become a stranger. Something in me has withered. I believe it's dead.

LAWRENCE. No—no,—will you listen?

HILDEGARDE. Oh, don't explain. I've had my fill of that. I'm not blaming you.

LAWRENCE. [*Choking.*] Listen!

HILDEGARDE. You'll only end by asking for something that I cannot give. I can't help it, Larrie; but the truth is, we don't need or want each other any longer.

LAWRENCE. But I want *you!* I can't live without you. I'd give up everything I ever hoped to get, to have you happy as you were!

HILDEGARDE. We never used to think about happiness. It just came.

LAWRENCE. [*With a cry.*] I wish I'd never met her! It's all been futile!

HILDEGARDE. No. It hasn't been. She's taught us both a great deal.

LAWRENCE. What's the good of that, if I've lost *you?*

HILDEGARDE. [*Continuing.*] And then I like to think the factory people are a little happier for our knowing Mr. Knollys.

LAWRENCE. [*Reproachfully and helplessly.*] How cruel you are! What do I care about all those things? It's only *you* Hildegarde! [*Going to her.*] You! You! [*Tearfully.*] You're all I want! [*Weeping.*] If I lose you, what will become of me? [*Clutching her childishly and accusingly.*] I'll just lose myself! [*Shaking her.*] Don't you see that I *belong* to you? Don't you see *that!?* Don't punish me any more. [*Hoarsely shaken with sobs, he falls and clutches her knees.*] You can't treat me like this! I can't stand it! I've been wrong; but don't punish me for what I couldn't help!

> [LAWRENCE *has delivered this last speech in a torrent of choking tears and with a sobbing incoherent vehemence.*

HILDEGARDE. Larrie—Larrie. . . . Don't be absurd. [*Comforting him.*] Don't cry, Larrie,—you foolish, foolish boy!

LAWRENCE. [*Still holding her tightly.*] And you won't leave me?

HILDEGARDE. [*Helplessly.*] How can I? You're such a child.

[*She takes him in her arms.*

Curtain.

PLOTS AND PLAYWRIGHTS

A Comedy

By

EDWARD MASSEY

EDWARD MASSEY was born in New York City in 1893. He received his elementary education in New York and Canada. For his college he chose Harvard, where he graduated in 1915. At Harvard he was especially interested in the drama, and associated himself with "The 47 Workshop" with which he acted and for which he wrote both before and since his graduation.

Plots and Playwrights was written for the English 47 course at Harvard and given at "The Workshop" in 1915. The Washington Square Players acted it about a year later, in March, 1917. It has since been played by several "little" theatres throughout the country—Providence, Cincinnati, Chicago, Kansas City—and in 1918 was revived at one of the large War Camps.

[Copyright, 1915, by Edward Massey; copyright, 1917, by Little, Brown and Company]

CHARACTERS

(Arranged in order of their appearance)

CASPER GAY
MAGGIE
JOSEPH HASTINGS
MRS. HAMMOND
TOM BURCH
MOLLY HAMMOND
FRANK DEVOY
ALICE MERRIAM
BESSIE DODGE
EDME JACKES
WILLIAM LLOYD
DICK GRIFFITHS
SIDNEY GRIFFITHS
BOB DOUGLAS
A WAITER and TWO POLICEMEN

PLOTS AND PLAYWRIGHTS

PROLOGUE

[*The scene is the front of a house on West Eleventh Street, New York City—a three-story building exactly like all the other houses in the block. It is about nine p.m. so the street is dark, and the house does not show up distinctly. A flight of steps leads to the front door and vestibule, and there is a light burning in the hall, for it can be seen through the glass of the door. Off stage a hurdy-gurdy is heard.*

CASPER GAY comes unsteadily along the street—a chubby, self-satisfied man. He wears evening clothes, a dark overcoat, white muffler, and a silk hat. He is slightly intoxicated, and looks much worried. He pauses by the steps, surveys the house, comes to a decision, and then mounts the steps. He rings the doorbell.

MAGGIE opens the door. She is an Amazonian servant.]

CASPER. [*Politely.*] Good evening.
MAGGIE. Yes, sir?
CASPER. How do you do.
MAGGIE. What do you want?
CASPER. Inspiration, my good girl, I'm looking for an inspiration.
MAGGIE. A what?
CASPER. An inspiration—comedy, tragedy, romance.

MAGGIE. Young man, this is a respectable house.
[*She shuts the door.*]

CASPER. Dear me, how very annoying. [*Descending steps.*] What shall I do, what shall I do? [*He reaches the foot of the steps and lands in the arms of a young man—JOSEPH HASTINGS.*] My dear sir, can you give me an inspiration?

HASTINGS. [*Amused.*] I'm afraid not. [*Tries to pass.*] Will you excuse me?

CASPER. Oh, you must help me. I'm in great trouble.

HASTINGS. Trouble?

CASPER. But it's no use, you wouldn't understand. Nobody can appreciate the troubles of an ausher.

HASTINGS. Why, are you an author?

CASPER. Am I an ausher? My dear fellow, I wrote "Sinfully Rich."

HASTINGS. Good Heavens! You're not Casper Gay, *the* Casper Gay?

CASPER. That's me.

HASTINGS. Are you the dollar dramatist, the great Broadway playwright?

CASPER. Yes, indeed.

HASTINGS. Well, this is most interesting. Whatever brings you to this part of West Eleventh Street?

CASPER. Do you write plays?

HASTINGS. No—short stories.

CASPER. Then it's all right. I can talk to you. What's your name?

HASTINGS. Hastings, Joseph Hastings.

CASPER. Mr. Hastings, I'm walking the streets in sheer desperation.

HASTINGS. What's the matter?

CASPER. A manager 'phoned me he must have a play. And I—Casper Gay—must write it—in just one month.

HASTINGS. Well?

CASPER. I can't get started.

HASTINGS. What!

CASPER. I've got nothing to write about. I need some material to start with.

HASTINGS. You don't have to search through this city for material. Look about you, man, look about you.

CASPER. [*Does so.*] Nothing.

HASTINGS. You're wrong there. Any street in this city can serve you. What's more, take this particular street, and any house in the block will do.

CASPER. They're ugly houses.

HASTINGS. Maybe, but you'll find they're chock full of material.

CASPER. I don't believe it.

HASTINGS. Look at this one here. It's a lodging house, of course, like all the others. Now I'll bet you there's a play on every floor of that house.

CASPER. Not a real play.

HASTINGS. I tell you there is.

CASPER. Nonsense.

HASTINGS. But it's true.

CASPER. No, no—you can't get drama that way.

HASTINGS. Why not?

CASPER. These people are nobodies. There is no drama in nobodies.

HASTINGS. You Times Square dramatist! It's up to me to show you you're wrong.

[*He runs up the steps and rings bell.*

CASPER. What's that?

HASTINGS. I'm going to prove my theory.

[MAGGIE *appears.*

MAGGIE. Well?

HASTINGS. I want a room. Can I get one here?

MAGGIE. Why, yes. [*Sees* CASPER.] Is it for that swell, too?

HASTINGS. No, a single room. It's for myself.

MAGGIE. Just a minute till I see the lady of the house.
[*She goes.*

HASTINGS. Now you'll have to admit I'm right.

CASPER. What are you going to do?

HASTINGS. Show you there's a drama on every floor of this house.

CASPER. How?

HASTINGS. I'll write a play to prove it. [CASPER *exclaims.*] Where can I reach you?

CASPER. The Authors' Club, of course.

HASTINGS. Good. You'll be hearing from me before long.

CASPER. But you can't write plays.

HASTINGS. Why not?

CASPER. You're a short story writer.

HASTINGS. Is that so? Just you wait and see.
[*He enters the house, and the stage is darkened. The hurdy-gurdy starts playing. Curtain.*

The intermission between the Prologue and Part I should be as brief as possible.

PART I

SCENE I. THE FIRST FLOOR

[*The room is the first floor front of the house seen in the introduction. The house is an old one, and at one time fulfilled a destiny higher in the social scale. So there is a high ceiling with a heavily decorated gas chande-*

lier hanging from the center, and the wall paper is dark and faded. The furniture is a combination of cheap new chairs and heavy old pieces—all very hideous. The windows are on the left, a door at back leads to the hall, and there is another door right.

Bed and wardrobe at back, small table up front on the right, large table and chairs, center.[1]

When the curtain rises it is evening, and the chandelier is lit. The center table is covered with a white tablecloth and laid for supper—with two places. There is also a small vase of flowers. On the side table there is an alcohol stove, not yet lighted, and other preparations for supper.

MRS. HAMMOND *is fussing round the center table. She is a motherly old woman with white hair. Is dressed cheaply, but looks neat. She hums to herself as she fusses away.*

There is a knock on the door. It opens at once, and MAGGIE *appears. She carries a parcel done up in paper.* MRS. HAMMOND *turns round with a little start.*

MAGGIE. Now what did you jump for?

MRS. HAMMOND. I knew it wasn't her—I know she couldn't get here so soon—I guess it's 'cause I'm all worked up.

MAGGIE. You're wrong to get excited like this.

MRS. HAMMOND. It ain't often, Maggie. But my little girl's been away for a long time now.

MAGGIE. [*Handing her the parcel.*] Here's your meat come at last.

---

[1] The same set should be used for all the boarding-house scenes. The rooms can be differentiated by changing the pictures and the furniture. This is desirable so that the intermissions between the scenes shall be as brief as possible, and also because the arrangement of the rooms would be similar.

Mrs. Hammond. Thank you.

 [*She crosses to the side table and unwraps the parcel there.*

Maggie. Miss Purcell wants you to be careful with that alcohol stove.

Mrs. Hammond. I won't put this on till Molly comes. I've some soup to warm first.

Maggie. Miss Purcell don't like her lodgers to use them things.

Mrs. Hammond. I'll be real careful. But I told Miss Purcell Molly was comin' home to me, and I wanted to cook supper for her—just as a kind of surprise.

Maggie. I guess she'll be finding us quiet here, after traveling around with those show folks.

Mrs. Hammond. I want her to rest for a while.

Maggie. We had some actresses stay here once. They was working at a theater down on Seventh Avenue. But Miss Purcell didn't like them—they stayed in bed all day.

Mrs. Hammond. You'll be sure and thank her for me, Maggie.

Maggie. Oh, Miss Purcell don't mind favorin' you, ma'am. It's them as don't pay their rent that she's down on. [*A knock on door, and* Tom Burch *puts his head in. He is a plain looking fellow of twenty-eight, but is always smiling and good-natured. He wears the uniform of a street-car conductor.*

Tom. Good evening to ye.

Mrs. Hammond. Come in, Tom Burch, and how are you?

Tom. I thought I'd drop in on my way to work.

Maggie. Don't be you bothering her, Mr. Tom. She's a bit nervous.

Mrs. Hammond. Oh, Maggie!

MAGGIE. I'm looking after you, ma'am, and I don't want him to talk you to death.

MRS. HAMMOND. I'm all right, Maggie.

MAGGIE. Well, when you get tired, you just call for *me*.
[*They laugh and she goes out.*]

TOM. Why, what's up?

MRS. HAMMOND. You see, Molly's coming home to-night.

TOM. You don't say so. When does she get here?

MRS. HAMMOND. Her train gets to the Grand Central at 5.20. What time is it now, Tom?

TOM. Five minutes to six.

MRS. HAMMOND. [*Going to window.*] I wonder what could be keeping her.

TOM. Them trains is always late. Won't you be having the fine time now.

MRS. HAMMOND. It seems so wonderful. Oh, Tom, isn't your Ma glad when you go up to see her.

TOM. Sometimes. But you see there's so many of us.

MRS. HAMMOND. It's been awful hard to see her growing up and growing away from me. I often pray that she was little again. [*Smiling.*] I'm cooking all the things she likes, but I don't know what she'll think of her Ma's cooking.

TOM. Believe me, she ain't had nothing like it.

MRS. HAMMOND. It'll be so different when she's here. She'll brighten the place up.

TOM. Well, I've got to be getting along now. I'll look in and see Molly to-morrow.

MRS. HAMMOND. Do you have to work on the cars all night?

TOM. Yes, indeed. It's a sweet job. They've moved me over to the Banana Line.

MRS. HAMMOND. Banana Line?

TOM. That's what they call it. The cars run in bunches.

[MAGGIE *opens the door.*] It's all right, Maggie. I'm going of my own accord. [*He goes.*

MAGGIE. [*Entering.*] Now don't get wrought up, Mis' Hammond, but I think she's come.

MRS. HAMMOND. What!

MAGGIE. There's a taxi just stopped outside.

MRS. HAMMOND. A taxi? Molly wouldn't take a taxi.

MAGGIE. Well, I saw a young lady get out. I'm on my way down now.

[*She goes.*

> [MRS. HAMMOND *trembles with joy, hurries to the window, and looks out. She exclaims happily, and taps on the glass. She crosses to side table, lights the stove, and puts on the saucepan of soup. Then she turns towards the door trembling so she can hardly reach it.*
>
> [MOLLY *opens the door. She is twenty-four; typical in dress and manner of the three-a-day vaudeville actress.*

MOLLY. [*Running to meet her mother.*] Mother, Mother, my own sweet mother.

MRS. HAMMOND. [*Tries to speak but cannot. She takes* MOLLY *in her arms and hugs her closely. Then she releases her.*] Oh, I've been so anxious. Was your train late?

MOLLY. We were on time, but some friends kept me at the station.

MRS. HAMMOND. Take off your things and sit down. Supper'll soon be ready. Oh, I got so much to ask you. Did you have your trunk checked?

MOLLY. I thought I'd better wait till my plans were more certain.

MRS. HAMMOND. [*Fear in her voice.*] You're going to stay home, aren't you?

Molly. I'll be here a week, anyway. I'll tell you all about it, only wait till I get Frank.

Mrs. Hammond. Frank?

Molly. I left him down in the hall. [*Calls.*] Oh, Frank, come on up!

Frank. All right. What will I do with the bags?

Molly. Bring them up. [*To* Mrs. Hammond.] Didn't I ever write you about Frank?

Mrs. Hammond. No.

Molly. That's funny.

Mrs. Hammond. You're not—you're not engaged to him.

Molly. Engaged to that Brooklyn hick! I should say not.

[Frank Devoy *appears, carrying a hat box and two suitcases, a long young man with sleeky hair and other earmarks of the vaudeville profession.*]

Molly. For heaven's sake, put those things down and come here. [*He does so.*] I want you to meet my mother. This is Mr. Devoy.

Mrs. Hammond. I am pleased to meet you.

Frank. How d'ye do, Madame? This is a great honor.

Molly. How much was the taxi?

Frank. Two-fifty.

Molly. Gee, didn't he soak you!

Mrs. Hammond. You came in a taxi?

Frank. We had to—such a fierce rush, you know.

Molly. Frank met me at the station. I'm here to rehearse with him.

Mrs. Hammond. I thought you was going to stay home.

Molly. Now sit down, Mama, and I'll tell you all about it. I didn't have time to write. Can you find a chair, Frank? [Frank *balances himself on one of the suitcases.*] You got my telegram?

Mrs. Hammond. Oh, yes, it came yesterday evening. Maggie brought it up to me.

Molly. I expected to stay home and rest, but this chance came, and it's too good to miss, isn't it, Frank?

Frank. Yes'm.

Molly. You see, Frank's on Loew time. That's the three-a-day vaudeville, Mama. He does a song and dance act with Margie Norton—she's Mrs. Heely now, but Devoy and Norton's what they call the team.

Mrs. Hammond. You're an actor too, Mr. Devoy?

Frank. Yes'm. Society acts.

Molly. And Norton had to quit, didn't she, Frank?

Frank. Yes, you see her husband—

Mrs. Hammond. He don't want her to act?

Frank. He don't mind, but she's going to have her third.

Mrs. Hammond. Oh!

Molly. Of course that lays her off for the season—

Frank. And she never warned me.

Molly. No. Frank had booked up a six month's tour —and of course he didn't want to give that up.

Frank. Why should I? Norton's the rotten half of the team.

Molly. So he wrote to me, and asked me to take her place. They played Boston last week, and I saw the act. Now I'm to rehearse with Frank, and then I'll be ready to step in. Margie'll hold out this week, won't she?

Frank. She's good for a fortnight, but Heely don't take chances.

Molly. Isn't it great for me, Mama. We're going right out to the Coast.

Frank. It's a grand little place, 'Frisco is; ever been there, Mrs. Hammond?

Mrs. Hammond. [*Out of the conversation and very*

uncomfortable.] No, sir, I ain't gone much outside of New York.

FRANK. Well 'Frisco's got 'em all beat. We'll take you to see Chinatown, Moll.

MOLLY. I bet it's swell.

FRANK. And Chicago. Oh, that College Inn!

MRS. HAMMOND. Do you think you ought to go? It's an awful long ways.

MOLLY. Why, Mama, it's the chance of my life.

MRS. HAMMOND. I guess you know best, dear—

[*She is silent.*

MOLLY. [*Breaks pause.*] Oh, say—I ain't going to wear a white dress in that last number.

FRANK. Why not—Margie always does.

MOLLY. 'Cause I've picked out a swell gown in pink.

FRANK. What do you want to do? Queer the act?

MOLLY. How?

FRANK. I wear a green suit—pink and green: say, that'll be grand; that'll make a hit.

MRS. HAMMOND. [*Trying again.*] Haven't you got a white dress, Molly?

MOLLY. [*Decidedly.*] It's all right, Ma. I'll dress my half of the act in my own way.

FRANK. Say, who the—[*He breaks off.*] Oh, I beg your pardon, Ma'am. [*Then in slight embarrassment.*] If we're going to meet Norton and Tad at Churchill's, we've got to hustle.

MRS. HAMMOND. Ain't you going to stay to supper now? We'd be glad to have you, Mr. Devoy.

MOLLY. Sorry, we can't, Ma. I made this date in Boston.

MRS. HAMMOND. But it's your first night home.

MOLLY. We're awful late now, but I told Frank I had

to come and see you first. [*Hugging her.*] Dear old Momsie. What's the time, Frank?

FRANK. Six-thirty. Honest, we ought to go.

MOLLY. Go out and hustle up a taxi. You may have to 'phone.

FRANK. You'd better come with me. It'll save time.

MOLLY. All right.

FRANK. Good night, ma'am.

MRS. HAMMOND. Good night, sir.

FRANK. I'm charmed to have met you. [*He goes.*

MOLLY. Good-by, dear old Ma. [*Kisses her.*] It's so good to be home. I'm sorry I got to go out, but I'll be in early—not later than ten or half-past. Good-by.

[*She follows* FRANK.

MRS. HAMMOND. Good-bye, my dearest.

> [*The door has been left open.* ALICE MER-RIAM *comes upstairs and passes along the hall.*

MAGGIE. [*Calls up to her.*] Oh, Miss Merriam, Miss Merriam.

ALICE. [*Leaning over the balustrade.*] Yes, Maggie?

MAGGIE. There's a letter for you in the hall.

ALICE. [*Waving the letter.*] I got it, thank you.

[*She goes upstairs.*

> [MRS. HAMMOND *crosses the room and shuts the door. She goes to side table, takes up a plate, fills it with soup and carries it to the large table. She sits down, and begins her supper. The hurdy-gurdy plays.*

Curtain.

Scene II. The Second Floor

[*The second floor front is very much the same as the room below it. The windows are at left, the door at back leads to the hall, and a door to the right to an adjoining room.*

A dresser and chair between the windows; sofa and wardrobe at back, bed on the right, and round table and chairs at center.

ALICE MERRIAM *enters at once from the hall. She is reading her letter.*

ALICE *is about twenty-eight; medium-sized, not very good looking. She wears a neat tailor-made suit and shirt-waist. She carries a sketch book. She comes to the center table, lays down the book, and then removes her coat and hat. She brings an alcohol stove from the wardrobe and lights it. Then she returns to her letter.*

BESSIE DODGE *enters from the right. She is wearing a kimono instead of a dress. She has Forty-Second Street mannerisms and naturally has acquired the very latest style in doing up her hair. She is twenty-five, but wouldn't admit to it.*

BESSIE. Who is he?

ALICE. You're all wrong, Bessie. It's from Morrisburg—from my father.

BESSIE. [*Disappointed.*] Oh! [*She sits down and starts to manicure her nails.*] Where on earth have you been Alice? You're awful late.

ALICE. [*Looks at watch.*] It's only half-past six.

BESSIE. I suppose you've had your supper.

ALICE. Yes, I stopped off at Child's.

Bessie. I knew it. And I came straight from the office.

Alice. I'm sorry. Where's Edme?

Bessie. Not home yet.

Alice. You can wait for her.

Bessie. Oh, she'll stop off for her supper too. You girls are bound I'll eat alone.

Alice. Are you going out to-night?

Bessie. Yep!

Alice. You know, it's disgraceful, Bessie. You've been out every night this week.

Bessie. Well, why not? I'm working from eight to six. If I had the easy time you do—

Alice. [*Laughs.*] Easy time!

Bessie. Sit down and draw the Venus de Milo ad lib —that's not work. Now, I'm kept busy at the office, and when I get away, it's the bright lights for little Bessie.

Alice. Any one who comes home at 4 a.m.!

Bessie. [*Sarcastic.*] Oh, did I disturb you this morning?

Alice. I heard you.

Bessie. I tried to be quiet. Edme slept like a rock.

Alice. Where were you?

Bessie. I had a swell time—party of fellows from Pittsburgh—Ella Fisher brought them round. They had a car, and we went way up the Hudson.

Alice. Were you riding all night?

Bessie. Oh, no. Went to the Winter Garden first— and Churchill's.

Alice. I don't see how you're fit for work.

Bessie. It never annoys me. Nice party! One of them's coming to take me out again, and I can't remember his name.

Alice. Good gracious!

BESSIE. Here's something for you, Alice. Did you ever hear of a Chaste Minerva?

ALICE. A what?

BESSIE. I knew you hadn't. It's a new drink—One of the fellows mixed it for me last night. I wasn't so crazy about the drink, but it's got a classy name, hasn't it?

ALICE. Very.

BESSIE. And it was a classy party too—they were regular fellows—lots of money—

ALICE. I don't see how you can go on parties like that, Bessie. It's so dreadfully vulgar.

BESSIE. Now don't talk like that to me. There's some of the girls in our office—" Go out with a fellow—my goodness, the very idea!" It makes them shudder. Well—I ride off to Shanley's and have a good time. They go down to a dairy lunch and flirt with the cashier so they won't have to pay their check. That sort of thing makes me sick!

ALICE. You'll never see it in my way.

BESSIE. I'm out to have a good time. And *voila, qu'est que c'est*—

ALICE. [*Smiles.*] You don't understand. But it's such a wild extravagant way of living—

BESSIE. Extravagant! Think of all the meals I get for nothing.

ALICE. I don't mean that—

BESSIE. And speaking of food. Will you make me a cup of coffee? I certainly can't last till supper, and I don't want to go out and eat alone.

ALICE. All right, but suppose Maggie catches us—

BESSIE. We should be annoyed by Maggie.

 [ALICE *goes to wardrobe and brings back a tin of coffee and a bag of sugar.*

BESSIE. [*Sitting by table.*] What did you do to-day?

ALICE. I went to the Museum.

BESSIE. My goodness, did you enjoy the antiques?

ALICE. Not to-day. I put all my time in on the Japanese Department. They have some gorgeous screens there.

BESSIE. Well, I wish I had some of your leisure time. You make me and my regular hours look sick.

ALICE. I was sketching—

BESSIE. [*Looking at sketch book.*] Did you draw these broken up gentlemen?

ALICE. No, that's class-work.

BESSIE. They're kind of sick-looking, aren't they? Ha-ha-ha. What do you call this one? Ready for the plunge—

ALICE. Oh, goodness—

BESSIE. This stuff ought to make a hit with the Morrisburg Johns; but [*Has an idea*] say, Alice, why don't you do magazine covers.

ALICE. I wish I could.

BESSIE. There's a lot of money in it.

ALICE. I know there is, but not for me—

BESSIE. Why not?

ALICE. Because I'm a failure, Bessie, I can't do anything. I don't know why I ever thought I could draw.

BESSIE. Why, Alice!

ALICE. Oh, up in Morrisburg, I was all right—but down here.—Well, when I see what the others are doing, and compare it with my work—it's pretty discouraging.

BESSIE. Why your drawings are real good. I like them.

ALICE. And I went away to show them what I could do. I can't go back a failure.

BESSIE. Look out, that's boiling. Gee, I'm sorry.

ALICE. [*Laughs.*] Thanks. Don't worry, Bessie, I'll peg away this year, and see what comes of it.—Got the coffee in your cup?

BESSIE. Yes, Ma'am.

ALICE. Steady, then. [*Pours the water into cup.*]
Want some crackers?

BESSIE. The coffee'll do. I'm going out to supper.

ALICE. You can make it up then.

BESSIE. I wish I could, but to-day's Friday.

ALICE. Friday?

BESSIE. Yes—I'll have to eat lobster.

[MAGGIE *knocks on the hall door and immediately enters.*

MAGGIE. Is Miss Edmy here? I've got a message for her.

BESSIE. She hasn't come in yet.

[MAGGIE'S *eyes have lighted on the alcohol stove.*

MAGGIE. Now, Miss Merriam. You know perfectly well that Miss Purcell don't allow them stoves in the house.

ALICE. We're very careful. There!

[*She puts out flame.*

MAGGIE. You may be careful just so many times, and the next time you'll be caught.

BESSIE. Do you want us to cook over the gas jet?

MAGGIE. There ain't no call to do your cooking here.

BESSIE. Well, Miss Purcell's got no kick coming. We pay regular.

MAGGIE. That may be, Miss, but we have to stand a great deal from our lodgers. Miss Purcell don't like the hours you keep, and she don't like the way you say good night to your young men.

BESSIE. You tell Miss Purcell to mind her own business.

MAGGIE. If you've any complaints to make, take them to Miss Purcell yourself. But I should think, Miss Bessie, that you'd like to set a better example—now that Miss Edme has a young gentleman.

[*She flounces out.*

BESSIE. You know some day I'll forget I'm a lady.

ALICE. She should know her place better.

BESSIE. Well, she hit me hard, all right. And so I should set an example to Miss Edme [*Mimicking*] now that she's got a young gentleman. She's always telling me I'm a bad example for the kid.

ALICE. Poor little Edme.

BESSIE. Edme with a fellow! Ha-ha-ha, that's funny.

ALICE. But Edme doesn't know a soul. [BESSIE *suddenly stops laughing.* ALICE *looks up.*] Does she?

BESSIE. Holy St. Michael! Say Alice—Maggie's right. I bet that kid's gone and put one over on us.

ALICE. Edme?

BESSIE. Yes, Edme. Of course she's got a fellow. That's what's been on her mind for the last two weeks. That's why she's been moping round the room.

ALICE. She's been a little paler than usual.

BESSIE. Love-sick, my dear.

ALICE. But Edme is a child. Oh, it would be dreadful—Who is he? Where did she meet him?

BESSIE. That's just what we've got to find out.

ALICE. I'm so fond of Edme.

BESSIE. No more than I am. I wouldn't see her in trouble for the world.

> [EDME *enters right. A pretty little girl of seventeen. She carries a large hat bag, which she keeps behind her back.*

EDME. Hello, Bessie.

BESSIE. When did you get in, you little buzzer?

EDME. About five minutes ago. Good evening, Alice.

ALICE. Hello, Edme.

BESSIE. What made you so late?

EDME. I had supper before I came home.

BESSIE. It's way after seven.

EDME. But I went shopping, too!

ALICE. Shopping?

EDME. Wait just one second.
[*She dances over to the bureau, produces a hat from the bag, and puts it on.*
ALICE. [*Quickly.*] Do you think she heard us?
BESSIE. No, not a word.
[EDME *dances back again. Her hat is very fetching—but very extreme.*
BESSIE. Look at the hat!
ALICE. My goodness!
EDME. Do you like it? Do you think it suits me?
BESSIE. Oh, it's perfectly darling! Where on earth did you get it?
EDME. I like it, I think it's lovely. Do you like it, Alice?
ALICE. Isn't it rather too old for you?
EDME. Oh, no, indeed. You don't like it.
ALICE. Oh, no, I didn't mean that.
BESSIE. I think it's adorable. And you're a darling.
ALICE. Where'd you get it?
EDME. A shop on Sixth Avenue—it was in the window.
ALICE. Straymayer's—he's having a sale.
EDME. That's the place. It was only $2.47.
BESSIE. $2.47. I don't believe you.
EDME. Yes. They're selling out—
BESSIE. $2.47! Why, it looks like a regular creation, doesn't it, Alice?
ALICE. Yes, I'm afraid it does—
EDME. [*Taking off the hat and looking at it.*] I thought it suited me—just as soon as I saw it.
ALICE. We want to talk to you.
EDME. [*Putting her hat on the table.*] I can't stay long, I may be going out.
BESSIE. Where are you going?
EDME. I don't know.
BESSIE. Didn't he tell you?

EDME. I don't understand.

BESSIE. Oh, we know all about him, only we want to know his name. [EDME *gives her a look of surprise.*] Don't look like that. Maggie told us.

ALICE. We want to help you, dear. We're older than you and can advise you.

EDME. I don't want advice.

BESSIE. Who is he?

ALICE. Please tell us, dear.

EDME. I don't know what you mean.

BESSIE. Come on, tell us the mutt's name.

EDME. Oh, he's not; he's very nice—

BESSIE. There you are! These innocents!

ALICE. And you never told us—

BESSIE. I'm very much hurt.

[*Turns away and pretends to be angry.*

EDME. I'm very sorry, I'm awfully sorry. I would have told you, Bessie, only then everybody would have known. I wanted it to be a secret. Maggie knew, 'cause she saw him bring me home, but I didn't think she'd tell. It was real mean of her.

BESSIE. Come and tell us about him? We don't know a thing.

EDME. You won't tease me?

ALICE. Of course we won't.

EDME. He—well, he's coming to take me out to-night.

BESSIE. What's his name?

EDME. Roy—Roy Wetherton; isn't it a nice name?

ALICE. Beautiful!

EDME. And he took me to the Strand, and we saw Mary Pickford in a lovely picture. Oh, I think she's a darling—

BESSIE. Cut the movies, and tell us about the fellow. How old is he?

EDME. [*Rapturously.*] Eighteen.

ALICE. Babes in the Wood!

BESSIE. That's good. I thought you might have fallen for one of these oily-haired floorwalkers.

EDME. Bessie!

BESSIE. What does he do? Does he work in your store?

EDME. Oh, no, his father's a lawyer.

BESSIE. What!

EDME. And Roy's going to college next year—that is, if he can pass his examinations.

ALICE. What was his name?

EDME. Roy?

ALICE. Yes.

EDME. Roy Wetherton.

ALICE. Is his father the Wetherton of Wetherton and Bond?

BESSIE. Do you know him, Alice?

ALICE. I've heard of him—a well-known firm.

BESSIE. Rich?

ALICE. Very. An only son.

EDME. That's Roy.

ALICE. Good gracious, child.

BESSIE. Well, I must hand it to you. Where did you meet him?

EDME. He came in the store one day to buy candy, and he saw me; I wasn't serving sodas then, I was only washing the glasses.

BESSIE. Well—

EDME. After that he came in every day and had a soda, and one day he asked me for a glass of water, and one evening he waited till I came out, and—and I let him take me home. [*She is fussed.*

BESSIE. Oh, you funny kid!

EDME. I used to be very lonely, and you go out so much, and Alice is always busy. I wanted to go out, too.

BESSIE. Why on earth didn't you tell us? I'd be real glad to hear you'd got some one to take you round, but honestly, hon', I don't think this fellow will do you much good.

EDME. Roy is awfully nice. I don't know why you say that.

ALICE. Let me talk to her, Bessie. I think I can explain—

BESSIE. Better than I can, anyway. And I want to get my dress on. I don't mind keeping a fellow waiting; still, when he's got a car— [*She goes right.*

ALICE. Now, dear—

EDME. I don't want advice. [*Gets up.*

ALICE. I just want to talk to you. Please sit down.

EDME. [*Settles herself on the bed, pouting.*] I knew you'd all scold if I told you.

ALICE. You know, Edme, just as well as I do, that you shouldn't have spoken to that boy.

EDME. I couldn't help it. He asked me for a drink of water.

ALICE. But you shouldn't have let it go any further?

EDME. I liked his looks.

ALICE. My dear, it's not respectable; you didn't know the boy.

EDME. I know him now.

ALICE. And Roy and you move in different circles.

EDME. Roy doesn't mind that.

ALICE. But, my dear, his parents do. His father is a prominent man—and he wouldn't want his son to go about with a shopgirl.

EDME. He hasn't told them about me.

ALICE. And do you think it's nice to go out with a boy you can't meet on his own level—who has to slip away from home every time he wishes to see you. Just now it amuses him to take you out, and he will go to some trouble to accomplish it. But by and by the novelty will wear off, and what will you do then, dearest?

EDME. Roy's going to marry me—as soon as he's of age.

ALICE. Edme, child, are you silly enough to believe that?

EDME. Of course I am; why shouldn't I?

ALICE. Did Roy propose to you?

EDME. Yes—and I accepted him.

ALICE. I never in my life heard anything so shocking! Don't you realize, dear, that boy can't possibly marry you.

EDME. Well, anyway, I like to go out and have a good time.

ALICE. Oh, Edme, it's not *nice*. You know it isn't.

EDME. I do like him.

ALICE. You shouldn't see him again, Edme.

EDME. Oh, Alice, I don't think it's wrong.

ALICE. It is, dear, it's very wrong.

BESSIE. [*Calls.*] Alice, will you help me into this dress, I'm stuck—

ALICE. Just a minute, Bessie. [*To* EDME.] You must decide now, dear; are you going to do what is right?

EDME. Yes—I suppose so.

ALICE. I have your promise? Really?

EDME. Yes.

ALICE. That's my brave little girl. [*Kisses her.*] I knew you'd do it.

EDME. [*Disconsolately.*] It's awfully hard. He promised to take me to Shanley's.

BESSIE. [*Calls again.*] Oh, Alice.

ALICE. All right, Bessie. [*Smiling at* EDME.] I thought I could depend on you.

[*She goes. Knock on door and* MAGGIE *enters.*

MAGGIE. Miss Edme?

EDME. Yes, Maggie.

MAGGIE. I got a message for you.

EDME. Oh, Maggie, tell me, is he coming, can he get away to-night?

MAGGIE. That he can, Miss.

EDME. [*Jumping up and down.*] Oh, he's coming, he's coming. I knew he would—I knew he could get away. Oh, you dear old Maggie. [*Hugs her.*] I just love you to death. [*Suddenly serious.*] Oh, Maggie, you don't think it's wrong to go out with him. You don't think I ought to stay home?

MAGGIE. Well, Miss Edme, if I may make so bold—

EDME. What is it? Please tell me.

MAGGIE. I would advise you to ask him right out what his intentions may be; ask him straight—" Young man, do you mean well by me? "

EDME. Oh, Maggie, he does!

MAGGIE. Ask him, Miss; pin him down to it. Young men is slippery creatures—

[BESSIE *enters. She has put on her dress but carries her hat.*

BESSIE. Any one called for me yet?

MAGGIE. No, Miss. [*Eyeing stove.*] And Miss Purcell says if you're going to cook on them stoves, she'll have to ask you for your rooms.

BESSIE. That's just too sweet of her. Give her my love, Maggie.

[MAGGIE *glares at her, tries to speak, and departs.*

BESSIE. [*Puts hat on dresser.*] The old crow!

EDME. Oh, no, I like her.

BESSIE. Come here, hon'; I'm going out, but I want to talk to you first. How do I look?

EDME. Oh, you're lovely, Bessie—you look kissable.

BESSIE. I tried to—

EDME. You really shouldn't, Bessie.

BESSIE. Never mind about me. All I ever do is drink a cocktail or maybe smoke a few cigarettes. And what's wrong with that? It pleases a fellow—makes him think you a good sport. I want to talk to you about Roy. You've promised Alice you wouldn't see him again.

EDME. Yes—

[*She brings a cushion from sofa and sits at* BESSIE'S *feet.*]

BESSIE. Now I was talking to Alice, and I brought her round to my way of looking at it.

EDME. You think it's all right; I knew you would.

BESSIE. Roy's a rich fellow, and he's willing to spend his money, isn't he?

EDME. [*Surprised.*] Why, yes, of course he is.

BESSIE. Then there's no reason why you shouldn't run round with him and have a good time. Let him take you to shows and dinners and suppers—that's all right—but don't go any further—don't take him seriously.

EDME. Oh, I see.—But, Bessie—

BESSIE. Can't you do that?

EDME. Bessie, I love him.

BESSIE. And what does Roy say to that?

EDME. He wants to marry me.

BESSIE. Oh, I'm so sorry.

EDME. He means it. I know he does.

BESSIE. The two of you are a pair of babies. Honey, dear, I want you to believe what I'm saying. I'm trying to advise you like your own mother would; it's all right to go out with him so long as you have a good time, but if you kid yourself into lovin' him, then he's going to break your heart.

EDME. But what will I do?

BESSIE. Alice was right. You mustn't see him again.

EDME. What will he do—what can I say to him.—Oh, Bessie—I can't—I can't.

BESSIE. Now I'll fix it up for you. I'll tell him you've gone away.

EDME. No, no—don't lie to him—

BESSIE. I won't lie—I'll just string him along.—You must trust me, honey. Because I love you.

[*She kisses her. Knock on door, and* MAGGIE *enters, beaming.*

MAGGIE. The young gentleman's here, Miss Edme.

EDME. [*Dismally.*] All right, Maggie. Thank you.

[MAGGIE *goes back to hall.*

BESSIE. I'll go down, hon'. Let me manage it.

EDME. [*Crying.*] I suppose it's the right thing.

BESSIE. Yes, hon'. You'd better let me do it.

EDME. All right.

BESSIE. [*Wipes her eyes with her handkerchief, then feels her lips.*] Oh, gee, I've got to freshen up first. I can't see him like this.

[*She goes out right. A man's voice*—WILLIAM LLOYD—*calls from up-stairs angrily;* "*Maggie, Maggie, is that you?*"

MAGGIE. [*Looking up; in hall.*] Yes, Mr. Lloyd.

LLOYD. Come right up stairs this minute; I want to see you.

MAGGIE. [*Wearily.*] Yes, Mr. Lloyd.

[MAGGIE *goes up-stairs.* EDME *realizes she is alone. She glances at door right. It is closed. She rushes to the table, picks up her hat and coat, and flies out the center door.* ALICE *and* BESSIE *enter.*

BESSIE. I'll go right down, Ed, oh, Ed.—Where is she?

ALICE. Bessie, that child! [*The front door slams.*] They're going out.

BESSIE. Well, we done our best. [*She sits down in front*

of the dresser and starts to put on her hat.] It's up to her now.

>   [*The curtain falls and the hurdy-gurdy is heard once more.*

>   *Curtain.*

Scene III. The Third Floor.

[*The third floor front looks exactly like the corresponding rooms on the first and second floors. The furniture is arranged as follows:—small table and armchair left; two beds at back; wardrobe blocking up door at right; and large table and chairs at right.*

On the small table is a green-shaded lamp—connected with a gas jet on the wall between the windows. The light from it shines full upon the armchair, while it leaves the rest of the room in shadow. This lamp is lit when the curtain rises, and is the only light used during the scene.

Dick Griffiths, *a clean looking boy of seventeen, is seated in the armchair. He is studying intently.*

Out in the hall William Lloyd *and* Maggie *can be heard in loud argument. Some of their talk can be distinguished, but* Dick *continues to work and pays no attention.*

Lloyd. Not another word, Maggie. You had no business to disturb it.

Maggie. Miss Purcell gave me them orders.

Lloyd. It's outrageous!

Maggie. You know Miss Purcell don't allow them stoves in the house.

LLOYD. I shall certainly remonstrate—
MAGGIE. She'd be more pleased if you'd pay what's owing on your room.
LLOYD. That will do, Maggie. You may go.
MAGGIE. [*Sarcastically.*] Thank you, sir.
  [*There is quiet. Then comes a rap on the door.*
DICK. Come right in, Mr. Lloyd.
  [WILLIAM LLOYD *enters. He is about fifty-five—the remains of a once vigorous and intelligent man—but evidently he has broken down through dissipation. He has not yet lost all his dignity, and carries himself well. But his clothes are shabby. In one hand he holds an alcohol lamp.*
LLOYD. That woman can be most annoying—
DICK. What was wrong, sir?
LLOYD. It is very ridiculous. You see this lamp—well, while I was out to-day, Maggie emptied the alcohol out of it.
DICK. [*Laughing.*] Oh, they're death on alcohol stoves.
LLOYD. It is a trifle, but it led me to argue with her, and to argue with Maggie is a great mistake. She has me at a disadvantage. Dick, my boy, may you never be lacking in ready money. I little dreamed—but then, things did not go as I expected, and now I am at the mercy of *la belle dame sans merci.*
DICK. Maggie means all right.
LLOYD. I know, but it's downright insulting to empty the thing behind my back. Let it rest, however; the incident is closed. [*He puts the lamp down on large table.*] What are you working on to-night, my boy?
DICK. It's some Greek reading.
LLOYD. For your school?
DICK. Yes, sir.
LLOYD. Let me see. [*Takes the book.*] Ah, Xenophon.

I don't think I could read him now. Do you find it hard?

DICK. Not this part. It's all marchings, and the words are easy.

LLOYD. What other readings have you done? Homer?

DICK. Oh, I won't get beyond Xenophon this year, but if I go to college—

LLOYD. Is it decided? Will your brother let you go?

DICK. I don't know. Sid's pretty set against it.

LLOYD. That's a pity—it would be a shame to let a chance like that go by.

DICK. Mr. Harvey's held the scholarship for me, but if I don't take it now, he'll have to give it to some one else.

LLOYD. Your brother should go to see him.

DICK. I wish he would. Mr. Harvey wrote and asked him to call.

LLOYD. Why, what objections can your brother have?

DICK. He wants me to go in the hat shop with him—

LLOYD. But you wouldn't like that, would you?

DICK. I couldn't bear it, sir. I worked there last summer, and it was bad enough then, when I knew I had this year at school to look forward to.

LLOYD. You want to learn something more—

DICK. Oh, yes, indeed; there's so much I want to know.

LLOYD. Haven't you talked to your brother?

DICK. He doesn't understand.

LLOYD. You should make him—

DICK. There isn't any one here who understands why I want to go to college,—that is, except you, sir.

LLOYD. See here, if I drop in later on, will you do me a favor?

DICK. What's that, sir?

LLOYD. Let me read the Anabasis with you. I'd like to see what it feels like to work at it again.

DICK. Oh, sir, I'd love to. Do you really want to?

LLOYD. Of course I do. Well, I'm off now.

DICK. And you'll be back?

LLOYD. Very shortly; I generally go out for a drop of —well—spirits about this time. It's medicine to an old man like me. But I'll be back.

DICK. That'll be fine; it'll be great to have some one to work with.

LLOYD. By the way, you don't happen to have a quarter, do you, I'm quite out of change.

DICK. Yes, sir, I think I have. [*Producing money.*] Yes. Is that—is that enough, sir? [*Gives him coin.*

LLOYD. Quite, thank you. Sorry to have to trouble you. Well, see you later.

DICK. Good evening, sir.

> [LLOYD *goes.* DICK *settles back to his work. His face is radiant. After a moment* SID *enters, he is twenty-seven, much coarser-looking than his brother.*

SID. What did Old Man Lloyd want?

DICK. Nothing. He was talking to me.

SID. Met him on the stairs. Going to get tanked up, I guess. What are you doing?

DICK. Working.

SID. Why don't you give it a rest?

DICK. It's for school—on Monday.

SID. Well, go ahead. I won't bother you.

> [*He takes off his coat.*

DICK. Did you see Mr. Harvey?

SID. No.

DICK. He wrote you.

SID. I got the letter. He asked me to call and see him.

DICK. Won't you go?

SID. I don't want to talk to your school-teacher. What good will it do you to go to college?

DICK. I want to learn something. I don't know anything now.

SID. That's your fault. You've had all the education you need. I didn't even go through High School, and I get along all right. I don't know what put this nonsense into your head.

DICK. I didn't think of it till I got the scholarship.

SID. Two hundred dollars won't see you far.

DICK. But I'll work in the summer—and there's Dad's money—

SID. You can't touch that till you're twenty-one.

DICK. You can advance some.

SID. Well, I won't. Dad didn't leave his money for you to throw away on a college education. It's all very well for a lot of rich fellows, who haven't anything better to do with their time or money, but you've had all the education I can afford to give you.

DICK. I wish you'd be reasonable.

SID. That's just what I am. So I'm going to put you in the hat shop, and keep you there as long as I've got control over you.

DICK. Don't do that, Sid.

SID. Why not? They liked you last summer, and they want you back.

DICK. But I hate the work—you never get anywhere.

SID. If it's good enough for me, it's good enough for you.

DICK. Sid, all I want you to do now is to go round to see Mr. Harvey.

SID. Where's the good? I've made up my mind.

DICK. He can tell you things so much better than I can.

SID. It'll be a waste of time.

DICK. You might do that for me, Sid. It's not asking much of you.

SID. Oh, I suppose I've got to go, or you'll never be quiet. Where's my coat?

DICK. Gee, that's great of you. You're awful good, Sid.

SID. I'm not as stubborn as you are.

DICK. Here's your coat.

SID. Well, aren't you going to give me the address?

[*Knock on door.*

SID. Come in.

[BOB DOUGLAS *enters—about thirty—short and fat with a chubby moon face. Sporty clothes. He carries a package.*

BOB. Greetings, friends. Surprised you, eh?

SID. [*Shaking hands.*] Well, I'm mighty glad to see you.

BOB. Thought I'd drop in and spend the evening.

SID. Fine. But where's your wife, Bob?

BOB. Hush, I have no wife.

SID. What!

BOB. Well, I haven't got one to-night, I'm taking the evening off.

SID. Where's Jane?

BOB. Paterson. Her mother's sick again, and Jane's gone to nurse her over the week-end.

SID. That's hard lines.

BOB. Hard lines! I've been married two years, and luck's been against me till now. Boy, it's three months since I've had a decent drink.

SID. Sit right down and make yourself comfortable. I'll go round the corner—it won't take a second.

BOB. Nay, nay; I brought the party along with me. I wasn't taking chances. Behold! [*He unwraps parcel and produces two quart bottles of whisky.*] Oh, you beauty!

[*He kisses one.*

SID. [*Laughing.*] You don't lose any time!

BOB. I'm making it up, boy, making it up. You know

Jane may look like a drooping lily, but she'd do credit to any police force.

SID. When did she go?

BOB. To-night. I saw her to the ferry with tears in my eyes, then I bought these and came hither. Am I welcome?

SID. You sure are.

BOB. All right. Let's to business. You'll find me out of practice. How are you?

SID. Fit as ever—only I've got to go to work to-morrow.

BOB. So've I—but Saturday—short and easy. Got any glasses?

SID. Surely—Dick, where are the glasses? My kid brother. You know Bob Douglas, Dick?

DICK. How do you do?

BOB. I think I met you before. Is this the student?

SID. Yep.

BOB. [*Pointing to book.*] What are you reading, son?

DICK. Greek.

BOB. That let's me out. I never was any hand at learning. [*He takes out a pocket corkscrew and commences to open a bottle.*]

SID. Get the glasses, Dick.

[DICK *goes to the wardrobe and brings two small glasses to the table.*]

BOB. I wish I could have learnt in my time.

SID. I was put to work when I was twelve and it did me no harm. Now the young gentleman here wants to go to college.

BOB. What!

SID. Get a prize or something.

DICK. A scholarship.

BOB. Good for you, kid. [*Filling the glasses.*] You take it straight.

SID. Sure.

Bob. When?
Sid. Fill it up.
Bob. That's the right spirit—I like to see that. [*Fills his own glass up.*] Will you join us, kid?
Dick. No, thank you.
[*He has retired to the armchair and is preparing to read there.*]
Sid. No. He don't drink.
Bob. Well—Over the hot sands—
Sid. Here's to you.
[*They drink.*
Bob. Ah, that's the stuff.
Sid. Mighty fine.
Dick. Oh, Sid.
Sid. Well?
Dick. You said you'd go to see Mr. Harvey? You could be back soon.
Sid. Say, what's wrong with you?
Bob. What's the matter?
Sid. It's this kid and his college—
Bob. Why don't you let him go?
Sid. He's too stuck on himself now. No, sir, he's going in the shop.
Dick. I don't want to go in the shop.
Sid. It's not what you want.
Bob. Be easy on the kid, Sid. Here, have another drink.
Sid. Thanks. [Bob *fills up the glasses.*] [*To* Dick.] And you'd better keep your mouth shut.
Bob. Come on—Over the hot sands—
Sid. Here's to you. [*They drink.*] Where'd you pick up that?
Bob. Down at Coney last summer—a dame taught it to me—left Jane sitting on the beach—and fell in with the cutest little skirt. Nita—some name, eh? Nita Delorme.

Gave me her telephone number. Guess I'll call her up to-morrow.

Sid. Jane may come home.

Bob. Say, don't even suggest it. How's your kid brother with the skirts. These quiet fellows are always devils with the women.

Sid. Not Dick. He does nothing but study.

Bob. Hand over your glass. [*He fills the two glasses up.*] You know—even if I'm not in condition—I can drink you under.

Sid. You'll have to travel far.

Bob. Oh, you think us fat fellows can't stand anything, but I'll show you. Over the hot sands—

Sid. Here's to you.

Bob. Yes, Nita taught me that—cute Nita. Ah, I was a happy man that day. [*He laughs.*] Jane sat on the beach till the tide came in—

Sid. [*To* Dick.] Put away that book. Can't you be polite? [Dick *looks at him, surprised.*] I don't want you reading when there's company. Put it up, d'you hear me?

[Dick *shuts book.*

Bob. That's right, come over here and be sociable; don't you want a drink?

Dick. No, thank you.

Sid. Stubborn as a mule. Here leave him be and fill up my glass.

Bob. Just a minute, and I'm with you. [*Finishes his glass.*] There. [*Fills the glasses.*

Sid. He'll stay home with me—I want to keep an eye on him.

Bob. Oh, hang it all, man, if he wants to go to college—let him go—a little college can do nobody any harm.

Sid. No, no, I'll knock that nonsense out of him.

Bob. I wish Jane would go to college. I'd pay all her

expenses—there and back. Come on now, we'll drink to Jane—lovely Jane—and may she ever be—Over the hot sands—

[SID *murmurs and they drink. Knock on door.*
BOB. Holy Saints—it's Jane!
SID. [*Irritably.*] No, no. Come in.
[WILLIAM LLOYD *enters—slightly flushed.*
LLOYD. Oh, I beg your pardon—hope I don't disturb—
[DICK *rises to go to him, but* BOB *gets there first.*
BOB. How d'ye do, sir—I'm glad to meet you; how d'ye do—I didn't get the name.
LLOYD. Lloyd.
BOB. Have a drink, Mr. Lloyd, have a drink. Open up the other bottle, Sid. Insist on the other bottle for Mr. Lloyd. Get another glass, Sid—
LLOYD. Really, I shouldn't—
BOB. Oh, you must—I insist upon it—so does Sid—we all do—just a minute.

[*He opens the second bottle.*
SID. [*Brings glass to table.*] Stick around, Lloyd.
LLOYD. Well, I promised Dick—but we can read again—some other night, eh?
DICK. [*Blankly.*] Certainly, sir.
LLOYD. [*Turns away relieved.*] This is very—very nice indeed. Just one, gentlemen—I've already had my usual allowance.
BOB. Glasses, please. [*Filling the glasses.*] There you are, sir. Come on, Sid. Well—[*He pauses.*] Over the hot sands—

[*They drink,* LLOYD *saying "Your health, gentlemen."*
LLOYD. Ah, that's medicine to me, Mr.—eh—what is the name?
BOB. You can be real friendly and call me Bob.
LLOYD. Quite so, sir. Why, Dick, you're not working?

DICK. [*Rather white.*] I've laid off for the evening.
[*Throughout the scene* DICK *is sitting in the armchair. The light falls on him; the others are in shadow.*]

LLOYD. That's right—You know "All work and no play makes Jack a dull boy." [BOB *fills his glass.*] Oh, thank you, sir.

BOB. Ready, Sid.

SID. [*Staring moodily at floor, looks up.*] Thanks.
[BOB *fills* SID's *glass.*]

LLOYD. Your brother is so anxious to go to college. I hope you will give your consent.

SID. No, I won't, Dick and his high-toned notions don't suit me. I'm going to show him who's head of this family.

BOB. [*Gesticulating.*] Don't you agree with me that if the kid wants to go to college, let him go to college.

LLOYD. [*Becoming garrulous.*] The higher education is indeed an accomplishment.

BOB. We're all against you, Sid.
[LLOYD *and* BOB *bow elaborately to* SID.

SID. He's not going to college. I'll see to that.

BOB. Now, if I was real clever, wouldn't you send me to college?

LLOYD. And deprive us of your company, sir.
[*They drink.*

BOB. Sid, if you'll send the kid to college, I'll let Jane go and keep house for him.

LLOYD. Education, my dear sir, is a very great attainment. The lower orders lack it—if a certain domestic in this establishment were only imbued with the first principles of education—I once made a speech on the subject of education—May I quote from it to you?

BOB. Go ahead, old scout—quote it to me—and I'll quote it to Jane.

LLOYD. The Greeks are—

[*He continues to mumble.*

BOB. Come on, Sid. Another drink. I'm ahead of you—

SID. Just a moment.

BOB. Not another. You're a quitter. We'll drink without you.

LLOYD. Hear, hear.

[*They drink.*

SID. [*Shouting.*] I'll be damned if he goes. [*To* DICK.] Come here, come here. Do you hear me? [*Dick approaches—very white.*] Now, listen to me—if I hear you mention college again—whether I'm drunk or sober, I'll beat your head off—D'ye get me? [DICK *stands wide-eyed.* SID *swings round.*] Now give me a drink.

> [*He fills his glass, then sits down and stares at the floor.* DICK *returns to the armchair. He sits there, nervous and twitching.*

LLOYD. Education is a funny thing—but Greek, ah, noble, inspiring Greek.

[BOB *starts to sing a Broadway Hawaiian ditty.*

LLOYD. I admire the Greeks and their customs.

[BOB *continues the song.*

LLOYD. [*Commences to recite the Iliad; after several lines he cries:*] Shades of Maggie, Shades of Purcell—[*He raises the bottles and pours whisky over the alcohol lamp.*] Where are you?

> [DICK *trembles from head to foot—the Greek book is in his hands—he takes it and tears it in two. He stares straight before him. At this moment there is a sharp rap on the door.* BOB *stops short on a high note,* SID *looks up,* LLOYD *is silenced.*

MAGGIE. [*Off stage.*] Miss Purcell says you've got to keep quiet—You're making too much noise.

> [*But they pay no attention. And with an increasing force, the hubbub proceeds. At this point the curtain falls.*
>
> *The hurdy-gurdy starts in. The curtain rises again, and it is once more the street in front of the lodging house.* BOB *appears on the steps in a very intoxicated condition. He disappears up the street— singing his Hawaiian ditty.*
>
> HASTINGS *follows him from the house. He watches* BOB *out of sight. Then he sits down on the steps, chuckles to himself, pulls out a little notebook, and proceeds to take notes.*
>
> *Curtain.*

PART II

[*A restaurant. A table and chairs at one side of the stage. (An elderly, stooping waiter, with white hair, ushers in* JOSEPH HASTINGS. HASTINGS *is wearing a dinner jacket, etc.*)]

WAITER. A table, sir?

HASTINGS. I'm expecting Mr. Gay. He 'phoned you to reserve a table.

WAITER. Oh, yes, sir. For Mr. Gay, the playwright; right here, sir, this is the table. Mr. Gay is seldom punctual, if you'll pardon me, sir.

HASTINGS. You know him, then?

WAITER. Yes, sir, I have quite a theatrical acquaintance, sir.

[CASPER GAY *enters. He is in evening dress.*
WAITER. Here is Mr. Gay now.
HASTINGS. Oh, I'm so glad to see you.
CASPER. How do you do. Sorry if I'm late.
HASTINGS. You're not.
WAITER. Good evening, sir.
CASPER. How are you. [*To* HASTINGS.] I thought I should never get here.

[*They sit at table.*

WAITER. What will you have, sir.
CASPER. Something to drink now. We'll dine later.
WAITER. Very good, sir.
HASTINGS. A Manhattan for me.
CASPER. To honor Mr. Hastings, I think I shall try a Chaste Minerva.
WAITER. Yes, sir. [*He goes.*
HASTINGS. Did you read my manuscript.
CASPER. Yes, indeed. Thank you so much.
HASTINGS. And what do you think.
CASPER. [*Looking oracular.*] I can see there's a play in it.
HASTINGS. I thought I could convince you. Now you'll admit I was right.
CASPER. Oh, I suppose so; but, my dear chap, that sort of thing won't go on Broadway.
HASTINGS. What?
CASPER. It's, it's not playwriting.
HASTINGS. Why not?
CASPER. Why! Because no manager will touch it.
HASTINGS. Can you tell me what's wrong.
CASPER. For one thing, there's so little connection between the scenes.

HASTINGS. Why should there be. I'm showing you there's a play on every floor of the house.

CASPER. Oh, you've got a play on every floor—and a lot of exposition too.

> [*The waiter brings the drinks and serves them. He remains an interested listener through the rest of the scene.*

HASTINGS. Surely you like my people. They're real enough.

CASPER. Yes, they are interesting. Of course you intend to write another scene and tie the whole thing up.

HASTINGS. Certainly not, my play is finished.

CASPER. Oh, you can't break off like that. Take that second little tragedy. I want to know what happens to Edme.

HASTINGS. That second play is a comedy.

CASPER. A comedy! Heavens! It's a good thing you let me read this. I think I can be of some help to you.

HASTINGS. Thank you, so much. Have you anything else to suggest?

CASPER. Some of your jokes—well—"The cars run in bunches"—that's pretty bad.

HASTINGS. Yes, I'm afraid it is.

CASPER. Now I'm interested in your play, or rather your episodes from life. I can see possibilities in them.

HASTINGS. So.

CASPER. I could take your material and write it up—write it up so it would go in any New York theater.

HASTINGS. The great American drama?

CASPER. I can turn it into a big Broadway success.

HASTINGS. That sounds interesting. How would you go about it?

CASPER. To begin with—look at Miss Purcell. For three acts you've talked about a character who doesn't appear on the stage. Why not make your old Mother the landlady?

HASTINGS. All right.

CASPER. Now your play is laid on West Eleventh Street—a New York play—therefore somebody is wanted by the police. Who will it be? Dick. No, he's the juvenile.

HASTINGS. Frank?

CASPER. No, indeed; Frank's a villain's name. I have it—Sid Griffiths. Sid is wanted by the police. What crime has he committed? Murder. That's too brutal. Robbery, that's it.

HASTINGS. Good.

CASPER. And the police suspect him. But they need some proof. Who will they turn to? His sweetheart? They won't learn much from her. His old pal—of course. There we have our starting point. There's where our play begins. [*The stage is darkened, and the restaurant scene gives place to the lodging house much as it appeared in the other scenes, with the door to hall at back, a door at right and windows at left. But the room is now a drab sort of sitting room, and electricity has replaced gas. There is remarkable atmosphere about it. Gold framed enlargements will give exactly the right effect.*

FRANK DEVOY is pacing up and down before the windows. He is obviously expecting somebody. The hall door opens, and TOM BURCH enters. He now wears the uniform of a police inspector. FRANK turns eagerly, and starts back.

TOM. Evening, Frank. Didn't expect me, did you?

FRANK. No, not exactly.

Tom. I thought I'd drop in, and pay you a visit.

Frank. Won't some other time do? I'm going out now. [*He starts to go.*

Tom. [*Blocking the way.*] Don't be in such a hurry.

Frank. What's your game? You got nothing on me.

Tom. Look here, Frank, what do you know about this Lloyd necklace?

Frank. Nothing.

Tom. You can't bluff me. You know who did the job.

Frank. No, I don't. Honest to God.

Tom. Now listen to me. I want the name of the man who glommed the Lloyd mansion last night. I'll give you half an hour to get it to me.

Frank. Say, what do you think I am?

Tom. Now don't forget I got two or three little things against you—enough to send you up the river for four or five years.

Frank. But see here—even if I do find out who it is I can't go to headquarters.

Tom. You can find me in the square—and I won't wait more than half an hour, remember that.

[*He goes.* Frank *mutters an oath. He starts to light a cigarette with trembling fingers, throws it away.* Edme *enters.*

Edme. [*Running to him.*] Frank! [*He pushes her away.*] What's the matter? I'm sorry if I was late.

Frank. It's not that. I'm in the devil of a scrape.

Edme. What is it? Oh, tell me, dear.

Frank. Naw, you wouldn't understand.

Edme. Oh, Frank, you should tell me. If you love me as much as you say you do, then you ought to trust me.

Frank. I can't tell you now. I've got to clear out of this.

Edme. What do you mean?

FRANK. I'm going West.
EDME. But, Frank, you aren't going to leave me?
FRANK. I got to—unless you come with me.
EDME. Oh, I couldn't.
FRANK. Why not?
EDME. It wouldn't be right. We're not married.
FRANK. That don't matter. We can get married as soon as we reach Chicago.
EDME. But it isn't right—even then—
FRANK. You see you don't trust me.
EDME. Oh, I do, Frank.
FRANK. You're going to let me go away alone.
EDME. Oh, no.
FRANK. And maybe you'll never see me again. How'd you like that?
EDME. It would be terrible. I couldn't stand it.
FRANK. Then you'll come?
EDME. Yes, yes, I'll come—of course I will.
FRANK. That's much better. Can you get ready in fifteen minutes? I'll have to go out and get the tickets.
EDME. Yes, yes.
FRANK. If you're going to back out, now's the time to do it.
EDME. I'm not, Frank.
FRANK. Good.

> [*He kisses her quickly and starts to door.* DICK GRIFFITHS *enters right.* FRANK *turns back.*

FRANK. Where will I meet you?
EDME. I'll wait for you here.
FRANK. All right. We got to get away to-night.

> [*He goes.*

EDME. [*Sees* DICK.] Oh, Dick, were you in your room?
DICK. Yes, I've been reading Xenophon.

EDME. Did you—could you hear us talking?

DICK. No, you can't hear a thing in there. [*He comes over to her.*] Edme, it's none of my business, I know, but I wish you wouldn't go round with him—with Frank so much.

EDME. Why not?

DICK. I don't think he's quite your sort.—I don't think he's good enough for you.

EDME. Oh, Dick, he's much too good. If you knew him, you wouldn't say that.

DICK. I don't know—

EDME. And I may as well tell you, Dick, that we're going to be married.

DICK. Oh, no!

EDME. Yes, isn't that wonderful?

DICK. I'm sorry I spoke now, I didn't know things were like that. [*He takes her hand.*] I hope you'll be very happy.

EDME. Thank you, Dick.

DICK. Gee, but he's a lucky fellow. You tell him that from me.

[BESSIE *enters.*]

BESSIE. Hello, kiddies. [*To* DICK.] Where's your brother?

DICK. I haven't seen him to-day.

BESSIE. I'm worried about him. You been studying hard as ever?

DICK. Yes, and I'd better get back on the job, or I'll never get to college.

[*He goes out right.*

BESSIE. That boy thinks the world of you, dear. You ought to be nicer to him.

EDME. Oh, he's always working, and he never goes out anywhere. I don't like that.

BESSIE. He may be a bit quiet—but I know a real fellow when I see one, and you won't find a better kid anywhere.

EDME. I'm not so sure.

[MRS. HAMMOND *enters. She carries a newspaper.*

MRS. HAMMOND. Good evening, Miss Dodge. How are you, Edme?

EDME. Very well, thank you.

MRS. HAMMOND. You look so pretty to-night. My little girl was pretty too. I must show you her picture some day. Would you like to see it?

EDME. Oh, yes, Mrs. Hammond.

MRS. HAMMOND. You remind me of her at times. There, there, I'm a silly old woman to talk about the past. Run along, dear. [EDME *goes, and she turns to* BESSIE.] I feel so sorry for that little girl with nobody to protect her.

BESSIE. Poor little kiddie.

MRS. HAMMOND. And when we see so much wickedness in the world. Did you read to-night's paper?

BESSIE. No.

MRS. HAMMOND. It's simply terrible. No one is safe. Some men broke into the Lloyd mansion on Fifth Avenue.

BESSIE. What!

MRS. HAMMOND. Yes, and stole the famous diamond necklace. It's worth a fortune, they say. Here's a picture of it.   [*She shows her the paper.*

BESSIE. [*Anxiously.*] Did they catch the man? Does it say?

MRS. HAMMOND. No, but the police have a clue.

[*A long whistle is heard outside.*

BESSIE. [*Starts.*] Oh!

MRS. HAMMOND. Why, what's the matter, dear?

BESSIE. Nothing, nothing at all. When did it happen?

MRS. HAMMOND. Last night, I believe. Mr. Lloyd's niece from Morrisburg was visiting him. It was she who

discovered the thief. [MAGGIE *opens the door.*
MRS. HAMMOND. Yes, Maggie?
MAGGIE. There's a person to see Miss Dodge.
BESSIE. Tell him to come up, please.
MAGGIE. Yes, miss. And, ma'am, could I see you for a few minutes?
MRS. HAMMOND. Certainly, Maggie. Will you excuse me, Miss Dodge.
BESSIE. Of course.
> [MRS. HAMMOND *and* MAGGIE *go out.* BESSIE *hurries to window.* BOB DOUGLAS *enters —the pessimistic comedy crook.*

BOB. Hey, Bess.
BESSIE. Good Lord, you scared me. What is it?
BOB. There's the devil to pay—
BESSIE. For heaven's sake, tell me—
BOB. Sid's outside.
BESSIE. I got his signal. Go on.
BOB. The police are after him.
BESSIE. Bob, it's not that Lloyd robbery?
BOB. Yes.
BESSIE. Oh, my God!
BOB. [*Ruefully.*] We'll all get ten years if he's caught.
BESSIE. [*Bitterly.*] What a fool thing—
BOB. He wants you to flash the lights, if he can come in.
BESSIE. Is he out in the street alone? [BOB *nods.*] Oh, the poor kid. [*She flashes the lights.*] There—
BOB. I hope he ain't found there. Sing Sing's too far from the bright lights to suit me.
BESSIE. What made him do it, Bob?
BOB. You better ask him that. They saw him get away. He's been followed close ever since—
> [*The door is thrown back.* SID GRIFFITHS *enters, pale, agitated.*

Sid. They're after me, Bess; they're after me.

Bessie. Oh, Sid, Sid, why did you do it? You promised me you'd go straight.

Sid. It looked like a sure thing.

Bessie. Oh, Sid!

Sid. Now listen, girl, I want you to get the straight of this. Frank Devoy's in it too. He gave me a plan of the house—

Bessie. Well?

Sid. I was to get the necklace and hand it over to him. He promised me five thousand. That was for us to start on.

Bessie. Oh, Sid, I'd rather start honest.

Sid. Well, it's done now.

Bessie. And you got the rocks, you got the rocks.

Sid. Yes, but they saw me.

Bessie. And the rocks, where are they?

Sid. I've got them on me.

Bessie. Good God. Oh, Sid, it's going to break my heart.

Sid. If I could only get the necklace to Frank. They won't suspect him—

Bessie. Where is he?

Sid. I was to meet him at the old shack. Here's where you come in, Bob.

Bob. I'm ready. What is it?

Sid. Tell Frank to come over here at once. Tell him if they find the necklace here, it'll mean the big house for all of us.

Bob. I get you.

Sid. Now, hustle.

Bob. I'll take a jitney.

[*He goes.*

Bessie. If you get out of this, you'll go straight—for my sake.

SID. God help me—I will.

[*He embraces her passionately.*]

BESSIE. You'd better stay in your room till he comes. I'll keep watch down-stairs and let you know.

SID. All right. Not a word of this to Dick, mind.

BESSIE. Of course not.

[*She goes.* SID *takes out the necklace and looks at it. Then he puts it back, crosses to door right, and goes out.*

After a minute the hall door opens, and EDME *enters with a traveling bag. She is very nervous. She puts the bag on the table.* MRS. HAMMOND *comes in.*]

MRS. HAMMOND. Why, Edme, where are you going?

EDME. I—I—nowhere—

MRS. HAMMOND. But you've got your hat and coat on. And your bag here—What does it mean? Are you going away?

EDME. Yes, I am, Mrs. Hammond.

MRS. HAMMOND. But where to? [EDME *does not answer.*] Can't you tell me? Surely it's nothing to be ashamed of.

EDME. I'm going away with Mr. Devoy.

MRS. HAMMOND. What!

EDME. We're going out West.

MRS. HAMMOND. But, Edme—you—you can't go with him alone—

EDME. He's going to marry me as soon as we get to Chicago.

MRS. HAMMOND. Chicago!! Oh, you poor little girl.

EDME. He promised me he would. I wouldn't go till he'd promised me.

MRS. HAMMOND. My dear, you mustn't run away like that. You don't know what you're doing.

EDME. Yes, I do. Frank wouldn't deceive me.

MRS. HAMMOND. You don't know the world, dear.

EDME. I wasn't going to do anything wrong.

MRS. HAMMOND. Of course not, dear. Now, I want you to sit down, and listen while I tell you a story. Please—it won't take long. [EDME *sits at her feet.*] I had a daughter once. She was a beautiful little girl, and I called her Molly. Well, Molly grew up, and she got restless at home. I guess I was too quiet for her. Anyway, she left me and went on the stage. Then I didn't hear from her for a long time—and I worried and one evening—it was in this very room—Maggie was trying to comfort me—

> [*A loud whistle is heard off the stage. The lights go out. They come on again, slowly, until the stage is in half-light.* MRS. HAMMOND *is still sitting by the center table.* MAGGIE *is standing beside her.*

MAGGIE. You do wrong to get excited like this.

MRS. HAMMOND. I can't help it, Maggie, I haven't heard from Molly in over a month.

MAGGIE. There, there. It'll be all right. You're tired out with this worrying. Come and lie down for a while.

MRS. HAMMOND. [*Rising.*] I know I'm foolish, but I can't help feeling that something must have happened.

> [*They go out right.* MOLLY *enters from hall. She is deathly pale. She staggers to the center table.* MAGGIE *re-enters.*

MAGGIE. Miss Molly.

MOLLY. [*Starting.*] Oh, my God!

MAGGIE. Glory be, you've come back to us.

MOLLY. My mother, where is she?

MAGGIE. Lying down in there. Wait till I tell her.

MOLLY. No, no, you mustn't do that. I'm going right

away. [*She sees writing materials on the table.*] Wait. [*She scribbles a note.*] I want you to give her this.

[*She turns to go.*]

MAGGIE. Oh, wait, Miss Molly. You're in some trouble, I can see that—What is it, tell me what's wrong?

MOLLY. It's nothing—no one can help me.

MAGGIE. Oh, tell me, honey.

MOLLY. No, no.

MAGGIE. You must tell me. You must tell your Maggie.

MOLLY. Oh, Maggie, I'm going to become—

[*She breaks down.*]

MAGGIE. Not that, honey, not that.

MOLLY. Yes, yes.

MAGGIE. Oh, Miss Molly.

MOLLY. I trusted him. I thought he'd marry me, but he lied to me, he tricked me.

MAGGIE. My poor little girl!

MOLLY. I can't face my mother. It would kill her.

[MRS. HAMMOND *calls* "Maggie, Maggie."]

MAGGIE. It's your mother, she's waked up. You mustn't go. Wait and see her, Miss Molly.

MOLLY. No, no. Give her my letter. It will explain everything. Oh, Maggie, I can't see her.

MAGGIE. Then, Miss Molly, take this. [*She gives her a necklace that is on the table.*] It's your mother's necklace. She got it when she was married, and I know she'd want you to have it.

MOLLY. God bless you. [*She goes.*

[MRS. HAMMOND *enters.*]

MRS. HAMMOND. Why, Maggie, who were you talking to? I thought I heard voices.

MAGGIE. There wasn't anybody.

MRS. HAMMOND. You have a letter. It's for me—it's from Molly—give it to me.

MAGGIE. No, ma'am, no.

MRS. HAMMOND. Give it to me, Maggie, there's something wrong; give it to me. [*She takes letter.*]

MAGGIE. Don't read it, ma'am.

MRS. HAMMOND. [*Reads.*] "I have gone away. You will never see me again." [*She breaks off.*] Oh, Molly, my little girl, my little girl.

> [*The whistle sounds again. The lights go out. They come on again slowly.* MRS. HAMMOND *is talking to* EDME.

MRS. HAMMOND. I never, never heard of her again. And that was sixteen years ago. It was terrible, terrible. I thought I should die.

EDME. [*Crying.*] Oh, I'm so sorry.

MRS. HAMMOND. And you know how I've watched over you, ever since you came to stay here. It would break my heart if anything should happen to you.

EDME. Don't cry, Mrs. Hammond. I couldn't go now. Not after what you've just told me.

MRS. HAMMOND. If he is an honorable man, he will wait and marry you here.

EDME. Yes, yes, I know he will. I'm going up-stairs now to unpack my things.

> [BESSIE *enters, followed by* BOB.

EDME. [*Drawing back.*] Oh, I can't talk to any one.

MRS. HAMMOND. [*Taking her in her arms.*] It's all right, dear. You must excuse us; this little girl isn't feeling very well.

BOB. Poor kid, what's the matter?

MRS. HAMMOND. She'll be all right. Just leave here to me. [*She goes out with* EDME.

BOB. Gee, I'm glad they didn't stay. Get Sid.

BESSIE. [*Going to door right.*] Sid, Sid,—come here.

[SID *enters from right.*]

SID. Did you get Frank?

BOB. He's coming right along—but look here—

SID. Where was he?

BESSIE. Tell him, Bob.

BOB. I passed Frank in the Square. He was talking to Inspector Burch.

SID. My God, no.

BOB. He's trying to double-cross you.

SID. Where is he?

BOB. He's here by now. I kept just ahead of him.

BESSIE. [*At door.*] Frank's on the stairs.

BOB. What're you going to do?

SID. Leave that to me. I don't want you to mix up in this.

[FRANK DEVOY *enters.*]

FRANK. Evening, everybody. [*There is a silence.*] Well, what's wrong?

SID. [*To* BESSIE.] I want you to go down-stairs and keep watch by the front door. Take Bob with you.

BOB. Oh, say—

SID. Do what I say. This is my affair.

BESSIE. Come along, Bob.

BOB. Oh, gee, I wanted to see the excitement.

[*They go.*

SID. Now take these rocks. Quick.

FRANK. You bungled the job, and you want me to take the consequences.

SID. We went pals on this.

FRANK. The jewels are no good now. They're marked everywhere.

SID. Well, they're after me hard. I've got to get rid of them.

FRANK. Oh, is that it?

SID. I don't want your money. I'm sorry I messed up with you at all. But take this. [*He hands him diamonds.*]

FRANK. Oh, I don't mind. [*Takes necklace and lays it on table.*] As a favor to you.

SID. Now look here, you rat, what were you talking to Inspector Burch about?

FRANK. I wasn't, Sid; who told you that?

SID. Don't lie. Bob saw you.

FRANK. He stopped me, honest he did.

SID. I'll have to let it go at that, I suppose. But I don't trust you, and I'm glad to be through with you. And get this—if you ever try to double-cross me, Frank, I'll kill you.

FRANK. Don't you try to threaten me.

SID. I mean what I say.

FRANK. I'm not afraid of you. [*He draws a revolver.*] Now you keep away, or I'll shoot. [*He points gun at* SID.]

SID. Put that down, you fool. D'you hear me, put it down. [*He walks straight up to* FRANK *and takes the gun out of his hand.*

FRANK. For God's sake, don't hurt me. I didn't mean it.

SID. [*Throws gun on table with great contempt.*] You dirty coward! Now I'm coming back in five minutes, and I don't want to find you here. [*He goes out right.*

FRANK. Damn you.

[*He puts necklace in his pocket. Enter* EDME.

FRANK. Aren't you ready? We've got to get away quick.

EDME. I'm not going, Frank.

FRANK. What's that?

EDME. It isn't right. You shouldn't ask me to.

FRANK. Don't be a fool. I've no time to waste.

EDME. No, Frank—it's no use.

FRANK. Come along now.

EDME. I can't I tell you, I can't.

FRANK. Listen to me, girl, I love you. I'm crazy for you. Do you think I'll let you turn back now. No, sir, you've got to come with me. [*He crosses over to her.*]

EDME. Don't you touch me. [FRANK *laughs at her.*] If you come near me, I'll scream.

FRANK. We'll soon stop that. [*He catches hold of her, and tries to cover her mouth with his hand.* EDME *breaks away from him. He follows her, and she switches off the lights.*] Here, where are you? [*No answer.*] Come, on: you can't play tricks with me. Speak up. [*No answer.*] Well, we'll soon find out. [*He flashes a pocket flashlight. It falls on* EDME.] Oh, there you are, you little fool. [*He advances toward her. She screams.*] Be quiet, d'you hear me! [*The flashlight falls on the revolver on table.* EDME *gives a cry and seizes it.*

FRANK. [*Putting off flash.*] Put that down, put that down.

EDME. [*Rushes to lights and switches them on.*] Now you keep away, or I'll shoot.

FRANK. Cut out this foolishness.

EDME. I mean it.

FRANK. I've stood enough from you.

[*He starts towards her. She shoots.*]

FRANK. You little vixen.

[*He falls.* EDME *screams. The hall door is opened.* MRS. HAMMOND *and* MAGGIE *enter.*]

MRS. HAMMOND. What has happened? What's the matter?

[BESSIE *enters.*]

BESSIE. Sid, where are you, Sid, Sid—

[SID *enters from right.* BOB *appears in hall doorway.* DICK *follows* SID. *He crosses to* EDME.

SID. [*Examining* FRANK.] Dead! I've got to make a get-away.

BESSIE. Try the hall. Quick!

[SID *goes out by the hall door.* EDME *is standing by table, holding revolver.*

DICK. Edme, what have you done? Edme—

EDME. [*Hysterically.*] Oh, I've killed him, I've killed him!

MAGGIE. What is it? What is it?

EDME. I couldn't help it. I had to.

MRS. HAMMOND. Edme!

EDME. It's true—I swear it's true. Oh, what shall I do—I've killed him.

[*She tears at her collar; it comes undone and reevals a necklace underneath.*

MAGGIE. Oh, my God, where did you get that necklace?

EDME. I couldn't help it—it was to save myself.

MAGGIE. That necklace—where did you get it?

EDME. It was my mother's—it was my mother's necklace.

MAGGIE. Mrs. Hammond—it's yours—it's the one I gave Miss Molly!

MRS. HAMMOND. Great heaven, child—who was your mother?

EDME. I never knew her. She died when I was born.

MAGGIE. It's Miss Molly's child—it's her little girl. Oh, God be praised.

MRS. HAMMOND. [*Embracing her.*] My child, my child, is this how I've found you!

SID. [*Rushes back.*] The police—they're out front!

BESSIE. We'll stand together, Sid, we'll stand together.

[TOM BURCH, WILLIAM LLOYD—*now a dignified old gentleman—and two policemen enter.*

TOM. Now, then, what's the row here? [*He sees the*

body.] My God! [*To a policeman.*] Watch that door. [*To the other.*] You get over there. [*He points to door right.*] Now, then, who's done this?

EDME. I have.

TOM. You murdered this man?

EDME. Yes.

TOM. Put the bracelets on her, Ned.

EDME. Oh, no, not that, not that.

SID. Leave her be. She did it in self-defense.

TOM. Oh, there you are, Sid. Where's Bessie?

BESSIE. Here I am.

TOM. Glad to see you. Why, hello, Bob. So you're here too.

BOB. [*Dismally.*] Hello.

TOM. Who's going to explain?

EDME. I shot him; I had to.

TOM. That don't go.

BESSIE. What's wrong?

TOM. [*Wheeling.*] Sid Griffiths, you shot Frank.

SID. What!

TOM. You shot him because he double-crossed you.

SID. It's a lie.

TOM. Where's the necklace?

SID. How should I know?

TOM. You're mixed up in this.

SID. No, sir,—not this time.

TOM. We'll see. Where's the necklace?

BESSIE. Most likely he's got it himself.

[*Pointing to* FRANK.

TOM. Well, I'll look and see. [*Finds necklace.*] Good God! Is this your necklace, Mr. Lloyd?

LLOYD. Why, yes. Of course it is.

TOM. Which of you put it there?

SID. I never saw it before.

BESSIE. Nor I.

TOM. It'll be hard to prove that. Now, then, you'd better confess. You shot him for revenge, didn't you?

DICK. But, sir, he couldn't have.

TOM. Why not?

DICK. He was in that room with me.

TOM. Can you swear to that?

DICK. Yes, sir. [*Sensation.*

BESSIE. The girl tells you she did it.

EDME. I had to.

TOM. It'll be up to you to prove that.

EDME. I will, I will.

TOM. Then I guess I can't hold you on that charge, Sid. [*General sighs of relief.*

EDME. Oh, Dick, can you ever forgive me?

DICK. Of course I can.

[*He takes her in his arms.*

SID. Is that all you want?

TOM. Just a minute. Mr. Lloyd, is this the man you saw in your study?

LLOYD. I can't say, Mr. Inspector. It was my niece who discovered him.

TOM. Quite so. Where can we reach her?

LLOYD. I sent her a telegram—I thought you might need her. [*Enter* ALICE.

ALICE. Oh, Uncle, I received your telegram. What is it? Have you found the thief?

TOM. Miss Merriam, would you know the man who broke into your uncle's house if you saw him again?

ALICE. Oh, yes, I saw him plainly.

TOM. Good.

ALICE. [*Discovering* SID.] Oh, my God. There he is! That's the man.

TOM. Aha! Thank you very much, Miss Merriam.

[*With Triumph.*] Well, I'll hold you for the robbery, Sid, and I guess you'll get ten years for it.

BESSIE. We were going to go straight if we got out of this—we were going to the country. Oh, Mr. Lloyd, don't let them take Sid—we were going to get married.

LLOYD. He's a thief.

BESSIE. It was that man [*Points to* FRANK] got him to do the job, and that's the truth, so help me heaven. And he did it for my sake. He thought I wanted the money. [EDME *produces a handkerchief and weeps.*] But I didn't. I wanted to go straight and live honest. [MRS. HAMMOND *and* DICK *are crying.*] If he goes up the river now, it'll be all up with us, we won't be able to start in again, we'll be too old.   [BOB *and* MAGGIE *weep.*

LLOYD. You sound as if you meant it.

BESSIE. I do, I do. Give us our chance, Mr. Lloyd, give us our chance.

> [*She breaks down; sobs loudly. The policemen have turned away. Their shoulders heave. Everybody is weeping.*
>
> [*Tense pause.*

LLOYD. [*Very quietly.*] Don't cry, my girl, I'm going to withdraw the charge.

> [*Every one exclaims with joy. The stage is suddenly darkened. The lights come on again, and the scene is the restaurant once more.*

HASTINGS. [*In horror.*] Stop, stop. It's unbelievable. I refuse to hear another word.

CASPER. My dear man, that play will run a year on Broadway.

HASTINGS. My God, no! Impossible!!

CASPER. Do you mean to say—

> [*They rise angrily. The waiter intervenes.*

WAITER. [*Quickly.*] Gentlemen, gentlemen, I can't stand by and see you misunderstand each other in this way. You are both unfair. You, sir, have written a good play, and so have you. But if you compromise, gentlemen, taking a little from your play, and a little from yours, sir, you will have a better play—a play that is both artistic and popular.

CASPER. How do you know so much about the drama?

WAITER. I've had experience sir.

CASPER. Experience! Who are you?

HASTINGS. Wait a bit. I've seen him somewhere before.

WAITER. Very possibly, sir. I used to work for Mr. Shaw, sir.

[*He goes.*]

CASPER. And, by Jove, he's right. That's it: you and I must collaborate.

HASTINGS. Collaborate! My dear sir, even your public won't stand for that. [*He turns to the audience.*] Will you?

Quick Curtain.

(*The End.*)

www.ingramcontent.com/pod-product-compliance
Lightning Source LLC
Chambersburg PA
CBHW031304150426
43191CB00005B/73